DISTINGUISHING THE RIGHTEOUS FROM THE ROGUISH

Distinguishing the Righteous from the Roguish

THE ARKANSAS SUPREME COURT, 1836–1874

J. W. LOONEY

The University of Arkansas Press
Fayetteville
2016

Manufactured in the United States of America

ISBN: 978-1-68226-004-3
e-ISBN: 978-1-61075-590-0

20 19 18 17 16 5 4 3 2 1

Designed by Liz Lester

♾ The paper used in this publication meets the minimum requirements of the American National Standard for Permanence of Paper for Printed Library Materials Z39.48-1984.

Library of Congress Control Number: 2016931016

To my wife, Era Brown Looney,
whose great-great-grandfather, John W. Brown,
left a wealth of historical information to Arkansas
historians through his mid-nineteenth-century
diary. Her interest in this subject and her unwaver-
ing support made completion of this project possible.

CONTENTS

PREFACE

If, as suggested by Bertram Wyatt-Brown, one function of the law in the antebellum era was to distinguish the righteous from the roguish, the role of the Arkansas Supreme Court in that effort would seem important.[1] Unfortunately, the history of Arkansas law in the antebellum era has yet to be written. In particular, the role of the Arkansas Supreme Court in the development of the law has received little attention. Legal developments during the territorial period have been the subject of some scholarship. Stephen A. Smith was one of the first who reviewed the role of attorneys during the years of territorial status.[2] For the most part, the members of the bar and of the judiciary came from prominent families outside the state and were of "adequate legal ability."[3] Smith provides descriptions of the conditions under which court was held in the territory and of the nature of law practice. Also included are snippets of information concerning a number of the most successful attorneys and amusing anecdotes arising in the course of their advocacy. Another study of the territorial courts is that of Lynn Foster. She examined court files from 1808 to1814 to show how a frontier court dealt with early disputes and the role lawyers and judges played in the development of a functioning court system.[4]

A more extensive study, Morris S. Arnold's *Unequal Laws unto a Savage Race: European Legal Traditions in Arkansas, 1686–1836*, traces the legal transformation in "Upper Louisiana" from the French civilian legal system to a fully functioning common law adversarial system. "It was," Arnold says, "as much a social and political change as a legal one."[5] The major difference in the two legal systems, as operated in the early years of the Territory of Arkansas, was procedural, not substantive. The operation of a common-law procedural system required a professional class of lawyers. It was this lawyer class that came to include "some of the richest and most powerful men in the territory."[6]

These studies, focused on the territorial period, are complemented by an article dealing specifically with the Arkansas

Supreme Court after statehood, in which L. Scott Stafford reviews the treatment of slaves in cases before the Arkansas Supreme Court and the legal status of slaves in Arkansas generally.[7] Their treatment in criminal law as both defendant and victim is addressed with particular attention to emancipation suits and to how slaves fared in civil cases. When slaves were prosecuted for crime, they were treated as persons, not property. Interestingly, in capital cases, slaves "fared rather well" upon appeal; during the antebellum years only one conviction was upheld; five were reversed.[8] In non-capital cases, whites could be sentenced to longer periods of confinement than slaves convicted of the same offenses because of the legislation which prohibited slaves from being imprisoned in the penitentiary.[9]

In the 1836 statehood constitution the legislature was given the authority to establish separate courts of chancery. Chancery courts had a long and important period of growth and development in England, providing equitable relief in cases where an adequate remedy could not be found in the common law. The American colonies and early states began to merge law and equity. This was the model followed by most states. In Arkansas in the early 1850s, interest increased in having a separate chancery court to deal with controversies surrounding the unraveling of the two state banks. It is this story that is related in two articles by Morton Gitelman.[10]

An important work that provides biographical information is C. R. Stevenson's *Arkansas Territory—State and Its Highest Courts.*[11] This work contains brief sketches of those who served on the Arkansas Supreme Court and is an invaluable starting point for information on the justices.

As can be noted, attention to legal developments in Arkansas during the antebellum period is limited. With the exception of the single article by Stafford dealing with slavery, no analysis has occurred relating to the work of the Arkansas Supreme Court during this period. Even the general works on history of the state ignore legal developments and the court, except for the infrequent mention in the context of political controversies. For example, Walter Lee Brown, in his masterful work on the life of Albert Pike, discusses Pike's role in litigation before the Arkansas Supreme Court during the banking controversy of the late 1830s and early 1840s. Brief mention is made of the effect court decisions on banking had on the re-election of the members to the court. (Two were not re-elected.) Pike himself served on the Confederate court during the Civil War, and this receives a brief mention in the biography, primarily focused on an opinion he wrote relating to the legitimacy of the Confederate state government.[12]

More general works, like Jeannie M. Whayne, Thomas A. DeBlack, George Sabo III, and Morris S. Arnold, *Arkansas: A Narrative History*, S. Charles Bolton, *Arkansas, 1800–1860: Remote and Restless,* and John Gould Fletcher, *Arkansas*, mention legal developments only in the context of social and political changes and then only in passing.[13] The Arkansas Supreme Court is seldom mentioned.

The work of the Arkansas Supreme Court is the focus of this study. This study is an attempt to place the court and the role it played in the center of the state's early economic and political development. The cases, controversies, and conflicts dealt with by the court mirror the greater society.[14] While a cursory review of individual cases can in no way be considered a scientific study or provide much statistical data for objective analysis, such a review does provide a series of snapshots of the evolution of the law and, in a real sense, the economic, social, and political changes underway in the state. It also provides a glimpse of some of the major actors involved in law and in the state's development.

The approach of this study is simple; the task, laborious. The state's highest court, like all such courts, has, from the beginning, issued opinions written by one of the justices that reflect the decision of at least a majority of the members of the court. These decisions were originally compiled by "reporters," who at first had their names associated with the case reports. The court later adopted a uniform system of citation for what are now called the "Arkansas Reports." From 1837 through 1861, following the outbreak of the Civil War, the court issued 2,126 written opinions. From 1862 to the end of Reconstruction in 1873, the court issued 615 more. Each has been examined. The Superior Court of the Territory of Arkansas issued 123 written opinions during its existence, and these are analyzed as well to provide a foundation for the future work of the state court.

Those cases that appear to have some particular legal significance are noted, along with those of some economic, social, or political import. This selection process, arbitrary at best, was sometimes easy because of attention given to the case at the time. Some were selected because they provide a picture of societal attitude (or that of the court) relating to a particular controversy. Others were noted only for amusement due to curious facts, interesting parties, or unusual results.[15] Overall they do provide the desired glimpse into the workings of the court and the issues confronted by it in its formative years. As suggested by Robert Kagan and others, the distribution of cases will, no doubt, be influenced by variation in legal thought or "judicial culture."[16]

A content analysis of the cases reveals not only the detectable changes, over time, of the type of cases before the court but also the emphasis the court placed on specific issues during each time period.

A review of the major cases, conflicts, and controversies within seven categories is included: (1) land titles, (2) banks and banking, (3) transportation, (4) slaves as property, (5) family law and family property, (6) debt and contract, and (7) criminal law and procedure. This is followed by a more general discussion of the court during the Civil War years and during Reconstruction. In addition to this review of the primary sources, secondary sources were consulted to place the actions of the court in the context of the social, economic, and political climate of the new state. These sources also provide valuable information relating to members of the Arkansas Supreme Court and the role they played in the development of the law.

CHAPTER 1

"A Hegemonic Function of the Law"

An Introduction

Legal history is only social history, political history, educational history, urban history and labor history in a fashionable, mystical, and somewhat impenetrable and awesome disguise.

WYTHE HOLT, "Now and Then: The Uncertain State of Nineteenth-Century American Legal History"

In the old South, slavery, along with the social and economic system it supported, was defended by white southerners not only as a constitutionally protected right but as a "socially beneficial institution," a "positive good."[1] The defense of slavery took on a moral tone. Southerners believed in what Bertram Wyatt-Brown summarizes as a "rule of honor," the moral code to which they adhered. In their view they conducted "their lives by the highest ethical standards."[2] This "inner conviction of self worth" was reflected in their neighbors as "mirrors that return the image on oneself."[3] The public confirmed the self-assessment. Reputation was evidence of character.[4] This personal attribute of honorable character was the "psychological and social underpinnings of Southern culture."[5]

The planters constituted a small portion of the population but dominated southern politics and society.[6] The slaveholding elites would, naturally, wish to preserve their ordered society and would comfortably exercise social control through the legal system. As Wyatt-Brown notes,

> the law served to distinguish the righteous from the roguish and, to some degree, the rich from the poor. Finally, the community, the final arbiter of morals and justice, acted to invest its worthy members with collective power in the name of tradition and order.[7]

Eugene D. Genovese refers to this as a "hegemonic function of the law," where the legal system becomes an "instrument" by which the socioeconomic class of slaveholders "imposes its viewpoint upon the class as a whole and the wider society." He continues,

> The law must discipline the ruling class and guide and educate the masses. To accomplish these tasks it must manifest a degree of evenhandness sufficient to compel social conformity; it must, that is, validate itself ethically in the eyes of the several classes, not just the ruling class. Both criminal and civil law set standards of behavior and sanction norms that extend well beyond strictly legal matters.[8]

It was the opinions of a relatively few that mattered, but these few, acting to preserve their own image of self worth (honor), could assert their moral authority by rendering powerless those who questioned "the premises of the social order."[9] One such premise was the morality of the slave economy. They came to see slavery as the "very foundation of a proper social order and therefore as the essence of morality in human relationships."[10]

In addition, the "democratization" of honor extended to men of the lower class who could participate through acts of citizenship, such as service on juries. They were, then, "equal" to the upper classes and, of course, honorable. Blacks were not.[11]

Arkansas in the early nineteenth century was a curious mixture of a changing frontier and an emerging southern culture. As a newly founded state with a developing economy, a critical question would be whether the legal system would be used to promote growth or whether legal developments would, in the end, be more attuned to the need to defend slavery as an institution and to protect the interests of the landed elite. While state leaders often used "release of energy" rhetoric associated with a developing economy, in reality, the "great agricultural interests" were first served and progress was retarded.

Interestingly, while it is often suggested that southerners maintained a distrust of law and wished to avoid legal experimentation, as expansion into new territories occurred in the early nineteenth century, the settler, according to Edward L. Ayers, "built his courthouse almost before he built anything else."[12] This was necessary to handle not only criminal matters but the increasing number of civil cases, often disputes over rights to property. James W. Ely Jr. and David J. Bodenhamer suggest that more recent interpretations lead to the conclusion that the South, like much of the frontier, was in actuality "a peaceful place where settlers tried to maintain and recreate community."[13]

The first reported case from the Superior Court of the Territory of Arkansas is a prosecution for rape in 1820 in which the jury found the defendant guilty. The judge overruled objections concerning the indictment and the selection of the jury and ordered that the defendant be "castrated according to the law." The case report made reference to the "old notion" that if a woman conceived, rape had not occurred because, the theory went, she must have consented; and it referred to a medical jurisprudence text and to other sources in reaching the conclusion that this idea was no longer accepted.[14] Few other criminal cases were appealed during the territorial period although the superior court judges sat as trial judges and conducted criminal proceedings.[15]

When Arkansas became a state in 1836 the area was still a frontier in every sense of the word. The populace was scattered and was an odd mixture of those interested in market opportunities offered by the undeveloped area, particularly in land speculation, and those who lived off the land as hunters, engaged in Indian trading, or eked out an existence by farming. According to visitors to the territory, it was a rough and violent place with little evidence of "civilized" conditions. The inhabitants of Upper Louisiana (which included Arkansas) were described by Elizabeth Gaspar Brown:

> Uneducated, unaware of and uninterested in events beyond their immediate daily concerns, they were not particularly concerned with the abstract question of what were to be the laws in force.[16]

As might be expected, disputes were often settled without resort to the courts. Dueling was common, and often those in positions of authority or power resorted to this method of dispute settlement. For example, during the territorial period, in 1824, one of the first members of the superior court, Andrew Scott, killed another judge in a duel in an apparent dispute that arose during a card game.[17]

Violent resolution of disputes continued into the statehood period. During an early statehood legislative session, the Speaker of the House, John Wilson, was offended by a remark made by a member of the legislature, J. J. Anthony. The Speaker came down from the podium, engaged in a confrontation with the offending member, and, when another house member tried to intervene, plunged the knife "to the hilt" into Anthony's heart. Wilson calmly cleaned the knife, walked back to the Speaker's desk, and entertained a motion to adjourn. He was later tried and acquitted in an adjoining county midst allegations that he had improperly influenced the judge and jury. It was reported that Wilson, his friends, and the jury adjourned to a dram-shop where Wilson paid for drinks and the entire group spent the night celebrating in the streets.[18]

When the Territory of Arkansas was created in 1819, the population exceeded fourteen thousand, most of whom depended on hunting and trade to survive. Largely French or of mixed blood, these inhabitants had little use for a legal system or a judicial structure.[19] Judge Morris Arnold quotes the naturalist Henry R. Schoolcraft, who visited the area in 1818 and 1819, describing those living in the territory:

> Composed of the unruly and the vicious from all quarters, insulated by a pathless wilderness, without the pale of civil law, or the restraints upon manners and actions imposed by refined society, this population are an extraordinary instance of the retrogression of society.[20]

Schoolcraft also described these persons as having "fled from society to escape the severity of the laws" and suggested that settlement of disputes among the Arkansas hunters was done through self-help.[21] He adds: "Justice, which in civilized society is administered through the formalities of the law, is here obtained in a more summary way."[22]

Other visitors to the territory were no more impressed. Thomas Nuttall described "hunters and voyagers" he encountered at a Red River settlement in what is now southeastern Oklahoma:

> These people, as well as the generality of those who, till lately, inhabited the banks of the Arkansas, bear the worst moral character imaginable being many of them renegades from justice, and such as have forfeited the esteem of civilized society.[23]

On his return trip through Arkansas Post in 1820, he noted that "men of education and wealth" had been drawn to the territory with an influx of lawyers among them.[24] On this visit Nuttall arrived just in time to observe the trial of what became the first reported case of the Superior Court of the Territory of Arkansas, referred to above, *United States v. Dickinson*.[25] Nuttall provided some detail concerning the crime in which the defendant was accused of rape of his young stepdaughter. The jury found the defendant guilty and imposed the punishment provided by law: castration. Nuttall described this punishment as "no less singular and barbarous, however just, than the heinous nature of the crime itself."[26] As indicated, the defendant appealed his conviction, citing errors in the indictment and in jury selection, but the superior court affirmed the decision.

The violence and lack of "civilized" conditions, as noted by Nuttall, were described by John Gould Fletcher as the "special breed of lawlessness produced by Arkansas during this period." The lawyer, he says, rapidly became the "arbiter of society," and the courts were soon clogged with "long-dragged-out lawsuits, endless legal battles over land claims."[27] Continuing, he adds,

> As regards robbery, murder, and violence, the earliest settlers harassed from the start by gangs of horse-thieves, bandits,

> land and river pirates, soon learned not to depend on the courts but to take the law unto their own hands and invoke Judge Lynch.[28]

For a variety of reasons, it was difficult to bring suspects to trial, and, if accomplished, juries were not anxious to convict.[29] Court was held only twice each year in each judicial circuit during the territorial period. The judge, along with most lawyers, rode the circuit.[30]

Attitudes toward law and legal institutions had not much changed by statehood. Arkansas continued to be isolated by geographic barriers. The population, though increasing in number, was homogeneous, and a "traditionalistic" political culture prevailed.[31] The population exceeded fifty thousand, and the new state was ruled by "fine Arkansas gentlemen."[32] The ruling gentry could be contrasted to the larger part of the population, which continued to consist of self-sufficient hunters and small farmers to whom state government and its institutions were largely irrelevant.[33] As described by Diane Blair:

> For most Arkansans, then, whose lives would proceed in the same path regardless of any election outcome, politics was simply a spectator sport.[34]

During the early statehood period settlers came to Arkansas looking for economic opportunities, frequently seeking land. The state's population doubled by 1840. The settlers were nearly all farmers, either acquiring their own land or "squatting" on government land they hoped to purchase in the future.[35] The highlands were home to a society of small farmers, and the lowlands were home to a "small class of market-oriented planters."[36] With the expansion of plantation agriculture, slaveholding also increased. Planters who owned slaves were identified as the "elite" in the social hierarchy.[37]

While there were class distinctions in the antebellum years, society in the state was "relatively cohesive." Carl Moneyhon wrote,

> The agrarian base of society added to the dominant social ideal. The plantation, farm, and rural village typified the world of individual Arkansans and provided a setting that

> reinforced the white egalitarianism of southern culture. The majority of individuals were bound together, from the richest to the poorest farmer, in a common struggle to wrest a living from nature.[38]

This social ideology was not one that generated class conflict but, rather, a common worldview that individual hard work could result in upward social mobility. But this egalitarianism for whites meant that the institution upon which the success of the elites rested, slavery, must be protected. The state's economy was tied to the interests of the minority—the slaveholding planters—so these agrarian and commercial leaders could advocate legislative policies that played "upon the hopes of the majority of people that they would at some future time benefit from particular policies."[39]

The elite in antebellum Arkansas, like those of other southern states, regarded slavery as not only economically necessary but a matter of morality. The system was necessary to provide moral guidance and discipline to the slaves—an ideology of paternalism that provided a rationale for slavery.[40] The controlling "slaveocracy" was concerned with the "orderliness" of society. This effort to maintain a common morality was, in this sense, a part of the effort to protect the institution of slavery upon which the common social ideology rested.

"Promotion of Enterprise" or "Hegemony"?

As the first Arkansas state legislature was about to convene in the fall of 1836, newspaper editor Albert Pike, an "emerging Whig partisan," urged the leaders to adopt a progressive platform for the future of the state.

> Give us two good banks, with a proper number of branches —open the country with rail-roads, and in twenty years not a state shall compete with us. Our progress in population, wealth and comfort will astonish even ourselves.[41]

He went on to warn that if the state pursued " a niggardly, penurious, and timid policy," development of the resources of the state would await "the superior energy and broader policy" of a later generation.[42]

In 1851 Pike traveled in several northern states and was impressed by the industrialization and extent of railroad construction: "the hum of industry, the rattle of machinery, the puffing of the locomotive." He recounted the lines of railroad in operation and the "abundant openings for employment" and observed that "education and knowledge as well as enterprise and comfort, kept pace with railroads." Pike then described what he observed when he returned to Arkansas.

> The contrast was enough to make one heartsick. A dull stupid apathy broods over the whole state like a great leaden-colored cloud. All along our roads are abandoned huts, shattered fences, deserted fields overgrown with weeds. Except for a few cotton-planters, nobody seems to have energy, confidence, or hopefulness.[43]

He went on to describe the lack of progress.

> Not a foot of railroad; not even a foot of planks—road or turnpike in the State. No manufactures; hardly one public school to a county; the roads almost impassable. . . . Even the roads which the General Government made for us we have been too lazy to keep up.[44]

What happened? How could one so enthusiastic about the future of a new state lose all optimism in a period of less than twenty years? In 1836 "imagination in its highest flight" could not keep pace with reality. Now reality was "a great leaden-colored cloud" of "dull, stupid apathy."

Pike felt the "cure" was to move forward with railroad construction and internal improvements in the state and in the South. Over the next several years he devoted his considerable energies to the unsuccessful promotion of such internal improvements, urging that this goal was "above politics."[45] All was to no avail. A correspondent to the *Little Rock Whig* on May 25, 1854, said it best:

> The South desires to do a great many things—practicable and impracticable; but between politics, chivalry, jealously, and the have-all-or-none disposition, together with the real, comparative disadvantages, growing out of her peculiar institution —she is on a first rate train to do nothing at all.[46]

It was the devotion to the "peculiar institution" that, in the end, diverted the energy of the state, and of the South.

In his prize-winning book, *The Transformation of American Law, 1780–1860,* Morton J. Horwitz argues that the early years of the nineteenth century in the United States evidenced the emergence of an "instrumental conception of law." This, he says, "encouraged innovation," and judges acted on a "self conscious consideration of social and economic policies."[47] He adds:

> In a whole variety of areas of law, ancient rules are reconsidered from a functional or purposive perspective, often before new or special economic or technological pressure for change in the law has emerged.[48]

These areas of law included transformation in the conception of property, the "triumph of contract," the absorption of pro-commercial doctrine into private law to accommodate "expanded values of a market economy," a fundamental shift in favor of competition, and, in a real sense, the use of the legal system to promote economic growth and encourage social change. Judges saw themselves as agents of change with a new policy orientation.[49]

Lawrence M. Friedman adds that the thrust of law during this period was "promotion of enterprise." The aim was to provide a basis for economic growth. For example, government was to provide transport, currency, and credit to aid in the growth and expansion of the economy.[50] Friedman indicates that as a market economy developed in the nineteenth century, American law had to change to "conform to the vast increase in the number of consumers." Law "for the millions," the middle class, had to develop. At the same time, the protection of property was increasingly seen as a function of law.[51] This transformation, he suggests, is seen in the areas of public land and settlement policies, real property, credit, and banks and banking.

Horwitz and Friedman draw on the precepts of James Willard Hurst, who, in his seminal work, *Law and the Conditions of Freedom in the Nineteenth-Century United States*, suggests that "law exists for the benefit of people" and sets out the concept of "release of energy" as a dominant value in making "affirmative use of law." It was Hurst who recognized the "instrumentalist" view of the law in the nineteenth century.[52] He concludes:

> We were all Republicans, we were all Federalists, in possessing a common instrumental belief which shaped the nineteenth-century legal order.[53]

The type of economic dynamism described by Horwitz and Friedman and envisioned by Hurst did not take deep root in the South though. Eugene D. Genovese attributes this to the "retardative effects" of the plantation economy. He summarizes these effects:

> A low level of capital accumulation, the planters' high propensity to consume luxuries, a shortage of liquid capital aggravated by the steady drain of funds out of the region, the low productivity of slave labor, the need to concentrate on a few staples, the anti-industrial, anti-urban ideology of the dominant planters, the reduction of Southern banking, industry, and commerce to the position of auxiliaries of the plantation economy."[54]

To this list he adds "the retardation of the home market for both industrial and agricultural commodities."[55] An economy dominated by a few large estates provided a limited market for industrial goods.[56]

James W. Ely and David J. Bodenhamer agree with much of the analysis of Horwitz and Friedman. They suggest that the South, however, was different. The southern system was more inclined to protect landed and slaveholding interests and was less receptive to new business techniques.[57] It may have operated actually to retard development. Ely and Bodenhamer identify four characteristics that define southern legal heritage: "unusual degree of attention to matters of race and caste, a rural culture, a hierarchical society, and pervasive localism."[58] The unusual degree of attention in the South to matters of race and caste curtailed legal experimentation. "Indeed, any change in the status quo was viewed with suspicion."[59] Southern law became a collection of "archaic provisions and conservative rulings."[60] In addition to the curtailment of economic advancement, the unique aspects of southern heritage also contributed to the southern approach governing personal status. Rules relating to marriage and the rights of women reflected patriarchal notions of the hierarchical society.[61] The status of slaves, of course, was dependent on their treatment as a unique form of property.

Tony A. Freyer agrees and suggests that southern law, particularly in the areas of transportation, credit, and property, accommodated diverse class interests, but in doing so, social and political stability were preserved at the expense of economic development.[62]

> One fundamental result of this accommodation was that, in return for policies that protected their property rights, small property holders ultimately acquiesced to a slave regime upon which depended the planter's and the merchant's wealth and influence.[63]

This can be no better illustrated than in the attention southern law focused on the protection of landed interests and slaveholders. Slaves were a unique type of property, and the slave population in the South was linked to economic development. In Arkansas the statehood constitutional convention debated the status of slavery in the new state. The original constitution addressed certain aspects of slavery, guaranteeing slaves as property.[64]

An example of the tension generated in efforts to protect the institution can be seen in the conflicts that arose when the Arkansas legislature authorized the manumission of slaves under certain circumstances. Arkansas appeared to be more flexible on this issue than some other slave states. Slaves could be made free by the will of the owner or by other written instruments, although they could be seized by creditors if the owner had debts.[65] However, attempts by the owner to carry out the intent to free particular slaves were frequently challenged in court. Suits for freedom were not uncommon and generally generated considerable controversy. A number of these cases reached the Arkansas Supreme Court, especially in the years leading up to the Civil War. These conflicts illustrate the tension between the property rights of individual owners and the greater societal interest in defending the institution of slavery.[66] As Ely and Bodenhamer suggest, "the need to support white domination dwarfed all legal concerns."[67] Genovese refers to this as "a hegemonic function of the law," where the legal system becomes an "instrument" by which the social and economic class of slaveholders "imposes its viewpoint upon the class as a whole and the wider society."[68]

A basic tenet of Marxist analysis is that the ideologies that exist in a culture are shaped by the economic base. One such ideology is that of the elite group or ruling class, which perceives its interests to be the "natural order of things."

> A corollary of this is that laws enacted according to the dictates of a dominant ideology will appear to the members of that society as rules designed to preserve the natural social and economic order.[69]

This "class instrumentalist theory of law" suggests that the dominant class uses the law to pursue their own interests. This may be deliberate or it may simply evolve from the view of the ruling class as acting to preserve the natural social or economic order.[70]

A step beyond class instrumentalism is the hegemony of law with the law as a body of discourse. The ruling class "educates with the consent of the governed in such a way that the lower classes come to view the rule of the ruling class as 'right rule,' obedience to which and acquiescence in which should be exacted and given."[71]

Becoming "Lords of the Soil": Land, Credit, and Slaves

In his acclaimed story of the growth and expansion of Arkansas agriculture, *Territorial Ambition: Land and Society in Arkansas, 1800–1840*, S. Charles Bolton refers to land, readily available in Arkansas, as the "wellspring of economic opportunity in an agricultural society." He quotes an early newspaper in Little Rock in its effort at boosterism as promoting Arkansas as a place where enterprising yeomanry could, by "a single manly effort," become "lords of the soil they cultivate."[72]

Bolton's account of the development of agriculture in early Arkansas, set out more fully in *Arkansas, 1800–1860: Remote and Restless*, tracks the development of dual agricultural economies in the state:

> The highlands area was becoming a society of small farmers, many of them subsistence farmers, while the lowlands region was gradually developing a small class of market-oriented planters.[73]

Arkansas historian Jeannie M. Whayne emphasizes that agriculture was the "prime motivator" in the economic and political development of Arkansas. She suggests that plantation agriculture did not expand significantly during the territorial period because of the problems associated with uncertain land titles and the lack of a developed court structure to permit settling of land claims.[74]

But expand it did, especially during the two decades from 1840 to 1860, which saw the "maturation" of the slave-dependent plantation society in the lowlands.[75] This expansion was linked to the growth of slavery in the state. It was the slaveholding elite that exerted influence "in social and political affairs far out of proportion to their actual members."[76] As Thomas DeBlack has noted, even in the highlands, where slaveholdings were generally smaller, the slaveholders "enjoyed great social and political prominence."[77]

In his groundbreaking study of slavery in Arkansas, Orville W. Taylor challenged the traditional view that the divisions within Arkansas over the question of slavery could be attributed to the absence of slavery in the uplands. He points out that slaveholding existed in all counties in the state but, with extensive documentation, shows the dominance of large slaveholdings in the cotton-producing areas.[78] He reflects: "These widely distributed small holdings, along with the large ones of the plantation areas, served to maintain a consciousness of slavery in every section of Arkansas."[79]

The 1836 statehood Constitution of Arkansas empowered the legislature to create banking institutions. One bank would "promote the great agricultural interests of the country."[80] A second bank would "promote business activities throughout the state."[81] This was a recognition that for the economy to expand, lending institutions in the state were necessary. A separate concern was the absence of an institution within the state to hold funds received by the state itself, primary from the sale of public lands.[82]

The solution was to create two banking institutions: the Real Estate Bank and the Bank of Arkansas ("State Bank"). The Real

Estate Bank, designed for the planters, permitted shares to be issued in return for agricultural real estate and crops. This became collateral for bonds that the bank sold (backed by the state), the proceeds of which were then loaned to the shareholders.[83] The State Bank was a state agency that could issue bank notes, sell bonds backed by the state government, and lend money to "attract and promote business."[84] Both banking efforts ended in failure.[85]

Another ongoing concern was internal improvements, especially transportation. The geography of Arkansas posed limitations in land travel, with swamps in the east and south and mountains in the west and north. Most transportation was by river. As the economy developed, so did interest in better roads and, eventually, railroads. However, sectional jealousies and "localism" delayed any significant progress. The focus of energy during the 1850s was away from transportation and toward protection of property and the institution of slavery.

It is interplay of these essential economic inputs—land, slaves, credit, and internal improvements—that is the story of the development of the agricultural economy of Arkansas in the antebellum period. As with all stories, it is fraught with legal controversies.

The story of the public lands is, in reality, a reflection of social policy—to create a country of free (white) citizens, living independently "on their own little farm!"[86] The goal was to settle and distribute this public asset in an orderly fashion, not to enrich government coffers, but to "vest land and power in the hands of smallholders."[87] The federal government set out to transfer land as rapidly and as widely as possible. A minimum price was demanded to encourage sales (and was reduced from time to time). The minimum unit of sale was, over time, also reduced. Credit was available. The states acted as de facto land agents, and thousands of acres passed from federal hands to the states and then into private ownership.

Speculators played no small role in the process. For example, portions of Arkansas were made available to veterans of the War of 1812 as "military bounty" lands. Not many veterans actually settled in Arkansas; these grants were bought by speculators. Later, the Swamp Land Act provided that the states could use profits from the sale of such lands for drainage projects and to build levees. The contractors who worked on these projects were paid in scrip that could be used to purchase public land at low prices. Again, speculators often acquired the scrip, and then the land, which could be later sold privately.[88]

The conflicts between those who acquired land as settlers (squatters) and those who acquired land otherwise (speculators) not only were the subject of much of the policy debate in a frontier state like Arkansas but occupied the courts as well. Both squatters and speculators appeared in the West (including Arkansas) in advance of any official survey or formal date of sale. Both federal and state legislative efforts were directed at resolving these conflicts. For example, in 1841 Congress passed a general preemption law favoring the squatters. One who had actually settled on the land and made improvements had a first claim to buy the land at a minimum price.[89] On sale days these settlers often intimidated outside bidders to keep the sale price near the legal minimum.[90] In Arkansas courts, conflicts between these groups often played out.

Land in early nineteenth-century America was the most basic form of wealth, especially as the land settlement policies saw disposition of the public domain into private lands. "In the popular mind, land was a commodity like everything else."[91] This meant that the law relating to private land evolved from English feudal notions into a view of property as "dynamic" and "instrumental."[92] Land had to be easily transferred in an active market. Disputes over land had to be resolved with less technicality. Rules of capacity to own and deal in land had to be revamped.

> The goal was economic growth, a rising, spreading population, a healthy, aggressive middle class. Sometimes the market principle had to give way. Legal doctrines sometimes deviated from strict market principles, usually to protect a politically potent class—the small-holders.[93]

Change was seen in concepts related to use and development of land (and other natural resources) as well. Movement occurred away from an idea of absolute dominion over property rights to a view of property that emphasized the newly paramount virtues of productive use and development."[94]

Lawrence Friedman says that in the nineteenth century the economy "sailed on a sea of credit," but, in bad times, "banks drowned in a sea of debt."[95] Much of the law governing debtor-creditor was, like contract law, judge-made. "They took their guidance, often, from actual business practice, which they simply ratified."[96] Cases related to promissory notes and other negotiable instruments were frequently before the courts. The rights and obligations of makers, endorsers, "accommodation" parties, and sureties, as well as creditors, were at issue.

While the law of debtor-creditor tended to be judge-made, the related questions of currency and banking were matters of public policy. "Everybody. . . needed credit."[97] Monetary policy, then, was the focus of political debate.

At the federal level, two banks of the United States rose and fell. In early Arkansas, two public banks, the State Bank and the Real Estate Bank, likewise rose and fell. The courts devoted much political energy and considerable time dealing with the banking controversies. While many of the cases reaching the Arkansas Supreme Court involving these entities were routine "debt and contract" cases, a number were of greater importance, dealing with the structure and nature of the institutions themselves and the state's role (and obligation) in both the founding and operation of the banks and in their ultimate demise. Intertwined in the legal controversies involving the banks was the political drama that focused on the banking question but, in reality, was a struggle for dominance in the state.[98]

In Arkansas, as the cost of land and slaves increased into the 1850s, credit was necessary for entry into farming or for expansion by many planters and farmers. In the absence of state banking institutions, merchants extended credit for needed supplies, primarily through New Orleans. Credit for the purchase of land or slaves also came from outside the state.

Since slaves were essential to the plantation system and outside creditors were often reluctant to extend credit with only the slaves as collateral, land and other property were often included in the borrowing arrangement. Many borrowers found themselves with debts exceeding their resources. By the 1850s concerns that Arkansas was "debt-ridden" and dominated by outside creditors began to surface.[99] Thus, even though Arkansas agriculture prospered into the 1850s, it was tied to a single commodity—cotton. Not only was the economy tied to cotton, the capital needed was controlled from outside the state by those "who had little interest in investing in anything locally other than the production of more cotton."[100] This limited the state's economic development prior to the war.

Bank failure was not the only unsuccessful effort to promote the economy in Arkansas. Transportation was an intractable problem. Only the rivers provided a reliable means of travel. Early efforts at road building proved lackadaisical at best, and such roads that did exist were impassable much of the year. The legislature did direct some effort at road improvement by creating a position of "overseer," who was mandated to see that roads were kept free from obstruction. Local residents were conscripted to work on the roads, but these efforts seemed largely ignored.

The push for railroads emerged in the 1850s. In spite of the supposed policy of using revenues from public land sales to support railroad construction, by the end of the 1850s only sixty-six miles of railroad had been built. Local interests prevailed. In the end, the push for internal improvements, such as it was, paled in comparison to other concerns. As summarized by Moneyhon:

> Even before the emergence of railroad interests that could subdue the spirit of localism, other concerns had forced local elites to unify. The greatest outside threat to their propertied interests came in the form of the antislavery movement and the emergence of the Republican party. Arkansas' leaders saw the movements as endangering their property. How to meet the menace occupied more and more of their attention and dominated political discussions of the 1850s.[101]

In the postwar period the same basic pattern re-emerged: a cotton culture hampered by a lack of credit and capital. This, Moneyhon suggests, meant that little changed "economically or socially over the next decades," but this did set the stage for the efforts of the "landed interests" to protect themselves by regaining control of state government.[102]

In his study of slavery in Arkansas, Taylor asserts that slavery was a "vital and growing institution during its existence in Arkansas."[103] He cites as evidence the fact that from 1820 to 1850 the percentage increase in slave numbers in Arkansas was the highest of any state and was second only to Texas from 1850 to 1860.[104] The slave population increased at a much faster rate than did the white population, especially in the lowland cotton-producing areas.[105] As cotton production expanded, so too did plantation size and growth in the size of slaveholdings.[106]

Taylor reviews the debate regarding the profitability of slavery and concludes that in the cotton-producing regions of the state, where favorable conditions prevailed, the great rise in agricultural wealth in the prewar years provides sufficient evidence that planters were making profits.[107] While the issue of profitability in the South, generally, may yet be unresolved, it is clear that agricultural success in Arkansas by 1860 may, in large part, be attributed to slave labor.

This reliance on slave labor, according to Genovese, gave the slaveholding elites an outlook that resisted economic change and created an "aristocratic, antibourgeois spirit" that served to emphasize values that were "socially desirable to a slave society." The accumulation of slaves and land "carried the badges of honor, prestige, and power."[108] This often required debt. Bolton reports, "Setting oneself up as a planter could cost between $15,000 and $36,000 for the necessary six hundred acres and between $20,000 and $40,000 for twenty slaves." Financing was difficult to obtain and, except for the failed attempts to create financial institutions within the state, was largely from outside the state.[109]

The availability of cheap land added to the potential profitability of plantation agriculture in Arkansas. However, this also increased the demand for slaves and the price. Slave prices in Arkansas remained among the highest in the South.[110] Thus, slaves themselves became an important source of collateral for expansion of agriculture.

After the adoption of the constitution, the legislature adopted laws relating to slaves and slavery. They were defined as "chattel property," as distinct from real estate, but deeds and other documents transferring ownership would be recorded similar to real estate.[111] The ability of creditors to seize slaves for payment of debts was limited in many southern states. Arkansas followed suit by declaring slaves as part of the "personal estate."[112] The question of the legal status of slaves as property appeared frequently in litigation and before the early appellate court.

Other Areas of Law: Family Law and Family Property, Debt and Contract, Criminal Law and Procedure

The late eighteenth and early nineteenth centuries were, in words of Michael Grossberg, the "formative era" of domestic relations law in the United States. A "republican family" evolved, and courts emerged as the proper forum for resolution of family disputes.[113] These disputes included not only those related to intimate family relationship—divorce and child custody—but also those involving family property. Courts increasingly dealt with cases related to inheritance and family "succession" and the efforts of families to protect wealth from creditors.

A part of this change was the emergence of special acts to protect married women's property. At first blush these acts might appear contrary to the hierarchal and patriarchal tradition, especially in southern culture. However, when viewed as a means of preserving and protecting family property—a goal of many landholding fathers—these acts, too, may be seen as a means of furthering the goals of the plantation economy.

Likewise, dower and homestead rights were accepted in the prewar years as debtor protection measures designed to protect family property. Any effort to recognize the role of the wife in planting "seed of domesticity" and to protect family property would be in line with southern paternalism.

During this period the family changed to create a republican concept of domestic relations, and judges were at the forefront in the legal developments related to a "dynamic law of the family."[114] However, in a plantation-dominated economy, such as in Arkansas, the patriarchal and hierarchical tradition continued. This tradition is reflected in the family law and family property cases that reached the Arkansas Supreme Court during the antebellum period. While affording broad protection to family property, the court continued to see the role of the wife as "planting seeds of domesticity" and to recognize the paramount position of the husband and father.

In the early nineteenth century the rise of the market economy also saw the emergence of the "will theory" of contract.[115] The source of the obligation of contracts was the convergence of the will of the contracting parties. Equity, while not ignored, played a more limited role in contract interpretation and enforcement. And, contract was placed on a constitutional pedestal: states could not impair the obligation of a contract. This "root notion" of the law of contract was at the base of the approach of courts to contract questions. Basic concepts of contract law, recognized and applied, supported a broad, free market.

One area of special concern was with regard to debt. Debtor-creditor law, a subset of contract, for the most part, evolved from existing business practices. Credit dependency, especially in a slave economy, involved an intricate web of contractual rights and obligations. And trial courts functioned as instruments to facilitate the credit economy. At the same time, this intricate web of credit dependency meant that a certain social interdependence was also created. The slaveholders, while themselves debtors, were also creditors. Exceedingly complex financial arrangements were often involved in an emerging economy such as Arkansas's. Frequently, the role of the judiciary was to unravel these complexities and determine priorities among competing claimants for collateral or for payment.

For the most part, debtor-creditor law evolved from existing business practices. Civil litigation frequently involved debt, and the courts served as instruments to facilitate the credit economy. The credit dependency of a slave economy generated a degree of "social interdependence that gave non-slaveholders "a stake in the slaveholder's world."[116]

Courts were called upon to unravel the complex arrangements that characterized the intricate web of credit transactions. This can be seen in the work of the Arkansas Supreme Court, in which debt collection cases dominated the court's docket. Many involved routine application of legal principles once the relative rights of the parties could be sorted out.

Contract law, in general, also evolved during this period. As the "will theory" became the accepted view, equity played a lesser role in the interpretation and enforcement of contractual obligations. The market economy demanded no less.[117] Generally accepted concepts of contract law were easily applied by the Arkansas Supreme Court once the often confusing facts were sorted out. Concepts such as specific performance, liquidated damages, warranties and misrepresentation, legal capacity, consideration, interpretation of terms, and application of the Statute of Frauds were applied with the will theory as the guiding principle. In some areas, particularly situations involving mistakes, custom in trade and warranties and misrepresentation equity could still intervene to prevent enforcement but only reluctantly.

In the Old South crime was not a great concern. According to Edward L. Ayers, "Southerners believed that crime was far more characteristic of the North than of their own ordered agrarian society."[118] They had their own explanation as to why this was so, frequently attributing the licentiousness they saw in northern society to "universal freedom and equality," which produced "demoralization and anarchy."[119] Industrial growth and urbanization seemed to be causes of the "melancholy phenomenon."[120]

Official case reports of the Arkansas Supreme Court in the early years of statehood indicate that a relatively sparse number of criminal cases were appealed. Frequently, the court wrestled with procedural questions, and, only with time, did a system evolve that allowed for effective prosecution of criminal matters. Lawyers and judges were generally unfamiliar with criminal procedure, and early state legislation offered little guidance as to what was expected of the courts in such cases. In fact, much of the state's early criminal law was copied from other states and dealt with substantive matters, not procedural matters.

The generally accepted view regarding criminal law during the antebellum period is that prosecution for crimes against property increased while those for offenses "against God and religion" decreased.[121] This was not necessarily true in the South, where crimes against morality continued to be prosecuted. Gaming, liquor-related offenses, and sexual immorality occupied much court time in the South.[122] This is reflected in the criminal cases before the

Arkansas Supreme Court, which were "mirrors" of social ideology. A close analysis suggests that the moral authority of the elite was asserted through an insistence on protection of public morality to aid in enhancing the existing economic order. A certain "legal puritanism" can be detected in the approach of the Arkansas court.

The War Years and Reconstruction

In spite of secession, in May 1861, the Arkansas Supreme Court issued nineteen opinions in that term. None followed in December 1861 and only one in June 1862. However, the court attempted to continue functioning as a part of the overall effort to keep state and local government in operation in those areas of the state under Confederate control. It issued twenty opinions in December 1862 and twelve in June 1863. Seven additional opinions were released but "lost" until recognized by a subsequent court once hostilities ceased.

Of the court's opinions during this period, a number related to slaves and slavery, and three important cases involved the interpretation of the secession constitution and state legislation under the Confederate government.

As the Confederate court attempted to continue functioning, in those areas of the state under federal control a new constitution was adopted under the supervision of the military authorities. A new court was elected in 1864 but only decided one case, that in December 1865. This case, *Rison v. Farr,* paved the way for voting by former confederates in absence of an oath relating to aiding or abetting the Rebel cause after April 1864.[123] As a consequence, in the election of 1866, "Conservatives" regained control of state government and elected three members to the state supreme court. A number of significant issues confronted this court in the eighteen months of service prior to removal by federal congressional actions. The questions of great public interest involved the legal effect of secession, the effect of emancipation and the rights of slaves, validity of delayed court actions, and the seizure of property by military authorities.

Congressional control of Reconstruction meant that a new

constitution was demanded before Arkansas could be readmitted to the union. A new Reconstruction court was elected (now five members) and immediately became embroiled in the political controversies surrounding the administration of the Republican state government. These public interest cases involved questions related to currency, contracts entered into during wartime, local political disputes and control of county government, the legal effect of secession, and the validity of actions of the Confederate state government. Most important were questions of the court's power and authority to resolve election disputes and to order public officials to take specified actions. The court's involvement in these highly charged controversies contributed to the decline in prestige of the court and, ultimately, to impeachment of three members of the court.

Ties of individual court members to competing political factions influenced many of the decisions of the court. In the end, the court's involvement in these issues was but a part of the overall political turmoil that ended with the reassertion of control of the legislature by the Democrats in 1874. A new constitution was approved and new state officials were elected, including three former Confederate judges in a revamped state supreme court. This, as Moneyhon notes, meant that Arkansas was restored "to those who had dominated it before the war."[124] He concludes:

> For the economic elite as a class the war brought great material loss but little changes in their local social and political powers. . . . The same group—even the same individuals—who had been on top in 1860 remained to a large extent the masters in 1874. The Civil War unquestionably visited real suffering upon the people of Arkansas. The war ended slavery and changed the institutions connected with that particular labor system, but it did not alter other basic institutions of the antebellum world.[125]

A Critical Question

The areas of law set out above reflect the mass of questions that confronted courts in the early nineteenth century. Horwitz,

Friedman, and others suggest that this period was one of a major transformation in many of these areas of law, largely brought about by the emergence of a budding market economy. Ely and Bodenhamer agree with this premise but point out that the South was different, so much so that the transformation seen elsewhere may have been curtailed in the South. This, they suggest, is largely a function of the larger societal need to defend the institution of slavery but also because of other characteristics that define southern legal heritage, such as "a rural culture, a hierarchical society, and a pervasive localism."[126]

The question is whether Arkansas, as a newly founded state, with a developing economy, sought to use the legal system to promote broad economic growth and encourage social change or whether the state, in the end, focused on the protection of slavery: whether the hegemonic function of the law was evident and whether this retarded the development of the economy. As indicated by Kagan and others, state supreme courts serve as "simple mirrors of social changes," and a "powerful relationship" exists between changing social and economic conditions and the work of a supreme court.[127] Even that tiny proportion of litigation that reaches state supreme courts reflects social and economic changes; the legal system, even at the apex of the judicial system, must reflect what is going on in society.[128]

During the critical period of Arkansas's development, 1836–1874, the work of the Arkansas Supreme Court serves as that mirror. It reflects not only social change but the development of the legal system in the new state and the role the judiciary was to play. This can be seen in the general categories of issues that would come before the court in the areas outlined above. From statehood until the end of Reconstruction, one organ of government played a vital role in the state's history—the Arkansas Supreme Court. While the legislature could, and did, indicate through legislation what matters were considered of importance to the populace, the court determined the efficacy of the legislation and set limits on how the law was to be carried out. The supreme court provided guidance to lower courts on how trials were to be conducted and how civil and criminal procedure was to be applied. Appellate decisions offer a series of snapshots of what issues were of public interest and how these were viewed by litigants and those involved in the administration of justice.

From a review of the work of the Arkansas Supreme Court, it can be concluded that Arkansas did not follow the transformational patterns outlined by Hurst, Horwitz, and Friedman in the approach to law in the early nineteenth century. Because it had a rural culture and was a slaveholding state, the limits suggested by Ely, Bodenhamer, and Freyer are evident in the work of the court. If Arkansas, as a frontier state with a developing economy, saw the legal system as a means to achieve the "release of energy," to use Hurst's terminology, this should be reflected in the opinions of the appellate court in the areas of law analyzed. Instead, what is evident is that in Arkansas, the court attempted to accommodate diverse class interests, but, as a slaveholding state, the institution of slavery was to be preserved at all costs—a "hegemonic function" of the law, as described by Genovese. The ideology of paternalism and the protection of an elite class of interests ultimately are reflected in the decisions of the court. Social and political stability was preserved at the expense of economic development.

CHAPTER 2

"Peculiar Province and Duty"

Organization, Procedures, and Trends in the Early Arkansas Courts

During the territorial period, 1803–1836, Arkansas was "frontier" but its character was changing rapidly. A part of the change is reflected in the developing political institutions, including the courts, as the area progressed toward statehood. The prominent participants in this process included a number of young lawyers who saw the potential of political careers in the new territory.[1] Various economic opportunities attracted many of these men, especially in the early years when the potential for living on a lawyer's income was limited. Many engaged in other activities, especially land speculation, and supported themselves with a variety of public positions. Judicial appointments were particularly attractive, and many future state politicians were, at some point during the territorial years, members of the judiciary. The superior court was the plum appointment. Not only did it provide a steady income, it served as a base of operation for political activities. No better example is found than that of the superior court judge Benjamin Johnson, whose brother Richard was vice president of the United States from 1837 to 1841. His son-in-law, Ambrose Sevier, was a congressional delegate and later a United States senator. His son, Robert Ward Johnson, served both in Congress and the Senate. The elder Johnson died "rich in this world's goods, rich in honor, and rich in the esteem of the entire people of the State."[2] Judges Thomas P. Eskridge and William Trimble were frequently cited as examples of poor men who made money quickly. Trimble, it was said, came to Arkansas "clad in homespun and dreams and in just ten years left the state with $20,000 in gold honestly made, something better than any lawyer in the Mississippi Valley had been able to do up to that time."[3] Judge Andrew Scott "acquired a fortune in private life."[4] Judge James Woodson Bates, founder of Batesville, was, in the early years, a real estate agent. He eventually "married a wealthy widow and became stationary on a rich farm near Van Buren."[5] Edward Cross, after service on both the superior court and the state supreme court and in Congress, took an active part in organizing the Iron Mountain Railroad and was its president for seven years.[6]

The issues before the court reflected the changing nature of the society as well. Prominent among the disputes were those surrounding claims to land. These controversies involved not only the political leaders and other citizens but, sometimes, members of the judiciary themselves. Conflicts over debts and other obligations dominated the workload of the courts, and some evolution of other commercial disputes is noted. Interestingly, a relatively small number of suits involved criminal matters or tort claims (personal civil liability). Presumably, many disputes of a personal nature were still handled outside the structure of the legal system. Dueling remained a common means of dispute settlement even among prominent leaders.[7]

A professional class was evolving as society changed. The initial group of lawyers in the territory was, at best, marginally qualified to practice law. Those appointed to the bench had limited training in the law. For example, of the fourteen superior court judges to serve during the territorial period, none had attended law school. Only two were college graduates.[8] Even with these limitations, it is clear that a professional class of leaders, including the bench and bar, would soon emerge. The "rich and powerful" in the territory by statehood included a significant number of lawyers and judges.[9] Drawn by opportunity, many capitalized on that opportunity by using the legal system as one means of achieving social and economic success.

Territorial Courts

By the time of statehood in 1836, Arkansas had seen seventeen years of formal court organization with a superior court and circuit courts established in the territory. Little legal formality existed prior to the organization of the Territory of Arkansas, effective July 4, 1819, although, while a part of the Territory of Louisiana, some futile efforts were made to organize courts of general jurisdiction. For example, in 1808, lay judges were appointed to serve in various judicial posts at the Arkansas Post.[10] This lay judiciary continued to function until the County of Arkansas was organized as a part of the Territory of Missouri in 1813. A professional judgeship was created to sit "near the village of Arkansas."[11]

When the Louisiana Territory was transferred to the United States in 1804, it brought with it an established civil law tradition with French roots but with almost forty years of Spanish experience. Arkansas Post, like other areas, was under the jurisdiction of the post commandant, a military officer who also served a judicial function. Legal formality in such places was an "inefficient complication."[12] When the transfer to the United States occurred, old legal approaches continued for a time. The resident military commandant continued to hear disputes even after the District of Louisiana, which included all of present-day Arkansas, was separated from the Territory of Orleans and some semblance of government was established under the Indiana Territory with Vincennes as its capital.[13] An elaborate court system was adopted in October of 1804, and the common law was imported wholesale as to public law. Private law was left to Spanish tradition for a time.[14]

At the same time, the "Lower Louisiana" inhabitants objected strongly to any change in the civil law scheme, and, in the end, it was left in place.[15] In "Upper Louisiana" the objection to the common law was weaker and less effectual, ironically, because of the absence of a "professional lawyer class."[16] As suggested by Brown, the inhabitants of upper Louisiana were

> uneducated, unaware of and uninterested in events beyond their immediately daily concerns, [and] they were not particularly concerned with the abstract questions of what were to

be the laws in force. The French of lower Louisiana were the reverse. They were the dominant group in all levels of society. They were attached to the civil law and its institutions and a certain nostalgia for a Latin rather than an Anglo-American civilization intensified this attachment. These facts are illuminating in explaining the different development of legal systems in lower Louisiana and in the remainder of the area.[17]

In 1805 the District of Louisiana became the Territory of Louisiana. Arkansas was within the District of New Madrid. Judicial authority, such as was exercised at Arkansas Post, continued under the military commandants.[18] This situation apparently continued for another three years until some effort was made to organize an American-style court in Arkansas Post in 1808, albeit one consisting entirely of lay judges: a Court of Common Pleas and a Court of Quarter Sessions. At the same time, a new District of Arkansas was created (for the second, but not the last, time). The convening of the Court of Common Pleas at Arkansas Post on December 5, 1808, was likely the first such court to sit there.

This untidy situation prevailed until 1814. The Missouri Territory had been officially created on June 4, 1812, and the County of Arkansas, finally, was created on December 13, 1813. A new Court of Common Pleas was established, and in 1814 an additional judge was authorized for the Missouri Territory and given exclusive jurisdiction to "reside at or near the village of Arkansas." George Bullitt, from Ste. Genevieve, was appointed to that judgeship as the first professional lawyer to sit on an Arkansas court. He served for five years, until the Territory of Missouri was divided into two parts, one of which became the Territory of Arkansas, effective July 4, 1819.[19]

When Missouri Territory was divided, the act dividing the territory provided for the appointment of three superior court judges. These first judges, along with the appointed executive branch officials, were authorized to serve a legislative function until such time as a regular legislative body could be organized in the territory. Under the laws of the Missouri Territory, which were extended to the newly established territory, superior court judges were assigned to districts and were required to hold court as circuit court judges in addition to their duties on the superior court. This aspect of the court structure was initially rejected by the first regular territorial legislature, but in 1821 the legislature reestablished the circuit court structure with superior court judges serving both capacities. By an act at the same time, the superior court was given original jurisdiction in criminal cases, concurrent jurisdiction with inferior courts, and exclusive appellate jurisdiction in civil cases, with any two of the judges empowered to sit on appeals.[20]

During the three years from 1824 until 1827, the superior court reported only nineteen cases. In what may have been the most interesting, *United States v. Cha-to-an-Na-pe-sea and Wa-Na-sea-shiner, Osage Indians*, the court held that Congress had the constitutional power to give the court jurisdiction of offenses committed by Indians.[21] The Indian defendants had claimed their attack upon certain territorial citizens was an act of war against the United States and that the Osage Indians were a sovereign and independent nation that possessed the right to declare war and commence hostilities against the United States. The court did not accept the argument and indicated that, even if it was a sound position, the Osage Nation was "in amity" with the United States and had disavowed the act of the defendants and had surrendered them, along with others, to be tried for the offense. The court upheld the verdict and sentenced the prisoners to be executed.

When sitting as an appellate court, the cases heard dealt primarily with collection of debts, with a limited number of criminal cases mixed in. An exception is a case of particular interest, *Grande v. Foy,* where the court concluded that the common law had been adopted in Louisiana Territory as far back as 1807 and "indeed prior to that time."[22] This opinion by Judge Cross has been characterized by Judge Arnold as "discursive" and "incoherent."[23] But it is the only opinion in which the Arkansas territorial court addressed the question of the adoption of common law instead of civil law.[24]

Early Statehood: An Overview

From the time of statehood until the Civil War, those associated with the celebrated Conway-Sevier-Johnson families—all interrelated by marriage, often connected professionally, and all Democrats with ties to Andrew Jackson—dominated politics in Arkansas.[25] The same "ruling dynasty" exerted considerable influence on the competing Whig Party.[26] The family influence in the first state elections resulted in the election of James S. Conway as governor, his brother Elias Conway as auditor, and Ambrose H. Sevier and William S. Fulton, Conway relatives, as the state's first US senators. The Conway faction handpicked Archibald Yell as congressman, Robert A. Watkins as secretary of state, and William Woodruff as treasurer. The domination of state politics by a single ruling faction was relatively easy. Conventions, arranged by party leaders, nominated both local and statewide candidates, and only after the selection of the nominees did public campaigning commence.[27]

Arkansas continued to be isolated by geographic barriers. The population, though increasing in number, was homogeneous, and a "traditionalistic" political culture prevailed.[28] The population exceeded fifty thousand, and the new state was ruled by "fine Arkansas gentlemen."[29] The ruling gentry could be contrasted to the larger part of the population, which continued to consist of self-sufficient hunters and small farmers to whom state government and its institutions were largely irrelevant.[30] Diane Blair described this: "For most Arkansans, then, whose lives would proceed in the same path regardless of any election outcome, politics was simply a spectator sport."[31]

During the early statehood period, settlers came to Arkansas looking for economic opportunities, frequently seeking land. The state's population doubled by 1840. The settlers were nearly all farmers, either acquiring their own land or squatting on government land they hoped to purchase in the future.[32] The highlands were home to a society of small farmers; the lowlands, home to a "small class of market-oriented planters."[33] With the expansion of plantation agriculture, slaveholding also increased. Planters who owned slaves were identified as the elite in the social hierarchy.[34]

Donald P. McNeilly in his study of early Arkansas society concludes that the planter elite controlled the wealth and manipulated the electoral process, always "unwaveringly ruled by the dictates and needs, in every detail and to the exclusion of everything inconsistent with it, of plantation society." He describes this "durable hegemony" as follows:

> They managed to reestablish then their thoroughgoing consensus among all of white society even in a frontier society energized by hyperdemocracy. In their crowning achievement—defining freedom as the right to own slaves—they had drawn all of yeoman society into their orbit and under their durable hegemony.[35]

While there were class distinctions in the antebellum years, society in the state was "relatively cohesive." As Carl Moneyhon says,

> The agrarian base of society added to the dominant social ideal. The plantation, farm, and rural village typified the world of individual Arkansans and provided a setting that reinforced the white egalitarianism of southern culture. The majority of individuals were bound together, from the richest to the poorest farmer, in a common struggle to wrest a living from nature.[36]

This social ideology was not one that generated class conflict but, rather, a common worldview that individual hard work could result in upward social mobility. But, this egalitarianism for whites meant that the institution upon which the success of the elites rested, slavery, must be protected. The state's economy was tied to the interests of the minority—the slaveholding planters—so these agrarian and commercial leaders could advocate legislative policies that played "upon the hopes of the majority of people that they would at some future time benefit from particular policies."[37]

Throughout the period, Democrats controlled the legislature. For example, in 1838 the state senate had thirteen Democrats and four Whigs; the House, thirty-two Democrats and seven Whigs.[38] While the Democrats dominated the period, the "opposition" would occasionally achieve some success. Thomas W. Newton, a Whig from Pulaski County, won election to Congress to 1846 to fill the vacancy created when Archibald Yell resigned to enter the Mexican War. And Whig David Walker was elected to the Arkansas Supreme Court in 1848. In April 1849, a Democrat, John S. Roane, defeated Whig Cyrus W. Wilson by only 89 votes out of 6,545 cast in a special election for governor.[39]

The Know-Nothing Party replaced the Whigs in the mid-1850s as the opposition party. Its leaders included such old Whigs as Albert Pike and Absalom Fowler. However, it did not successfully challenge the Conway faction. The real challenge to the ruling faction, by then called the "Johnson Machine," came in the late 1850s as the growing western part of the state began to demand a stronger voice in state politics.[40] An independent wing of the Democrat Party steadily grew in influence and successfully split the Conway-Johnson dynasty in the 1860 election. Henry M. Rector, a Conway relative, who had been placed on the state supreme court in 1859 to "get him out of the way," resigned from the court, denounced the Johnson faction's policies, and won election as governor with support of the opposition.[41]

The Civil War disrupted government functions, including the courts, and while the court continued to function, the number of opinions was limited. The justices elected prior to the war continued to serve under the Confederate state government throughout the war period, except for Justice Hulbert Fairchild, who resigned in 1864 to be replaced by Albert Pike.

In the meantime a new state constitution was adopted in 1864 under federal auspices and under the supervision of the military authorities. Only federal soldiers and those who had taken an oath of allegiance to the Union could vote. This constitution differed little from the original 1836 constitution, except it repudiated secession and outlawed slavery. It provided for election of members of the state supreme court, and a slate of officials were presented to the voters along with the constitution itself in March 1864.[42] Those eligible to vote, excluding the area of the state under Confederate control, approved the constitution by a vote of 12,177 to 266.[43] A new three-member supreme court was elected, but its contribution was limited. This court did issue one critically important decision in 1865, *Rison v. Farr*.[44] This decision construed a provision of the new constitution regarding voter qualification to override restrictions enacted by the legislature. This decision paved the way for ex-Confederates to reassert political power in Arkansas.

The ex-Confederates gained control of the legislature as "conservatives" in the election of 1866. At this election David Walker, John J. Clendennin, and Freeman W. Compton were elected to the court. This trio functioned efficiently through December 1866 and both terms of 1867 before their removal from office by the federal Reconstruction Acts. On March 2, 1867, Thaddeus Stevens of Pennsylvania introduced the first Reconstruction Act in Congress, which declared that no legal state government existed anywhere in the South. Arkansas was placed in a military district along with Mississippi, and the military commander was empowered to substitute trials before a military commission for civil courts. Naturally, no appeal was to be heard to a civilian court. The Reconstruction Act demanded new constitutions of the southern states.[45]

The dissatisfaction of the congressional radicals with President Andrew Johnson's amnesty proclamation of May 29, 1865, and the clear reassertion of control of state government by the former Confederates led to the eventual assertion of congressional control of Reconstruction.[46] The first Reconstruction Act, passed over presidential veto, declared that no legal state governments existed in ten of the former confederate states, including Arkansas, and established military districts to maintain law and order and to protect life and property. The act also called for a convention in each state to draw a constitution acceptable to the US Congress.[47] The qualification for electors to select members of the convention restricted the vote to those who had not been "disfranchised for participation in the rebellion." The second Reconstruction Act provided for elector registration.[48] The third Reconstruction Act of July 19, 1867, attempted to clarify just who was disfranchised and excluded all "executive and judicial officers" as those who had held any "civil offices created by law for the administration of any general law of a State, or for the administration of justice."[49]

General E.O.C. Ord, who commanded the Fourth Military District, including Arkansas and Mississippi, followed a strict interpretation of the acts.[50] The registration of voters was completed under General Ord's direction so that by November 9, 1867, he certified that 68,805 persons were on the rolls. The question of holding a constitutional convention was put to a vote on the first Tuesday in November. According to Ord's December report, 41,134 actually voted, and the proposition carried 27,567 for to 13,558 against.[51] Delegates to the convention were selected at the same election. Among those delegates were John McClure and Thomas M. Bowen, who would both later serve on the Arkansas Supreme Court.[52] Bowen was chosen as permanent chairman and McClure served as one vice president.

The proposed constitution was submitted to the voters on March 14, 1868, and election to all state offices was held on that date as well.[53] According to the reports of the military commander, the Arkansas Constitution was adopted by a vote of 27,913 to 26,597, a majority of 1,316.[54] State election officials declared approval of the constitution, 30,380 to 41.[55] A Republican slate of officers was declared elected, including Bowen and McClure to the state supreme court.[56] Members of the constitution convention supposedly were prohibited from seeking office, but these delegates and others were elected nonetheless.[57]

Since a large number of the registered voters did not participate in the March election, a majority did not vote *for* the new constitution. However, Congress passed a special act of February 28, 1868, which declared that a majority of *votes cast* was sufficient for passage.[58] In June Arkansas was readmitted to representation in Congress. However, Reconstruction was coming to an end. Controversy over the control of state government dominated politics in Arkansas during the early 1870s. The struggle resulted in the adoption of a new constitution in 1874 and the election of a new three-member court. All three members had served before. The powerful elite of the state had resumed control of state government, and the court members were clearly of that group.

Organization of the Arkansas Supreme Court

The last territorial legislature in Arkansas called for a constitutional convention to meet January 4, 1836. The January convention developed the state's first constitution, based on the constitutions of other recently admitted slave states, in less than a month and presented it on January 30. Congress formally approved admission on June 15, 1836, effective July 4.

At the constitutional convention a judiciary committee, chaired by a former territorial superior court judge, Andrew Scott, presented what was described as an "elaborate report" related to organization of the courts.[59] Most of the recommendations of this committee were incorporated into Article VI. The Arkansas Constitution provided for a three-member supreme court elected by a joint vote of both houses of the legislature. The terms of the supreme court judges were to be eight years, but the first three members would draw lots for four-, six-, or eight-year initial terms. The court was given appellate jurisdiction with general superintending jurisdiction over inferior courts.[60] The court was to exercise original jurisdiction only as provided in the constitution itself. The jurisdiction of the court was not restricted to purely appellate matters. In fact, much of the time the early court was devoted to writs, such as writs of mandamus, habeas corpus, supersedeas, quo warranto, and certiorari.[61] The petitions on such writs required daily sessions of the court during the early years.[62]

The 1836 constitution provided for circuit courts (also elected by the legislature) with original jurisdiction in criminal cases. This jurisdiction was exclusive with regard to felonies.[63] As to civil matters, the circuit courts were given original jurisdiction with regard to contracts over one hundred dollars and for other civil cases not "cognizable" before a justice of the peace.[64] Much of the minor work of the courts was left to either justices of the peace or county courts. The general assembly was given the authority to confer jurisdiction on justices of the peace in cases less than one hundred dollars and in penal offences that were punishable only by a fine.[65] County courts were given probate jurisdiction.[66] One matter that was to become crucial in later years was the authorization given to the general assembly to create chancery courts when it was felt expedient to do so.[67]

The inclusion of a judicial article in the first Arkansas Constitution was typical of other state constitutions, which, for the most part, had recognized the concept of an independent judiciary and had either established separate courts prior to the adoption of the federal constitution or, if admitted thereafter, had adopted the concept of a separate branch of government consisting of courts of general jurisdiction and a superior court with appellate powers.

The new state constitution provided for the election of supreme court justices by joint vote of both houses of the legislature. Daniel Ringo, Townsend Dickinson, and Thomas J. Lacy, the first members of the supreme court elected by the general assembly, were not related to the ruling families, and at least two, Ringo and Townsend, were regarded as Whigs. In future years, however, others with direct family connections would serve on the court. For example, Thomas Johnson, Ringo's replacement on the court in 1845, had married a Conway relative. His replacement, George C. Watkins, likewise married (twice) relatives of the Conways. A Conway brother, William B, served on the court in 1847 and '48. In 1859 and '60, future governor Henry M. Rector, a cousin on the Conway brothers, likewise served. During the antebellum years, a number of other justices would have personal and professional connections to the ruling families. The justices during this period are listed in tables 1, 2, and 3.

TABLE 1

JUSTICES OF THE ARKANSAS SUPREME COURT, 1837–64

CHIEF JUSTICE	JUSTICE (1)	JUSTICE (2)
Daniel Ringo, 1837–44	Townsend Dickinson, 1837–42	Thomas J. Lacy, 1837–45
Thomas Johnson, 1845–52	George W. Paschal, 1843	Edward Cross, 1845–46
George C. Watkins, 1852–54	William K. Sebastian, 1843–44	William Conway B, 1846–48
Elbert H. English, 1855–64	Williamson S. Oldham, 1845–48	David Walker, 1849–55
	Christopher C. Scott, 1848–59	Thomas B. Hanly, 1856–58
	Henry M. Rector, 1859–60	Felix I. Batson, 1859
	Hulbert F. Fairchild, 1860–64	Freeman W. Compton, 1859–64
	Albert Pike, 1864	

TABLE 2

JUSTICES OF THE ARKANSAS SUPREME COURT, 1866–68

CHIEF JUSTICE	JUSTICE (1)	JUSTICE (2)
T. D. Yonley, 1864–66	C. A. Harper, 1864–66	Elisha Baxter (did not serve)
David Walker, 1866–68	Freeman W. Compton, 1866–68	John J. Clendennin, 1866–68

TABLE 3

JUSTICES OF THE ARKANSAS SUPREME COURT, 1868–74

CHIEF JUSTICE	JUSTICE (1)	JUSTICE (2)	JUSTICE (3)	JUSTICE (4)
W. W. Wilshire, 1868–71	John McClure, 1868–71	Lafayette Gregg, 1868–74	Thomas M. Bowen, 1868–71	William M. Harrison, 1868–72
John McClure,* 1871–74	E. J. Searle,* 1871–74		J. E. Bennett,* 1871–74	M. L. Stephenson, 1872–74
E. H. English, 1874	John T. Bearden (did not serve)		Freeman W. Compton, 1874	

**Impeached.*

The newly established supreme court first met for organizational purposes on November 7, 1836. The court met later in November for the purpose of enrolling attorneys who desired to practice before the court. The general assembly had enacted legislation requiring examination either by the court or by a committee before attorneys could be licensed to practice. Apparently, the court examined and licensed the first two—Samuel S. Hall and William Cummins—and then appointed them as a committee to examine other applicants. Nine other attorneys, among them future members of the court John J. Clendennin and Albert Pike, were licensed during this session on November 11, 1836.[68]

Before the Arkansas Supreme Court could effectively deal with the host of questions it would face concerning land titles, banks and banking, transportation, slavery, family law and family property, debt, and contract or criminal law and procedure, it was necessary for the court to sort out jurisdictional questions arising in the various courts established in the new state constitution. Procedures for all courts and, indeed, for the appellate court itself were a necessary prerequisite for a functioning judicial system.

These questions occupied a significant portion of the court's caseload, particularly in the early years. Even in some cases primarily focused on substantive issues, procedural and jurisdictional questions arose and had to be dealt with before the court could address the merits of the cases. For example, in the first of the banking cases to reach the supreme court in 1839, the issue was whether the court had any direct jurisdiction to determine whether directors of the Real Estate Bank could be ordered to appear and show cause why criminal information should not be issued against them for usurping their positions. The court denied the request and indicated that it was a court of appellate jurisdiction only. However, soon thereafter the court was considering such questions as a part of its "writ practice" in civil proceedings.[69] The court was literally writing its own history as it set out the rules to govern procedures in the courts, drew the jurisdictional boundaries for the court's operation, and established guidelines for attorneys and politicians working with and in the fledgling government. As the court grappled with its own procedures, it did so in the context of the political controversies and conflicts of the time.

The Ringo Years, 1836–1845

During the eight-year tenure of Daniel Ringo as chief justice, much of the court's workload centered on jurisdictional and procedural matters, as might be expected with a newly organized government and an untested court structure. Much of the work of the court in the early years was devoted to establishing procedures for attorneys to follow in matters before the court itself as well as in the lower courts. The rules of the court were included in the first volume of reported cases, and the first four published cases were procedural in nature. In 1842 the court adopted a specific rule regarding the nature of the briefs that would be published as a part of the report of cases. Apparently, some of the briefs submitted had become quite lengthy, and to include these detailed arguments in the case reports was unwieldy. Lawyers could continue to submit the lengthy arguments, but they would not be published in the case reports.

One reoccurring issue was the question of the jurisdiction of the various levels of the judiciary, particularly the Arkansas Supreme Court itself. The exact role each level was to play under the judicial article was of some importance. The judicial article had expressly granted powers to the circuit courts, the county court, and probate courts. The exact limits of each court's role were, at best, unclear.

The legislature had in 1843 authorized circuit courts, under certain circumstances, to re-adjudicate, to revise or reverse their own judgments. In *Byrd v. Brown*, the court found this to be unconstitutional in that re-adjudication must be by some tribunal other than that in which it was previously decided, and superior to it.[70] The court found that the legislature had no power, under the constitution, to divest the supreme court of its appellate authority, and once an inferior court had pronounced judgment, its authority ceased and that of the supreme court attached.

On the other hand, the court protected its authority to intervene in lower court proceedings. In *James C. Woods, Ex Parte*, the court analyzed the constitutional power of the supreme court, which it labeled "appellate (ordinary)" and "extra ordinary" (where a lower court has exceeded its powers and required some correction).[71] The court confirmed that the court, or a single justice, could act using various writs to correct improper lower court proceedings.

However, the justices were concerned that if the supreme court allowed questions of law to be brought directly to it from inferior courts that it would be "oppressed":

> Were appeals or writs of error allowed to bring up cases direct from the most inferior courts, it is easy to imagine the

mischiefs that would ensue. The man of moderate means, the diffident suitor, and the lover of quiet, will yield to the presumptuous and overbearing; and the rights of the poor will frequently be crushed by his more wealthy opponent. The spirit of litigation would be engendered, strengthened, and differed, and the usefulness of this court, in a great measure destroyed, by crowding its docket with cases in many instances without a shadow of law or justice to sustain them, to the annoyance of meritorious litigants, and the exclusion of its legitimate business.[72]

Much of the court's early work involved the "writ practice," which evolved from the grant in the constitution of authority to issue a number of specific writs. Early in the first term the court confronted a case, political in nature, but focused on the use of a writ. *Taylor v. The Governor* dealt with, first, whether the supreme court had the power to issue a writ of mandamus to the governor.[73] The court found this writ to be expressly authorized in the constitution. The main question was whether the governor should be ordered to issue a commission to John F. Taylor as sheriff of Pulaski County. Taylor claimed he had been properly elected to the office. The governor had refused the commission, claiming Taylor had not properly accounted for public funds collected while serving as sheriff during territorial years. The court found Taylor had defaulted on his obligation and was ineligible to hold an "office of profit and trust" under the state constitution, so no mandamus should issue.

Two years later the court revisited the question addressed in *Taylor v. The Governor* related to the issuance of a writ of mandamus to the governor to issue a commission to a public official—this time to the commissioner of public buildings.[74] In part the controversy focused on the relative powers of the judiciary and the executive, and the parties argued points raised by *Marbury v. Madison*.[75]

Judge Lacy reviewed in some detail the implications of *Marbury* and concluded that a court had no constitutional power to compel the executive to perform such an act. He discussed the legal or constitutional theory of separation of powers and reached conclusions regarding jurisdiction similar to those in *Marbury*. Regarding the power of the judiciary the court stated:

> It is, however, the peculiar province and duty of this court to interpret and decide upon the laws and the constitution in the last resort. If two laws are opposed to each other, the court must determine which shall govern; so if the constitution and a statute stand in irreconcilable variance . . . [t]he constitution regards the judiciary as the final arbiter and interpreter of its will, and its language is in many instances addressed to the courts. It would be wholly impossible without the agency or action of the courts, to preserve inviolate the rights of personal liberty or of private property.[76]

The fact that the court spent so much time it its early years on procedural questions is not surprising. This was typical of courts in the early years of a state. As Lawrence Friedman has concluded, a certain level of "record worship" was a part of appellate review during the entire nineteenth century; that is, appellate courts tended to be "sticklers for technicality" and "spent their lives looking at formal records and may have come to believe in them too much."[77]

During these initial years, the banking controversy dominated political discussion in the state. Likewise, cases involving the banks were regularly before the court. Beyond the cases relating to courts and procedure, the banking cases and others characterized as "public interest" or "debt and contract" cases dominated the court's docket. Few criminal cases and none involving family law or torts were heard. Slavery cases were beginning to appear but were not a major part of the caseload in the early years.

The public interest cases dealt with the balancing of power between the three branches of government and, in particular, the court's role. Banking questions still occupied the court, particularly in the July 1842 term, when four important cases were resolved just before the expiration of the term of Justice Townsend Dickinson (who was not reelected). A small number of slavery cases were before the court during these years, including the first conflict over whether a transaction was a sale or a loan of a slave and the first slave warranty case.

The Johnson Years, 1845–1852

An "era of extreme fussiness," to use Friedman's term, was most evident during the period of Chief Justice Thomas Johnson's leadership (1845–1852). The court set a "high value on regularity of procedure" and would overturn cases on the slightest technicality.[78] For example, in a debt case, the argument was made that one of the parties to the contract was "Semon," but had been identified on the declaration (statement in this suit) as "Semons."[79] The court analyzed the effect of the addition of "s" as to whether these were the same party. The test used was "whether they are the same in sound." The court found the final "s" to be "as full and distinct as that of any other letter preceding it" and, as a result, the variance in names rendered the judgment in the case invalid.[80]

During the Johnson years the court reported 804 opinions. Over one-fourth dealt with procedural issues or the jurisdiction of the various courts. While routine procedural questions dominated the court's docket in raw numbers (along with the debt and contract cases), the clear emphasis in importance was on the jurisdiction and authority of the various courts. In addition, constitutional amendments during this period modified the way circuit courts were chosen and dealt with the legislature's authority regarding the court system. A significant number of cases related to these changes. Other questions involving court procedure included the important distinction between law and equity.

In what may have been the most significant case of the 1845 term, *Hempstead & Conway v. Watkins*, the court analyzed the distinction between law and equity.[81] It was certainly the longest case. The court directed summaries of the arguments of counsel be reported due to the "importance of the principles involved in the case."[82] The underlying case dealt with complicated issues surrounding the relationship of creditors, principals, and sureties. However, the issue of most public importance related to the exercise of equity jurisdiction by the circuit courts. The constitution had provided that the circuit courts were to exercise equity jurisdiction until such time as the legislature created separate courts of chancery. At this time, circuit courts were authorized to exercise chancery jurisdiction as the legislature had not yet created any separate courts of chancery. In exercising this jurisdiction the circuit court would sit "on the chancery side." Arkansas law recognized the distinction between cases at law and those in chancery. The legislature had passed a statute that suggested that the equity jurisdiction was to be exercised in "all cases where adequate relief cannot be had at law." The legislature had also passed a special statute dealing with sureties, which the court apparently felt limited court jurisdiction. This the legislature had no authority to do since the constitution clearly gave the circuit courts power to exercise full equity power. The court concluded that circuit courts have jurisdiction over equitable matters, but not because the general assembly had not yet established courts of chancery. The jurisdiction vested in the circuit courts "must remain there" until abolished or limited by the legislature.

The court, in analyzing the law in other states, included a sprightly defense of chancery jurisdiction:

> It may be also observed that many eminent jurists, like those of former times, entertain great jealousy against courts of chancery, and constrained to regard the ancient landmarks of the jurisdiction of chancery, and will endeavor to uphold, so far as in us lies, that magnificent fabric of judicial ethics, which has been reared in resplendent majesty by the most profound geniuses that ever erected a superstructure of human wisdom, or fashioned a system for the administration of human justice. We feel no disposition to display a Vandal barbarism by lending a helping hand to demolish and destroy so splendid an edifice, replete with everything calculated to demand our admiration and reverence; nor would we remove a single stone or efface a single feature by which the harmony of the super-structure might be endangered, or which might mar the beauty of its fair proportions.[83]

Beyond the constitutional issues confronting the supreme court relating to lower courts, other questions related to the procedures for securing new trials, appeals, and judgments. One can read these cases as the court's effort, in part, to educate attorneys regarding proper procedures. For example, in *Hopkins v. Dowd* the court focused on motions for a new trial and reminded lawyers that the court had "repeatedly decided" that the court would, on appeal, limit inquiry to specific causes set forth in a motion for a new trial.[84] Likewise, the court indicated that it had "repeatedly held" that it would not reverse a decision of the circuit court where the only ground was mere weight of the evidence.[85]

In this second stage of the court's history, questions of procedure still played a major role in the workload of the court, although in raw numbers cases related to debt and contract became the leading type of case before the court. When combined with cases characterized as "bank and banking," many of which were actually debt collection efforts, this area of law was increasingly important. Property-related cases, including those called "public land" cases and slavery cases, were also emerging as significant during this period, including a number relating to slaves as inherited property.

The Watkins/English Years, 1853–1861

By the time that Chief Justice George Watkins assumed his duties in 1853 many of the procedural issues and questions involving the jurisdiction and authority of various courts had been resolved. Likewise, as the history of the state banks drew to a close, fewer bank cases occupied the court's time as well. Since fewer procedural and bank questions reached the court, they were replaced with a greater number of cases dealing with property, including slaves. In addition, more criminal matters were appealed. As the banking controversy wound down, the court was confronted with other cases related to development of the economy: internal improvements and transportation. Following the grant of swampland to the state by the 1850 federal legislation, struggles over control of the disposition of this land and over the proceeds from its sale would evolve as a constant source of strife. Likewise, as efforts to develop railroads generated sectional jealousies and political conflict, questions began to reach the court related to legal issues surrounding those business entities. The increase in public land cases during this period may be attributed to the swampland cases; the increase in cases related to business entities, to railroad controversies.

As public attention began to focus on the issue of slavery, so to did the court. A total of seventy-seven slave cases were heard by the court in the years leading up to the Civil War. In those cases, the court dealt with the consuming issue of the nature of slaves as property, how they would be treated in inheritance and probate matters, as separate property of married women, and, of course, as collateral for debt. Warranty issues were frequently litigated, as were other contract issues. Perhaps most important were the suits for freedom and emancipation cases as they reflect the court's attitude toward protection of property and the acknowledgment of a paternalist/hierarchical view of slave society.

In the early years the work of the Arkansas Supreme Court was dominated by jurisdictional and procedural matters. During the Ringo years, 1837–1844, 52 of the 168 cases (31 percent) were procedural in nature. In the Johnson years, 1845–1852, 186 of 802 cases (21 percent) were of this type. Even in the Watkins/English years, 1853–1861, procedural questions continued to confront the court; 196 of 1,157 cases (17 percent) were predominately procedural questions.

Over time other cases emerged in importance. Debt and contract issues were the most significant. During the Ringo years only 17 of 608 cases (3 percent) were debt and contract cases. During the Johnson years 242 of the 802 cases (30 percent) were of this type. In the third stage 262 of 1,157 cases (23 percent) involved debt or contract. If many of the banking cases are combined with these, especially during the Johnson years, the number related to debt rises even more.

Another striking feature of the caseload trend is the significant increase in the number of cases involving slaves or slavery. The raw number of cases never reached the level of other case types, but the increase from 7 cases in the early years to 36 in the middle years and to 77 in the prewar years is noteworthy. Much of the "law of slavery" was set out in the decade prior to the outbreak of the Civil War as the court struggled to apply existing legal concepts to the "peculiar institution."

The War Years and Reconstruction

During the first year of the war potential economic collapse in Arkansas was a great threat. Credit was unavailable, debtors were unable to pay on loans, and creditors were unwilling to extend further credit.[86] Shortages of supplies followed. Planters were unwilling to abandon cotton production in favor of foodstuffs.[87] The military situation in the state added to the instability. General Thomas Hindman attempted to stabilize matters by declaring martial law in mid-1862. This move was generally resented, and civilian authorities expressed concern over the usurpation of authority.[88]

Initially, attempts were made to keep state and local government in operation. The Arkansas Supreme Court issued only one opinion in the June term 1862, but in December it issued twenty, and in June 1863, twelve. Predictably, the court was called upon to resolve a number of issues related to slaves. This court, composed of Justices English, Compton, and Fairchild, was disrupted with the resignation of Fairchild, who felt the military authority had gone too far.[89] He was involved in three important cases involving interpretation of the secession constitution and state legislation under the Confederate government. Albert Pike took his place on the court. This court issued seven opinions that were "lost" until included in a subsequent issue of the *Arkansas Reports* after the conservatives regained temporary control of state government after the war concluded.[90]

The court's workload declined as the war progressed, and, eventually, the court would cease to function altogether. This was a reflection of the fact that local courts were, for the most part, closed during much of the period.

A second state supreme court was established by the constitution of 1864 in those areas under federal control. This court, elected in March 1864, began to function only in late 1865 after courts were reestablished in the state. This court did decide one important case in December of 1865, *Rison v. Farr,* involving the new constitutional provisions related to voter qualifications.[91] This decision, which found voter qualification restrictions enacted by the legislature to be in conflict with the new constitution, paved the way for ex-confederates to reassert political power in Arkansas. An oath that a prospective voter had not taken up arms or supported the Confederacy since April 1864 was not a valid qualification.

The appellate workload increased significantly when a completely new court was elected in 1866 as Democrats asserted control of the civil government in the elections of that year. However, this return to normalcy was not to last, nor would this court remain in office much longer. On March 2, 1867, Thaddeus Stevens of Pennsylvania introduced the first Reconstruction Act, which declared that no legal state government existed anywhere in the South. Arkansas, along with Mississippi, was placed in a military district, and the military commander was empowered to substitute trials before a military commission for civil courts. New constitutions were demanded of the southern states. The members of the Arkansas Supreme Court were removed from office.[92] Congressional Reconstruction had arrived.

The 1868 constitution, developed in response to the Reconstruction Act, provided for a mixed system with the chief justice of the Arkansas Supreme Court appointed by the governor but with the associate justices elected by "qualified electors." The justices selected in 1868 served during a period of increasing political controversy in Arkansas. Some members of the court became embroiled in the political turmoil; some were impeached by the legislature; others managed to avoid personal controversy. However, the court itself was caught up in the issues of the day and, on more than one occasion, had to resolve questions growing out of the political situation.

The political questions before the court occupied much of the court's time during this period. These opinions reflect greater thought and analysis and sometimes generated vigorous, dissenting opinions, especially as the major split in the Republican Party developed in the early 1870s. The cases that involved important political issues can be classified into five major categories. First, the court dealt with a series of cases related to currency. Contracts entered into during the war often referred to "dollars" or "Confederate money." Questions continued to arise as to the effect of obligations during the conflict where specific currency was referenced. A second group of important cases also dealt with questions arising out of contracts entered during wartime, such as those related to use of property for war purposes or those for the sale of slaves. A third group of cases arose out of local political disputes and conflicts between various groups who were vying for control of local government. These conflicts were of particular consequence because of Republican actions undertaken to finance government programs and the growing opposition to these programs at the local level. A fourth category focused on the legal effects of secession and the effects of federal action on Arkansas citizens and the validity of actions of the Confederate state government. But the most important category dealt with political controversies related to election disputes, the rights of individuals to hold office, and contests for offices, including the Brooks-Baxter contest for the governorship.

The involvement of the court in these political controversies ultimately led to impeachment charges against some members, specifically, Chief Justice John McClure and his close associates. These charges came amidst the turbulent struggle for control of state government, which ended with the adoption of a new constitution in 1874. The powerful elite in the state resumed control once again.

CHAPTER 3

Finding "Repose" from the "Nagging Concern" of Title Insecurity

Cases, Controversies, and Conflicts Relating to Land Titles

"Ruralness," in the words of Charles S. Sydnor, "lightens the weight of law."[1] In the rural culture of the South the ideal of social progress was "from frontier to plantation."[2] And, according to Sydnor, not only did this ruralness shape the southerner's view of the law, but the law was shaped by it: not only because of the agricultural population, but also "because of the prominence of countrymen in economic, social and political life."[3] Rural culture was, according to James Ely and David Bodenhamer, one of the defining characteristics of southern legal history.[4]

An illustration of preserving stability and protecting the status quo is provided by the Arkansas Supreme Court's ultimate approach to land title cases. To move "from frontier to plantation," stability and security in land titles would be one area where the rural southerner would see the law as useful, a means of bringing stability to the social order. Land-law reform in early America was a part of the effort to stimulate growth.

> But law, policy and public opinion had most respect for productive property, property put to use, property that was dynamic rather than static.[5]

An active land market meant conveyancing was simplified; the law of real property was turned "into a more usable tool."[6] A "chronic problem" was title. Land titles were complicated by the very efforts to transfer public land into private hands, which added a layer of confusion with the various "certificate," "bounty warrants," "land scrip," and preemption claims that were used to evidence an interest in land.

> The land law aimed to make land freely marketable. But this was not an end in itself. The goal was economic growth, a rising, spreading population, a healthy, aggressive middle class.[7]

As land became considered a commodity, a marketable good, it was traded "with speed and fury."[8] As Friedman suggests:

> Even when genuine settlers arrived, built houses, and planted crops, the turnover was still exceedingly rapid. Farmers themselves were speculators who gambled on the rising price of land. Many farmers worked their land for a while, then eagerly sold out (at a profit) then moved on to a newer frontier.[9]

Conveyancing had to be simplified; land documents, standardized. This occurred early in the nineteenth century. However, the release of the public domain introduced new complexities. The issuance of new types of government documents—e.g., scrip, warrants, certificates—as evidence of title meant new types of disputes. These documents were traded and transferred, leading to new types of claims and frequent disputes. Fraud and abuse were common. Forgery was frequent; corruption in land offices and among local officials contributed to the problem.[10]

One doctrine adopted to the new conditions was adverse possession, which seemed to favor settlers against absentee owners.[11] The idea was that a person who occupied land for a specified period, remained in possession, added improvements, and did so "openly and notoriously" could establish a better right to the land than even a record owner. This was a reaction to "chaotic" land titles; it was a way to cure mistakes if one stayed in possession long enough.[12] This concept was the means by which many of the title conflicts were ultimately resolved. The "retooling" of the legal principle of adverse possession was an example of promoting economic growth in agriculture, favoring development and settlement over speculative ownership.[13]

Land title disputes demanded considerable attention of early Arkansas courts, including the Arkansas Supreme Court. The court was drawn into numerous disputes over land titles. Many of these were conflicts between speculators who had acquired presumed rights from holders of claims to military bounty lands, New Madrid certificates, claims to Indian lands, and, later, swampland. In some cases they had acquired rights from holders of preemption certificates.

While the court initially lacked sympathy toward preemption claimants (and was sometimes reversed by the United States Supreme Court), over time many of the disputes were resolved in favor of protecting the existing order. Occupancy was valued and the concept of adverse possession provided a basis for resolution of disputes and a recognition that stability in land titles was important.

Many disputes in early Arkansas courts were between holders of preemption claims and other types of unconfirmed claims to public land. These included claims under Spanish land grants under terms of the Louisiana Purchase. Under legislation confirming the Louisiana Purchase, grants made by the Spanish government that were settled by October 1, 1800, or settlements made prior to the purchase date of December 20, 1803, were to be protected. A number of these claims were in Arkansas Territory. In addition, portions of Arkansas Territory were made available as "military bounty" lands, which had been reserved to pay individuals who enlisted during the War of 1812.[14] A million or more acres of such land north of the Arkansas River was granted.[15] In addition, following the New Madrid earthquakes of 1811–1812, the government issued certificates to those whose property was destroyed, and these could be redeemed by claims on property elsewhere in Missouri Territory, including Arkansas.[16] Few of these claimants actually attempted to settle on public lands in Arkansas. Speculators purchased these claims, sometimes at the risk of legal disputes with preemption claimants.[17]

Hardly had the Revolution ended when restless settlers began to move westward seeking "a piece of the West" as a "moral right."[18] These pioneers were often squatters, with no legal title, who simply preempted tracts by moving onto the land, making improvements, and commencing farming. They soon came in conflict with speculators who sought to "convert western lands into commodities."[19] This conflict was reflected in the debate over national land policy. On one side were those, such as Henry Clay and the National Republican (later Whig) Party, who advocated a planned settlement of the West with revenue from land sales distributed among the states. Clay's view was that to legitimate squatting would encourage a "lawless rabble" to settle upon the public lands.[20] The Jacksonian Democrats supported preemption rights and favored a reduction in land prices to assist cash-poor settlers in their quest for land.

As the political debate continued, westward movement proceeded rapidly. Squatters not only exerted political pressure for recognition of their rights but, at a local level, disrupted the land auction system by active intimidation of land officials and prospective purchasers.[21] Congress reacted, starting in 1830, by enacting a series of temporary preemption laws that applied to all squatters on federal lands.[22] These laws were renewed in 1832, 1834, and 1838 and made permanent in 1841. Under these acts squatters no longer had to bid at competitive auctions but could prove up their claims and pay a minimum price for the preempted tract.

The public land policy of the Jacksonians was designed to accommodate the goal of Thomas Jefferson: to create a country of free (white) citizens, living independently "on their own little farm."[23] The goal was to settle and distribute this public asset in an orderly fashion and to "vest land and power in the hands of small holders."[24] These objectives ran afoul of those who wished to "convert western lands into commodities."[25] Even Henry Clay, who generally opposed preemption, criticized "fraudulent, heartless, scandalous, abominable speculation."[26]

When the Arkansas Territory was created in 1819, a significant portion of the population consisted of Arkansas Cherokees who had moved to the area with the approval (and encouragement) of

Jefferson. The president had, in 1809, promised to give land to those Cherokees who wished to immigrate west of the Mississippi in exchange for existing Cherokee lands in the East. This was only a first step, in Jefferson's view of "civilization," and over time, with space to develop, the tribes could transition from hunting on communal lands to farming on individual plots. Even in encouraging this move into segments of the Louisiana Purchase, Jefferson was not thinking in terms of permanency. Rather, Arkansas could "simply be a place where acculturation could proceed at a more leisurely pace."[27]

This policy set the stage for future conflicts over land in Arkansas. Whites moved into the area more rapidly than even Jefferson had imagined. The territory, at least much of it, proved suitable for cotton production. The international market for cotton caused "land-hungry whites" to "flood the region."

> By the second decade of the nineteenth century, all that white settlers in Arkansas needed was for Indians to vacate their land. Resistance was futile, and even those who most successfully adapted to white culture and customs, such as the Cherokees, would find that accommodation was no refuge from the onslaught of land hungry whites.[28]

Land disputes with Indians, particularly the Quapaw in southeastern Arkansas, inevitably slowed widespread expansion of plantation agriculture. Negotiations with the Quapaw and with the Osage in northern Arkansas were carried out, in part, to aid white settlement and, in part, to facilitate relocating of the Cherokees from the East to Arkansas. These negotiations let to a series of treaties with both the Quapaw and Osage and their ultimate relocation to Oklahoma. In the process, a tract of land north of the Arkansas River was purchased from the Osage to serve as buffer between them and the Cherokees. Conflicts involving this tract, known as "Lovely's Purchase," along with disputes regarding claims to Spanish land grants, claims based on New Madrid certificates issued to victims of the earthquakes of 1811 and 1812, "military bounty" lands for veterans of the War of 1812, and preemption certificates (secured by squatters who made claims of ownership) generated considerable litigation in Arkansas courts.[29]

Legal Actions in Arkansas Territorial Courts

Arkopolis was moved in a single day. About one hundred painted and masked men, working "amid songs and shouts," used ropes, chains, and logs to move each building of the settlement a few hundred yards onto Quapaw land. Buildings too big to move were burned by the "merry company" that "seemed tolerably drunk." This report was from an eyewitness account of the moving of the settlement at Little Rock from the original townsite awarded by the Territorial Superior Court to William Russell, a holder of preemption rights. The losing parties, who had planned to call the town "Arkopolis," claimed ownership under New Madrid certificates. The court ruled these to be invalid for lands south of the Arkansas River. Russell won the case but lost the town.[30]

Disputes involving land in or around Little Rock commenced before the decision was made to move the territorial capital from Arkansas Post. A driving force for that relocation was William Russell, a large-scale land speculator, who had purchased a number of land claims on the site of the future capital. Competing speculators settled nearby. Land allotted to the Quapaw Indians was a prime target of squatters and speculators alike. One rival of Russell was Stephen F. Austin, who, along with a number of associates, acquired unused New Madrid certificates issued after the earthquake of 1811–1812. In the meantime, Amos Wheeler had settled on the Little Rock townsite and began to lay out the new town.[31]

While the legislature initially failed to agree to Russell's proposal to move the capital, the Austin group was more persuasive and the legislature approved a plan that designated the capital as Little Rock and provided that Wheeler would construct a building for use of the legislature. Russell then filed suit and convinced the superior court that Austin's New Madrid certificates should be ruled invalid for lands south of the Arkansas River. The Austin group was ousted. Russell became sole owner of the townsite but found the town relocated to land outside his claim. Austin, in the meantime, conveyed his interest in the claims to Chester Ashley, who was to become one of Arkansas' most prominent (and wealthiest) leaders. Russell and Ashley reached a compromise whereby each owned one-half the claim. Little Rock was reborn.

Perhaps, the most important case in the early territorial period is the second case reported, *Russell v. Wheeler*, heard by Judges Scott and Johnson in June 1821, before Selden joined actively in the court's work.[32] This case grew out of the controversies surrounding the removal of the seat of government from Arkansas Post to Little Rock, and, in particular, the competing land claims for the town site. Following the New Madrid Earthquake of 1811 the victims had been permitted by Congress to obtain certificates for 160 acres of public land anywhere in the United States. William O'Hara had obtained three of these certificates related to the site of Little Rock. He had assigned a partial interest to Stephen F. Austin and Austin's brother-in-law, James Bryan. Amos Wheeler represented these claimants. This area partially overlapped a claim (by preemption) made first in 1814 by William Lewis but claimed in 1820 by William Russell and Benjamin Murphy. The competing interests both sought to have Little Rock named as the capital, and a number of prominent individuals had invested in one claim or the other. Judge Andrew Scott apparently had invested in the Russell-Murphy preemption; Governor James Miller, for example, had an interest in the Wheeler New Madrid claim.[33]

Wheeler had offered to the legislature, on behalf of the New Madrid group, certain lots for use of the territory and promised to furnish accommodations. Russell then brought a suit for trespass on behalf of the preemption claimants. On appeal, the superior court (Scott and Johnson) ruled in favor of Russell and upheld the jury decision in favor of the preemption claimants. The reaction of the New Madrid claimants was to move the town. They immediately demolished some buildings and moved others, an action colorfully described by one visitor as follows:

> First we saw a large wood and stone building in flames and then about 100 men, painted, masked and disguised in almost every conceivable matter, engaging in removing the town. These men, with ropes and chains, would march off a frame house on wheels and logs, place it about 300–500 yards from its former site and then return and move off another. They all seemed tolerably drunk, . . . and by nightfall they had completely changed the site of the town.[34]

A compromise was soon reached by the exchange of part interest in the competing claims so that the capital could be established.[35]

Conflicts over land titles began during the territorial period and continued into statehood. As indicated earlier, the most detailed and lengthy opinion of the territorial era involved such a dispute. The case is of significance because it resolved dozens of controversies growing out of Spanish land grants that dated to 1781.[36] The case, *United States v. Samperyac and Stewart*, involved claims that had been confirmed by a previous decree in December 1827 in favor of Bernardo Samperyac and others for four hundred "arpens" of land each.[37] The former decree had been based on purported land titles, which reflected that Samperyac had acquired the land by a grant signed by Spanish territorial governor Esteban Miro. The title showed a subsequent transfer to John J. Bowie and from him to Joseph Stewart. Part of the testimony in the prior case involved one John Hebrard, who claimed to have been an alcalde in Louisiana under the Spanish government from 1789 to 1791. He claimed to recognize the signature of Miro and testified to the legality of the grants. He further claimed to have known Samperyac. Judges Benjamin Johnson and William Trimble had confirmed the grants in December of 1827, along with 130 other grants of four hundred arpens each. No appeals were lodged in any of the prior cases.

The United States now took the position that the decrees were obtained by fraud, that the documents in question were forgeries, that Hebrard had committed perjury, and that Samperyac was a fictitious person. The government requested that the court annul the former decree. The court reversed all the prior decrees based on new evidence produced by the government. The court made special note of the fact that numerous transfers that purported to have been made to Bowie were attested by the same witness, John Cook. They questioned whether this same person could have been present in several different locations to witness the transfers from different original claimants to Bowie. The court said:

> Bowie must have had a talisman, possessed of the magical power of Aladdin's lamp, by which he calls up, at his bidding, this omnipresent witness. We have no doubt that this witness, like the genius in the Arabian tales, having performed

> the office for which he was invoked, has vanished into air, and disappeared forever.[38]

The court's reversal of the prior decrees was appealed to the United States Supreme Court and argued at the January 1833 term. The high court held that the original decree was a nullity and that Bowie had never acquired any title in the property and, given that fact, the transfer to Stewart passed no right or title to him.[39]

Legal Actions Involving Preemption Claimants

Disputes continued into the statehood years. Litigation between squatters and speculators (or competing speculators) was common. The nature of these conflicts is illustrated by two land cases involving title by preemption, *Wynn v. Morris* and *Wynn v. Garland,* where the court had to determine the effectiveness of efforts toward establishing preemption rights under the May 29, 1830, act.[40] The question was important enough that Chief Justice Elbert English, who dissented in the first case and partly so in the second, indicated in his dissent that he understood the cases would be taken to the United States Supreme Court, where the matter would be "finally and authoritatively" settled.[41]

These disputes arose out of preemption acts relating to a land grant in the vicinity of the Red River. The original act of May 29, 1830, allowed one to assert a preemption right based on occupancy and cultivation of acreage within the unsurveyed grant area. This act was extended in 1832. Subsequent preemption acts of 1838 and following years allowed purchase of land from the government if no one had a superior right under one of the prior acts. In 1840 and 1841 the lands were surveyed, and the next year a 500,000-acre parcel was selected by the governor for sale to raise money for public improvements. The governor proposed to planters along the Red River that they locate and be prepared to purchase the land at a price to be determined by the legislature. This was done by act of December 31, 1842, with the price set at two dollars per acre. Upon payment, deeds would be issued on up to 320 acres. Subsequently, the legislature allowed an additional 1,280 acres to be purchased at five dollars per acre. These arrangements were subject to any valid rights of claimants under the original 1830 act as a preemption entry. Such an entry would "nullify" selection and location under the 1842 act.

The first case arose when Keziah Taylor appeared and requested a preemption entry based on cultivation in 1829 and possession as of the date of the 1830 act on certain land in Lafayette County. She received a certificate of purchase and immediately conveyed the land to Morris. Wynn objected and claimed that he had been cultivating the land in question for several years and that Mrs. Taylor had been residing in Texas for some twelve years. He had acquired rights, he claimed, through a chain of transfers dating back to the time Mrs. Taylor left the state and had been in possession of the tract for some time.[42]

The problem was that preemption rights under the original act could not be sold. The land was unsurveyed, and no occupancy and improvement on public lands made the right transferable. However, by supplemental legislation, the right could still be exercised in 1842, and the inception of title would relate back to the original occupancy. (Any sale of improvements on public land was not a sale of the preemption right itself.) As a result, Wynn had received no enforceable right or title. Morris took subject to any valid preemption rights of Mrs. Taylor. Since her cultivation in 1829 and possession in 1830 was established, her right became a legal right. The only issue was whether she forfeited the right by remaining out of state and becoming "an alien." The court did not distinguish between right and title and found her right to be vested. It was on this latter point that Chief Justice English most strongly disagreed. He believed Mrs. Taylor had sold her improvements and abandoned the land, and since she was a citizen of Mexico on July 14, 1832, when the act extending the preemption system was passed, she had "placed herself without the pale of the spirit and policy of the pre-emption system," which should apply only to "continuous settlers or occupants."[43]

In the second case, Wynn claimed preemption under the 1838 act, showing that he had purchased the land from the government under that act. Garland asserted a right under the 1830 act (through one Samuel Hemphill), which the General Land Office recognized as the senior right. Wynn alleged "abandonment, fraud, and mistake" and showed to the court's satisfaction that cultivation had not occurred on the land in question in 1829 or 1830 but on adjoining lands instead. As a result, the preemption right of Hemphill was a nullity and Wynn's rights under the 1838 act were recognized. Justice English agreed with the conclusions on the facts but made it clear that to the extent that this ruling was based on the decision in the first case, he disagreed with Justices Scott and Walker.[44]

The disputes in *Wynn v. Morris* and *Wynn v. Garland* represent a common conflict between claimants who actually intended to occupy and use the land in controversy. Many of the disputes in Arkansas courts were conflicts between squatters and speculators or between competing speculators. For example, those representing the preemption claims in and around Little Rock were in no way the agrarian small holders for which preemption policy was designed to accommodate but, rather, were speculators who had taken advantage of the preemption policy to assert claims to what became valuable, non-agricultural land.

The Fight over Little Rock

The story commences with Matthew Cunningham, a physician from Missouri, who, along with his wife, arrived in the Little Rock in time to be involved in the Russell-Austin conflict and to assert his own claims as a preemptor. In *Cunningham v. Ashley and Beebe*, he asserted that he had, in July 1821, settled on and commenced to improve land south of the Arkansas River, a portion of which he had continued to reside upon and upon which he had constructed a dwelling facing a street in the town of Little Rock.[45] In addition, he claimed that he had acquired the interest of a holder of a "Cherokee pre-emption certificate," granted to those who had a right of preemption on lands ceded to the Cherokee Indians, and that this certificate entitled him to a preference in becoming a purchaser of the tract in question. When he attempted to do so in 1839, his claims were rejected. He discovered that Chester Ashley and Roswell Beebe had entered claims on the same land under

New Madrid certificates. This, he asserts, was done while he was in Washington, D.C., arguing his position that the New Madrid claims were invalid (to no avail).

Cunningham was not successful before the Arkansas Supreme Court. In an opinion by Justice Christopher Scott, the court found that Cunningham had not presented evidence of the validity of the series of assignments of the Cherokee preemption claims. Furthermore, Cunningham's own preemption claim was deemed insufficient because he failed to comply with the law to establish proof of occupancy and cultivation. The court carefully avoided ruling on the validity of competing New Madrid claims, only referring to the defendants as "honestly presenting what they supposed to be their rights" and indicating that the location of the New Madrid claims had been "afterwards declared void."[46]

Cunningham lodged an appeal in the United States Supreme Court. That decision was published in 1853, along with the Arkansas Supreme Court's decision on remand.[47] The United States Supreme Court opinion indicated that the denial of Cunningham's claims, though not stated in the records, was on the basis that the tract was covered by New Madrid locations "laid on" in April and May of 1820. The higher court upheld Cunningham's claims and found that the two New Madrid claims serving as the basis for Ashley's and Beebe's claims were void as interfering with Cunningham's preemptive rights. Ashley's heirs (he was by now deceased) and Beebe were ordered to quit claim the land to Cunningham upon payment to them of the minimum price for public land plus interest from the June 1838 date they had made their entries under the New Madrid claims. In reality, Cunningham only received one-half because one Brumback had actually had possession of one-half the quarter section and had conveyed his rights to Ashley.

The Cunningham-Ashley saga did not end with the decision of the United States Supreme Court. After the Arkansas Supreme Court ordered the mandate to be carried out, the parties (or their heirs) disagreed on how the division of the 160 acres should occur. (Ashley had acquired the interest of Brumback to one-half.) The problem for Ashley was that no entry had ever been made on the Brumback preemption. While the state supreme court decision recognized the preemption as superior to the New Madrid certificate claims, it had not recognized the Brumback preemption as giving title to Ashley. Cunningham was entitled to have the land divided so as to include his improvements.[48] Upon reconsideration, the court found that Cunningham might be entitled to rents and profits for the time the land was held by Ashley.[49]

Cunningham also sued the Brumbacks, who had been in possession of the premises since 1827 and during the entire pendency of the litigation between Cunningham and Ashley and Beebe. The court stated, "Christian Brumback, Jr., who was born on the land, is now in the prime of life, and has always resided on the land up to this day."[50] The court found that while the Brumbacks originally had no legal right, the plaintiffs had delayed so long they no longer had a remedy. In recognizing the concept of adverse possession as applicable, the court stated, "There shall come a time when even the wrongful possessor shall have peace; and that it is better that ancient wrongs should go unredressed, than that ancient strife should be renewed."[51] Cunningham lost after all.[52]

If Cunningham was a determined litigant, even more so was Nathan Cloyes (and his heirs).[53] The first of the Cloyes cases to reach the Arkansas Supreme Court was *Lytle v. State of Arkansas*, which was appealed to the United States Supreme Court.[54] The opinions of the Arkansas court and the United States Supreme Court were published together. On April 23, 1831, Nathan Cloyes filed for preemption on a tract that he had occupied since 1826. As it turned out, a part of the tract formed part of what Governor John Pope selected and sold to William Russell to raise money for the building of a courthouse and jail, acting under the authority of an act of Congress granting land to the Territory of Arkansas for erection of public buildings.[55] The heirs of Cloyes sued those who had purchased various interests in the tract sold by the governor. (Among those were Ambrose Sevier, James S. Conway, and Samuel Hempstead.) The US Supreme Court found that Cloyes had complied with the statutory requirements, so his right was perfected and was not affected by the subsequent legislation. This decision overturned the Arkansas Supreme Court's earlier ruling in the case.

The Arkansas court had ruled that Cloyes could not claim a

right of preemption beyond the fractional quarter section upon which occupancy and cultivation were confirmed but that his claim, even to that, must fail as conflicting with the act of Congress granting land to the territory. They read the federal act as preventing the exercise of preemptive rights on land that the governor had disposed of under authority of the grant.

The United States Supreme Court agreed with the first conclusion but not the second. The court found that Cloyes had not only held an "accrued" right but proved it prior to the June 15, 1832, grant to the state. He had "done every thing that he could do to perfect his right. The act of Congress could not impair vested rights."[56] The case was remanded to determine if the defendants could show that they were bona fide purchasers.

In *Lytle (Cloyes Heirs) v. State of Arkansas,* the matter was again before the Arkansas Supreme Court following a decision on remand to the Chancery Court of Pulaski County.[57] On issues not decided earlier, Justices Christopher Scott and Thomas Hanly considered the case "at great length." Justice Elbert English did not sit.[58] The primary question now was whether there was fraud involving the preemption right. Overriding the entire proceeding was the concept that a decision of the United States Supreme Court was "law of the case" and conclusive on all points decided. The main contention was that Cloyes had engaged in fraud and that one of the claimants, Absolom Fowler, had engaged in "champerty."[59]

The case had been in litigation since 1843 and following the US Supreme Court decision had been remanded to the chancery court to allow both sides to amend the pleadings and to fully argue the case on the merits. The basic contention was that Cloyes had been in possession of the land prior to his death in 1831 and his widow and children remained on the tract and paid for the property. They contend they were "unceremoniously put out of possession thereby by Governor Pope and other influential men."[60] The subsequent patent was issued by Governor Pope, and the plaintiffs claimed it should not have been issued on lands on which they held a preemption claim. The defendants claimed that Cloyes engaged in fraud and that Governor Pope's actions were proper.

The court recognized the superior position of the decision of the US Supreme Court but saw this as "substantially" a new case. In reviewing the history of the conflict, the court concluded that the claim of Cloyes rested on "occupancy and possession," but it expressed doubt as to legality due to some deficiencies in land office procedures. More important, the court interpreted the Statute of Limitations as foreclosing any remedy against the defendants arising out of the amended complaint filed in 1853. The court recognized adverse possession on the part of the defendants following the sale by Governor Pope in 1834.[61]

The court examined the alleged fraud by Cloyes in the occupancy and possession of the land in question. The court was not impressed by the evidence of cultivation, saying it was presented with "as little regard to the truth" as that related to occupancy. The chancellor could disregard the findings of the land office in this regard. While there were some statements from Governor Pope and his successor, Governor William Fulton, that were favorable to Cloyes, the chancellor's consideration of the testimony, quoted in the opinion, came down clearly against those claiming under Cloyes. The alleged preemption right was "but colorable, and was not substantial and was fraudulent in law, and found in favor of Cloyes by the Register and Receiver at Batesville, upon false testimony."[62] The main opinion was written by Justice Scott. Justice Hanly concurred in the result but disagreed with some conclusions, none of which affected the outcome.[63]

Another determined litigant was Henry Rector, elected in 1859 to fill a vacancy of the Arkansas Supreme Court. One of the cases heard by the court during his first year on the bench was *Ashley v. Rector.*[64] Justice Rector, obviously, did not hear the case, and the opinion was written by Special Judge Thomas Johnson. Rector, as a major holder of land claims, was sure to be involved in the fight for Little Rock land. The litigation commenced when the widow of Chester Ashley, along with Roswell Beebe, filed a quiet title action against Rector with regard to a tract of 640 acres in the city of Little Rock. This tract was purchased in 1838 by Ashley from the state as part of five sections granted to the state for completing public buildings. Rector's claim came from a succession of transfers from a holder of a New Madrid certificate who had located on the land in 1825. Interestingly, Ashley had also acquired a 3/10 interest in that claim. The issue was, once again, the validity of the New Madrid claim.

The court reviewed the provisions of the 1815 act, which allowed for the New Madrid certificate and indicated that strict compliance was required to create legal rights in the land. Upon examination of the factual record in this case, the court found no evidence of an acceptable survey of the tract by the New Madrid claimants. The purchase by Ashley (and sale of one-half to Beebe) was on the public records and Ashley and Beebe had held possession of the land dating back to 1825. In fact, the New Madrid claim had previously been declared invalid during the territorial years and "from that time been actually abandoned, and surrendered, as utterly invalid and worthless."[65] Rector's claim was, thus, held invalid.

The Fight over Hot Springs

Disputes over preemption were not limited to the growing area of Little Rock. Another center of controversy was around "the hot springs of the Washita," recognized for their remarkable thermal and reputed therapeutic qualities. The Dunbar-Hunter Ouachita River expedition of 1804–1805, sent by President Thomas Jefferson to explore the southern limit of the Louisiana Purchase, found that camps around the thermal waters already existed for those who sought health restoration in the waters.[66]

In *Gaines v. Hale*, heirs of a holder of a preemption claim ("the Belding heirs") sought to eject a holder of a New Madrid certificate.[67] They submitted correspondence from the Land Office reflecting that a preemption entry had been permitted on the land, subject to any interest of the United States (which had reserved the land). The land office recognized the Gaines claim as superior to that of New Madrid holders, and the court gave credence to this finding, indicating that any conflict between the Gaines preemption claim and the government would have to be resolved in a separate proceeding.[68] Evidence of the preemption claim would be admitted in a proceeding between the preemption claimants and the New Madrid claimants.

Such a conflict was soon before the court in a series of cases involving Gaines (the Belding heirs). In the first of these, the defendant was a future state supreme court justice and future governor, Henry Rector, who had inherited considerable land holdings from his father, Elias Rector, a land surveyor and speculator.[69] Among these were claims to the land surrounding Hot Springs. The conflict was between preemption claimants who claimed legal title by virtue of receipts and certificates of purchase from the land office and conflicting claims by those who asserted equitable claims under the New Madrid acts. The court followed the US Supreme Court as the "constitutional expounder of the acts of Congress" but not from "the deliberate and clear convictions of our own minds."[70]

The New Madrid claimants wished to introduce documentary evidence, including surveys showing the land surrounding Hot Springs, to be that of a New Madrid certificate holder, Francis Langlois. Their claim grew out of the act of February 17, 1815, authorizing those owning land in the county of New Madrid who had been injured by earthquakes to locate similar land on "any of the public lands of the Territory." New Madrid patent certificates specified a quantity of land but "floated"; that is, no specific tract was named. The court found that unless such claims were "fixed" on a particular premises prior to the date of a preemption claim, the preemption was superior. The New Madrid right had not vested. One way of showing that the right had vested was by a return and approval of a purchase of a specific tract by the land office.[71] The court again emphasized that the only dispute before it was the dispute between the parties to determine their respective rights. The effect of any government reservation on the ultimate rights of the prevailing party was not to be determined. The court distinguished the nature of the preemption right and the New Madrid right (which it called a "float") as follows:

> On the other hand, a pre-emption right, when not a float, constitutes a specific claim to the particular tract from the very first inception of the claim. It grows out of the particular tract of land cultivated and occupied at the time contemplated by the act of Congress which creates it, and inheres in that tract. The floating right, on the contrary, constitutes

> a specific claim to the particular lands on which it may be located, not from the inception of the claim located, but from the time of its location.[72]

Rector was not the only claimant in conflict with the Belding heirs. Others tried different tactics. In *Hale v. Gaines,* the claimant attempted to offer a Cherokee preemption certificate to support his claim.[73] The court said that the land in question was not subject to be located with the Cherokee preemption. In *Sweeptzer v. Gaines,* the claimant wished to offer proof that he was an independent settler on the public lands and that the Belding ancestor was not within the provisions of the preemption law.[74] The court rejected this argument, having previously found to the contrary.[75] While the court confirmed the priority of the Gaines (Belding heirs) claims to land around the springs, the ultimate conclusion was that the springs themselves were reserved for public use.[76]

Part of the difficulty for New Madrid claimants was interpretation of the New Madrid Act. The act permitted the location of a like quantity of land on any land of Missouri Territory then authorized to be sold.[77] Attorney General William Wirt had, in 1820, issued an opinion that New Madrid certificates could only be located on previously surveyed lands, limited by section lines. Congress, in 1822, provided that previous locations on unsurveyed lands could be perfected.[78] Elias Rector took no action to perfect his title at that time, and in 1832 Congress reserved the hot springs and four sections of land around the springs.[79] In 1831 Henry Rector had the original claim resurveyed and recorded. The litigation referred to earlier resulted. Rector's certificate was also rejected on the basis that the United States had reserved the hot springs in 1832.[80]

Indian Lands

As white settlers moved into Arkansas Territory they were confronted with Quapaw claims to much of the southern and southeastern portion of the future state. This area, suitable for plantation agriculture, became a target of those dedicated to appropriating Quapaw land.[81] A treaty with the federal government on August 24, 1818, accomplished this goal, in part. By this treaty the Quapaw ceded all but two million acres and retained hunting rights on the remainder. A subsequent treaty in 1824 forced the tribe to relinquish the remaining lands. The final removal occurred in 1833 when they were assigned reservation lands in the Indian Territory.[82]

The Osage were a different type of obstacle. They were a threat to the relocation of eastern tribes to central Arkansas. Friction between the Osage and both the Choctaw and Cherokee erupted into violence as the eastern tribes settled in the territory. Initially, a tract of land north of the Arkansas River was purchased from the Osage to serve as a buffer zone between the Osage and Cherokee. However, hostilities between the tribes continued until the Osage were finally removed to Indian Territory in 1825. Similarly, the Choctaw were removed in 1825 at the insistence of white settlers who already occupied land ceded to the Choctaw.[83] The Cherokee posed a more difficult problem. Early settlement by some Cherokees along the White and St. Francis Rivers was augmented by location of a larger number of eastern Cherokee to Arkansas in 1817. They remained until 1828, when they too were resettled in Indian Territory.[84]

White settlement in the Arkansas Territory progressed more rapidly than even Jefferson had imagined. The attraction of the new land as "unspoiled forests and uninhabited prairies . . . teeming with possibilities" meant that removal of the tribes became a goal of both "humble settlers" and the "emerging elite."[85]

As for the acres of land vacated by the tribes, a generation of litigation arose relating to claimants who were displaced by the initial efforts to secure tribal lands and those who settled on the land during Indian occupancy and never left. One such controversy arose out of the land purchased from the Osage to serve as a buffer between them and the Cherokee. This area, known as "Lovely's Purchase" (for Indian agent William Lewis Lovely, who made the purchase), included part of the northwestern corner of Arkansas Territory. White settlers were ordered to leave the area and, in return, each head of household could receive 320 acres of public land elsewhere in Arkansas Territory, a so-called Lovely donation claim.

Similar claims arose when white settlers were required to vacate areas ceded to the Cherokees. Many refused to move.[86] In

1828 when the Cherokee were forced to leave Arkansas, the lands they vacated were immediately overrun by white settlers vying to lay claim to improvements made by the departing Cherokees. The improvements were to have been appraised and the Cherokees reimbursed. The conflicts over this land were not finally resolved until federal legislation in 1886 recognized existing preemption claims and certain homestead rights.[87]

An example of the type of conflict that arose over Lovely claims is *Logan v. Moulder*.[88] There Logan agreed to convey to Moulder the Lovely claim of one Peter Mercer and warranted the claim to be good and valid. By doing so he had, according to the court, a duty to produce evidence of his title when legally demanded. Justice Thomas J. Lacy, writing for the court, spelled out in some detail the evidence necessary to prove title. A certificate from the Land Office, endorsed with the proof taken before them of the compliance with the law, complied with a right to location or entry on particular land, was enough to require a patent be issued to the holder or his heirs. Logan apparently was unable to sustain the burden of proof.

Swamp and Overflowed Lands

A major support for internal improvements was the donation by the federal government in 1850 of five million acres of swampland to be used to encourage the construction of levees, ditches, and drainage projects. This failed to accomplish the goal due to control of the funds by local interests along with outright abuse and fraud. The Arkansas Supreme Court was drawn into the controversies over the administration of the program and over conflicting claims to land.

The federal government conveyed "swamp or overflowed" lands to certain states in September 28, 1850.[89] The purpose was to facilitate conversion and development of these lands by permitting the states to sell the lands and then apply the proceeds to reclamation of the lands.[90] This grant to Arkansas was seen as a "means of salvation from bankruptcy," given the precarious financial situation the state was in following the collapse of the state-sponsored banks.[91] The secretary of the interior was to identify the swamplands, but one option given the states was that they could, through their own agents, present claims for lands they believed to qualify.[92] Arkansas created the Board of Swamp Land Commissioners to fix the price for the lands, determine the location of levees, classify the lands, and let contracts for building levees and drains.[93] The board created three districts and appointed "locating agents" to identify the lands for which claims would be submitted. Difficulties ensued and the initial selections were rejected. During this period of uncertainty, land settlement continued by those who held various types of claims or were squatters.

Attempts were made to withhold land from entry, but this was not successful.[94] The US surveyor general for Arkansas expressed his concern in a letter to the commissioner of the General Land Office in February 12, 1852. He questioned the wisdom of impeding the sale of the land but, at the same time, leaving the lands "free and open and accessible to the separate and combined interests of speculators and monopolists" who were, he felt, taking "immense advantage" of their positions as levee contractors, commissioners, and locating agents to select "choice bodies of land" and secure them by location using the various methods available to holders of "State Scrip."[95] This situation resulted in "much tangling of land claims, many of which clogged the State and Federal Courts for the next 30 to 40 years."[96]

When Elias N. Conway took office as governor in late 1852, he expressed his displeasure with the operation of the Board of Swamp Land Commissioners. In response, a law was enacted in January 1853 creating a new set of land agents to handle sale of the swampland at public auction. Lands not sold at auction could be obtained by use of "swamp land scrip."[97] The scrip involved was issued to contractors who worked on the levee and drainage projects. They could then use the scrip to purchase land at the auctions or afterwards, if the land was not sold. Speculators often acquired the scrip, then the land, which could be sold privately.[98]

The conflicts in authority between the newly established land agents and the existing Board of Swamp Land Commissioners led to great confusion and faulty administration of the entire program. In 1856 the legislature abolished the board, assigned its duties to the governor, and set dates for location and cancellation of the scrip.

The controversies continued up to the outbreak of the Civil War. In fact, just prior to entry into war the legislature approved the investment of proceeds from swampland into railroad stock, as earlier suggested by Governor Conway (and over the objection of Governor Henry M. Rector.)[99]

Some 8.6 million acres were received by Arkansas under the Swamp Land Act. Railroads and, eventually, levee districts ended up with significant amounts of the land. As summarized by Harrison and Kollmorgan:

> Many a great plantation was eventually made from the tracts granted to levee contractors in the years just before the Civil War. There is little doubt but what State officials and levee contractors got the "pick" of the lands. In many cases they obtained lands easy to protect from overflow and relatively well drained. Tracts selected by administrative officials as payment for services and those selected by contractors working on public projects were considerably larger than those purchased by actual settlers. Many of the great lumber companies as well as agricultural holdings found their start in the lands obtained under the Swamp Land Grants.[100]

Controversies over the administration of the swampland program generated considerable litigation. For example, in one such case, the authority of the land agent was challenged. Legislation gave the land agent some authority to resolve conflicting claims. The constitutionality of this was questioned. The court found it to be mere ministerial power and did not prevent a challenge in court of conflicting claims between those who received swampland certificates and those claiming preemption.[101]

The swampland program gave the administrators of that program the responsibility of acting for the public good in constructing levees and drainage systems. In *Martin, ExParte,* landowners claimed that the commissioners were filling in a levee in such a way as to stop drainage from a bayou, which, in turn, would flood their farmland during the construction process.[102] They requested an injunction on the basis that they would be entitled to damages for injury but that the swampland legislation containing no provisions for such a remedy.

The court took the opportunity to discuss the right to compensation when private property is taken for public use. The Arkansas Constitution contained no provision that provided for compensation, but the court said that it was "implied from the nature and structure" of the government. Eminent domain is an inherent power and, if private property is taken,

> the duty of making compensation may be regarded as a law of natural justice, which has its sanction in every man's sense of right, and is recognized in the most arbitrary governments.[103]

They cited cases from other states and the United States Supreme Court in support of the view that liberty consists of the security of private property, which is one of the primary objects of government. Even though it was not mentioned in the state constitution or in the swampland legislation, the court found such a right to exist. Since it did, an injunction was not necessarily the optimal solution since damages could compensate for any injury to the property. Since this was a temporary situation, the lower court was given the responsibility of finding a solution.

Another question was the issue of whether such lands were exempt from taxation.[104] When the lands ("swamp and overflowed . . . made unfit thereby for cultivation") were conveyed to the state in 1850, the legislature provided that sale of the lands carried a tax exemption until reclaimed or for ten years. Subsequently, in 1855, the legislature attempted to repeal the tax exemption and to tax the lands from the date of sale. Unlike earlier decisions in land title cases, the court found this would violate the provisions of the United States Constitution restricting laws "impairing the obligation of contracts," which the court characterized as "justly ranked about the wisest provisions contained in the Federal Constitution."[105]

The legislature also enacted legislation that authorized an annual special levee tax that raised funds for the improvement of levees in a county.[106] One major landowner, using scrip issued upon levy contracts, had located on some 90,000 acres of swamplands in 1855, 1856, and 1857. He objected to the payment of the levee tax. The court, apparently not enamored with speculators, distinguished the provisions in the 1851 act that permitted contractors the option of taking lands or scrip. If they had taken land in kind, this was considered a purchase and the tax exemption applied. If they took scrip instead of land in kind, they did not become a purchaser and did not acquire the exemption.[107] The court stated:

> In the offer of the State, the exception was held out as an inducement to purchasers and contractors to purchase, or, in the language of the act, "to take up" the *lands*, and not as an inducement to contractors to take *scrip*. Until the offer was accepted, or, in other words, until a purchase was made, there was no contract. Did the State not have the right to withdraw her offer? Was she bound to wait, in order that the holders of scrip after speculations had ceased to be desirable, might have an opportunity to secure the exemption? The State was under no obligation, legal or moral, to do so.[108]

The court went on to describe the nature of the scrip that could "be floated." The contractor might sell the scrip and realize the present cash value rather than purchase and select swampland lying anywhere within the swampland grant.[109]

One issue not decided in this case was the issue of whether the tax could be levied and collected on lands not subject to overflow or not protected by levees although within the levee district. The court interpreted the concept of alluvial lands "that would be benefitted by levees" to include lands in the vicinity that might not themselves be subject to overflow but would be more easily accessed as a result of the levees.[110]

The tangled web of land titles was complicated by the actions of various agents working at the same time. For example, in *Fletcher, ad v. Pool,* one holder of an apparent title had purchased land at the land office of the United States in January 1851.[111] Thereafter, the other purchased the same land with swampland scrip at the state office. The court found that the federal officials had acted by inadvertence on an erroneous opinion as to the state's rights and that the title to swamp and overflowed lands had vested in the state as of the date of the Swamp Land Act (September 15, 1850). The holder of title from the state prevailed.

Another complication arose when there were preemption claimants on land included within the swampland grant area. By the original 1851 act they were given twelve months from the transfer to the state to prove their right of preemption and enter the land. By 1853 legislation, this was limited to the date of public sale by state land agents. While these parties were not before the court in *Hempstead Land Agent v. Underhill Heirs,* the court raised the question of whether these conflicting claims might affect the title of the Underhill heirs who were challenging the actions of the state land agents.[112]

The Underhill heirs were before the court in another controversy growing out of a contract their father had entered to purchase jointly a tract of swampland.[113] He had agreed to furnish swampland scrip for full payment of the lands, and the joint owner was to deposit with a Memphis bank one-half the sum for the credit of Underhill. This was done, but Underhill apparently did not make entry to all the lands anticipated (only about 2,416 acres in his own name). The lower court found that over 4,336 acres should have been entered and ordered that the Underhill heirs convey an undivided one-half of the agreed acreage. The supreme court agreed this solution was equitable.

Another type of conflict in title is shown in *Deloach v. Brownfield.*[114] There both parties had supposedly purchased the land in question. Deloach claimed under one Frazier, who had applied to a land agent to purchase the lands in exchange for scrip issued to him for levee work. Later, the lands were offered for public sale by another land agent and were purchased by Brownfield and Watkins. The problem for DeLoach was that at the time Frazier applied to enter the lands in controversy the land agent had no authority to sell the lands as he had not yet received plats or maps of the lands and his authority did not commence until October 1853. (The application was made in September.) By December when the Board of Swamp Land Commissioners issued a certificate to Frazier, they no longer had authority to act due to the change in the law replacing the commissioners with state land agents.[115]

More successful was the levee contractor in *Brodie v. Moseby.*[116] There the contractor agreed to do levee work along land he already owned in anticipation of obtaining a preference right to purchase adjacent lands. He obtained scrip for his levee work in 1854, which, under a change in law, was actually issued in dollars and cents rather than representing land per se. He maintained that he never wavered in his intention to take the adjacent land and took the scrip as a mode of settlement. Once the lands were confirmed as swamplands in 1855, he exchanged the scrip and, eventually, in 1857, a deed was issued to him. In the meantime, Brodie applied to enter the lands and attempted to buy them, claiming that Mosley's claim was irregular in that he did not obtain the lands for work done prior to the change in the law. The court felt that Mosely had acted consistently throughout and that he had the better claim.

As late as the December 1861 term the court was still dealing with swampland controversies. Three opinions that term dealt with these issues. The most detailed was *Walworth v. Miles.*[117] The land in question was about 4,600 acres of land known as "Point Chicot," which Walworth had occupied from 1828 to 1836. These lands, along with some held by Miles, were included within what was known as the "DeVillemont claim," which was resolved in the United States Supreme Court in 1851 greatly due to the efforts of Walworth.[118]

In the meantime, Miles had contracted to do work as a levee contractor, and, upon approval of estimates of the work done, he applied for payment in the lands in question and in scrip. The Board of Swamp Land Commissioners soon thereafter suspended the application when Walworth objected to the sufficiency of the work, and then the commissioners rejected the Miles claims altogether. Walworth then requested to enter the lands. The court upheld the decision of the commissioners to reject the work of Miles. It did not regard the work by Miles as payment for the lands. The court reviewed other disputes between Miles and Walworth, including an attempted settlement agreement, an attempted arbitration, and a mortgage debt apparently owed by Miles. The court ruled for Walworth on all issues.[119]

Controversies involving swampland continued after the outbreak of the Civil War. The court, still functioning in December 1862, issued three opinions relating to preemption claimants and the sale of swampland. In the first of these, *McIvor v. Williams*, the land agent had permitted McIvor to purchase the land by virtue of a preemption right.[120] Williams claimed that he had a preferred right due to improvements made on the property by those from whom he had secured an interest. Unfortunately, by the time the land was sold to McIvor little evidence of the improvements remained. The original improvement had been the deadening of trees on an acre or so in 1855, which had become overgrown by bushes and vines by 1859. Similarly, in *Wright v. Green,* deadening of trees along a property line was not sufficient to establish a claim.[121] Two surveyors could not find the dead trees. Furthermore, the court found that, even if this had occurred, it was not for the purpose of improvement of the strip of land now claimed but rather to improve the land of the adjacent property owner. In the third case, *Paty v. Harrell,* the contesting claimants each asserted a preferred right to purchase the land based on improvements each claimed to have made on the same land.[122] However, the evidence suggested that the improvements of Paty and his predecessors in interest came before those of Harrell.

In the last term of the Confederate court in which Justice Fairchild participated, June 1863, three additional cases arising out of the swampland program were resolved. In the first of these, *Marlow v. Adams,* the evidence reflected that improvements were made at the time Adams purchased an interest in the property[123] Those of Marlow came later, so Adams was the preferred purchaser. Likewise, in the second case, in which the court found the evidence to be "painfully embarrassed by conflicting testimony," the court upheld the preemption status of what seemed to be the earlier improvements.[124]

The third case involved Albert Pike, who would soon replace Justice Fairchild on the court. The other party was the widow of George Underhill.[125] Pike and Underhill had entered into an agreement to jointly enter and locate swampland south of the Red River. Pike was to select at least 20,000 acres or more as Underhill furnished scrip obtained by him as a levee contractor. Over 50,000 acres was selected and final certificates of purchase were obtained for most of the lands. Underhill's widow claimed dower in each of the specific tracts, and the lower court decreed her as entitled to one-sixth life interest of all the lands (one-third of Underhill's one-half). The supreme court recognized her interest but felt it more equitable to first set aside one-sixth of the proceeds of each sale in interest-bearing accounts for her benefit rather than attempt to partition the land. The sale would be of sufficient land to extinguish Pike's debt. Once this was accomplished, the land could be partitioned between Pike and the Underhill heirs, with her dower protected in the Underhill land.

When Pike replaced Fairchild on the court, he had the opportunity to write his own opinion in a swampland case. In *Branch v. Mitchell*, in a detailed opinion, Pike considered a conflict between a claimant under the swampland program and one holding "Choctaw scrip."[126] Mitchell apparently owned lands on the Arkansas River adjacent to swampland that passed to the state under the September 28, 1850, grant from Congress. Under the state's implementing legislation, preference was given to those owning lands on the bank of a river to take the contract to levee the lands. Mitchell contracted to do so, and the records of the swampland commissioners indicated he had purchased certain of the lands in question.

In the meantime, John Jordan received patents from the United States for the lands in question with Choctaw scrip and conveyed an interest to Branch, the contesting party. Mitchell had selected the lands he intended to enter well before he completed the levee work, and even if a certificate had not been issued he was entitled to the land once the work was completed. The primary basis for the court's opinion was that these lands had been conveyed to the state under the swampland program and Jordan's purchase from the federal government gave him no title since the lands no longer belonged to the United States.

The second swampland case resolved by the Confederate court was *Rice v. Harrell.*[127] In this case, the court interpreted provisions of the 1857 act permitting preemption rights to be asserted on lands on which a claimant resided, cultivated, or reclaimed swampland. The evidence indicated that Rice had made improvements (although limited) on the lands in controversy. Although Harrell had also filed for preemption, his supported affidavits were apparently altered after filing, which meant his claim was not adequately presented.

Swampland issues continued well after the war. In the December 1870 term *Trulock v. Taylor* was finally resolved.[128] The case had originally been filed in 1862 but no action was taken. A new suit was filed in 1866 and the original suit was dismissed. The conflict was between a purchaser who had selected and entered the lands under the swampland program in 1858 and one who had purchased after a preemption claim had been established. Apparently, the land was included in lands selected by the state as part of the grant from the federal government to be sold as swampland. However, the plaintiff claimed the land was not overflowed or swampland and, in any event, had been possessed by him and his predecessors in interest since 1836, although no patent was issued to the original preemption claimant. The court resolved the dispute by applying adverse possession and suggesting the state had made a mistake in including this land in the swampland grant. Given the long period of occupancy, the state, as well as the defendant, presumably had actual notice of the plaintiff's claim.

In December 1871, the court heard yet another swampland case. *Harrison and Stewart v. Lewis,* was an example of problems that had arisen in management of the swampland program.[129] The plaintiffs presented proof that they had complied with the requirements of the program, had received a certificate of entry as paid for the land in question. The land agent could later find no record showing entry and payment, and as a result, a patent could not be issued to the claimants. The court ordered that the patent should be issued.

A June 1872 case, *Casselberry v. Fletcher*, followed *Branch v. Mitchell* and applied adverse possession to resolve the issue.[130] The facts, as in *Branch*, showed a long period of occupancy followed by efforts to claim under the swampland program. The competing interest was affirmed two days before that of Casselberry. In ruling for the party in possession the court stated:

> It is very clear that the general policy of the land laws, both national and State, has been and is to favor the actual settler;

> to prefer those who, with their families push forward to clear up the forests. Such being the general policy of the government, a court of equity, where the language of the statute will justify, should so construe it as to carry out that public policy.[131]

The last swampland case by the postwar court was in 1873. *Pence v. Sanford* involved competing patent certificates issued by the state land agent within three days of each other.[132] Sanford asserted that while he had the later certificate he should be given priority because he filed an application to purchase the lands many years earlier. The court said that to fully understand this equitable claim it would be necessary to "go at some length into that bundle of confusion known as the swamp land laws."[133] The court then reviewed the legislative history of the swampland program and the efforts of Arkansas officials to administer the program.

Sanford's certificate for location of 1853, issued by the swampland commissioners, was apparently an application to purchase, not a "full certificate" as contemplated by the original swampland legislation. In 1855 the legislature attempted to legitimize such prior actions by permitting holders of such certificates to present them and purchase the land if there was no conflicting claim to the same land. However, the court interpreted the 1855 act as applying only to certificates issued in conformity with law. The application of Sanford gave him no vested right against the homestead of Pence, who had been in possession at least since 1856.

Legal Discourse in Arkansas Public Land Cases

Many in the South initially supported the policy of preemption, not only as "vital to a society of liberated, self-directing, enfranchised individuals" but as a "blow against 'land speculators,' identified more and more as the scheming equivalent of eastern corporate monopolists."[134] This Jacksonian view prevailed through the politically turbulent 1830s and resulted in the adoption of the various "squatters' rights" acts in Congress, permanently codified in the Pre-emption Act of 1841. As increased agricultural competition occurred as a result of cheap-land policies, and as slavery expanded and the slave-holding elite ascended to power, there is evidence that support for preemption eroded in the South.[135]

Interestingly, in the cases reaching the Arkansas Supreme Court during this period relating to public land, few were conflicts between squatters and speculators per se but, rather, were fights between groups of speculators, some of whom had acquired their rights by purchasing preemption claims. This was particularly true in the conflicts concerning the land in and around Little Rock.

Close analysis of the language of the Arkansas court's opinions and an analysis of the outcomes suggest coolness to preemption claims. By contrast, in those Arkansas cases appealed to the United States Supreme Court (in which the Arkansas court was reversed), the higher court was supportive of the "adventurous pioneer." The highest court adopted the view suggested by Friend: "But pioneering as an activity, as a verb, was a *revolutionary* idea."[136] For example, the United States Supreme Court in *Lytle v. State of Arkansas*, in an opinion by Justice McLean, set out its view of preemption claims.

> The claim of pre-emption is not that shadowy right which by some it is considered to be. Until sanctioned by law, it has no existence as a substantive right. But when covered by the law, it becomes a legal right, subject to be defeated, only by a failure to perform the conditions annexed to it. It is founded in an enlightened public policy, rendered necessary by the enterprise of our citizens. The adventurous pioneer who is found in advance of our settlements, encounters many hardships, and not unfrequently dangers from savage incursions. He is generally poor, and it is fit that his enterprise shall be rewarded by the privilege of purchasing the favorite spot selected by him, not to exceed one hundred and sixty acres. That this is the national feeling is shown by the course of legislation for many years.[137]

Justice McLean was an obvious choice to author opinions relating to public lands. He had served as commissioner of the General Land Office in 1822, appointed by President James Monroe. He was then postmaster general under Presidents Monroe, John Quincy Adams, and Andrew Jackson and was elevated to the United Supreme Court by Jackson in 1829 and served until his death in 1861.[138]

McLean was not truly a Jacksonian Democrat and, at various times, sought the presidential nomination of other parties, including the Whigs. On the court he became increasingly nationalistic but tended to support vested economic interests.[139] As a westerner of humble beginnings and a former land commissioner (who as a young man had also worked for the federal land office), Justice McLean no doubt developed an empathy for the "adventurous pioneers" and a favorable view of preemption.

Of course, this view was not at all related to the actual parties before the court in the Arkansas cases. They were in no way the poor "adventurous pioneers" pictured by Justice McLean. They were, in fact, speculators who, in the end, did not prevail although asserting claims based on preemption, wishing to purchase a "favorite spot."

The concept of adverse possession was adopted as a means of ultimate resolution of many of these conflicts. The adoption of this concept is an illustration of the transformation of an ancient doctrine by nineteenth-century American courts in recognition of the occupier as having the superior right.[140] The English requirements of "residence, cultivation, fencing or other improvement" were relaxed to the key American elements of "actual possession, hostility, exclusivity, continuity, openness and notoriety." This gave "constructive" notice of the claim of the user even if "actual" notice might be unlikely.[141] However, in applying the concept in areas already developed, the courts were reviewing adverse possession as a "limitations model." That is, to bring some stability to title which would promote marketability.

> At some point, however, the true owner's opportunity to challenge the possessor's title must end. Delay decreases the availability and reliability of evidence; witnesses die, memories fade and documents are lost. Adjudications premised on such stale evidence are prone to error. Moreover, the possessor is ultimately entitled to "repose," or freedom from the nagging concern generated by title insecurity.[142]

In accepting this doctrine as a basis for ultimate resolution of the cases, the Arkansas court was weighing preservation of the existing order as more important than the disruption that might be entailed in displacing occupiers already in place. For example, as ultimately decided by the Arkansas Supreme Court, the Cloyes claims were found to be based on fraud and mistake. Adverse possession was found to give the defendants the better claim.[143] The same turned out to be true for Cunningham in his fight with Ashley and Beebe (and the Brumbacks).[144]

Cunningham and Ashley were among the most powerful in early Arkansas. Their conflict over control of Little Rock did not extend to political matters. Both were aligned with the powerful Conway-Sevier-Johnson families who controlled Arkansas politics (and political offices) from 1820 to 1860. Chester Ashley was born in Massachusetts, grew up in New York, completed college in Massachusetts, and studied law under Tapping Reeve at Litchfield, Connecticut. After moving from New York through Illinois and Missouri, he settled in Little Rock in 1819 and was a major force in Arkansas until his death in 1848 while serving in the US Senate. He was not only a successful lawyer but a major land speculator and by 1827 was considered the wealthiest man in the territory. He owned vast plantation holdings in southeastern Arkansas in addition to his Little Rock land.[145]

Ashley's opponent in the major land litigation was Dr. Matthew Cunningham, who had arrived in Little Rock about the same time as Ashley. Cunningham, a graduate of the University of Pennsylvania Medical School, was Little Rock's first doctor, and his wife was, apparently, the first white woman to settle there. The first white child born there was the Cunningham's son, named, interestingly, Chester Ashley Cunningham! Dr. Cunningham was later elected as Little Rock's first mayor.[146] Their land ventures and protracted litigation are indicative of the nature of the litigants most often before the Arkansas courts.

In the Cloyes's litigation, the nominal defendant was the State of Arkansas. In reality, the defendants were the trustees of Real Estate Bank, which included Chester Ashley. A separate defendant was William Russell. The end result (applying adverse possession) clearly favored the "elite" group of "influential men" who had "unceremoniously" put Cloyes out of possession. The Arkansas court had seemed impressed with Cloyes's preemption claim and appeared to be searching for a basis to decide against Cloyes in spite of the decision of the United States Supreme Court finding in favor of the validity of the Cloyes's claim. The court members, themselves aligned with the political dynasty, appeared to be inclined toward an outcome that would preserve the status quo and favor the controlling faction.

Henry Rector's claims were never looked upon with favor in the Arkansas courts. This might appear surprising given that Rector was a cousin of the Sevier and Conway families and, in his early years, benefitted from his familial relationship. This relationship was, however, "never secure." He was, some said, elevated to the supreme court in 1859 to "get him out of the way." He served only fifteen months, resigned to run for governor in 1860 as the anti-dynasty candidate, and won. By the time his cases reached the supreme court, his disenchantment with the domination of state politics by the ruling dynasty was evident.[147]

In the end, the Arkansas court found solutions that favored the status quo and permitted those in possession to remain so. These were members of the ruling elite who controlled the political process in the state.

CHAPTER 4

"Coon Skins and Peltry"

Cases, Controversies, and Conflicts Related to Banks and Banking

If states were to stimulate and encourage economic growth, the two main demands for public goods were for credit (and currency) and transportation. Arkansas, as a developing frontier, found itself disadvantaged in both. In 1851 when Albert Pike lamented over the "dull stupid apathy" over the whole state, some efforts to stimulate the economy had been tried and had failed. Most notable was the effort to create state banking institutions. The court's role in this controversy is noteworthy. While it cannot be concluded that the court acted "instrumentally" to promote banking, it is clear that the court was caught up in the political turmoil and may have molded decisions at any given point to fit the political climate. The court was at first reluctant to enter the controversy, then supportive of the bank leadership, then, ultimately, more protective of the state's interests. This saga illustrates how the powerful elite—primarily slaveholders—exercised their influence.

Future United States Supreme Court justice John Catron, then a member of the Tennessee Supreme Court of Errors and Appeals, wrote essays in the *Knoxville Register* in 1829 linking the economic interests of "the cultivators of the soil and the laboring people in Tennessee" to political liberty. The focus of his attacks was the investors in the national bank, which he chastised as a "monied aristocracy" that "care nothing for our wants, or opinions; the money is upon us like a cloud of Egyptian locusts to eat up our substance and be withdrawn."[1] Catron was expressing the frustration of many Jacksonians and, as a judge serving in the midst of economic expansion, saw the law as a means of promoting the public interest, not special privilege. Pioneer settlers found a sympathetic ear. On slavery, Catron saw paternalistic relationships as here to preserve the established racial order.[2] He adopted, according to Timothy S. Huebner, a "southern perspective on law and Constitutionalism."[3]

In this period of economic expansion, the "market revolution" was characterized by Charles Sellers:

> As pent-up demand galvanized commodity production, as masters of slaves and capital followed a flood of pioneer farming folk across the Appalachians into the heart of the continent, Americans first realized that they were indeed undergoing a market revolution.[4]

Thus, the three elements necessary for southern expansion—land, slaves, and capital—were much a focus of Jacksonians like Justice Catron. However, in spite of the political turmoil over the national bank, credit in the South was not largely supplied by banks, but channeled through third parties for the large planter and from the storekeeper for the smaller middle-class farmer. The planters themselves lent money and sold goods on credit to their less prosperous neighbors.[5] In spite of political rhetoric criticizing bank credit, and especially the national bank, no producers or traders could have survived without credit. As Tony A. Freyer has pointed out, local and nonresident traders were bound to producers in an "intricate web of contractual rights and obligations" that arose over the credit dependency.[6] Honest credit, as opposed to speculative credit, was seen as necessary.

> This reliance, moreover, helped to explain why anticapitalist rhetoric to the contrary notwithstanding, even mainstream democrats throughout the period supported state banks.[7]

In Arkansas that support was reflected in the 1836 constitution, which authorized the legislature to create two banks. One, the State Bank, would become a repository of state funds and would make loans throughout the state. The second, the Real Estate Bank, was "calculated to aid and promote the great agricultural interests of the country."[8]

During the December 1837 session of the Arkansas General

Assembly, the legislature had under debate a bill aimed at the extermination of wolves. The bill authorized a bounty for the scalps of wolves. During the debate on the "wolf bill," it was suggested that massive fraud might be practiced by those who would claim the bounties. Representative J. J. Anthony of Randolph County offered an amendment to the bill requiring that the "signature of the president of the Real Estate Bank should be attached to the certificate of the wolf scalp," apparently implying that the possibilities for fraud in presenting wolf scalps was similar to some of the actions taken by the unpopular Real Estate Bank of Arkansas. The Speaker of the House, John Wilson, who was also president of the Real Estate Bank, took offense at the remark, drew a large knife, and advanced on Anthony. When another house member tried to intervene, Wilson plunged the knife "to the hilt" into Anthony's heart. Wilson calmly cleaned the knife, walked back to the speaker's desk, and entertained a motion to adjourn. He was later tried and acquitted in an adjoining county midst allegations that he had improperly influenced the judge and jury. It was reported that Wilson, his friends, and the jury adjourned to a dram shop, where Wilson paid for drinks and the entire group spent the night celebrating in the streets.[9]

This incident illustrates the passions generated by a single issue that dominated Arkansas politics for almost fifty years, 1836–1884. Only during the period leading up to the Civil War was public attention focused elsewhere. The issue was the state debt arising, to a large degree, from the activities associated with the State Bank and the Real Estate Bank, both created during the state's first legislative session. Controversy related to the banks arose from the beginning and lingered well past Reconstruction until resolved by "repudiation" via constitutional amendment in 1884. As the controversy brewed, a series of lawsuits focused on the operation of the banks, their control, their assets, the debts and obligations generated, and the state's ultimate responsibility for these obligations. A generation of lawyers and judges were involved in the resolution of the various legal questions. And, naturally, the state's highest court played an important role in the saga.

That role is intertwined with the political intrigue surrounding the efforts of the state's powerful elite to create banking institutions to benefit agricultural interests in the state, that is, plantation agriculture. Promoters of the banking institutions were, whether Whig or Democrat, representative of the strongest political force in the state—large landowners. While the legislature gave voice to the idea that the banks would give "new impulse" to industry, the real intent was to "promote the great agricultural interests of the county," as stated in the state's constitution.[10]

This political intrigue is reflected in the evolution of the court's opinions during this era. At first, the court appeared to be reluctant to enter the banking controversy. Once it did, the initial decisions seemed to favor those in control of the banks. As the drama unfolded, and as the composition of the court changed, the court's opinions reflected a less favorable attitude toward those in control of the institutions and a more protective attitude toward the state itself. (The United States Supreme Court reversed the Arkansas court on three separate occasions related to this conflict.)

Creation of Banks in Arkansas

Territorial leaders in Arkansas had considered establishing banks prior to statehood. Specie, especially that spent on the purchase of federal lands, was leaving the area to be deposited in banks in nearby states.[11] These banks retained specie reserves (gold or silver) and issued their own notes, which could be legally transferred from one person to another as currency. The scarcity of specie made credit transactions all the more important and the push for local banks all the stronger.[12]

The first act of the state legislature in 1837 chartered the State Bank and the Real Estate Bank. The former was chartered as a state institution, the latter as a private operation backed by state funding.[13] Branches of each were authorized as well. The joint legislative committee that recommended that the banks be chartered indicated that if the state did not charter the banks, it would be "20 years behind." The committee's report proposed the banks as a means of giving "new impulse" to industry and controlling "our circulating medium." The banks, according to the committee, would be of "infinite value to the state." As a way of justifying the creation of the State Bank, the committee suggested that $1 million in state funding could be repaid in twenty years if the banks borrowed at 5 percent and made loans at 8 percent. The banks were to act as repositories of state funds, secure funds from "foreign capitalists," and lend money throughout the state.[14] Governor James S. Conway approved creation of the banks, along with $3 million in financing borrowed by the state, against the advice of Democrat leader Chester Ashley and Whig leader Absalom Fowler. The leading proponents of the state banks were John Ringgold of Batesville and Anthony H. Davies of Chicot County, both Whigs. The major opponent was Absalom Fowler, the Whig candidate for governor in 1836. However, only one Whig member of the legislature voted against the institutions. And, control of the banking institutions was largely in the hands of the "dynasty" leaders. Democrat Chester Ashley became intimately involved in bank operations.[15]

A national financial panic, combined with mismanagement and downright corruption, led to the failure of both institutions, along with the various branches, soon after they began operation. A hint of the difficulties to come appeared in the report of the president of the State Bank submitted to the general assembly in November 1837. While the report asserted that a "respectable surplus" had been generated through a "prudent course" and an "honest adherence" to the pledge to give "due regards to the honor of the state," the report also recognized the "present deranged state of the country" and reflected that only $100,000 of an expected $300,000 in state bonds had yet been realized.[16]

The state apparently could not sell state bonds due to the general economic conditions in the country, and the state's drafts for its share of the surplus federal revenue could not be cashed for specie. Only paper money from out-of-state banks was obtained, and the notes of those banks were the only funds available for operation of the banks in Arkansas.[17] Each branch experienced similar problems. Each was able to lend and did so magnanimously, but each had difficulty in collection. Each suspended specie payments within a short time.[18]

Following this report, the senate concurred in a house resolution for a joint committee to examine the State Bank.[19] During the remainder of the session legislators introduced various resolutions that expressed frustration with both banks. For example, Senator George Izard introduced a resolution on November 13, 1837, to require a report of the president of the Real Estate Bank concerning all bonds and mortgages used (intended) to secure bank stock. The resolution in its original form referred to the creation of the bank as "calculated, from its nature, to enrich the few at the expense of the many." This language was deleted by amendment, but the resolution passed.[20] By the end of 1839 the banks were clearly in trouble, and specie payments were suspended. In 1843 the State Bank was closed and the Real Estate Bank was assigned to private trusteeship, a matter of controversy and intrigue until 1855, when it too was closed. From statehood until the Civil War, the state's debt increased significantly, largely because of the bank fiasco.[21] The state's involvement in the banks provided political fodder for an entire generation and became the central issue in Arkansas politics prior to the Civil War. Both Whigs and Democrats became entangled in the problems created by the failure of the two institutions.[22]

As a result of the use of state bonds to fund the banks, state debt steadily increased so that by 1858 it was over $1.2 million in principal and interest on the State Bank bonds.[23] Among these obligations were $500,000 in "Holford" bonds that the Real Estate Bank sold for $121,366 cash to a trust company in New York and resold to James Holford and Company of London for $325,000. The Holford debt remained uncollected through the Civil War and Reconstruction but was finally repudiated, along with some other state obligations, in 1884.[24] The legality of those bonds was one of many questions concerning the banks that reached the Arkansas Supreme Court during the antebellum period.

Control of the Banks

During the January 1839 term of court, the justices encountered the first controversy arising from the operation of the banks. The state, represented by Chief Justice Daniel Ringo's brother-in-law,

Frederick Trapnall, asked the court to order the purported directors of the Real Estate Bank to appear and to show cause why a criminal information should not be issued against them for usurping their positions as directors. Among the defendants was Ringo's former partner, Chester Ashley. The court denied the request on the basis that the supreme court was a court of appellate jurisdiction only and could not exercise the requested power without legislative authorization.[25]

Soon thereafter the same parties appeared before the court in a civil proceeding to request that the supreme court order the directors to appear and show by what authority they held office (technically called a writ of *quo warranto*). Justice Thomas Lacy, rendering the court's opinion, found the directorships to be public offices since the state had created the banks. The plea of Ashley failed to show that he and the other directors had been properly elected. The court held that the directors had unlawfully entered into and exercised their office.[26]

This was followed by the most significant banking case in the 1841 term, *State v. Harris*.[27] This involved a writ of *quo warranto* issued against Carey A. Harris that required him to show by what right he exercised the office of president of the Real Estate Bank. Harris was unable to show that he met all the technical requirements to act as president, so an order of ouster was entered based on an opinion by Chief Justice Ringo. The challenge to Harris was spearheaded by Chester Ashley. Albert Pike and Absalom Fowler represented Harris. This was but the opening round in the skirmish over control of the Real Estate Bank.

As the controversy surrounding the banks grew, the legislature became concerned with the growing state debt, estimated to be about $3 million in 1840.[28] In the 1842 legislative session, extensive investigations were made of the financial dealings of both banks, and the State Bank was closed. At the beginning of the session, Governor Archibald Yell criticized the "deplorable condition" of the banking institutions, referred to "embezzlements" and "short-sighted" policies, and suggested that liquidation of the banks was the only course open, although he also suggested that the state's financial condition would not permit the payment of interest on state bonds sold by the banks. He likewise opposed increased taxation as a means of meeting obligations on the bonds.[29]

A legislative committee examined the condition of the Real Estate Bank and reported numerous grounds for forfeiture of its charter, including "monopoly and favoritism on the part of the *stockholder and officers, in their own behalf*."[30] During this period, the assets of the Real Estate Bank were put under the control of a board of trustees.[31] This action prompted litigation brought by Chester Ashley and others to set aside the "deed of trust" by which the assets had been transferred to the trustees. Albert Pike had drafted this instrument and acted as attorney for the trustees during the trial and subsequent appeal to the Arkansas Supreme Court. Thomas Lacy and Townsend Dickinson, with Ringo dissenting, upheld the validity of the transfer.

Ashley and William Cummins, one of the directors, argued that the assignment of all assets to the trustees was an absolute nullity because Central Board members selected as trustees acted for themselves and not in the interest of the bank. They also argued that the Central Board members had no authority to make an assignment to themselves. They indicated, in argument, that the total assets were valued at $2,200,000 and that some $1,500,000 in state bonds were outstanding. They suggested that the state debt be paid rather than allow the trustees to control and manage the funds. The court's opinion by Justice Lacy upheld the assignments. Chief Justice Ringo dissented. He declined to rule on the validity of the deed of trust but maintained, on technical grounds, that the court should not intervene based on the pleadings before it. He apparently believed the power existed if the issue had been properly presented to the court.

Following the decision, Cummins asked for reconsideration by the court but was refused. He then submitted a letter from Governor Yell requesting that the issue be re-argued and re-heard by the court. Justice Dickinson refused the motion in a strongly worded, but tactful, reply in which he defended the decision of the court and warned the governor:

> If the *executive* department shall so far lose sight of its boundaries, as to *encroach* upon, or *usurp* the powers of the judiciary,

> or attempt, under the pretext of a deep interest in the general welfare, to influence its judgment, or control its action, such interference should be repelled with firmness, but with dignity.[32]

This decision created considerable controversy, fomented by W. S. Oldham and Thomas B. Hanly, who had been elected to the upcoming legislature. (Both were future members of the court.) Talk circulated during the legislative session of impeaching Judge Lacy, but the matter was not pursued.[33] Albert Pike, apparently acting on his own, requested opinions of the Chancellor James Kent of New York and Judge Joseph Story of the US Supreme Court regarding the validity of the deed of trust. Both jurists indicated that they believed the deeds to be valid, and, based on this evidence, some of the furor in the legislature subsided.[34]

Constitutionality/Corporate Existence

Following the 1842 decision confirming the action of the directors of the Real Estate Bank, the court faced an increasing number of cases involving both that bank and the State Bank of Arkansas. In the January 1842 term, the court addressed the question of the constitutionality of the State Bank. In *McFarland v. State Bank,* the court applied decisions of the US Supreme Court "with the utmost cheerfulness, and in good faith."[35] And it declared the law incorporating the Bank of the State of Arkansas to be constitutional.[36] In later cases they refused to reconsider the question.[37] They also upheld the creation of the State Bank against a challenge that the act establishing the bank created no corporation. The court found the corporate nature of the bank to have been established by implication and allowed it to pursue debt collection as a corporate entity.[38]

During the January and July terms of 1843 and 1844, the court dealt with eighteen cases involving either the Real Estate Bank or the State Bank. Many of those cases involved routine questions of law. Some did not. For example, in *Gray v. Real Estate Bank*, Chief Justice Ringo, writing for a unanimous court, held that the Real Estate Bank was barred from maintaining a debt collection action in the name of the bank because of the assignment of all the bank's rights to the trustees.[39]

In a case of some political consequence, *Real Estate Bank v. Rawdon*, the court attempted to sort out transactions that had occurred during the sale of state bonds belonging to the bank.[40] Senator Ambrose H. Sevier and Thomas T. Williamson had been appointed commissioners to sell the bonds in Washington. The obligation of the bank to Williamson was at issue in the case, which resulted in three separate opinions complicated by changes in court membership during the pendency of the case.

The first opinion was delivered in July 1842 by Justice Dickinson, joined by Justice Lacy. Ringo dissented. Dickinson lost re-election and was replaced on the court by George W. Paschal. The court reopened the case in January 1843, when Paschal joined the bench. Paschal, for some reason, served only about six months before he resigned to be replaced by William K. Sebastian, who served through 1844. A third and final opinion in the case was then delivered by Sebastian, joined by Lacy, with Ringo again dissenting. The final decision relieved the bank of responsibility for certain obligations to Williamson.

In the 1844 election the controversy over the bank affair resulted in some loss of prestige for the ruling Conway faction. Ambrose Sevier had been censured by the Arkansas House by a vote of 33 to 27 during the 1842–43 session for his role in establishing the bank and handling its bond transaction in Washington. In his attempt to defend himself, he sent a series of letters from Washington that were "vituperative," reflecting "incredible arrogance and "tastelessness."[41] During the 1844 campaign Archibald Yell, then running for Congress, criticized Sevier. William Woodruff, the *Gazette* publisher, expressed his disenchantment with the Sevier-Conway faction.[42] This was in part because of its inability to keep him as treasurer.[43] He had previously moved closer to Chester Ashley, who had represented him in a contest over state funds he claimed were due for his service as treasurer. The legislature elected Ashley to the US Senate.[44]

The most important of the bank cases during the remainder of Chief Justice Ringo's term came during the July 1844 term in

State v. Real Estate Bank.[45] The proceeding had been brought for the purpose of seizing the franchises of the Real Estate Bank. Among the various allegations were those that the bank had suspended specie payment on November 2, 1839, became insolvent on April 2, 1842, and on that same date assigned all assets to the trustees and became wholly incapable of continuing the business of banking. Since the bank ceased to exercise its franchises as chartered, the court pronounced that the corporate existence of the Real Estate Bank had ceased. Little was to be learned of the operations of the trustees and their handling of bank assets until the administration of Governor Elias Conway in the 1850s, when the operation was finally brought to an end.[46]

While the court had resolved the question of the corporate existence of the Real Estate Bank in *State v. Real Estate Bank*, it had left the question of the corporate existence of the State Bank unanswered.[47] The legislature had on January 31, 1843, placed the bank in liquidation and had indicated an intent to close the bank for business. The court, in *Underhill v. State Bank*, in the July 1845 term, held that while the act of liquidation limited and modified the operation of the bank, it still retained a corporate existence for the purpose of collecting and paying debts.[48] Justice W. S. Oldham, an anti-bank addition to the court, wrote the opinion.

Validity of Legislative Action

In the July 1846 term of court, the chaos surrounding the two banks continued to generate problems for the court. Interestingly, former Chief Justice Ringo now successfully appeared as an attorney for a Real Estate Bank stockholder who was being sued by the trustees on a mortgage foreclosure.[49] Moreover, a future member of the court, David Walker, successfully argued that the original fifteen trustees of the Real Estate Bank lost their authority to sue for debt collection upon the election in 1844 of five "residuary" trustees vested with sole authority to act.[50]

The case that drew the most attention was *Woodruff v. Attorney General Pro Tem*, which challenged an act of the 1845 legislature repealing a section of the State Bank charter.[51] The act had repealed the section of the charter allowing notes of the bank to be received in payment of debts due the state. An action was originally brought against William E. Woodruff, the former treasurer, to recover funds he had allegedly retained during his time as treasurer. Woodruff maintained that he had a cross-demand against the state for amounts owed him. A judgment was rendered against Woodruff in circuit court. He attempted to pay the judgment in notes issued by the Bank of the State of Arkansas. Frederick Trapnall, acting by appointment as attorney general, refused Woodruff's appeal because of the 1845 legislative action.

Woodruff then brought an action to force the state to accept the notes. Woodruff was represented by George C. Watkins, by then the attorney general, who continued his representation of Woodruff, which had started in the earlier case. Also acting as Woodruff's attorney was James Curran, the nephew of former Justice Townsend Dickinson's wife. Trapnall was former chief justice Ringo's brother-in-law.

The unanimous opinion of the court, written by Chief Justice Thomas Johnson, upheld the legislation. The court believed that since the legislature created the State Bank, it could totally repeal the charter, making all notes worthless. In the same way, it could modify the charter to make the notes invalid after a certain date.

Woodruff then appealed to the US Supreme Court. There, former justice and now Senator William K. Sebastian presented the state's argument.[52] The US Supreme Court, in a split opinion, held that the law of repeal did not affect the notes in circulation and that the state could not impair the obligation of its own contracts. The dissenting justices took the position that the state did not personally guarantee the bank's obligations and should not be bound forever to receive the notes in payment. Thus the US Supreme Court reversed the Arkansas court.

In a second case relating to the repeal of the same section of the charter of the State Bank, *Paup v. Drew*, the Arkansas court held that notes of the State Bank were no longer legal tender and that the state was not bound to accept the notes in payment of bonds owed to the state by Paup.[53] This case was also appealed to the US Supreme Court but with a more favorable result for the state. In

Paup v. Drew, the high court upheld the decision of the Arkansas court because the contract Paup had signed called for payment "in specie or its equivalent."[54] Currency less valuable than specie was not anticipated by the parties.

When the Arkansas court convened for the July 1849 term, a new member was present. Christopher C. Scott had been appointed on July 12, 1848, to complete the term of Justice Oldham, who had resigned to run for Congress. (He was defeated.) The legislature then elected Justice Scott to complete the term. He was subsequently re-elected twice and served until his death in 1859.[55]

Another new member joined the court in the January 1849 term, Whig David Walker. While in the state senate, he had achieved a reputation for independence, and his Whig credentials were sometimes challenged.[56] He was appointed as commissioner to investigate the Fayetteville Branch of the State Bank in December of 1840, and in 1842 he was on the legislative committee organized to investigate and make recommendations concerning the Real Estate Bank.[57] He introduced the bill to liquidate the Real Estate Bank and maintained that the state had a moral obligation to pay debts created by the sale of bonds by the bank.[58]

The first major bank case to come before this court was *Wilson v. Biscoe,* in the January 1850 term in which Walker delivered the opinion of the court.[59] The effect of the decision was to overrule a prior case, *Duncan v. Biscoe*, which had restricted the collection of mortgages executed to the Real Estate Bank.[60] By this decision the trustees could foreclose the mortgages and sell lands to enforce payment of stock loans. Walker's opinion was consistent with his strongly held view that the debts of the state should be paid. He recognized that the bank trustees might not apply money collected from the mortgage foreclosure to payment of the state bonds, but he felt the legislative intent in the charter was clear and that the "present condition" of the bank was not to be considered in construing legislative intent.[61]

The most important bank case during the early 1850s may have been *State v. Curran* in the July 1851 term.[62] Curran was a holder of State Bank notes that the bank refused to redeem because, under the various liquidation acts, all bank assets had been made property of the state. Curran sued the state in chancery court, asking that the debts owed by the State Bank be satisfied by the state. The supreme court, in a unanimous opinion, upheld the constitutionality of the various liquidation acts and held that the assets were beyond the reach of bank creditors such as Curran. Curran appealed to the US Supreme Court, which reversed the decision. The high court held that the liquidation acts impaired the obligation of contracts (the bank charter). The court found the state to be the sole stockholder of the State Bank, and the charter constituted a contract with the holder of bank notes to pay the obligations of the bank.

End of the State Banking Era

The saga of the banks was drawing to a close. But first, an additional change in the court would occur. Chief Justice Johnson's term ended in 1852. Elected to replace him was former attorney general George C. Watkins, who had also served as William Woodruff's attorney in the ultimately successful challenge of the modification of the charter of the State Bank. Watkins, one of the first settlers of Little Rock, had entered a law partnership with Chester Ashley and, later, with James Curran. He had also married Sophie Curran, a daughter of William S. Fulton. His first wife was Mary Crease, a relative of the Conways.[63]

One of the first cases to come before the court under Chief Justice Watkins was *Ringo v. Biscoe, Trustees R.E. Bank*, a suit brought by former Chief Justice Daniel Ringo, holder of bills and notes issued by the Real Estate Bank for which payment had been refused by the residuary trustees.[64] The critical issue was whether the trustees, who had succeeded to all rights of the bank for the sale or recovery of property and assets according to the decision in *Wilson v. Biscoe*, also succeeded to the liabilities of the bank.[65] In a detailed opinion by the new chief justice, the court held that any holders of a right of action against the bank could follow assets into the hands of the trustees and proceed in court for collection of any debts or obligations due. On the same date, the court resolved a number of other cases on the same basis.[66]

In January 1854, *State v. Curran* was before the court upon reversal by the US Supreme Court.[67] Chief Justice Watkins did not sit in the case because Curran had been his law partner. The court affirmed a lower court decree that carried out the mandate of the US Supreme Court to permit Curran to obtain satisfaction of debts owed by the State Bank. In light of *Woodruff v. Trapnall,* the court also allowed for payment of state taxes for the years 1838 and 1839 in notes of the State Bank.[68] The two cases, in combination, served to resolve a number of matters pending before the court.

Governor Elias Conway had undertaken to investigate bank activities and to end the turmoil caused by the continued litigation. An action filed in Pulaski Circuit Court in 1854 would effectively kill the Real Estate Bank.[69] Governor Conway obtained legislative approval for the creation of a separate chancery court that could deal with the case. The court was created, and a Whig, Hulbert F. Fairchild, was appointed chancellor. He succeeded in stopping the apparent abuses that had continued even after the trustees assumed control.[70] Legislative efforts in the 1854–1855 session provided protection for State Bank assets as well.[71]

During the 1856 session of the legislature, the receiver appointed by the chancery court to take charge of the assets of the Real Estate Bank made a thorough report to Governor Conway on the financial status of the defunct bank.[72] In addition, an accountant's report, filed October 20, 1856, revealed that the trustees who had received the assignment of assets, along with their "particular friends," were among the greatest debtors of the bank, as was its attorney, Albert Pike. Justice Dickinson had defended the independence of the judiciary in upholding the validity of the assignment of assets to the trustees of the Real Estate Bank, to which he himself had been a debtor.[73] The accountants attributed the reluctance of the trustees to pursue payments of bank debts by others to this situation. "They paid nothing, or next to nothing, of what they themselves owed to the bank, and under these circumstances it was with ill grace that they could enforce payment on others."[74]

During the 1856 legislative session, a joint committee also examined the affairs of the State Bank. The committee found the liabilities remaining to be about $1.4 million with no assets to pay the debt other than uncertain obligations of the Real Estate

Bank.[75] Two years later, in his message to the legislature, Governor Conway reported that the debt of the Real Estate Bank was just over $1.8 million, but that lands mortgaged by stockholders would be adequate to pay the liability of the state. The debt of the State Bank remained at just over $1.2 million with inadequate means to pay the debt.[76]

Not all issues involving banks were resolved by the time war broke out. One of the decisions of Justice Fairchild (when he was serving as chancellor) reached the court in 1862, and, of course, he did not sit in the case. Justice English delivered the opinion that affirmed the lower court decision. The issue in *Whitney v. Peay* dealt with the so-called "Holford" bonds.[77] The state had issued to the Real Estate Bank five hundred bonds for $1,000 each for the purpose of raising capital. The North American Trust and Banking Company loaned $250,000 (in installments) to the Real Estate Bank with the bonds pledged to secure the loan. A total of $121,336.59 was advanced to the bank. The NAT&BC then pledged the bonds to James Hoford & Co., London Bankers, for a loan of $325,000. NAT&BC became insolvent, and a receiver was appointed in New York to settle the affairs of the company. The Arkansas bonds were found to have been legally assigned to Holford and had an actual value in 1857 of $425,000.

Whitney, in the meantime, proposed to pay the NAT&BC receiver the sum of $2,500 for the debt of the Real Estate Bank, which was approved by the New York court. Whitney then sued the receiver of the Real Estate Bank (Peay) for the amount of debt assigned to him. The court, referring to Whitney as an "adventurer" who purchased the debt for a "trifling sum," found that once the NAT&BC transferred the bonds to Hoford they could not compel the Real Estate Bank to pay the debt because the bonds could not be surrendered to the Real Estate Bank even if the debt was paid. Whitney was in no better position than NAT&BC and could be in no better position than the company.

After the war, issues relating to the bank were before the court again in *McCreary v. The State*.[78] A legislative act of January 16, 1861, designed to aid in the foreclosure of mortgages given to secure stock subscriptions was before the court. The state had brought suit to foreclose on real estate that was mortgaged to pay for stock subscriptions in the Real Estate Bank. The state had issued bonds for the raising of capital. The legislation in issue changed the remedy available but did not infringe existing rights, so it was constitutional. The court described the situation as follows:

> The State assumed a large liability. To indemnify her the bank promised to pay off her bonds, and the mortgagors bound themselves to pay off their stock bonds with all the interest that might accrue, or to pay such an amount of the bond of the State, issued in favor of the bank equal to the amount of stock granted to them respectively or their equity of redemption was subject to foreclosure.[79]

The act of the legislature was interpreted to permit the state to act on behalf of the holders of the state's bonds as well as the State itself. It was never intended that the bank itself would enforce these claims.[80]

In *Hanger & Moody v. The State,* the state brought a similar suit to foreclose on a mortgage given to secure stock in the Real Estate Bank.[81] However, the bank had previously sued on the original debt of $3,600 and sold the land to one of the trustees of the bank for $120 (for benefit of the bank). The receiver then transferred the bank's interest in the land to Hanger and Moody for $11,163 (to be paid in bonds of the state issued to the bank).

The court held that the purchasers were "junior mortgagees" receiving only an "equity of redemption." The lands were liable, first, to pay the prior encumbrance and any excess could not inure to the benefit of the original debtor nor to the purchasers, the presumption being that the purchase price is to pay the amount due on the prior bond and mortgage.

Summary and Conclusions

The banking fiasco had long-term negative effects for the state. The state debt plagued the state until well after the Civil War. No state leader could convince the legislature to increase taxes to pay the debt. Indeed, the legislature was pressured to grant tax relief during the late 1840s and early 1850s.[82]

In addition, the failure of the banking institutions meant that there was no ready source of credit or currency. The shortage of money meant reliance on bank paper of other states or "coon skins and peltry."[83] A controversy also arose as to circulation of small bank notes, and, in fact, the legislature restricted circulation of currency of less than a five-dollar denomination.[84]

The Arkansas Supreme Court played a pivotal role in the resolution of numerous legal questions generated by the banking controversy. The individual members of the court, as is always the case, brought to the court their political and personal connections. While the extent to which their attitudes and views affected their decisions related to the banking institutions cannot be clearly discerned, some general observations are merited.

The earliest promoters of the banking institutions in Arkansas were a curious mixture of Democrats connected with the ruling faction and some powerful Whigs. Democrat leaders like Chester Ashley, Edward Cross, and William Woodruff were initially involved in the operation of the banks. Ambrose Sevier was a bank supporter as well. Some dynasty Democrats, Governor James Conway and his brother Elias, for example, were apparently lukewarm to the idea. Archibald Yell was unabashed in his opposition.

Control over the banks centered around conflicts between Ashley and those connected to him and Whig leaders Albert Pike and Absolom Fowler. Fowler had originally opposed the bank concept, but once those connected to Ashley were ousted from bank control, Pike and Fowler (the "old Whigs") took charge of Real Estate Bank assets through trustees. Justices Lacy and Dickinson apparently fell in with the pro-bank group. Chief Justice Ringo remained opposed. His opposition led him to actively fight with those in control of the bank assets after he left the bench. Ringo's early position, though, contributed to his defeat for re-election at the hands of Thomas Johnson, more closely connected to the dynasty Democrats. Eventually, the ruling dynasty of Democrats became identified as anti-bank, although some anti-bank Whigs such as David Walker capitalized on the issue as well. The dynasty Democrats became identified as anti-bank and, presumably, their later selections to the court reflected this attitude. W. S. Oldham provides an example. He was openly anti-bank before appointment.

In some cases, personal situations may have influenced decisions. Justice Townsend strongly supported the trustees of the Real Estate Bank and, at the time, was a bank debtor. On the other hand, Chief Justice Ringo's inherent conservatism may have more greatly influenced his views than any deep-set political convictions regarding the banks. Justice David Walker's independence led him to oppose the banks, but he just as strongly supported payment of state debt created by the banks. He was identified as a Whig and was a major opposition figure during the period but was an opponent of the banking schemes from the beginning.

Certainly, it can be concluded that appointments to the bench, made by the general assembly, were influenced by the legislature's perception of the candidate's views regarding the banks. It is, perhaps, in this indirect way that the court's decisions were affected. What is clear from the banking controversy is that those in control of the political levers in the state used those levers to benefit their system of "special privilege."[85] The Arkansas Supreme Court was but a pawn in the greater game of financial control in the state. Only as connection with the banking institutions became a political liability did the court show some independence.

CHAPTER 5

"Pervasive Localism"

Cases, Controversies, and Conflicts Relating to Transportation

Lawrence Friedman expands on James Willard Hurst's and Morton Horwitz's thesis by suggesting that the first half of the nineteenth century "was a period of promotion of enterprise."[1] Railroads and other public improvements were generally supported, but "routes, terms and conditions, and other details were the stuff of intense political battle."[2] Bridges, roads, ferries, and canals were the subject of charters. Sometimes states granted money. This would seem to favor business over farmers and landowners, but these policies were generally popular. "Farmer-settlers had a desperate hunger for transport . . . to carry their goods to market to bring settlers to their region, to stimulate business to raise the overall value of their lands."[3]

In Arkansas the "intense political battles" were frequently resolved in favor of local interests—an illustration of James Ely and David Bodenhamer's concept of "pervasive localism."[4] No statewide scheme of improvement was successfully implemented. Eugene Genovese goes a step further and sees, in this "commitment to localism" by southerners, their view of "the highest form of liberty." The plantation was raised to a political principle.[5] This dwarfed all other concerns.

Poor transportation limited the economic growth in early Arkansas to areas near rivers. While riverboat transport was well developed, although problematic at times, roads were inadequate and often impassable in bad weather.[6] This meant that land without access to river transport was much less valuable, often selling for a fraction of the price for land along the major streams.[7] There were suggestions that speculators were holding onto this land (and preventing settlement) in hopes of future railroad construction in those areas to drive up land prices.

The efforts toward better roads were limited in the early years to requirements for roadwork by those whose land adjoined designated roads and by the appointment of "overseers" who were to see that the work was done as required. Criminal sanctions could be imposed for failure to work the roads and against negligent overseers.

By 1850 there was general recognition that the state had to expand basic services if economic growth was to continue. This included roads, levees, and railroads, but also a system of public education and a geological survey to encourage development of the state's natural resources.[8] However, no unified policy emerged. Localism and sectional jealousies impeded progress. In the 1850s the political focus shifted to protection of the property interests of slaveholders. Local disputes, sectional jealousies, and avarice subsumed the great objectives, and the courts became embroiled in the litigation that ensued.

When Arkansas Territory was organized in 1819, it was accessible primarily by river transportation. Flatboats and keelboats were used to transport settlers and their property, including animals and provisions.[9] Steamboats soon followed, with the first ascending to Arkansas Post in March of 1820.[10]

Roads were generally non-existent, and those that were found were little more than narrow trails. Swampy conditions in the eastern and southern parts of the state and rough mountains in the west and north made travel by land difficult. In the 1850s a military road was constructed, using federal funds, from the northeastern part of the territory to the southwest and the Red River. A road from Memphis to Little Rock was completed in the late part of the decade.[11] Other roads were built, but upkeep was a continuing problem.

Cooperation of landowners for road construction and upkeep was a difficulty. The legislature adopted a system of naming road overseers who were responsible for seeing that roads were kept in repair. They were provided a list of "road hands" who were obligated to work for specified periods on the road when notified by the overseer. The overseers were considered public officials with duties defined by statute.[12] They were sometimes prosecuted for failure to carry out their responsibilities.[13]

Travel by road continued to be difficult at best. Even into the 1850s travelers complained that Arkansas roads were "the most execrable ones to be found" in the entire county.[14] Governor Elias Conway urged a "good dirt roads" program rather than railroads, but even this effort failed.[15]

Railroads

Railroads became the focus in the 1850s. Competing railway companies were formed and charters issued for several proposed routes. Each had its coalition of political supporters, and one group received congressional backing and transfer of additional lands to the state for railroad construction. Hope was first placed in the sale of public lands permitted under the Swampland Act of 1850, which made swamp and overflowed land available for sale to finance public improvements.[16] However, strife delayed construction, and struggles among local interests meant that little progress was made by the outbreak of the Civil War.[17]

The state chartered some railroad companies in the hope that the local routes could be tied to a transcontinental route. Various companies competed for the lands, and major political battles ensued over route and terminus locations. These fights continued until the outbreak of the Civil War, which then delayed any significant progress.[18]

The Arkansas Supreme Court was asked to intervene in some of the railroad disputes. These disputes were often between the railroad companies and disappointed subscribers. In the first of these, *Hammett v. Little Rock & Napoleon R.R. Co.*, the defendant attempted to raise the question as to whether the corporation was in legal existence (a "nul til corporation" plea).[19] The court, however, determined that when a corporation was created by a public law, leaving nothing to be done as a condition precedent to the coming into existence of the corporation, the defendant could not raise the question. Furthermore, an individual could not raise the question of forfeiture of the charter. Only the state could sue to void the charter. The charter to the Little Rock & Napoleon R.R. Co. was granted by the Arkansas General Assembly.[20]

In 1859 a series of cases were before the court in which subscribers argued that they were relieved of obligations to pay assessments because the railroad had changed the location of the route or selected a different terminus in violation of the charter. These cases involved the Mississippi, Ouachita, & Red River R. R. Co., which had been chartered in 1852 to construct a railroad from the Mississippi River to Fulton and the Texas border.[21] This group, which organized in Camden, planned to issue fifteen thousand shares of capital stock at one hundred dollars each. Construction commenced on the Mississippi end.[22]

Congress approved land grants to aid in the construction, with six miles on each side of the line (and other lines) to be sold at $2.50 per acre. The surveyors reached Camden in 1854 amid great celebration.[23] At the same time grading commenced near Camden and a few miles of track were laid.[24] But, the project was never to be completed. A dispute arose as to the route to be followed from Camden to the Red River. A series of cases related to this dispute reached the Arkansas Supreme Court. The initial question related to the compliance of the railroad board of directors with provisions of the act of incorporation. Assessments were made against the stockholders who had subscribed, but proper notice was not given of the assessments.[25]

The precise issue in dispute regarding the route was before the court in *Witter v. M.O. & R.R. R. R. Co.*[26] The charter of the company made specific reference to a location at "some point on Red river, at or near Fulton," which contemplated intersecting a terminus of the Cairo and Fulton Railroad, which was organized to run through Little Rock and south. After the survey was completed, the company chose a route that went from Camden to a "cut-off," which would be the crossing of the Red River some twenty miles from Fulton. This route was on an elevated ridge instead of running through an overflow.

A subsequent act of the legislature sanctioned the route change, ignoring Fulton altogether. The original charter reserved to the company the authority to accept or reject any act of the general assembly amending the charter by a vote of a majority *of the stock*. In this case, the 1857 amendment was accepted by a majority *of the stockholders* but not necessarily of the stock.

The court found that the defendant would be released from his contract of subscription if the act sanctioned a material departure from the route prescribed in the original charter. The court determined that the change was material; the subscriber was released from the contract of subscription.[27] The court emphasized that the location specified in the charter became part of the contract with subscribers and that a material change in that location would release non-assenting subscribers.

In a similar case, *Mississippi Ouachita and Red River Railroad Company v. Cross*, the court addressed the questions of what remedy the subscriber had in such situations and what evidence could be introduced in a suit against the subscriber.[28] The principle adopted was that the subscriber could not show that the corporation had violated or failed to comply with provisions of the charter as a defense to his contract. That was a matter for a separate action. He could only show, as in *Witter*, that his contract with the corporation was breached.

The railroad was unable to accumulate sufficient funds to continue the project before it was interrupted by the outbreak of the Civil War.[29] The legal and political wrangling regarding the various railroad projects came to a halt as war loomed. The economic panic of 1857, coupled with the increased public attention to slavery, meant that little progress would be made until after the war.[30]

During the war, *Mississippi, Ouachita and Red River Railroad Company v. Gaster* was before the court a second time, focused on the remedy available to a subscriber who alleged that state legislation authorizing a change in the route of the proposed railway was not binding on the corporation itself.[31] Since it was not shown that the act was binding on the corporation, the defendant would not be released from his subscription but would be entitled to an injunction if the route was a material variation from that proposed in the charter. The court cited *Dartmouth College* for the proposition that the legislature may create a corporation but may not dissolve it or alter or amend its charter without its consent.[32] To permit otherwise would be to impair the obligation of contracts in violation of the constitution.

Following the war the number of railroad disputes did not reach the prewar level for many years. One such controversy involved the M.O. & R.R.R. Co.[33] In 1860 Chicot County issued ten $1,000 bonds payable to the railroad company in five years with interest. This was done to enable completion of a portion of the railroad and was apparently intended to be a subscription to the capital stock of the railroad from the internal improvement fund of the county. The legislature had, in 1855, authorized such subscriptions. The problem was that the legislation did not mention bonds and no other legislation authorized counties to issue bonds for any purpose. The power to subscribe the internal improvement fund did not include the power to obligate the county.

In *Whitehead and Wife v. The Arkansas Central Railroad Company*, an act of the legislature that set out a procedure for determining compensation to a landowner when land was taken by eminent domain for the construction of a railroad was challenged as being in conflict with the state constitution.[34] The constitution provided that full compensation was required irrespective of any benefit to the landowner and required that a jury determine the amount. The legislation attempted to streamline the process by providing for appointment of five commissioners to ascertain compensation and authorized them to consider real benefit or advantage to the landowners to be derived from construction of the railroad. This, the court found, was a direct conflict:

> Words more fixed and well understood, language plainer, more unambiguous and mandatory in terms than used in the constitution, it seems to us, could not have been employed and admit of a doubtful construction.[35]

Another issue that arose for the first time was the question of whether a laborer's lien applied to workers on railroad construction projects. The legislature had passed legislation in 1868 that gave laborers a lien on the "production of their labor for such work and labor." The court construed this language in *Dano v. M.O. & R.R.R.R. Co.*[36] The court referred to the granting of special rights and privileges through liens to "certain members of society such as mechanics, laborers and material men" and indicated that no branch of the law had been "so thoroughly changed by legislation . . . no doubt wisely."[37]

The court analyzed the statute thoroughly, searching for a means by which one who had worked on a railroad roadbed could assert the lien. Much of the law referred to movable property, for example, a crop on which farm hands had worked. This, the court said, could easily be seen to be the "production of their labor." But the laborer in this case had produced nothing to which the lien could attach. In part, the difficulty here was that the plaintiff was attempting to collect claims purchased or transferred to him by other laborers, and the court pointed out that the lien statute remedy was personal and could not be transferred. Justice Lafayette Gregg, in dissent, felt that a proper claim could be asserted against railroad property where the right of way was owned by the company.

Ferries and Bridges

Other transportation-related controversies arose over ferry franchises and toll bridges. The legislature in 1837 had authorized county courts to grant ferry privileges when located on county roads and to collect a tax for the privilege. Other ferry operations could be restricted within one mile "except or near cities or towns" and "where the public convenience may require it."

In *Murray v. Menifee,* the issue was whether Cadron, near the location of two ferries chartered on the same day by the county court, was a town.[38] When the ferries were chartered, Cadron consisted of one store, dwelling houses for two families, one warehouse, and a population of six. The supreme court, after looking at the history of Cadron, said that to call this a town "could be an obvious misapplication of the term."

Justice Henry Rector, in dissent, questioned the legislative scheme because the effect of allowing the county to grant a ferry franchise was to, in effect, designate a stream as navigable (which made it a public stream). The court, however, determined the intent was to declare a crossing at a private stream to be a "public ferry" and subject it to regulation as if it were on a public navigable stream.

A second ferry case the same year was *Lindsay v. Lindsay*, a similar conflict near the town of Powhatan in Lawrence County regarding ferries across the Black River.[39] The issue was raised in a chancery proceeding as to whether "public convenience" allowed the establishment of a second ferry. This had been considered by the county court and, in any event, could not be challenged in a chancery proceeding. Rector dissented, again, to the extent that he did not believe establishment of a ferry vested private rights.[40]

The court was explicit in reference to vested private rights in *Brearly v. Norris*, an 1861 squabble among family members.[41] One operated by license of Yell County; the other, from Pope County. The court agreed that the first franchise was a vested private right and could not be disturbed by the second grant, albeit from a different county.[42]

Controversies over ferry franchises continued after the war but were resolved following the earlier cases. In *Bell v. Clegg*, a landowner on the north side of a river obtained a ferry franchise from the county.[43] An owner on the south side of the river did the same, then leased the ferry privilege of the north side owner for five years and operated the ferry in both directions. In 1862 the county refused to extend the license of the owner on the north side but did so in 1866. In between these times, the south owner continued to operate the ferry in both directions. The north bank owner sued for one-half of the profits in the interim years but was unsuccessful. The court pointed out that ownership of the soil did not entitle the owner to a ferry franchise. A right to do so must be conferred by proper authority—in this case the county court. That authority, by statute, included the power to determine when to discontinue a ferry franchise.

In *Haynes v. Wells*, the question arose as to whether the ferry franchise could be transferred or conveyed separate from the land itself.[44] The court held that it was a grant from the state and was not "made to pass any title absolutely, or in fee," and was granted only to those "owning, or rightfully possessed of lands on the river."[45]

The court had two occasions to deal with the responsibilities of ferry operators. In *Jabine & Woodruff v. Midgett,* the plaintiff asked to be taken across the Arkansas River by ferry.[46] Some fourteen hours later the ferry took him across and he filed suit. The plaintiff prevailed in the lower court and, again, before a jury in circuit court. On appeal, the supreme court indicated that as a common carrier the ferry operator was required to provide "suitable means of transportation," that the public must be covered at "all reasonable hours without unnecessary delay."

> The law establishes ferries for the public good and convenience, and not for the individual profit of the keeper; and he who accepts this trust must provide himself with proper boats to accommodate the public at all states of water, or suffer the consequence of his neglect.[47]

In the second case, *Harvey v. Rose,* a ferryman was sued for the loss of a mule that fell from the boat and drowned.[48] The mule was part of a pair that was at first detached from a team of six mules pulling a wagon of cotton. Before the boat departed, the plaintiff himself ordered the mules brought onto the boat. The ferry operator did not object. The court pointed out that the ferryman, as a common carrier, if he accepted possession and custody of the mule, was insurer of property committed to his care. The presumption is that he took the property in his control. If he is able to show that the owner retained exclusive control himself, the duty is a lesser one—actual negligence. A new trial was ordered since the trial court did not properly instruct the jury on the responsibility of a common carrier.

An issue also arose with regard to a charter granted by the Pulaski County court to erect a toll bridge.[49] One provision of the grant was that the bridge was to remain "free and open" to the citizens of Pulaski County. The question was whether this meant only travel by foot or would include free "passage for carriages, carts, wagons, coaches, oxen, horses, servants, etc." The court gave it the broader construction.[50] Beyond ferries and bridges, the court also dealt on one occasion with a "plank road." The Memphis & St. Frances Plank Road Co. was organized with a required $50,000 subscription. The question arose as to whether this had been obtained prior to organization of the corporation and whether the company had a legal existence prior to construction of this road, the erection of toll gates, and the collection of toll.[51]

Summary and Conclusions

Harry L. Watson has convincingly argued that "yeoman families," "farmers and their families who owned their own land and depended almost exclusively on their own labors in cultivation," were either indifferent or, perhaps, hostile to state-sponsored efforts to expand commercial activity such as support for railroads, banking, or internal improvements.[52]

> When commercial interests sought to expand the sphere of the market place by publically funded "internal improvements," the yeoman saw a threat to public liberty.[53]

Watson also points out that the evolution of party politics was fueled by social tensions that pitted the commercially orientated Whigs, who supported state aid to internal improvements, against the Jacksonian Democrats, who saw the purposes of the state as "limited and were fearful of class legislation."[54]

> Democratic legislators were frequently unwilling to grant the subsidies and corporate charters which were usually essential for the success of development projects.[55]

They were, however, willing to see the state's share from the sale of public lands be used for development opportunities. The result was often bipartisan compromise on state aid to internal improvements but with "wide distribution" of "state largesse" so that local leaders "could not complain of neglect."[56] This could also mean that little progress was made, as exemplified the situation in Arkansas.

An example is support for public schools. The vast supply of available land was seen as a way of providing money to support education. Congress cooperated in 1836 by granting every sixteenth section of each township to be sold for the support of education. In Arkansas the legislature authorized, in 1843, that these revenues be placed in a common school fund.[57] Local interests pushed for a disbursement of the funds, first to the township in which the donated land was located and later to the county. The funds remained so small, once disbursed, that few schools were supported.

Arkansas even managed to dispute the provisions of the 1836 grant from Congress. In *Nayers v. Byrnes,* the issue was whether additional requirements added by Congress after the original grant were binding.[58] The court interpreted the provisions as to be absolute at the time of the grant; no new conditions could be subsequently added.

By 1850 in Arkansas, there were only 353 public schools serving 8,493 pupils. By contrast, Michigan, which was admitted as a state the same year, had 2,714 public schools serving 110,445 pupils. The big difference was in tax revenues collected for public schools. Michigan collected $88,879; Arkansas, $250.[59]

What is evident from this review of failed efforts to promote the economy in early Arkansas is that a "spirit of localism" prevailed to such an extent that no unified policy or program emerged. Sectional jealousies prevented progress.[60] Political interest shifted to concern with the antislavery movement and the emergence of the Republican Party, which was seen as a threat to the property interests of the powerful elites.[61] The goals for the state seen by Albert Pike as still attainable in 1851 were overshadowed by an even greater cloud. The narrow agenda of slaveholders "and their minions"—promotion of an economy based on land, slaves, and cotton—was threatened, and even the yeomanry was drawn "into their orbit and under their durable hegemony."[62] By defining freedom as the right to own slaves, sovereignty became defined in terms of protection of slavery. As Donald McNeilly states:

> More important, it unified Arkansas on the primacy of slavery clarifying their unanimity. Whig, Democrat, planter, and farmer were united on their view that an attack on slavery was an attack on sovereignty; the latter was a direct challenge to honor itself. Above it all, above union or secession, Arkansas had hoisted highest the flag of plantation slavery.[63]

CHAPTER 6

"Inspecting the Negro Foot"

Cases, Controversies, and Conflicts Relating to Slaves and Slavery

Issues involving slaves and slavery were an increasing part of the Arkansas Supreme Court's caseload during the antebellum years. A significant number of cases dealt with slaves as the court struggled to apply legal concepts to this unique form of property. At times the court was comfortable treating slaves like real property; at other times, less so. The slave cases often served as the vehicle by which the law of property was developed or confirmed. What becomes obvious in a review of the slavery cases before the Arkansas Supreme Court is the court's effort to protect the property interests of slaveholders and to attempt to preserve the institution to meet the goals of the slave economy.

In her study of slavery in the antebellum courtroom, Ariela J. Gross, like other historians, used as an organizing principle the dichotomy of slaves as property and slaves as persons. She explored the paradox of this "double identity as human subjects and the objects of property relation *at one and the same time*."[1] She recognizes that some historians explain any inconsistencies in the law of slavery by the efforts of slaveholders (and southern judges) to shape the law "instrumentally to serve their own economic interests or by the tendency of the common law to approach economic efficiency."[2] She emphasizes the dilemmas of courts in the South faced when attempting to apply existing legal rules to cases involving slaves. The major dilemma was the dichotomy she posits between slaves as property and slaves as persons.

This, too, is the focus of Mark V. Tushnet in his analysis of *State v. Mann* and the frequently cited North Carolina Supreme Court opinion of Judge Thomas Ruffin, who Tushnet labels an instrumentalist judge who was explicit in the policy goal of preserving slavery (rather than expanding capitalism).[3] Tushnet, however, recognizes the underlying need to resolve the contradiction of slaves sometimes treated as real property and sometimes as personal property. He states:

> Whether slaves were treated in legal rules as more like land (real property) or like other possessions (personal property) mattered in determining the liability of third parties for injuries to the slave, and—even more—in determining who would inherit which slaves.[4]

He could have added the importance of determining which debt-or-creditor rules were applicable. This distinction also came into play in determining the dower rights of widows, married women's property rights, possession and ownership questions, and contractual issues such as rights to specific performance or warranty upon sales of the slaves.

The efforts of courts to apply traditional common law rules to disputes involving slaves as property could be seen, according to Tushnet, as one of two approaches:

> One sees slavery as an institution serving masters' self-interest much in the way that industrial capitalism served capitalist entrepreneurs' self-interest. In this story slave law changed some common law rules to maximize the masters' economic return on their investment in slaves. Because the common law rules were developed to deal with other kinds of property, and slaves were human beings with individual wills who could resist their masters, the rules had to change.
>
> The other story sees slavery as fundamentally different from market society. Here slave law changed common law rules to acknowledge the openly hierarchical nature of slave society. If the common law of market society began to move from status to contract, the law of slavery reinscribed status in a law that elsewhere had begun to discard it.[5]

Thomas D. Morris argues, according to Tushnet, that each played a role but, in the end, "liberal capitalist ideas pervaded southern slave laws."[6] Others agree and suggest that Morris tracks the path outlined by Morton Horwitz: that property law moved, during this period, "from paternalism to formalism, from conservative republicanism to liberal capitalism."[7]

Morris recognizes the tension between "equitable paternalism and market individualism" but points out that commercialization of slavery was not a completed process and that a pure "law of slavery" had not emerged by the outbreak of the Civil War.[8] This lack of clarity is reflected in the struggle of the Arkansas court in determining how slaves as property fit into the legal system.

Slaves as Collateral

Morris traced the development of the law of chattel mortgages and, in particular, the mortgaging of slaves. He points out that as a market economy developed an emerging general law of contract encapsuled a "will theory." That is, individuals entered into contracts "to advance their future expectations."[9] The concept of the mortgage as a transaction in which land was used as security was well established in early American law. The creditor got legal title, but possession remained with the debtor. If the debtor paid as agreed, the creditor's rights would be reconveyed. If not repaid, the creditor took the property. However, an "equity of redemption" gave the debtor a certain time to "redeem" the land by payment. On the other hand, the creditor could use a "foreclosure" proceeding to force the debtor to pay or forever lose the equity of redemption.[10] The innovation was to extend the same concepts to chattels, generally, and slaves, in particular. The problem was that the common law had not recognized an "estate in chattels"—the nature of ownership was such that a mortgagee could not acquire a legal estate in chattels. This view eroded as a market economy developed.

Three differing concepts emerged when slaves were to be mortgaged. One view was that the chattel mortgage in slaves was equivalent to that in land. Legal title would be conveyed to the mortgagee. The second view was that the chattel mortgage was a conveyance that granted no legal title but created a lien on the property of the debtor.[11] A third approach was the "trust deed" by which legal title is transferred to a third party trustee who could sell the property for the benefit of creditors if the debt was unpaid. This mortgage equivalent provided a convenient mechanism for structuring the loan.[12]

During the colonial period many colonies exempted real property from the claims of unsecured creditors based on English law. This was more likely to be true in colonies that used slave labor. There the annual sale of staple crops provided the liquidity that creditors desired. However, these same areas were dependent on English credit to purchase slaves, and English creditors became concerned that colonial legislatures would characterize slaves as real property and, thus, protect them from unsecured creditors. Some colonies did so. Virginia, for example, did so in 1727. Slaves could function as ready collateral and could more easily be sold to pay debts than could land, so the protection of slaves from creditors raised concerns. The legislation in some colonial legislatures led to the 1732 enactment in Parliament of "Act for the More Easy Recovery of Debts in His Majesty's Plantations and Colonies in America" (the Debt Recovery Act). It made all property interests (houses, lands, slaves, and others) liable for all debts.[13]

After independence, the states, generally, adopted statutes similar to the Debt Recovery Act in order to promote the availability of credit and commercial expansion.[14] However, one of the major departures from the English remedy was frequent recognition of an equitable right of redemption if land was sold to pay debts. During the early nineteenth century not only did a number of states enact statutory periods of redemption, they also established other debtor relief measures to expand protection of certain debtor's assets from the claims of creditors.[15]

As these transformations regarding land were occurring, also emerging was the concept of chattel mortgage law applicable to slaves. This raised two important questions for courts. First, when chattels were mortgaged, was legal title conveyed to the creditor (as in the case with mortgages on land) with the debtor retaining only an equitable estate, or did the mortgage merely create a lien on the property of the debtor? Second, was the transaction a mortgage or a conditional sale?[16]

The Arkansas Supreme Court dealt with the first of these issues in the context of a mortgage on real estate by stating:

> For the protection of the interest of the mortgagee, and in order to give him the full benefit of the security, it is held that the legal estate passes by the mortgage: but for other purposes, the mortgage is, in general, held to be a mere security for the debt.[17]

The use of the conditional sale was common in Arkansas and was used in creative ways. Disputes arose when the presumed seller attempted to redeem or pay off what he claimed was not a conditional sale but a mortgage. The court attempted to clarify the distinction in a number of cases but, ultimately, decided that the "character of the conveyance is determined by the intention of the parties." Parol evidence could be used to show the intent of the parties.[18]

An apt illustration is in an 1841 case in which one Clements had signed a bill of sale to Sylvania Phillips for five slaves (named) for $400. The instrument provided that Phillips would reconvey them to Clements within two years and six months for $500 (if they did not "die, run away or be stolen"). Phillips immediately transferred four of the slaves to Porter for $400 under a similar agreement. The court analyzed the surrounding circumstances, including the fact that Clements was in financial difficulty at the time, and found the transaction to be a sale not a mortgage, and the right to repurchase was "only a collateral right." The court emphasized that if the slaves had died (and some had) the loss would have been sustained by Phillips.[19]

A similar result was found in *Johnson's Ex'r v. Clark*.[20] There the court emphasized that in conditional sales the condition (repurchase) must be strictly performed in accordance with the terms. They quoted a Virginia court:

> The reason for holding vendors to strictness in conditional sales, applies with peculiar force and weight where slaves are the subject of contract in this country. They are regarded by the law as perishable property, and may die the next day after the purchase. If they should not, their labor may become

> profitable, and their value greatly enhanced by their increase. Now, would it be just or proper for a vendor to lie by until their labor or increase had greatly exceeded the principal and interest of the money agreed to be paid, and then be allowed to come into a court of equity, and to redeem the slaves, when the purchases in the meantime had run all the risk of their lives, and had been at the trouble and expense of rearing, and, where, in the first instance, he had not only paid the full value of them, that would have been deprived of laying out his money for other slaves, unconditionally.[21]

Subsequent cases continued to emphasize that the intention of the parties was the key. For example, in *Williams v. Cheatham* there was no evidence that Williams owed any money to Cheatham or that Cheatham agreed to loan money to Williams.[22] Rather, it appeared that Williams was in financial difficulty and wished to sell the slaves to pay toward an obligation at a bank. Some discussion was had about a right to redeem, and Cheatham indicated a willingness to permit redemption within six or twelve months. No provision was included in the bill of sale regarding redemption. Questions were raised about what happened if the slaves died and Williams said the loss would be Cheatham's. He, in turn, apparently said that if he had to take the risk then redemption would be at his discretion. This indicated a conditional sale and not a mortgage.[23]

On the other hand, where the "clear and certain intention" of the parties indicated that there was a debt capable of being enforced, that the slaves were "pledged as security" for that debt, it would be deemed a mortgage. One indication was where the loan was for only a portion of the value of the slaves.[24] Furthermore, if there was doubt:

> Courts of equity will be inclined to construe contracts to be mortgages rather than sales, whenever their real character may be doubtful.[25]

Recording Requirements

Another ownership dispute involved a statute of 1846 that recognized deeds and instruments of writing for the sale of slaves and provided that they could be recorded the same as conveyances of real estate and could be used in evidence in the same manner.[26] In the end, this case, too, was resolved by a careful review of the facts.

In *Main v. Alexander,* a slave mortgage was the backdrop for the court's interpretation of certain acts of the legislature relating to recording liens and mortgages.[27] The court acknowledged that, as between the parties, their rights were unaffected by recording requirements but that filing was necessary to affect the rights of third parties—an important concept giving effect to recording statutes.

Possession Disputes

At common law, specific procedures had developed for requesting a court's assistance for the return of property held by someone alleged not to be the rightful owner. One such procedure was "replevin"; another was "detinue." Both are related to the recovery of personal property. Wrongful possession of personal property could be asserted by an action for damages in "trover." The procedures were adopted in early state statutes, along with "unlawful detainer," an action for the recovery of real estate. Another procedural device was a "quiet title" action, whereby a contested title to real estate could be resolved.

A defense in contested title actions involving land was the doctrine of "adverse possession." The occupier who held the land for a set period of time "openly, continuously, exclusively, adversely and notoriously" could assert a claim by adverse possession. As the Arkansas court stated, "The law wisely holds that there shall come a time when even the wrongful possessor shall have peace; and that it is better for ancient wrongs should go unredressed, than that ancient strife should be renewed."[28]

Although these were doctrines that developed at common law, the state adopted them by statute and also individual "statutes of limitations," that is, specific time limits following which the original owner's claims would be barred. A number of the possession disputes regarding slaves involved one or more of these concepts.

In 1845 the court approved the concept of replevin regarding the return of a slave wrongfully taken from the owner. This concept was generally applicable to personal property and, in spite of a legislative act making slaves real property for many purposes, the court applied replevin to slaves.[29] The court also approved the practice of permitting a seller to retain a right of possession for life in the same way as a life estate could be reserved in land conveyances.

Another court case involved a slave indirectly.[30] An action had been filed in replevin for a slave. The defendant died. The question presented was whether the action should continue against the administrator of the estate or against the heirs. The court treated the slave as real property and ruled that the action would have to be against the heirs. In another replevin case, where a father had claimed to have sold slaves to his son, the issue centered on the question of whether the sale had actually occurred, in light of evidence that the father exerted control over the slaves after the purported sale.[31] In another replevin case, it was determined that a suit for recovery of a slave could not be sustained during the term for which the slave was hired.[32]

Another case involved the application of another legal concept, "detinue," applied to a slave that had been in one's uninterrupted possession for a period of five years.[33] The concept of detinue was often applied to recover personal property loaned to another. Here, the statute under which recovery was sought applied to "pretended" loans and was not applicable.

Another slave case involved the question of "trover," that is, a suit for damages for wrongfully converting personal property belonging to another to one's own use.[34] The evidence showed that the plaintiff had in 1826 received a slave woman from his wife's father and had kept her in his possession until 1835 or 1836 (except for a year or so when she was back with his father-in-law). In 1836 she accompanied the father-in-law to Texas, but in subsequent years she was hired out with the plaintiff's other slaves. The plaintiff and his father-in-law lived and cropped together until about 1843. The slave was kept (and accounted for) as the plaintiff's property. However, in 1838 the father-in-law sent his son (the defendant) to take back the woman by force. She was then sold to the defendant. The defendant's claim was that his father had only loaned the woman to the plaintiff. The jury apparently did not believe this to be the case and returned a verdict for the plaintiff for $1,875 (the value of the woman and her three children), which the court upheld. The only legal principle of note was the court's finding that the bill of sale was not necessary to pass legal title to slaves; a gift accompanied by delivery and subsequent peaceable possession was sufficient.

In *Carter v. Cantrell*, the heirs of Matilda Carter sued to recover certain slaves that they claimed were owned by their mother at the time of her death and, thus, passed to them.[35] The defendant claimed to have bought the slaves from the husband of the deceased. The slaves were never actually in possession of either the husband or wife prior to her death. The court cited the reasoning of the common law, which gave a husband title to personal property of the wife because, upon marriage, he became liable for payment of her debts. But upon her death he ceased to be responsible for debts incurred before marriage. Any surplus over such debts would go to her heirs. Here the slaves would likely have passed to the daughters, but their claim was barred by a statute of limitation.

The first slave case in 1847 was, in reality, an inheritance case.[36] The decedent had a number of children by his lawful wife, but he then left her and cohabited with a woman he referred to in his will as his "beloved companion," Fanny Smith, with whom he had several illegitimate children. In his will he left "1 dollar and no more" to each of his legitimate children and his legal wife (who was named "Happy Trance") and left slaves to each of his illegitimate children. In addition, he left certain slaves to his companion for her life, with a provision that they would pass to such of her children "as she may think proper." The problem was that after the testator's death, Fanny married James Carr but never designated which of her children were to receive the slaves. Upon her death, Carr refused to deliver them to her children, and litigation resulted. An argument on behalf of the legitimate heirs was that the children of Fanny could not take as legal heirs of their father and that since their mother had only a life estate in the slaves, they could not pass from her to her children either. The court, however, looked to the intent of the testator and noted that he had "but little regard" for his children by his lawful wife, whom he had "discarded." Since Fanny, his companion, had failed to designate any one child in particular to receive the slaves, it would be "just and proper" to distribute the property equally among her children.[37]

What is most striking about the work of the January 1856 term is the number of cases (fourteen) that involved slaves in some way. Ownership disputes were the most common. For example, in *Sadler v. Sadler*, the dispute was over ownership of a slave, Ben, who may have been in possession of the deceased from some thirteen years prior to his death.[38] A state statute gave one who had held "peaceable possession" of slaves for five years a vested and perfected "right of property" and constituted a bar to any suit in law or equity. In subsequent cases, the court held that the five years must be peaceable possession but, if proved, would be presumed to be adverse.[39]

An illustration of the interplay between adverse possession and statute of limitations is *Pryor v. Ryburn*.[40] Here, the court construed the effect of an 1846 statute that provided that adverse possession of slaves for five years gave the party in possession a superior right to the slaves. In this case, the father conveyed all slaves to one son by bill of sale. After the father's death, some of his other children claimed that this was, in effect, a testamentary devise and that the son was to divide the slaves among the siblings upon the father's death. The son contended he received the slaves in consideration of his agreement to pay his father's debts, which he had done.

The court found that the evidence showed that the son had been in continuous possession of the slaves from the death of his father in 1844 until the suit was brought in 1852. The statute made five year's adverse possession sufficient to bar any suit in law or equity. The court explained the "grave considerations of policy" that induced the legislature to create the statutory protection for those in "peaceable possession," "openly and notoriously," "exercising control and ownership":

> Hard cases may arise under the statute, but more numerous cases of hardship might have arisen had the statute been less comprehensive in its terms.[41]

The court applied the same statute in *Ewell v. Tidwell*, where a mortgagor continued in possession of slaves, who were the collateral under the mortgage, after default.[42] The mortgagee had not attempted foreclosure. There had been other possible claims against the slaves as well, but the "peaceable, adverse possession for five years" barred any action. Interestingly, the holder of the slaves had left a will in which he bequeathed to certain "free negroes" (so stated in the will) lands, personal property, and a slave, Charles. The court accepted the notion that "free negroes" could own lands and make contracts, stating:

> The negro, though morally and mentally inferior to the white man, is, nevertheless, an intellectual being, with feelings, necessities and habits common to humanity. By the act of emancipation, the reciprocal obligations and duties between master and slave, by which the slave owes obedience and fidelity to the master, and the master owes to the slave support and protection are ended. Then this takes place, no one is interested in the protection of the negro. If, under such circumstances, he could not make and enforce contracts, it is difficult to understand how he could, with any certainty, supply his commonest necessities. Such a condition would be inconsistent with civilization. And, besides this, the negro having no power to acquire property, or certain means of gathering the fruits of his labor, every incentive to industry would be at once destroyed; and sinking into idleness and depravity, he would become an intolerable nuisance.[43]

However, the court was unwilling to condone the ownership of slaves by "free negroes," finding it contrary to public policy and "directly opposed to the principles upon which slavery exists among us."[44] This policy was justified by the court as follows:

> Without attempting to discuss slavery in the abstract, it may be said that it has its foundation in an inferiority of race. There is a striking difference between the black and white man, in intellect, feelings and principles. In the order of providence, the former was made inferior to the latter; and hence the bondage of the one to the other. For government and protection, the one race is dependent on the other. It is upon this principle alone, that slavery can be maintained as an institution. The bondage of one negro to another, has not this solid foundation to rest upon. The free negro finds in the

> slave his brother in blood, in color, feelings, education and principle. He has but few civil rights, nor can have, consistent with the good order of society; and is almost as dependent on the white race as the slave himself. He is, therefore, civilly and morally disqualified to extend protection, and exercise dominion over the slave.[45]

Warranties in Slave Sales

Breach-of-warranty lawsuits involving the "soundness" of slaves were common throughout the South. According to Ariela J. Gross, these were the most common cases involving slaves at the trial as well as the appellate level.[46] The slaves' mental or physical conditions were often at issue, but, also, "vices of character" such as dishonesty, running away, or drinking could be the basis of litigation.[47] In this litigation, slaves were treated in the same way as horses or machines. The law relating to warranties was not only applied but, in the South, developed as a part of the "law of sales" that departed from the common law.

Breach of warranty of title in the sale of land was commonly accepted as a basis for recovery by the end of the eighteenth century. The only issue was the level of damages to the purchaser who was ousted by one with superior title. The rule of English common law was that the purchaser could recover only the original purchase price. In America the states, by statute, protected the value of improvements. These "good faith possession" statutes allowed the purchaser to recover from the one who ousted him with superior title. The increased value of the land was not recoverable from either the superior title holder or the seller.[48]

With regard to sale of goods, in pre-nineteenth-century America (and perhaps in England) a "sound price" rule prevailed. Horwitz described it as the rule that "a sound price warrants a sound commodity."[49] If a jury determined that goods were unsound when sold, the price could be adjusted. In modern terminology this would be an "implied warranty" of soundness based on the price.

Horwitz suggested that the trend in the antebellum years was to move toward a "will theory of contracts," that is, toward rules that protected the expectations of the parties and their specific bargains. One aspect of this was to move from the "sound price" rule, which allowed equitable adjustment in the price the parties had agreed upon, to a doctrine of caveat emptor. Under this concept the buyer could recover only if the seller made an express warranty or if the seller knowingly made false or deceitful statements.[50] The development of caveat emptor was, according to Horwitz, "a dramatic overthrow of an important element in the eighteenth century's equitable conception of contract."[51]

This change in doctrine was consistent with the growth of a commercial market economy that, at least in the northeast, was emerging "from the subsistence farming and local manufacture of the early colonial days."[52] What is missing in this analysis is the development of a slave economy in the South.

As slavery expanded in the South and the domestic slave trade became more significant, slaveholders looked to the law to protect their interests. This included the need to protect slave buyers form unscrupulous sellers, "whether traders or fellow slave owners."[53] One way to protect slave buyers was to reject the concept of caveat emptor in favor of the warranty of soundness in the "sound price" rule or to insist on the presence of a clear and unambiguously written disclaimer.[54] This was the approach taken in South Carolina.[55] Other southern states took a different path, one somewhere between caveat emptor and the sound price rule.[56]

While the sound price rule was not accepted in other southern states, implied warranty of title was. Furthermore, the slave seller had a duty to disclose known defects to a buyer. Express warranties became more important with regard to unknown or hidden defects. Fraud and deceit were also used to expand seller's liability.[57] As Andrew Fede states:

> Although most antebellum slave law decisions analyzed cases that involved unknown defects as warranty, and not fraud cases, the same issues emerged, if in different doctrinal forms. The buyer was required to prove that the seller said something about the soundness of the slave in the negotiation process. The buyer also had to prove that the chattel was unsound when sold, and that this caused him damage.[58]

The Arkansas Supreme Court addressed all these issues at one time or another. The number of warranty disputes increased just prior to the Civil War, as did all types of cases involving slaves. The clearest statement of the warranty of title, when applied to slaves, was in the 1858 case of *Boyd Ex. v. Whitfield,* in which slaves were transferred in a complicated series of transactions.[59] The ultimate purchaser was then sued by residents of Virginia who claimed superior title to the slaves. The evidence reflected that the slaves had been sold at a fair price by one who was in possession of the slaves and claimed them as his absolute property. Under those circumstances "the seller is answerable to the purchaser, if it be taken from him by one who has a better title than the seller, whether the seller knew the defect of his title or not."[60] The court emphasized that the implied warranty was "personal to the vendor and the purchaser" and does not pass to a subsequent purchaser to give him a right of action against the first seller. He must look to his "immediate vendor."[61] The court made a distinction between sale of slaves or other chattels and land.

> There are covenants of warranty which pass from one to another by the mere sale and transfer of land, but this rule has no application to the sale of slaves or other chattels.[62]

One of the more interesting title questions arose in *Strayhorn v. Giles,* in which a mulatto named Bill was obtained in Indian County by one Houser, who placed him with Strayhorn for sale, providing a power of attorney.[63] Strayhorn sold Bill to the plaintiff, Giles, warranting him to be "a slave for life." Pending at the time of that sale was a suit for freedom that Bill had filed against Houser. This suit was resolved some two years later by a judgment of liberation for Bill. The lawsuit between Strayhorn and Giles was based on fraud, which would void the contract made for Houser, the principal, by his agent, Strayhorn. Giles had the right to sue either or both in "trover" for the value of a female slave given in part payment for Bill.[64]

The Arkansas court did not have occasion to speak on the issue of whether any sort of implied warranty existed in slave sales other than implied warranty of title. All cases before the court involved express warranties of soundness. The court did set out the rules applicable in such cases in a series of cases. For example, in *Jordan v. Foster* the court accepted, as a general proposition, the idea that an obvious defect that requires no skill to detect is not covered by an express warranty of soundness.[65] In this case, the testimony of a doctor was used to establish a distinction between the effects a disease ("paralysis") that could be observed and the nature or cause that could not be observed by an unskilled eye. The testimony of doctors "skilled in the science and practice of medicine" was accepted as competent evidence in a subsequent case as well, although the jury was instructed that the opinions were not conclusive. It was the province of the jury to give appropriate weight to the testimony.[66] The physicians who testified had examined the slave prior to his death and suggested he was afflicted with "hereditary scrofula" but admitted that they might be wrong in their conclusion. The importance of the case was not the evidentiary issue but the court's emphasis that if the slave was unsound, the measure of plaintiff's damages was the difference between what he would have been worth at the time of the sale if he had been sound, as he was warranted to be, and the actual value in unsound condition.[67]

The court returned to the question of the obvious defect in *Thompson v. Bertrand.*[68] It affirmed the proposition that an express warranty does not cover a defect that "is so apparent as to be obvious upon careless inspection, and to every observer, requiring no skill or pains for its detection."[69] The court also cautioned that one not skilled in science or the practice of medicine should not be permitted to express an opinion as to the causes of any unsound condition. Here an overseer went beyond his observations of the appearance and condition of the slave and gave his conclusions based on his years in the business of "management of negroes."[70]

The court, in these opinions, set out well-established rules regarding express warranties and applied those rules in the context of slave sales. The court showed no reluctance to do so regarding any consideration of the character of the chattels—slaves were property. The only expression of concern for the slave came in the earliest of the slave warranty cases, the only one which dealt with "unsoundness of mind," *Pyeatt v. Spencer* in 1842.[71] In that case a slave named Sophia was alleged to be mentally deranged. The buyer claimed that the seller knew she was so at the time of the sale. A number of witnesses testified that the woman had been "obstinate and disagreeable," "of vicious, bad disposition," but not deranged. Her attitude was attributed to her wanting to go to her children, to whom she seemed "much devoted." After she was sold to the plaintiff, he was seen whipping her. The witness testified: "He had her stripped, and staked down on the ground; her feet and hands extended, and fastened to stakes; and her face downwards. . . . Spencer had drawn some blood, but not a great deal. He took salt and cob, and salted her back." This witness "found her to look wild" and opined that she was "deranged and worthless."[72] The court concluded:

> It is with pain and sensibility that the court feels itself constrained to remark that whatever seeming wildness and aberration of mind might be perceived in the slave, it is but reasonable to suppose, was caused by grief and the excessive cruelty of her owner.[73]

The court reviewed two cases that were actions for deceit or false and fraudulent representations as to soundness, contrasting them to actions for breach of warranty. The court recognized that the more appropriate remedy would be for breach of the contract of warranty where an express warranty exists. In such cases the seller's knowledge of the falsehood of the warranty is immaterial. In the case of fraud or deceit, the basis for the allegation is not only that the representation was false but that the seller knew it to be so. This action may be more appropriate when no actual express warranty is made.[74]

The similarity in the two actions is that in a breach-of-warranty case, the buyer may either keep the property and sue for damages or rescind the contract within a reasonable time after discovery of the unsoundness and sue for recovery of the sale price. In the fraud or deceit action, the purchaser has the same options. The difference is in the nature of proof that must be offered. Interestingly, this conforms to the idea of caveat emptor and the rule that the seller must knowingly make false statements to be liable.[75]

Specific Performance of Slave Sale Contracts

Another indication of how southern courts protected slaveholder interests was their adaption of the rule of specific performance to slave sale cases. The traditional concept of specific performance applied to land sales. The seller could be compelled to transfer the land if sold under a valid contract because money damages did not provide an adequate remedy. The rule only applied to sales of personal property if the items were considered unique. Ordinary items of commerce were not considered unique.[76]

Slaves were treated differently. Although chattels, their "moral and intellectual qualities" meant damages at law would not be adequate compensation.[77] In *Sanders v. Sanders*, the Arkansas court evaluated the question of whether a court of equity should grant relief in these situations.[78] Not only did the court refer to the "intellectual and moral" qualities of slaves as making damages an inadequate remedy, but it quoted a Tennessee court as adding "social qualities—-in skill, fidelity and gratitude, as well as their capacity for labor" as reasons for protecting the interest of the slaveholder.[79] The court did caution that exceptions might be made if the slave was held by the owner as "mere merchandise," but that issue was not addressed.[80] This exception was apparently applied in sales to slave traders.[81]

Suits For Freedom/Emancipation

The decisions of Arkansas Supreme Court relating to emancipation of slaves reflect a certain ambivalence toward slaves as property. As summarized by Scott Stafford, this ambivalence was reflected as follows:

> A ruling in favor of emancipation cut off the property interest of the particular person who claimed to be the owner of the slave, but the property interest of a slave owner included the right to set the slave free, and any curtailment of that right infringed on the property rights of slave owners in general.[82]

And, aside from the lack of clarity as to property interests of slaveholders, public attitudes toward emancipation changed from the time of statehood until the outbreak of the Civil War.[83]

The statehood constitution authorized the legislature to permit voluntary emancipation of slaves by will or other written instrument so long as the rights of creditors were protected.[84] This was done by 1838 legislation.[85] A procedure was also established by which a person could petition the circuit court to commence a suit to establish a right to freedom.[86] By 1859 attitudes had changed and the legislature banned voluntary emancipation.[87]

In the meantime, a number of emancipation suits were appealed to the Arkansas Supreme Court. Interestingly, most of these were after 1850. One exception was an 1847 case in which the court dealt with the effect of a probate order that confirmed that the will of the testatrix had manumitted her slaves. The court, on appeal, gave a strict interpretation to the statute and held that a separate suit in circuit court was required to establish a right to freedom.[88]

While adhering to the strict statutory requirements to establish freedom, the court, in 1850, permitted an appellee to waive certain requirements so that an appeal could go forward. The appellee (a "man of color") had sued for freedom and obtained judgment in the circuit court. The appellant had failed to strictly follow all appellate rules, but the court heard the appeal anyway, finding that the particular requirements were set by statute for the benefit of the appellee, who could waive them and, in this case, had done so in the lower court.[89]

In one of the more interesting and, perhaps, important cases, the court was called upon to apply a combination of prior statutes applicable to emancipated slaves.[90] The legislature had in 1838 authorized the emancipation of slaves by deed or will (unlike some states that prohibited emancipation by the owner). However, the legislature had prohibited immigration and settlement of free Negroes in the state after March 1843. Those already residing in the state were required to record evidence of their freedom and give bond for good behavior.

In this case, Duncan Campbell had left a will in which he provided that $5,000 was to go to "Viney, a yellow girl" and that his sister was to take care of Viney until she reached age fifteen, when she was to be freed and receive her legacy. The slave was Campbell's daughter by one of his slaves and was about three when he died. The issue for the court was whether the terms of the will purporting to emancipate Viney were contrary to law and public policy and void. The argument was that the statute prohibiting emancipation of free Negroes into the state operated, in effect, to repeal the older provisions allowing for emancipation by will or deed.

The record showed that the bequest was essentially the deceased's entire estate. Viney's argument was, given this to be the case, she was entitled to her freedom immediately upon the testator's death and should receive her portion of the estate as well. The lower court agreed.

The Arkansas Supreme Court saw the matter, in part, as a question of will construction and wished to give effect to the intent of the testator. They believed he intended that Viney should be liberated immediately but "were loath" to sanction the idea that a mere bequest to a slave acted as an emancipation. They could find no indication that the testator intended for Viney to remain a slave, but rather that he confided her care and custody to his sister. The court believed his legacy to be vested and effective immediately. Apparently, another member of the family had been named as guardian since the sister, Mary, had been among those challenging the will itself.

In 1857 among the more important cases were two dealing with the question of manumission. *Jackson v. Bob* was instituted by Bob, a Negro, who sued for his freedom.[91] A jury found that he should be liberated. The trial started, according to the court, with the presumption against the slave, and he was required to prove his right to freedom. Bob was apparently able to meet this burden as far as the jury was concerned. The appellate court was another matter.

The evidence produced by Bob was that a former owner had conveyed his claim to one Robert Hamilton with the promise that once Bob reached age twenty-one he could "work out" his "valuation" and be freed. Hamilton signed an instrument to that effect which called for an appraisal followed by freedom once Bob "worked out" the sum of his appraisal.[92] The court allowed various oral statements of Hamilton along these lines to be introduced. The supreme court stated that there was no actual instrument of emancipation and that mere declarations of the master were not enough to establish emancipation. Hamilton's instrument did not meet the requirements of the statute allowing emancipation.

> Emancipation is an act of grace or benevolence on the part of the master to the slave. The slave can furnish no legal consideration for it.[93]

The second manumission case met a similar fate.[94] There, instruments were introduced in which the owner stated he wished the slaves to be free following service to his wife for her life and "upon condition of their being her faithful servants." These writings were witnessed by his wife and duly recorded. A statement of the wife was also shown in which she verified that the slaves had been "obedient and dutiful servants." Her will also stated that she wished the slaves to be freed. The appellate court, following *Jackson v. Bob*, found the statements of the owner to be ineffective and not in compliance with the statute. And the will of the wife was ineffective by itself because she was never the owner of the slaves nor did she hold them by adverse possession.

Another type of slave case, *Daniel v. Guy*, was of interest not only because it dealt with a suit for freedom but because the court set some specifics about how it could be determined what race a person was.[95] The underlying presumption was that if one was of the Negro race, whether of full or mixed blood, he or she was presumed to be a slave; whereas, if it appeared that one belonged to the white race, he or she was presumed to be free.

The plaintiffs, Abby Guy and her four minor children, had since 1844 passed as free persons and lived among white folks. They lived part of the time with a man named Guy and went to church, parties, and school as white persons. Abby grew her own crops and conducted business on her own. A short time before the suit, the defendant had taken Abby and the children into possession and treated them as slaves. He claimed that Abby's mother was a "bright mulatto" but had been a slave in his family and had passed by will from his father.

The lower court had instructed the jury that if it appeared the plaintiffs were less than one-fourth Negro, they were presumed to be free and the burden was on the defendant to prove them to be slaves. A statute regarding suits for freedom stated, "If a plaintiff be a negro or a mulatto, he is required to prove his freedom."[96] The court struggled with the definition of "mulatto" as used in the statute and concluded that the lower court's "one-fourth rule" was not acceptable. The correct rule, according to the court, was that the child "takes the condition of the mother" regardless of the classification. No statute fixed a limit to the rule. The court also allowed evidence of "physiology" to be presented to the jury from persons "skilled in the natural history of the races" who could testify as to distinguishing marks between the Negro and the white race.

There was a similar case in 1858, *Gary v. Stevenson.*[97] There, the court applied the presumption recognized in *Daniel v. Guy,* that a slave is also a slave regardless of racial appearance.[98] In this case the evidence revealed the complainant to be blue eyed, sandy haired, with "jaws thin, his nose slim and long," with no visible signs of Negro blood. One expert testified that it would take at least twenty generations "from the black blood to be as white as complainant."[99] Nevertheless, since evidence was presented to show that his mother (who also appeared white) was owned as a slave, there was no basis for his claim to freedom as a "white" person.

In another suit for freedom, *Bob alias Robert Crow v. Powers,* the basis for the claim was a written instrument purporting to grant manumission and emancipation to the owner's slaves "after [his] death."[100] The question was whether the instrument, while by its terms provided for emancipation in the future, was in compliance with the statute on granting emancipation. The court viewed the document as a "deed of emancipation" and did not purport it to be a testamentary instrument (a will). The appellate court felt the lower court erred in not allowing the jury (which was trying the suit for freedom) to see the document since it was in compliance with statutory requirements. A new trial was ordered.

Another important slave case involved the 1859 legislation that forbid any further emancipation of slaves.[101] The will of the master, made in 1853, provided for emancipation of his slaves seven years after his death. The slaves (Phebe and eighteen children and grandchildren) had sued for freedom in 1857. The court found that they had no right to freedom (or to sue) until the seven-year time period had expired (i.e., in 1860) and that the act did not apply to instruments, such as his will, made prior to the enactment of the law. The court concluded with an expression of concern about such a situation:

> The question of freedom should be determined like every other question made before the courts, solely upon the legal aspects, without partiality to an applicant for freedom, because he may be defenseless, and a member of an inferior race, and certainly without prejudice to his kind and color, and without regard to the sincere convictions that all candid, observing men must entertain, that a change from this condition of servitude and protection, to that of being free negroes is injurious to the community, and more unfortunate to the emancipated negro than to anyone else.[102]

In 1861 *Daniel v. Guy* reached the supreme court again.[103] A jury in Drew County (following a change of venue) had also returned a verdict for the plaintiffs upon retrial of the case. The court approved the decision of the trial court to permit the jury to examine the feet and to otherwise inspect the plaintiff and her children. The court stated:

> The experience of every intelligent observer of the race, whether in the instances of mixed or unmixed negro blood, will doubtless attest the truth of the testimony of the professional witnesses. No one, who is familiar with the peculiar formation of the *negro foot*, can doubt, that an inspection of that member would ordinarily afford some indication of the race—though the evidence of race, thus afforded, would, of course, be stronger or weaker, according to the extent of the admixture of the blood.[104]

The court affirmed the judgment of freedom with some reluctance.

The sad story of Abby Guy's effort to be free of Daniel did not end with her second case before the supreme court. She was there a third time as Abby Roper in *Daniel v. Roper*.[105] This time she had sued for the return of property—two mares and a colt, a yoke of oxen, and a cart—which Daniel had taken from her when he attempted to reduce her and her children to slavery. The court, still wondering what her actual race was, acknowledged that she had successfully sued for freedom on the basis of belonging to the white race. Since that was found to be true (by two different juries), she was under no disability to sue for return of her property or for its conversion.

> She must, then, have been acting under the claim of being a free person, must have been recognized and treated as such by others; for otherwise she could not have accumulated horses and oxen.[106]

However, since she was a free, white person, the statute of limitations was applicable and her suit could not be maintained.

Responsibilities for Acts of Slaves

At common law, a master could be responsible for the acts of a servant committed while the servant was engaged in employment. This relationship, based on contract, recognized the servant as having rights but also responsibilities to the master for the consequences of his actions. But, the master's liability did not extend to willful or malicious acts of the servant.

Slave-era courts attempted to distinguish the relationship of master and servant from that of master and slave. Different concepts of liability for the acts of slaves grew out of this distinction. As property, any injury to the slave by third parties could be redressed by actions of the master. At the same time, the slave had no civil liability for injuries done to third persons. Logically, this responsibility would be that of the master. This was the starting point for the court's analysis in *McConnell v. Hardeman*.[107] This was the first case addressing the responsibility of a master for the acts of his slave. In that case a slave was accused of having taken a horse belonging to the plaintiff.

The court attempted to distinguish the master-slave relationship from that of the master and servant, referring to slavery as a "domestic institution," a *status* not based on contract. The court recognized that under civil law a master could be liable for acts of slaves, but in the common law jurisdictions that was true only if the master commanded or approved the act of the slave. Acts done without the authority of the master or against his orders were a different matter. The court reviewed cases from other jurisdictions in an effort to find a basis for decision, ultimately suggesting that the efforts to distinguish between the master-slave relationship and the master-servant relationship gave unsatisfactory results. They turned to Arkansas legislation, which, on its face, seemed to resolve the question. The criminal law provided that masters could be held liable for acts of slaves that were indictable offenses, such as killing domestic animals or various trespasses on real estate. For offenses less than felonies, the master could "compound," that is, make restitution to the injured party and then punish his own slave for the offense. If the master failed to do so, a criminal legal proceeding could be had against the slave and a suit for damages could be made against the master.[108] The court noticed that these provisions gave "color" to the idea that masters were "unqualifiedly" liable for acts of slaves even if done without the consent or knowledge of the master. This, however, did not seem to be an entirely satisfactory outcome in the courts eyes. The court stated:

> We consider that the statutory enactments in this State are modifications of the general law, and, therefore, the master's liability for acts of his slaves in which he did not participate, must be restricted to those trespasses which are indictable offenses, or not being so, are specified in the statute.[109]

The court suggested that the legislature consider future provisions that would limit the liability to the value of the offending slaves. This was based on an apparent concern that if slaveholders were made liable for all trespasses of their slaves, the "true interests" of slaveholders would not be promoted unless some restrictions were imposed on the extent of liability.

In a second case the same year, *Ridge v. Featherston,* the allegation was that the slave had shot and killed a mare belonging to the plaintiff.[110] The slave, Wagoola, had apparently told the plaintiff a few days earlier that if he did not keep the horse off his master's plantation he, Wagoola, would kill her. The act of killing a horse, if done willfully and maliciously, was an indictable offense of the type referred to in *McConnell v. Hardeman*. However, the case was reversed because the court found that the statement of the slave should not have been admitted in evidence in a civil suit against the master. (It could have been in a criminal case against the slave.) The logic was, in part, because it would make the slave a competent witness against a white man.[111]

The issue was not addressed again until 1861 in *Graham v. Roark,* where an overseer of slaves ordered slaves to remove a crop of corn and peas and rail fences on land belonging to the plaintiff.[112] The slaveholder was out of state at the time and had no knowledge of the offense. A specific statute now detailed the remedy for such trespasses. If done under the direction of the master, treble damages could be imposed for destruction of the crop and double damage for damages caused by "throwing down" a fence and a penalty of five dollars for each "throwing down." If slaves committed the offense of their own will, the action could be the responsibility of the slaveholder (but single damages only). The court noted that this statute went beyond the rule of *McConnell v. Hardeman* and placed responsibility for injury caused by slaves on the slaveholder rather than the injured party. The court found that when slaves acted under the direction of an overseer, they were not his employees but were still the responsibility of the owner. (The court said this case could have proceeded under the sections permitting treble or double damages but noted the plaintiff was only seeking single damages.)[113]

The court refined its approach when dealing with the responsibility for crimes committed by slaves. It drew the distinction between criminal actions and civil actions in *Sarah v. State,* pointing out that a slave was not subject to a civil action but could be prosecuted for crimes.[114]

> The slave however, is a human being—he is regarded as a rational creature—a moral agent. He, as well as the master, is the subject of government, and amenable to the laws of God and man. In all things lawful, the slave is absolutely to obey his master. But a higher power than his master—*the law of the land*—forbids him to commit crime.[115]

This was true even if the slave could show he or she acted under the direction of the master. The court noted that in such cases "he ought not, in justice, to be punished so severely, as where the crime is voluntary on his part."[116] A jury should be permitted to consider this in mitigation of the punishment of the slave.

Responsibilities for Actions toward Slaves

The court was confronted not only with cases involving the responsibility for acts of slaves, but also, on occasion, with questions of liability for actions that harmed slaves in some way. For example, in *Henry v. Armstrong*, the issue was whether a master could recover for battery against a slave where it was alleged that slaves had been whipped by a "company of patrol" to the extent they could not perform labor or service for some time.[117]

The patrol, "being in discharge of their duties as patrols, visiting all negro quarters and other places, suspected of unlawful assemblages of slaves," saw the slaves in question "strolling about" without a pass and proceeded to administer "lashes, not exceeding twenty." The owner contended that these particular patrol members were outside their township and their lawful authority could not extend beyond the limits of the township in which they were appointed. The court agreed with the trial judge that testimony as to whether the patrol was invited to come into the township by inhabitants should not be admitted. The court outlined the patrol system, which was called a "police regulation," as a "slumbering power" that could be called into action when needed. But it would only be called to act in the township where it had authority.

> The presumption is, that the people of each township are able to quell all ordinary disturbances occurring in it, by or among their slaves, and this can be better and more appropriately done by those who are neighbors and friends, having a common interest to protect, and a common danger to guard against, than by strangers, whose interference has not been invited.[118]

The slaves in this case had apparently been attending religious service on Sunday (which had been "orderly and well conducted").

They were arrested by the patrol, tied, and whipped with no more than ten lashes each. The court said that this, if deserved, would not have been cruel or excessive even if their cries were heard "by persons at some distance."[119] However, since masters could not coerce labor from slaves on Sunday, the plaintiff could not show any loss of services from the whippings. The court was cautious about extending a right of legal action to masters in such cases where there was no loss of service because this might "tend to consequences, which would hardly be tolerated in a community where slavery exists."[120] It would encourage slaves, according to the court, to be insolent by word or demeanor.

In a second case involving liability for actions toward slaves, the court adopted the rule that one who hires a slave for a set period is obligated to furnish "proper nursing, medicine and if necessary, to call in a physician for his relief" unless an express contract with the owner provides otherwise.[121]

Criminal Actions Involving Slaves

As indicated above, the criminal law provided that a master could make restitution for injury by the commission of a criminal offense by a slave and then punish the slave on his own for the offense. As a result, many criminal cases involving slaves never reached the courts. Sometimes whites were prosecuted for certain activities involving slaves. For example, in *Powell v. State* the defendant was charged with the employment of a slave in a retail grocery where ardent spirits were sold.[122] Witnesses had observed the slave frequently in the grocery, where he apparently slept. He would bring water, roll out barrels, sweep, bring out the owner's horse, and go on errands. This was sufficient to constitute the offense. In a second case, *Edwards v. State,* the offense charged was selling ardent spirits to a slave without permission of his master.[123] The part of the statute under which the defendant was charged applied only to white persons. A second section applied to free Negroes or mulattos, where no exception applied to sales with consent of the master. It was not necessary to identify the defendant as white to sustain the charge.

In another illustration of the complexity of the social relationships, the court had to determine whether an indictment was sufficient under the act making it a misdemeanor for a white person to "harbor or entertain" a slave without the consent of the owner.[124] While upholding the validity of the statute, the court also upheld the lower court's decision to quash the indictment because it failed to state the name of the owner or overseer of the slaves, which the court regarded as an essential element of the description of the offense. The court took pains to distinguish this case (which involved a "trespass" against the property of another) from the gaming cases and the Sabbath-breaking cases previously considered by the court.[125]

And the court drew a distinction between a criminal indictment and a suit for freedom. In the latter, there is a presumption of slavery; in the former, where different grades of punishment attach to the offense depending on whether the defendant is slave or free, the indictment must describe the condition and the proof must conform.[126] In this particular case, the court was concerned that the defendant was only referred to as "a negro" and no testimony was adduced at trial that he was a slave. Punishment for free persons of color was the same as for white persons, but slaves were subject to different punishments for the commission of the same offenses.[127]

In a dramatic example of how carefully the court evaluated legal requirements for conviction, in *Sullivant v. State*, Joe, a slave belonging to Escanah Sullivant, was charged with attempted rape.[128] The witness testified that she awoke up with someone in her bed trying to rape her. She did not see the assailant but saw the direction he ran. The defendant was brought to the property and forced to place his bare feet in the track made by the fleeing offender. It "fit," and after the husband of the witness whipped the defendant, he confessed, according to her testimony. The court granted a new trial, calling the testimony "loose and unsatisfactory" since it only related a conclusion of law—not facts as to what happened that would provide basis for the jury to decide if those facts constituted the offense.

In *Charles v. State*, the court was confronted with two questions, one of law, one of sufficiency of evidence.[129] The defendant, a slave, had been convicted of attempted rape and sentenced to be hanged. The evidence suggested that he had entered the room of the victim (a white girl, aged fourteen), where she was sleeping with five other girls; had been partially undressed ("that portion of which I cannot decently speak"); took hold of her shoulder to try to turn her over; and she had awakened and raised an alarm.

The critical constitutional issue raised in the case was whether a provision in the state constitution requiring slaves to suffer the "same degree of punishment as would be inflicted on a free white person" when convicted of a capital offense meant that a statute mandating the death penalty for a black man who attempted to commit rape of a white woman was unconstitutional because a white man could only be imprisoned for the same offense. The court concluded that the provision simply required that the same mode of punishment be used for capital offenses for both black and white men. The court read this provision to grant a certain feeling of "humanity towards the unfortunate African race and in order to secure them against that barbarous treatment and excessive cruelty which was practiced upon them in the earlier period of our colonial history."[130]

The evidentiary question gave the court more pause. In order to find one guilty of the offense of attempted rape, it is necessary to find the same elements as for rape itself, particularly, intent to effect the purpose by force. The court was not convinced that the evidence was sufficient to show that the defendant intended to use force but only that he "intended to have such carnal knowledge of her while she was asleep."[131] The conviction was reversed.

One criminal case involved the prosecution of a slave for attempting to commit rape on a white woman (a capital offense).[132] A new trial was granted because the lower court refused to allow testimony that the complaining witness had proposed to the owner of the slave that she would not prosecute him if paid $200 and because the jury was not instructed that in order to find the defendant guilty they would have to be satisfied from the evidence presented that the complaining witness was a white woman. The statute at issue was previously before the court on the constitutional question of whether a slave could be punished capitally for an offense that, if committed by a white man, would result only in imprisonment. The court had upheld the statute as constitutional.[133]

At the trial in this case the witness testified and made references to "her husband" and "her brother" (presumably white men), but there was no evidence presented that she was, *in fact*, white. The court rejected the idea that the jury could make such a determination by visual inspection, saying, "A fair complexion is not inconsistent with the taint of negro blood."[134] However, the court was less concerned with proof necessary to show that the defendant was black, finding sufficient evidence in the record to sustain the proof.

In *Austin v. State* a slave was convicted of murder of a white man.[135] The killing had occurred after the slave, Austin, had a confrontation with his master in which he had "talked improperly" to his master. The evidence was that the slave had armed himself with a stick and had stated that he would "not be taken." The following day the master and others approached the defendant with the apparent purpose of "correcting" him. He was, at the time, carrying an ax with which he had been working and refused to lay down the ax. He said that he "would not be whipped" and would "kill the first man that attempted to take him." The victim approached Austin with a stick and attempted to strike him. The victim was hit on the head with the edge of the ax, which resulted in his death.

At the trial the slave argued that the killing was only manslaughter and that he acted without malice. He wished to introduce evidence concerning the events of the prior day to show that he had no premeditation or design with regard to the victim. The court felt the jury should have been allowed to consider this evidence as to the "motive of the heart."[136] In addition, the slave wished to elicit testimony of the master. The state objected because of his "pecuniary interest as owner," and the lower court excluded the testimony. The reviewing court considered decisions from other states in which this argument had been advanced and concluded that the better view was to allow the master as a competent witness for or against a slave.

> Society will not allow him to say, I have a pecuniary interest in the event of the trial, my testimony may subject me to a loss, and I will not testify against my slave. On the other hand, humanity forbids that society should say, you have such an interest and shall not be heard to prove a fact in his favor.[137]

The master's pecuniary interest would go only to his credibility, not to his competency as a witness. The case was reversed and the slave was granted a new trial.

Pleasant v. State was before the court a second time in 1853.[138] This case had previously been before the court and a conviction had been reversed.[139] The defendant, a slave owned by James Minton, was accused of attempted rape by Sophia Fulmer, a white woman. During the trial, the defense attempted to question the accuser about her relationship with her husband and her "criminal connection" with various other men. They also wished to inquire about allegations of rape she had made against others and, specifically, whether she had invited a female slave to sit at her table for dinner. Numerous witnesses were called and asked about these matters, but the trial court prevented questioning along these lines of either the accuser or the witnesses. On appeal, the court found that it would be proper to hear evidence of a general nature concerning character, truth, and veracity. This could, in cases of rape or assault to commit rape, extend to questions regarding general reputation for chastity but could not delve into evidence of specific incidents with particular persons. The court was persuaded that to do so would compel the witness to incriminate herself or to commit perjury or at least to disgrace herself. Since the trial court had not even allowed questions concerning general character, the conviction was reversed again. In addition, the court seemed convinced that some sort of bargain had been struck between the accuser and the owner of the slave, which would have resulted in the prosecution not going forward. The slave owner should have been allowed to testify as to these matters (as decided in *Austin v. State*).[140]

While the court was willing to reverse the conviction and send the case back for a new trial, the attitude of the court toward offenses of rape or attempted rape of a white woman was clearly expressed in the review of the evidence related to chastity. The court stated that the character of the female, "however abandoned," is no justification for the act and is relevant only for the purpose of raising the presumption of assent. The court added:

> But surely, it may not be unsafe or unjust to the prisoner to say that, in this state, where sexual intercourse between white women and Negroes is generally regarded with the utmost abhorrence, the presumption that a white woman yielded herself to the embraces of a Negro, without force, or want of chastity in her, would not be great, unless she had sunk to the lowest degree of prostitution.[141]

In the July 1856 term, criminal cases were a major focus and two of those involved slavery. One raised the question of whether a slave could be indicted for a criminal offense at all since slaves were "mere chattels."[142] The court indicated that slaves,

> though inferior in mental and moral endowments to the white race, and occupying a subordinate position, in the order of Providence, yet they are rational beings, and as such, are not only responsible for crimes committed by them, but are under the protection of the laws, and whilst their masters may lawfully exercise over them all necessary and proper authority to keep them in subjection and enforce obedience and submission, yet they are amenable to the law for any wanton and inhuman treatment on their slaves.[143]

A related question was whether the master was required to be informed of the transgression of the slave and pay any damages sustained as a prerequisite to indictment. The court found that this was necessary and that the master had to be given the option of "chastising his own slave" before the slave was subject to indictment.

Summary and Conclusions

The treatment of the "slave" cases as routine illustrates that the Arkansas Supreme Court harbored no particular sentiment toward recognition of slaves as anything more than another class of property. What is clear from the freedom suits and emancipation cases is that, in the end, the supreme court justified slavery based on the necessity to preserve racial dominance. While the court sometimes toyed with the concept of slaves as persons, ultimately, it was their reaffirmation of slaves as property that determined the outcome in all cases.

What is also apparent in the approach of the Arkansas Supreme Court to slaves as property is the judicial concern for the rights of slaveholders. As concluded by Fede:

> Slave owners dominated politics and the economy in the antebellum South, and both the courts and legislatures were populated with individuals who were, at the least, sympathetic to the slave owning interest.[144]

And as pointed out by L. Scott Stafford in his study "Slavery and the Arkansas Supreme Court," the justices had to "justify and preserve" slavery as an institution when addressing slave-related issues.[145] Slaves were valuable property, and the wealthy planters who held the largest number of slaves could insist on protection of their property interests. Whether the court viewed the law as an "instrument of social policy," as asserted by Horwitz and Hurst, or merely an acknowledgment of the paternalist/hierarchical nature of slave society, as Genovese suggests, is less clear. What is clear is that the court struggled, sometimes inconsistently, with the character of slaves as property but was willing to modify common law concepts to fit the goals of the slave economy.

CHAPTER 7

"Affording Peace and Quiet"

Case, Controversies, and Conflicts Relating to Family Law and Family Property

Michael Grossberg, in *Governing the Hearth: Law and the Family in Nineteenth-Century America,* calls the late eighteenth and early nineteenth centuries the "formative era" of domestic relations law in America. This, he says, is because of "converging family and legal changes."[1] The family changed from a "part of a hierarchically organized, interdependent society" to a "republican family" that stood apart "in an increasingly segregated, private realm of society."[2] A "refashioned" legal order emerged which included "popular acceptance of legal instrumentalism" and the increasing role of litigation in settling disputes.[3] The convergence of these transformative views created a republican concept of domestic relations, which produced a "dynamic law of the family" in the new republic.[4] Grossberg further suggests that the role of judges in this development is a critical part of the story.

> Judges figured prominently in the creation of domestic-relations law. Appellate opinions, in particular, offer the most thorough commentary on the law. They do so because one of the emerging realities of nineteenth-century family law was the primary role of the state judiciary in devising and applying its basic principles and policies. The unique nature of appellate opinions—their special character as public documents designed to persuade diverse audiences—also heightens their evidentiary value. In writing them, judges articulated their assumptions and ideas about family governance. The opinions thus reveal many of the fundamental values, fears,

and interests that governed the establishment of a distinctive category of laws to govern the family.[5]

As historian G. Edward White points out, judicial opinions are "products of their historical moments" and are "time-bound" but must be recognized as "documents designed to serve the purpose of resolving disputes and exhorting citizens to engage in one form of conduct rather than another." In so doing, they have a unique quality "emphasized by an internalist historical perspective."[6] White also notes that at the time of independence, American culture "centered on the agricultural household."[7] The agricultural household was "an economic as well as a social unit."[8] This was a household that was composed of four primary sectors: (1) land use (ownership, sale, and lease), (2) labor (slavery to masters and freeholders), (3) family relations (gender, age, marriage, child rearing, wealth accumulation, and inheritance), and (4) trade and commerce. Law had to respond to changes within each of these sectors; and, in doing so, with regard to family relations, the formative patterns described by Grossberg can be gleaned from the cases appearing in reports from the appellate courts during the early nineteenth century.

The family law and family property disputes reaching the Arkansas Supreme Court in the years from statehood, 1836, until the close of the Reconstruction Era, 1874, include the following categories:

(1) divorce and family relationships,
(2) married women's property,
(3) inheritance or succession,
(4) dower, and
(5) homestead.

When Arkansas became a state in 1836, many southern states had no general divorce law and legislative divorce was rare. Arkansas, which freely borrowed from Tennessee, enacted a divorce law that empowered the circuit courts to grant divorces for a number of specified causes. In the early years, the Arkansas Supreme Court rarely had the occasion to interpret this law.

More frequently, the Arkansas court dealt with issues related to family property and, in particular, married women's property. Prior to statehood the territorial legislature had enacted an elementary form of a married women's property rights act, which protected the property of a wife from the debts of a husband incurred before marriage. In 1846 the state legislature enacted a married woman's property law, patterned after an existing Mississippi statute. Married women could own property in their own names, free of liability of the debts of the husband.

The general inheritance provisions of "descent and distribution" or "succession" were apparently borrowed, with minor revisions, from New York. Following English common law, Arkansas adopted dower and applied the concept to both land (a life interest in one-third) and personal property (one-third outright) and to a similar provision regarding slaves. Finally, Arkansas adopted homestead provisions as a means of protecting family property both at death and against creditors.

Divorce and Family Relationships

Marriage has, historically, been easier than divorce. Marriage in the United States has been viewed in legal theory as a contract. Even the recognition in some states of common-law marriage was viewed in contract terms—a "verbal contract" between parties to consider themselves married. However, even if the view of marriage was that of contract, American states always considered it a "sovereign right" to prevent "undesirable" marriages.[9] Certain limitations were reflected in statutes, common law, or social customs, and judges and legislatures tried to balance nuptial freedom (the freedom to contract) with social protection.[10]

While the contractual nature of marriage emphasized consent of the parties, it was considered too important to leave entirely to private agreement. Public ramifications of the unique relationship meant that a distinct republican notion of family governance "evolved with social duties attached."[11]

> Making room for a larger public presence in nuptials followed from the view that matrimony was too vital to society to be left far beyond the regulatory reach of the state.[12]

As a result, limitations were imposed relating to physical qualifications (age, sexual incapacity, kinship, and mental incompetence) and to prevent "nuptial dishonesty" (fraud, coercion).[13] Eventually, bigamy and polygamy became the focus of criminal law.[14] Racial restrictions, however, were traced to common-law origins with not only bans on slave unions but anti-miscegenation laws in many states both before and after the Civil War.[15]

Just as states took greater interest in regulating the marriage contract, then too there was a growing movement toward specifying how that contract could be dissolved. However, regional differences were stark. Initially, legislative divorce was the norm in the New England states and was available in some southern states as well. In the South, however, divorce was minimal and change came slowly. The North soon replaced legislative divorce with a court proceeding. Judicial divorce gradually supplemented the cumbersome legislative process, which was a "nuisance" and a "pointless drain" on legislative time.[16] Legislation providing for judicial divorce specified limited grounds, frequently incest, bigamy, adultery, abandonment, or extreme cruelty.[17] Divorce could be had only by an "innocent" spouse, and the intent was to prevent voluntary, consensual termination of the marital contract.[18] Divorce laws were evidence of the public regulation of the relationship and the recognition that this was no ordinary contract. Divorce was a "public remedy" for a "public need" and, understood in this light, these laws were a part of the state's police power and did not "impair" the private contract.[19]

The South was not inclined to embrace easy divorce, in part, because the concept of patriarchal dominance prevailed, which meant a reluctance to intervene in household matters.[20] However, the adversarial nature of the proceeding meant that some "fault or moral wrongdoing" would be demonstrated that weakened the position of the errant spouse and reinforced the innocence of the other.[21] And some states broadened the definitions of grounds for divorce. "Mental cruelty" was included within cruelty, and "general indignities" that made cohabitation "intolerable" were also considered a part of cruelty.[22]

During the territorial period in Arkansas, divorces could be obtained either by court proceedings or in the legislature. The legislative divorce was, in effect, an ex parte proceeding, where the request was submitted for action without the other party given the opportunity to respond.

An early example of a court proceeding for divorce is found in the territorial records in *Allen v. Allen,* arising in Independence County, in which the husband, Samuel, filed a divorce petition claiming his wife was "ill natured and disobedient" and had deserted "his bed and board." He claimed she was "naturally impotent and incapable of procreation." The wife, Elizabeth, in turn, filed a cross complaint and claimed that she had "in all things demeaned herself as an affectionate wife" and that Samuel had used "rude and unkind language" toward her, and she alleged that her husband had used physical violence against her, which had forced her to leave his house. She requested a *divorce a mensa et thoro* (legal separation) and spousal support. The case was tried before a jury, which found that Elizabeth was not "naturally impotent" and that she had cause to leave Samuel's bed and board. The court granted her *divorce a mensa et thoro*, allowed her to live separate and apart from Samuel, and ordered him to pay an appointed trustee sixty dollars for her maintenance and support. Upon appeal to the superior court, the case was reversed on technical grounds and set aside. The basis was that Elizabeth had not answered the original complaint but had, instead, filed a cross complaint. According to the court, the answer was to be filed before a cross complaint could be heard. In addition, as a *femme covert*, Elizabeth could not file a proceeding except by a "next friend." The case was apparently resolved in the lower court because it was simply removed from the superior court docket later in the year.[23]

At the time of Arkansas statehood many southern states had no general divorce law and legislative divorce was rare. Divorce laws were common in the New England states and were in place in New York, New Jersey, and Tennessee.[24] The 1836 Arkansas Constitution provided that the general assembly could not pass on a bill for divorce but could prescribe how divorces would be granted in the courts (and how such cases would be "investigated" by the courts).[25] Identical language was included in the 1861

Confederate constitution.[26] No such provision appeared in the 1868 constitution or the 1874 constitution, presumably because the concept of legislative divorce was no longer considered a viable approach and court-directed divorce proceedings were well established. Arkansas, borrowing from Tennessee, enacted a divorce law in 1837. This act empowered circuit courts to grant divorces for a number of specified causes, including where one party was "addicted to drunkenness for the space of one year" or had been guilty of "such cruel and barbarous treatment as to endanger the life of the other." A less concrete cause was that one party "shall offer such indignities to the person of the other as shall render his or her condition intolerable."[27]

This "general indignities" provision came before the court in 1848 in *Rose v. Rose*.[28] This was the first case dealing with divorce to reach the higher court. The court, in an opinion by Justice Christopher C. Scott, reviewed the historical foundation for divorce in the ecclesiastical courts of England and indicated that the chancery courts "have rightfully, as to divorce and alimony, all the powers of the English ecclesiastical courts as well as additional powers conferred by our statutes."[29] The court then described conduct that, while not "legal cruelty," could be considered as rendering the marital state intolerable.

> And so it may be safely assumed of those personal indignities mentioned by the statute, which necessarily include rudeness, vulgarity, unmerited reproach, haughtiness, contempt, contumely, studied neglect, intentional incivility, injury, manifest disdain, abusive language, malignant ridicule, and every other plain manifestation of settled hate, alienation and estrangement, both of word and action, that they must be no less habitual, continuous, and permanent, to create that intolerable condition contemplated by the statute, and for which it provides relief.[30]

In reviewing the evidence, the court upheld the lower court decision that the wife had shown grounds. It was not necessary that the grounds reach the level of "cruelty" making it impossible to discharge the duties of married life; only that to continue in marriage would compel those duties "under such continuous extreme and unmerited suffering."[31]

In the next divorce case before the court, in 1855, the court indicated that a divorce proceeding could not be taken by default; some proof of the allegations would be necessary. The parties could "make the marriage tie" but could never break it without some proof being submitted.[32]

In a subsequent divorce case, *Bauman v. Bauman,* the court reviewed the circumstances under which a decree providing for alimony and child support could be revised.[33] The court indicated its view of the authority of chancery courts:

> The chancery Courts ought to employ the same rules of law which the Ecclesiastical Courts do, except in so far as they be found unsuited to our Courts, or in conflict with specific, constitutional or statutory provisions or the general spirit of our laws.[34]

The court then proceeded to cite an ecclesiastical court decision regarding an alteration of a decree for alimony and indicated that such occur only where there is a material alteration of circumstances, such as improved "faculties" of the husband.

An issue arose in early divorce litigation as to how attorneys might be assured of payment for professional services in representing wives in divorce actions. This issue arose because the common law held contracts made by a married woman to be void, unless the wife held separate property that could be used to pay the attorney. In *Viser v. Bertrand,* the court held that reasonable compensation to an attorney could be chargeable to the separate estate of the wife.[35] The court felt that a promise by her would be binding even if made *after* the divorce.

After the war the court had the occasion to comment on an ante-nuptial agreement and the method of appeal in a divorce action. The ante-nuptial agreement was upheld, but the court referred to the "awkward attitude" a divorce placed the parties in since the law allowed three years for an appeal following the decree.[36] The court did express some doubt as to the effectiveness of such appeals, saying, in this case, that even if the judgment had been reversed, the court had doubts that this would have restored the wife "to the loving embraces of Enoch H. Simpson."[37]

The court later dealt with the doctrine of condonation in divorce actions, where the alleged grounds were adultery yet the proof showed the plaintiff continued the marital relationship with full knowledge of the guilt of the defendant. This was in *Turnbull v. Turnbull.*[38] The evidence showed that the defendant was "a very light and imprudent woman, very fond of the society of other men besides her husband, and very unrestrained in her manner at all times."[39] She had been seen frequently with the "adulterer," who was an actor at a theater owned by the plaintiff. While the plaintiff was out of town, the man was seen going to her room late at night and remaining until the next morning. At other times she expressed her affection toward the man and was seen using "very indecent and unbecoming familiarities with him."[40] Not long thereafter, as the court succinctly states, "the Plaintiff shot Conner in his wife's room."[41] The husband was held in jail for one night after the shooting, but upon his release he and his wife renewed their relationship, living together as man and wife. He made notable effort to convince others of his wife's innocence and was "profuse in his expressions of conjugal affection" toward her in letters sent while they were apart. The court found that while there was no mention of condonation as a defense to an action for divorce under the Arkansas statute, this did not limit or destroy a well-known doctrine unless specifically mentioned. The concept of condonation recognizes that a basis for divorce may be waived or abandoned.

> The peace and quiet of families, the tranquility of society, and a proper regard for the welfare of the issue of the marriage which may be born or engendered after the time of the condonation, afford the most potent reasons on which the principle rests.[42]

The plaintiff filed for divorce long after knowing of the wife's actions and after seemingly to have forgiven her. Thus, the court upheld the defense. The court said there was little in the case that "can awaken the sympathy of the court on behalf of either party."[43]

In line with the patriarchal and hierarchical tradition, colonial law in America did little to alter the view that the father was the "natural" custodian of children, who were, in a real sense, his possessions.[44] Post-revolutionary republican views of the family, combined with judicial discretion, led to expanded maternal rights and greater concern for the best interest of the child.[45]

In the South the presumption of the father's superior rights to custody prevailed throughout the antebellum period. The father-child bond was the basis for social position and inheritance, and, particularly in planter families, the "way of life" required "subordination and dependence."[46] The position of the mother in the household was recognized thus: to plant "seeds of domesticity" but at all times to be deferential to the paramount role of the father.[47] While mothers were rarely named as legal custodians of children, the evolution of the "tender years" doctrine meant that children were often left in her care especially during the early years. Only in extreme case of paternal unfitness was the father deprived of his "legal, natural right."[48] Though courts were reluctant to exercise judicial discretion in favor of mothers, legislation in a number of southern states focused on the welfare of the child and gave courts more flexibility in custody decisions.[49]

The patriarchal nature of the family relationship, even as late as the 1860s, is illustrated by the case of *Patterson v. Thompson.*[50] The father of an adult daughter brought an action for seduction, alleging loss of service and expenses related to her pregnancy. The action was not for "lost virtue" but for the father's loss: "the injury, the suffering and the disgrace that the seduction and pregnancy of the daughter have produced to himself and his family."[51] The court reviewed the relevant law indicating that, had the daughter been under twenty-one, she would have been considered the father's servant and an action could have been maintained whether or not she was in his actual service. However, if she was of legal age, as in this case, there was no legal injury unless she resided with the family and did, "at least, such slight acts of service as a daughter and members of her father's family is expected to do."[52] Absent the master-servant relationship, no right of action would be available. "Sickness and expenses that are the direct conveyance of the illicit intercourse" are necessary. In this case the daughter conceived in August, went to live with her sister, and then moved out of state with the defendant, at whose home she had been teaching. She married (apparently, not the defendant) prior to the birth of the child. The court found that the father incurred no expenses and no loss of service. He had no cause of action under these circumstances.

The attitude of the court (and the state of the law) is nicely illustrated by a statement of the court in 1852 regarding the relationship of a husband to his wife's relatives. The issue was whether the husband of an aunt was related to the husband of her niece. The issue involved a judge's disqualification to hear a case.[53] The court said that affinity was calculated in the same way as consanguinity but that marriage created a different type of relationship altogether.

> It is upon the principle of a complete merger or incorporation of the very being and existence of the wife in that of her husband, and upon that alone that the relationship contended for, can be conceded.[54]

An interesting development in the area of family law was illustrated in *Magness v. Walker*, in which the court rejected the common law rule that a wife could not testify when called as a witness for the husband.[55] That rule was based on the concept that the interest of the two was identical. When offered as a witness against the husband, the testimony was excluded on the basis of public policy (to preserve "peace and quiet" of families."[56] The 1868 Arkansas Constitution provided that in civil actions no witness would be excluded because "he is a party to, or interested in the issue to be tried."[57]

In this case the wife had acted as agent for the husband in renting the farm during a period when he was out of state. Her testimony was offered to prove the terms of the contract. The lower court had not permitted her testimony. The case was reversed and remanded to permit her testimony. The court also criticized the trial court for permitting testimony of the brother of the opposing party regarding "loose and careless remarks" of the wife made subsequent to the contract and outside the presence of either party. Why, the court asked, could such evidence be used if her "solemn oath" could not be heard in the presence of the court and the parties? In a similar situation, the court reaffirmed the principle that a wife could act as an agent for her husband but had no legal authority to dispose of her property or bind him to a contract without his authority or his subsequent ratification.[58]

Separate Property of Married Women

At common law, upon marriage, the husband and wife were considered "one flesh," with the man as "owner of that flesh."[59] This meant that the husband acquired a right to use any real estate of the wife during her life (owned by her at marriage or acquired by her during the marriage). He controlled all "rents and profits" from the real estate. Any personal property ("chattels personal") came under the exclusive control of the husband.[60] If they had surviving children, then his right continued during his life ("tenant by curtsey").

An exception recognized by courts of equity was the separate estate created by a "marriage settlement," usually in the form of trusts in wills or by a prenuptial agreement between the parties.[61] The equitable estate, created by will, usually gave the woman possession and profits from the property but restricted her right to dispose of the property.[62] Creditors opposed such arrangements because, in absence of settlements, they could look to the property of the wife to pay the debts of the husband.[63]

An example of how narrowly courts viewed these arrangements is shown in *Harrison v. Trader and Wife,* where the husband and wife had entered into an agreement prior to marriage that the property of neither should be taken for the debts of the other.[64] The wife had, on her own, borrowed $2,500 before they married. The court suggested that, as between the spouses, the contract might be considered valid but, as to third parties, the common law still prevailed, so the husband was liable for the debts of the wife "created *dum sola*" (before marriage). The court seemed to be sympathetic to a situation where the wife retained property for her exclusive use and control but felt obligated to continue the common law rule in absence of legislation to the contrary.

During the territorial period, the Arkansas legislature passed an elementary form of a married women's property rights act, the first in the nation. This 1835 legislation protected property of a wife from the debts of the husband incurred before marriage. It did not protect the property from debts incurred after marriage.[65] This was enacted largely at the behest of planters who wished to see property protected from the mismanagement of their daughters' husbands.

In 1846 the state legislature enacted a married woman's property law patterned after an existing Mississippi statute. Under the new law, married women could own property in their own names, free of liability of the debts of the husband. While the initial section of this statute referred to real or personal property, the operative sections dealt with slaves. Wives wishing to protect their property were required to record or "schedule" the property in the public records.[66] This act was approved, in part, as a form of debt relief (given the "Panic of 1837") and in recognition of the "nature of plantation economics," in that families desired means of providing some security to female children, especially by passing down slaves.[67]

The Arkansas act had been introduced and passed in the 1840 legislative session but was vetoed by Governor Archibald Yell, who claimed it would free wives of obligation and disrupt families.[68] One of the most ardent opponents was David Walker, who was serving in the Arkansas senate at the time. Later, as a member of the Arkansas Supreme Court, Justice Walker would write an opinion that reduced the effectiveness of the act in protecting a woman's property from creditors of her husband. In that case, *Lovette and Wife v. Longmire,* the wife had received slaves as an inheritance from her mother.[69] Longmire had obtained a judgment against her husband prior to the inheritance. He attempted to enforce this judgment against the wife's. The statute allowed a wife to hold property acquired by bequest, devise, gift, or distribution in her own right during marriage or "coverture." Slaves held by a wife prior to marriage could be exempt from liability for debts or contracts of the husband. The court indicated that the statute would allow exemption for debts contracted by a husband after separate property was inherited by the wife. Unfortunately for the Lovettes, the court construed the statute as offering no exemption for debts of the husband dated prior to the passage of the act.

In a second look at a rule stated in a prior case relating to a wife's ability to stop the sale of slaves held as her separate property in order to pay a husband's debts, the court drew a distinction between slaves and other types of property.[70] What was really at issue was the question of whether a contract for the sale of slaves could be specifically enforced by a court or whether damages for breach of contract would be a sufficient remedy. The general rule was that specific performance could be ordered if the thing was of "peculiar value and importance."[71] The court recognized that this concept had been "aptly applied to slave property" in the southern states.[72] Where a wife was seeking to prevent a sale to pay her husband's debt, the nature of this property suggests that a court might intervene to prevent the purchaser from "removing the slave beyond the reach of legal process."[73]

In *Denson & Wife v. Thompson,* the court was called upon to determine the effect of a deed of gift to a married woman when the gift was for her life and then to the "heirs of her body."[74] Under English common law this created an "estate tail" in land but gave an absolute interest in chattels. Here the wife brought suit to recover the slaves from a purchaser who had bought them from her husband. She argued that as real property the slaves were not the husband's to sell. The court found the limitation language applied to give absolute title to her and, thus, the slaves passed as if they were chattels.

A similar question was before the court again in 1861, where the question was whether restricting language leaving a slave to the grantee for life, then to the "heirs of her body," when tied to a specification that the slave would not be subject to the debts of or disposition by the grantee's husband, meant the slave could not be subject to debts of the grantee's second husband.[75] The court, in a detailed opinion, found that the wife had acquired a separate interest in the slave and her increase, and this separate interest was never subject to the control of the second husband or subject to his debts, in seeming contradiction to the 1857 decision in *Denson and Wife v. Thompson*.[76]

In 1858 the court first determined that the failure of a wife to file a schedule in the recorder's office, as prescribed by statute, when she received a slave from her brother by will, meant that the slave did not become her absolute property. The court said the intent of the recording statute was to give a married woman the option to exercise "her ample legal capacity" to avoid encumbrances by the husband's debts.[77] However, in a second case the schedule was filed, as required, regarding four slaves acquired by the wife from her parents. The husband's right in such property was limited to "control and management" and the resultant "production thereof," which was his property. He had no other interest in the slaves that could be subject to his debts.[78]

Soon thereafter the court recognized the wife's right to protect her estate in land as well as slaves.[79] The 1868 constitution included a property rights provision for women.

> The real and personal property of any female in this State, acquired either before or after marriage, whether by gift, grant, inheritance, devise or otherwise, shall, so long as she may choose, be and remain the separate estate and property of such female, and may be devised or bequeathed by her the same as if she were a femme sole. Laws shall be passed providing for the registration of the wife's separate property, and when so registered, and so long as it is not entrusted to the management or control of her husband otherwise than as an agent, it shall not be liable for any of his debts, engagements or obligations.[80]

The 1874 constitution included a clause under "exemptions" that provided this:

> The real and personal property of any femme covert in this State, acquired either before or after marriage, whether by gift, grant, inheritance, devise or otherwise, shall, so long as she may choose, be and remain the separate estate and property and may be devised, bequeathed or conveyed by her the

same as if she were a femme sole; and the same shall not be subject to the debts of her husband.[81]

The question of a husband's control over the separate personal property of the wife continued to be an issue well after the war. In *Jackson v. Hill,* the court reaffirmed the position that personal property such as cattle, hogs, and sheep brought into a marriage by a wife vested absolutely in the husband.[82] The provisions for filing a schedule of the wife's property did not affect the husband's rights.

In *Parrott v. Nimmo,* the evidence showed that the husband and wife were married in Alabama.[83] The husband had no assets; the wife had a considerable estate. In 1858 the husband came to Arkansas and used a portion of his wife's property to purchase land in Arkansas, which he had deeded in his own name. They lived on the land until death, she in 1861 and he in 1865. The husband died with considerable debts and his administrator sold the land to aid in paying these debts. The three children of the couple intervened and claimed that by the laws of Alabama the property owned by their mother remained her separate property and that the deed to the Arkansas land was taken in their father's name against the express wishes of their mother. The court found that under Alabama law the property of the wife remained her separate property at marriage even if it came into possession of the husband. Any sale and reinvestment into other property was also the separate estate of the wife. The question became whether the move to Arkansas served to transfer the money and property into the husband. The court found the money used for the purchase was the separate property of the wife and her rights could be then traced to the land purchased with it.

Interestingly, in 1872 the court may have shown a more liberal attitude toward women's separate property. The court recognized that a married woman may bring suit, alone, when the matter concerns her separate property.[84]

Inheritance

Intestate succession in America diverged from the English rules early on. The rule of primogeniture was rejected; equality among the children became the norm.[85] The rules of intestacy that evolved were rigid, with a widow or widower favored along with children of the decedent.[86] Bloodline was influential as well.[87]

In 1855 a major case involving the Arkansas court's interpretation of statutory language on descent and distribution was before the supreme court. The case had been heard a year earlier by Justice Christopher C. Scott and Judge Samuel H. Hempstead, sitting as special judge. The attorney for appellant was Elbert English, now chief justice.[88] One attorney for the appellees was H. F. Fairchild, now chancery judge in Pulaski County and future supreme court justice. Both had submitted detailed briefs, which were published with the court's opinion, authored by Judge Hempstead. He referred to it as a "voluminous and really difficult case" involving construction of the inheritance law of the state.[89]

The situation involved a young man who died at age seventeen without a will. He had two half-sisters, the present claimants of his estate. His next closest relatives were his paternal grandfather and descendants of a paternal aunt. The scheme, adopted by the legislature, dealt with the inheritance of both real estate and personal property. However, some sections focused only on real estate and appeared to draw distinctions regarding ancestral estates, that is, real estate that "came by the father or mother." Such property passed to the "kindred, who are of the blood of the ancestor from whom it came."[90] A distinction seemed to be intended between such assets and those acquired by "exertions and industry."[91]

A specific statutory provision recognized "half-bloods" as equal to "whole blood" relatives except in cases of ancestral estate: "descent, devise or gift of some one of his ancestors." Those "not of the blood of such ancestor" would be excluded from inheritance.[92] One could have construed this portion of the statute to exclude only the descendants of the half-blood; and, according to the court, "such is the grammatical and logical construction.[93] However, the court would not give the statute this interpretation, saying:

> It would be unsafe to construe a statute according to mere grammatical rules, or to rely on punctuation, as any material aid in ascertaining the true meaning. Neither bad grammar nor bad English will vitiate a statute any more than a deed.[94]

Thus, half-bloods and their descendants were prohibited from sharing in the inheritance of ancestral estates "where they were not of the blood of such ancestor."[95] They shared equally if they could show they were of the blood of the ancestor from whom the property was acquired or with regard to "newly acquired" estates.

The court then set out seven conclusions relating to the Arkansas provisions, the last of which was the matter referred to above. Applying the conclusions to the facts here, the half-sisters would take no interest in the real estate because it came to the deceased from his father. (The half-sisters were children of the mother prior to her marriage to the father of the deceased.) By the same principle, only paternal kindred could inherit the real estate. The grandfather and the descendants of the aunt would be entitled to the entire real estate.[96]

As to the personal property (which included slaves owned by the deceased's father), the half-bloods would be treated equally to whole-blood relatives. The half-sisters, being the next of kin of the deceased, would share equally in his entire personal estate to the exclusion of all other persons.[97]

An interesting factual twist occurred in that the paternal grandfather, Greenberry Kelly, on February 20, 1847, purported to convey to a nephew, James Kelly, all real and personal property that he had received from his grandson (the deceased). The court was not favorably impressed by the circumstances in which this conveyance occurred, finding James Kelly to be "a shrewd, enterprising, business man, strong-minded, far seeing . . . well-calculated to have influence over a man in the condition of Greenberry Kelly . . . and not to have been over-scrupulous in its exercise for the benefit of himself."[98] On the other hand, the court set out in colorful detail the condition of Greenberry Kelly:

> The donor, at the time of this transaction, had passed the period usually allotted to human existence. He was in the last stages of second childhood, with his physical energies wasted, and his mental powers decayed. A century had passed over his head, and still he lived, as he had been living for at least twenty-five years previous—the recipient of the public bounty—an inmate of the poor-house—where, three months

> afterwards, he ended his long and profitless life. The hands of strangers smoothed his brow in death—the feet of strangers followed his remains to the grave. If he had not outlived his race, he appears to have outlived their affections.
>
> Long before the execution of the deed, his memory was so impaired as to render him unconscious of events, and he appears to have been ignorant of what was going on in the world, as if he had not existed at all. In stirring political times, when taken to the polls, to exercise the right of suffrage, he could not retain the names of candidates for whom he was expected to vote, although repeated to him over and over again, or, as one of the witnesses expressed it, repeated "an hundred times." It is true that the boisterous and riotous scenes of his early manhood shed their light, like a dim taper, on his memory, thus affording perhaps, the strongest evidence of his old age. It is a wise dispensation that those, who are no longer capable of mingling in the active scenes of life, or appreciating its enjoyments, should not also be deprived of the happiness, incident to longevity, of re-perusing the volume of earlier life.
>
> He was, undoubtedly, a very infirm and feeble old man—usually in bed—had been afflicted with general palsy for at least twenty-five years—was partially deaf—had been an intemperate man—would become intoxicated whenever opportunity offered—had been a county charge and under the control of keepers for about thirty years—was never known to have property; transact business, or make contracts—was indifferent to property, and incapable of managing or taking care of it. Surely, such a man must be the prey of the artful and designing, and is a fit subject of guardianship in a court of chancery. Indeed, the mind is shocked at the idea that such a man could understandingly dispose of a large estate, in a foreign jurisdiction.[99]

As a result the court set aside and canceled the conveyance, leaving the property to be distributed to the proper heirs of Greenberry Kelly.

A second factual twist occurred when the legitimacy of the paternal aunt, Mary, was called into question. The court accepted "hearsay" or "reputation" as admissible evidence on questions of "pedigree." Entries in a family Bible, correspondence, recitals in deeds and wills, inscriptions on tombstones, inscriptions on family portraits, and charts of pedigree were all accepted as evidence, as would be declarations of relatives or family members. The exception would be in prosecutions for bigamy or in the civil action for "criminal conversation," where actual marriage would have to be established. In this case the evidence was convincing that Mary was the daughter of Greenberry, although he had separated from her mother. Mary had lived with her mother and a son had lived with Greenberry.

The construction of the statute of descent and distributions, as set out in this case, served as the basis for resolution of at least three other cases in this term of court, presumably, with Chief Justice English participating. Perhaps, his experience as one of the lawyers in *Kelly's Heirs* gave him a sound footing to assist in these decisions. Justice Scott, however, authored the opinions.[100]

Some additional clarification of the inheritance provision came after the war in *Campbell and Wife v. Ware,* a case also dealing with "ancestral estates."[101] Ancestral estates (as opposed to new acquisitions) are those coming by inheritance. In this case the conflict was between the deceased's mother and his grandfather. Ancestral lands coming from the father's side go to the line of the father to the exclusion of the mother's side; if from the mother, the lands go to her side to the exclusion of the father's side. Here the mother was not regarded as a direct heir of the son. Harman H. Brewer died in 1859, survived by his son, Nicholas Brewer Jr., and by his wife, Susan F. Brewer, who later married Campbell. The estate passed from Harman to his son, Nicholas Brewer Jr., subject to the dower interest of Susan. Upon Nicholas Jr.'s death, the lands passed to his grandfather Nicholas Sr. and from him to his surviving grandson, James N. Ware (son of a daughter, Mildred).

In 1872 in *Norwood and Wife v. Holiman*, another complication arose regarding ancestral estates under a revision in the Arkansas statute.[102] The court wished to avoid ruling on the validity of the new statute and so decided the case on procedural grounds. The court did state that the distribution provided for under the statute might benefit the petitioner, Harriet, a daughter-in-law of James

Holiman at the time of his death in November 1868. Her husband, Elijah, one of James's sons, died the next month. They had a daughter, Eugenia Maria, who died in 1870, with her mother as her sole heir. The estate in question came by "line of the father," so it would come to Eugenia Maria from her father and then to her mother, Harriet, unless there were creditors of Eugenia Maria's father who made a claim.

The complications arising from such cases emphasized the desirability of testation. "Freedom of testation" became the standard rule, with an absolute right to disinherit children.[103] This right did not apply to spouses, who could claim a "forced share" even if the will left them out entirely.[104] Surviving spouses were also protected by provisions for dower and by homestead exemptions.

Dower

Under English common law, a widow was entitled to a life interest in one-third of her husband's land.[105] This protection extended to any real estate owned by the husband during the marriage unless the wife consented to a sale or mortgage.[106] This rule was designed to compensate married women for the denial of the right to own property separately and for the loss of property at marriage.[107] Dower was not recognized in personal property under English common law, although if a man died intestate the widow received one-third of the value if there were children and one-half if there were no children.[108]

This was of some concern in the plantation economy. Slaves were a valuable capital asset tied to the land in many ways. In some colonies, slaves were classified as real estate, making them subject to dower. In others, special statutes required all other personal property be exhausted to pay the husband's debts before slaves could be used.[109]

Under common law dower was important to protect the widow but was not strongly favored by legislators because the rights of creditors were defeated.[110] Some states eliminated the right altogether or provided the widow with a choice between dower and an absolute share.[111] The justification for dower was that it was a way of compensating wives for the property that they lost upon marriage. The dower right provided immediate support since women could not own property in their own names.[112] On the other hand, it was a "clog" on land titles upon the sale of land unless the interest of the wife was released. This created difficulties for an active land market.[113] Dower was seen as a means of preserving the social and cultural identity of the woman, tying her to her deceased husband and extending the "normative structure of coverture beyond the end of a marriage."[114]

In Arkansas it was not clear if the widow possessed a dower right in personal property, even if much of the estate came from the wife, until the issue was addressed by the Arkansas Supreme Court in 1842 in *Hill's Adm. v. Mitchell.*[115] Justice Thomas J. Lacy wrote the majority opinion, in which he reviewed the history of dower and the traditional requirements. He called it a "lien upon the estate of the husband from the date of the marriage" and recognized a preference over the rights of creditors "subsequently acquired."[116] The Arkansas legislature had incorporated the common law concept as far as land and had added a similar provision regarding slaves. The legislation also provided for the dower right of the widow to be one-third of the personal estate "in her own right." The majority interpreted the Arkansas statute as providing the widow a dower interest in slaves and in the personal estate that was, like land, not subject to the payment of the husband's debts.[117] As to the character of slaves, the court added:

> While slaves with us, in one sense of the term, are peculiarly personal property, yet in another they have all the sacredness and value, nay even more than real estate.[118]

Justice Ringo dissented with regard to the personal estate, which he did not find to be properly characterized as subject to dower but, rather, as an outright distribution to the widow after the debts and costs of administration were paid.[119] He did not dispute that slaves were to be treated in the same manner as real estate.

While the court in some cases appeared to be treating slaves in much the same way as real estate, in others this was not the case. For example, in *Cook v. Cook,* the husband acquired slaves from his wife upon their marriage.[120] He later conveyed those slaves by deed to his children by a prior marriage and reserved to himself their use and services during his lifetime. Upon his death the widow attempted to have the transfer set aside as fraudulent. The court refused to do so on the grounds that the wife had no existing right, no "vested present interest in the slaves," but only a dower interest in "such property as he may be possessed of at the time of his death."[121] A distinction was drawn between her rights to dower in slaves and in real estate. In fact, the court referred to the husband's acquisition of personal property upon marriage and compared the life estate in dower to all of his lands to what he gained "in a pecuniary point of view."

In another case considering slaves as property, *Menifee's Adm'rs v. Menifee, et al.*, the issue was the extent to which a surviving widow would be entitled to a dower interest in the increase of slaves accruing between the death of her husband and the time of allotment of her dower and in the "hire" of slaves.[122] As an initial matter, the court confirmed that issues of this nature could be determined in chancery court (as opposed to probate court). The court interpreted state statutes to have enlarged the common law concept of dower to now include slaves as personal property as well as realty, and the estate administrators held such property only as trustees until it could be allotted to the surviving widow.[123]

The following year, 1848, in *Gaines as Adm. v. Briggs*, a father had given a slave to his daughter, and the slave became her sole and absolute property.[124] However, when she married, under the prevailing law of the time, the slave (and her offspring) became the property of her husband, subject to the wife's dower right at his death. The husband's administrator had a right to possession of the slaves. In another case involving an estate that included slaves, the court found that a widow was entitled to not only a dower interest in a particular slave, but also an interest in the value of the services of the slaves during the period of administration of her husband's estate.[125] The administrators had a duty to "put the slaves at public or private hire" and were accountable for the ordinary value of the services of the slaves at hire.[126]

Arkansas legislation recognized the right of a wife to dower in the lands of the husband upon his death. This did not extend to mortgaged land as against the mortgagee even if she did not join in the mortgage.[127] Nor was dower available out of personal property transferred in trust to pay debts. The wife's acquiescence of the transfer was not necessary.[128] In *Street v. Saunders,* the widow claimed dower in seven bales of cotton she claimed were the property of her deceased husband.[129] The problem was that her husband had executed a "trust deed" to the growing crop in return for valuable consideration (in the nature of a loan). The widow claimed this was nothing more than a mortgage, but the language of the instrument referred to it as a sale. Saunders did not own the crop at his death but only had possession for the purpose of gathering the crop (technically, "emblements") and, if sold for more than owed to Street, he could retain the excess. (The crop was insufficient to pay the debt.)

Dower was not available with regard to partnership property bought with partnership funds until creditors and partners were satisfied. In *Drewry v. Montgomery,* the widow, Sarah E. Drewry, elected to "take against the will" of her husband and, instead, claimed dower in the real and personal estate.[130] This included property owned by the partnership Howell and Drewry and also a mercantile business, P. B. Wheat and Company. As previously recognized, her dower interest would be a life estate of one-third in real estate and one-third of personal property absolutely. She claimed this dower interest in partnership property free of debts of the partnership. To permit this interpretation would increase the burdens and liabilities of the surviving partners and would "work a manifest injustice" to these partners as well as to creditors of the partnership.

The Reconstruction court dealt with dower in what was a factual question of whether a presumed widow (Delilah) was a lawful wife of a decedent (Elbert Jones).[131] Evidence submitted indicated that Elbert and Delilah had lived together for many years and held themselves out as husband and wife. Delilah claimed they had married in Tennessee in 1831 and, as his widow, she was entitled to dower. The court defined marriage as a "civil contract" and that the parties must be capable of contracting to consent to a marriage:

> A lawful marriage may be defined to be a contract made by parties authorized by law to contract, and solemnized in the manner prescribed by law. To constitute a lawful wife, there must have been a lawful marriage.[132]

The problem for Delilah was that there was evidence that Elbert had been married to an earlier wife, Matilda, from whom he separated in about 1825 but never divorced. The court indicated that Delilah presented no evidence to the contrary (the evidence regarding coming from a brother of Elbert). Since it was within her power to produce such evidence, she had "no higher equities than the relations of the deceased." The court was critical of the arrangement, saying "If, instead of being married, she lived with deceased as his concubine, it was her own fault and she can blame herself alone."[133]

Homestead Exemption

The concept of exempting certain property from the claims of creditors (the "homestead") is generally credited to have originated in Texas prior to statehood. The origin may have been in Spanish law perpetuated by the Mexican government and then adopted by Texas in 1839, specifically in terms of the family home.[134] Texas had gained a reputation as a "refuge for debtors" by the mid 1820s.[135] Debts incurred by Texas colonists before they moved to Texas were difficult to collect and were the subject of discussion in the drafting of a commercial treaty between the United States and Mexico prior to Texas independence.[136]

Concerns over the difficulties that settlers encountered in raising capital, in light of the demands of outside creditors, caused Texas leaders, in particular, Stephen F. Austin, to propose postponement of debt collection by outside creditors.[137] This was accomplished by an 1829 act that included not only a debt moratorium but a property exemption for land and certain productive chattels.[138] The Texas act of 1839 borrowed from this predecessor and incorporated personal-property exemption and statutory provisions already in place in American states.[139] Some states exempted certain types of property; others placed monetary limits on types of property.[140] The Texas act exempted the family home, as well as specified chattels, from claims of *subsequent* creditors but specified that it was not to interfere with contracts already binding between parties.[141] From Texas the idea rapidly spread to the states, either by law or constitutional provisions, most often in the form of protecting the family home. It was expanded to protection of the surviving widow as a "probate homestead" and provided protection from creditors.[142]

Between 1848 and 1852 eighteen states passed homestead exemption laws, including Arkansas.[143] The laws exempted the homestead from certain debts, required consent of the spouse for sale or mortgage, and extended protection to the surviving widow.[144] These laws went beyond restrictions on creditors but "targeted families as the principal beneficiary of state paternalism, giving women new property rights."[145] They were promoted as family protection measures.[146]

The usual provision included a plot of land (160 acres or a town lot in Arkansas) that had to be actually occupied as a home. The "head of household" gained protection during his or her lifetime and, following death, the immediate family (usually the widow and surviving minor children) could continue occupancy even if creditors or other legal heirs held a superior title.[147] Exactly what the terms "head of household" or "families" were to mean was often left to judicial construction.[148]

The Arkansas court had few opportunities to interpret the 1852 statute prior to the Civil War. One of the few was the final, reported case of the Confederate court in 1863, *McKenzie v. Murphy*.[149] In this case, the defendant had lived in Arkansas since 1842, except for brief periods in New Orleans, and had served as a soldier for the United States in the war with Mexico. He had been married for ten years and had three children. Yet his citizenship was questioned by the plaintiff, and he could offer no actual documentation from a court of his naturalization. The Arkansas court interpreted the concept of "citizen" broadly as used in the homestead exemption statute and read the intent of statute to afford no individual benefit to the head of a family "disconnected from the family" but found that the benefit should extend to the family of a "domiciliated foreigner" as well as to family of a "citizen, native born or naturalized."[150]

The postwar court was called upon to interpret the provision of the statute exempting "one town or city lot." The issue was whether it was limited to one "lot" or piece of ground on which the dwelling was located or whether it included a more comprehensive area, which might include appurtenances on adjoining lots as laid out by the city.[151] The court gave the legislation the more expansive interpretation, reading the statute to be remedial and concluding that a narrow or literal reading was not consistent with public policy.

> The splendid mansion and the humblest cabin stand upon the same legal footing—each is the *home* of the citizen, as he has it, and as such the law protects it.[152]

The 1868 constitution elevated the homestead exemption to a constitutional principle. The first interpretation of this provision was in *Greenwood & Son v. Maddox and Toms*.[153] A complication in the case was that Toms was unmarried and held the property in an undivided tenancy in common with his two minor sisters. The land was 320 acres and Toms claimed an exemption on his undivided share. The court interpreted the constitutional provision (which was written more broadly than the original statute) to include an exemption for an unmarried man as "head of a family" as far as the exempt land itself was concerned. However, the court suggested that Toms would have had to seek partition of the land to secure the exemption (assuming the ancestral home would be on the portion he received in the partition). Furthermore, an additional complication arose because the "improvement" on the lands was a semi-portable cotton gin that Toms and Maddox, his partner, had purchased. This was partnership property subject to partnership debts and was not a permanent improvement for "betterment of the property," so it could not be claimed as exempt under the homestead provisions.

A final case involving the homestead exemption was *Norris v. Kidd*, in which a married man and head of a family occupied a house on the premises on which the plaintiff had obtained a judgment.[154] The debtor did not assert the homestead right until the date of sale, upon execution of the judgment. The court indicated that this was too late—the owner was required to select the homestead and file an application prior to the sale. (This method was set out in an 1871 statute.) Mere occupancy was insufficient. Failure to file was a waiver of the homestead right.[155]

Summary and Conclusions

Arkansas followed the lead of other southern states in providing for divorce by the courts and eliminated legislative divorce soon after statehood in 1836. Arkansas also provided for broader grounds by specifying "general indignities" as a basis for divorce. The Arkansas Supreme Court interpreted this provision in 1848 as permitting divorce on grounds other than legal cruelty if the conditions rendered the marital state intolerable. The court had few other opportunities to deal with divorce but did confirm that chancery courts were traditionally authorized to deal with alimony and support and also applied the defense of condonation as a basis to deny a divorce.

One aspect of family relationship was emphasized—the paramount role of the father as the presumptive custodian of children in the patriarchal and hierarchal tradition. Mothers were viewed as subject to "subordination and dependence," as required by the role they were to play, particularly in planter families. The merger of the "being and existence" of the wife with that of the husband was recognized. This had special relevance in considering the separate property of married women.

Under the common law, upon marriage, the husband and wife were considered "one flesh" and the husband legally acquired the right to use the wife's real estate during her life, and her personal property came under the exclusive control of the husband. Creditors could look to the property of the wife to pay the debts of the husband.

This situation continued until the enactment of Married Women's Property Acts, a version of which was enacted in Arkansas during the territorial period; it protected the wife's property from debts of the husband incurred before marriage. After a contentious debate in multiple legislative sessions, the Arkansas General Assembly in 1846 enacted a broader law, which permitted wives to own property in their own names, free of liability for debts of their husbands.

The Arkansas Supreme Court was called upon to interpret this legislation and, initially, took a restrictive approach, which reduced the effectiveness of the law. Just prior to the Civil War the court began to recognize greater rights of the married woman to protect her property, at least her land and slaves. This may have been, in part, as a result of the influence of planters who wished to see property protected from the mismanagement of their daughters' husbands. It was well after the war that Arkansas courts determined that married women enjoyed full property rights.

Related to the issue of property rights of married women was the question of inheritance. Rules of intestacy evolved that favored a widow or widower along with children of the deceased. One distinction in the nature of real property was a focus—that is, the concept of the "ancestral estate." A distinction was made between assets that "came by the father or mother" and those acquired by "exertions" of the decedent. The Arkansas Supreme Court dealt with this question in some detail and took pains to trace real property that would qualify as ancestral to those blood relatives who were entitled to inherit. Again, one conclusion is that an effort continued to protect the land in such circumstances. Interestingly, slaves were included as personal property for this purpose and passed like other personal assets, to the next of kin regardless of the origin. As a result, "freedom of testation" became the norm. However, a surviving spouse could not be completely disinherited and gained additional protection by enactment of dower statutes and homestead exemptions.

Dower, under common law, provided that a widow was entitled to a life estate in one-third of her husband's land and a share of personal property outright. This was designed to compensate wives for the loss of property at marriage. Dower was not favored by creditors because their rights were subservient to the dower interest. And it created some difficulties for markets in land in that titles could be "clogged" unless the interest of the wife was released. Related was the concern in the plantation economy if the slaves were classified as real estate. This position was, however, confirmed by the Arkansas Supreme Court as early as 1842. This was not always the case, and for some purposes slaves were treated as *both* real estate and personal property. The court struggled with this question during the entire period.

The concept of the homestead exemption was adopted in Arkansas, along with other states, in the 1848–1852 period to exempt the homestead from certain debts and to require the consent of the spouse to sell or mortgage the property. This offered additional protection to the surviving spouse. In this case southern paternalism was not extended to include slaves in the class of protected property. The supreme court, when called upon to interpret the exemption, gave it a liberal construction. In 1868 it was elevated to a constitutional principle.

An ultimate conclusion can be reached. The Arkansas Supreme Court, when called upon, took an expansive view of family property and, generally, interpreted the laws to afford the broadest protection to families. While reluctant to afford married women separate property rights, the court did, in line with southern paternalism, recognize the realm of the wife in planting "seeds of domesticity" and were sympathetic to efforts to protect family property to this end. Affording "peace and quiet" to families was a certain goal.

CHAPTER 8

"The Key to Republican Economic Morality"

Cases, Controversies, and Conflicts Relating to Debt and Contracts

In 1851 G. W. Cottingham, a Methodist preacher, became a promoter of a concoction known as "Newsom's Vegetable Tonic." He contracted with various parties (some were church members) for the rights to make and sell the medicine in specific counties. He claimed that the mixture was patented. In truth, the tonic was not patented and the ingredients were in common use among physicians.[1] Cottingham sold the rights for exclusive sale in specific counties to Rev. Fountain Brown. Others were sold to Peter German, who, in turn, sold the rights to Brown, who gave notes for payment. These notes were transferred to Wright, who sued to collect on the notes when they became due, and a jury ruled in his favor.

Among other evidence presented in the case (without objection) were letters from Cottingham to a committee of investigation of the Methodist Church, which had been appointed to investigate charges against Cottingham, as well as letters to some of the church members to whom Cottingham had sold the rights to the tonic. Cottingham denied any intentional wrongdoing but acknowledged that restitution might be necessary and agreed to transfer his property to the church district elder for this purpose. He begged to be permitted to continue to "offer to the starving thousands the bread of life." To suspend him, he said, would be his ruin. The outcome of this church proceeding is not set out in the opinion, and the trial court had instructed the jury to disregard the evidence but to focus on the transactions with Brown. The case was sent back for a new trial on procedural grounds, with regard to one of the notes, because there was no evidence before the jury that could have authorized them to find for appellee, Wright. (The jury decision was affirmed on a second note.) The evidentiary problem was that the contract between Brown and German was likely void (no patent existed) and the evidence before the jury regarding Wright's purchase of the note from German gave no indication of any effort on Wright's part to determine if the notes were valid before taking the assignment.

While no particular evolution of the law was involved, this case illustrates the interplay between contract law and debtor-creditor law. It may have been an entertaining diversion for the court, but it was resolved by applying general principles of law and strict procedural rules. Such was often the case in debt and contract cases in the antebellum court.

The "sea of credit" on which the nineteenth-century economy sailed, in Lawrence Friedman's words, meant that courts were at the forefront in developing laws governing the debtor-creditor relationship.[2] Exiting business practices formed the basis for much of the law used to enforce the "intricate web of contractual rights and obligations" arising from credit dependency.[3] Creditor-debtor disputes and debt collection efforts dominated trial court dockets in the antebellum years. Thomas D. Russell, in a groundbreaking study of local court dockets in South Carolina, confirmed that

> civil litigation dominated antebellum dockets; that debt cases comprised the preponderant majority of civil suits; and that these debt suits normally concluded with plaintiffs' judgments.[4]

Trial courts functioned as an instrument to facilitate the credit economy. And credit was essential in slave-based systems, just as was true in non-slave economies outside the South.[5] Creditors relied on the courts to secure and collect their debts. As Russell states, "One word characterizes most of the work of nineteenth-century trial courts: debt."[6]

Tony A. Freyer suggests that credit dependency generated a degree of "social interdependence" that gave non-slaveholders "a stake in the slaveholder's world." This occurred, the argument goes, because the small or non-propertied classes received assistance as debtors from the slaveholders and mercantile classes. This made them feel "beholden politically as citizens and voters."[7] The "intricate web" of economic association included credit supplied by the storekeepers or the wealthier planters who, in turn, depended on world markets with credit channeled through factors. Property-holding southerners (land and slaves) were themselves debtors dependent on crop sales.[8]

Freyer further suggests that as much as 20 percent of loans were never paid, which enhanced the feeling of interdependency in the economic system.[9] And, the law, on the whole, favored debtors.[10] Two examples illustrate the point: the concept of "preferential creditors" and that of "negotiability." The debtor would transfer assets to a preferred creditor by endorsement of a bill or note; the preferred creditor would take only a small portion of what was owed (an "accommodation") and the debtor would be able to start over yet be obligated to the preferred creditor. Negotiability made such transactions possible through assignment of the bills as notes.[11]

While courts might be called upon to unravel these sometimes complex arrangements, as Russell concludes, actions for debt in trial courts were often summary proceedings involving "confession judgments," whereby the defendant admitted the liability and a judgment was entered without an actual appearance in court. As a judgment-creditor, the plaintiff could then initiate execution at whatever pace seemed appropriate: perhaps, reaching an accommodation with the debtor but establishing priority as against other creditors.[12]

With the considerable volume of civil litigation at the trial court level involving debt, it is not surprising that such cases would also occupy a significant place at the appellate level. When debt cases are included within the "debt and contract" category (and many more were debt collection cases than any other contract dispute), the Arkansas Supreme Court heard more of these cases than any other type. Only procedural cases were of similar numerical significance. And, in cases classified as "banks and banking," many were debt collection cases in which one of the state banking institutions was plaintiff. Furthermore, within the category of "slavery" many of the disputes involved mortgages or conditioned sales where slaves were the collateral. For example, in the 1845–52 time period the Arkansas Supreme Court issued 252 opinions classified as "debt or contract." Only procedural cases, at 202 opinions, came close to this number.

Debt

Many of the debt cases can be called "routine" collection matters, often involving some "glitch" in the collection effort at the lower court level or, perhaps, brought for purposes of delay to permit the debtor additional time to recover financially. A few were of special significance in the development of the law of creditor-debtor relations. One such was the 1852 decision in *Bertrand v. Barkman,* which approved the concept of negotiability in Arkansas.[13] This case followed the United States Supreme Court decision in *Swift v. Tyson.*[14] This case, while establishing a general commercial law, left state legal institutions free to act with regard to local credit markets.[15]

Swift v. Tyson had given a broad interpretation to negotiability of accommodation paper in interstate credit transactions. *Bertrand v. Barkman* achieved the same result for transactions within Arkansas. Barkman, of Arkansas, had formed a partnership in New Orleans to act as "cotton and commission merchants" and executed a note, payable in eight months, to the firm. This note was endorsed and delivered to Townsend Dickinson (former Arkansas Supreme Court justice), who, in turn, endorsed it to Bertrand with the specification that, when collected, $3,720 was to be paid to Mrs. A. J. Clarke, with interest. Apparently, Dickinson had secured a sum of money from Mrs. Clarke's husband prior to his death, perhaps acting as an agent for the firm.

Bertrand sued Barkman on the debt evidenced by the note, and a judgment was entered. However, Barkman sued in chancery court to prevent execution on the judgment and argued that the transfer from Dickinson to Bertrand was not for value and, therefore, was subject to defenses he could assert. The Arkansas court agreed with this position and recognized the general concept of commercial paper as "currency." The court set out the rule and the reason for it:

> So long, therefore, as such paper may be exchanged for money or for property, or may be used to extinguish a debt, or may evidence the surrender of an available security, or of some valuable right upon the sole strength of the transfer of such paper, it does the office of a currency; but when it merely serves as indemnity against future probable loss or an existing liability, or of collateral security for a pre-existing debt, it does not perform that office in the sense of currency representing value, and as such, the medium of the transfer of rights and the extinguishment of obligations, and the facilitator and exporter of trade and commerce.

Since Bertrand had presented no evidence of the basis of the transfer from Dickinson (other than a receipt acknowledging a duty to pay the note, when collected, to Mrs. Clarke and the balance to Dickinson) the court considered it to be "collateral security" and not for value. If Bertrand was not a "*bona fide* holder or possessor for value in the sense of the mercantile rule, he could hold, defend, or recover under the mercantile law, either at law or in equity."[16] This failure "'still sticks to him as the poison shirt of Nesses" and equity cannot act in his favor.

This opinion, authored by Justice Christopher C. Scott, followed two decisions of the prior year in which the court set out, in some detail, the nature of remedies available to creditors. In *Whiting & Slark v. Beebe,* the complex financial dealings of James DeBaun were revealed, along with those of many of the prominent parties with which he dealt.[17] The recitation of facts related to the financial complexities alone occupies 87 pages of the 171-page case report. DeBaun had numerous judgments against him in both state and federal courts. That of the plaintiffs was on a mortgage on certain real estate in Little Rock. Other judgments against DeBaun had resulted in the public sale of much of DeBaun's property, including that mortgaged to the plaintiffs. DeBaun had directed the sheriff as to what portion to sell first, which operated to the prejudice of the lien of the plaintiffs. (The case report is replete with examples of the concept of "preferential creditors." The plaintiffs were not among them.)

Justice David Walker attempted to answer all the questions raised and to set forth guidance regarding creditors' remedies. An Arkansas statute permitted the debtor to select property to be sold to satisfy a debt. The creditor selected the means of procuring satisfaction of the debt. Here, the plaintiffs had secured a mortgage in February 1841 upon which there were prior judgment liens. In May 1843 the plaintiffs purchased the property at public sales held in enforcement actions on the prior liens. (These sales were apparently set aside by the chancery court, and the plaintiffs were now seeking specific performance of their contracts of purchase.)

The plaintiffs, according to the court, were not innocent purchasers and were aware of legal defects in the process leading to the public sale in May 1843. The defendant, Beebe, acquired a presumed title to the same property at a subsequent public sale in November 1843. However, Beebe asserted a claim for the whole amount of the prior judgments, although a portion had been satisfied in an apparent attempt to conceal from the plaintiffs the actual amount of existing prior liens. The court indicated that the sale by which Beebe claimed title would be set aside and that the plaintiffs had the "senior equitable lien" on the property in dispute. (Beebe was given the option of paying off the plaintiffs and retaining title to the property.) DeBaun was apparently aware of these actions and acquiesced in them. The court said he must come to court as an "honest debtor" who endeavored "in good faith" to protect creditors "against the effects of a fraud or injury perpetrated by a portion of them to the injury of himself and others."[18] The end result was that the court felt that lienholders such as plaintiffs here were entitled to know of any credits toward a senior lien when they purchased at a public sale. The senior lienholder could not conceal that fact and attempt to apply the sale proceeds in their entirety to a pre-existing lien where not all was still owed.

Many of the debt cases involved no particular evolution of the law but, rather, like *Whiting & Slark v. Beebe*, required the court to unravel complex financial dealings and then determine priority among multiple creditors. A good example is *Watkins and Trapnall v. Wassell.*[19] Here, Chief Justice George C. Watkins was one of the parties in a case that arose well before he became a member of the court. He did not sit in the case, and it was originally heard by Justices Walker and Scott with a special justice, Isaac Strain, sitting. Upon a motion for reconsideration, the final opinion was written by Justice Walker, without Special Justice Stain's participation.

The case involved a basic principle of debtor-creditor law, that is, that the interest of a judgment creditor is limited to the actual interest of the debtor at the time the lien attaches (i.e., when the judgment is received). This principle was brought in conflict with a basic principle of real estate conveyancing, that is, if one sells and conveys real estate to which he has no title but subsequently acquires title, this goes to the benefit of the grantee (purchaser).

In this case Richard Byrd purchased lots in Little Rock in 1833 at a public sale and assigned and transferred them to his son, William, who was then a minor. William received a deed from the governor in 1835. Richard constructed buildings on the lots, and in 1838 William, still a minor, conveyed part of the property to Richard. In 1843, when William reached adulthood, he confirmed the 1838 deed to his father.

In the meantime a judgment was obtained in federal court against Richard in 1840, and the property was sold under that judgment to Watkins in November 1844. Watkins also purchased some of the property on behalf of judgment creditors in cases arising in state court.

Trapnall obtained judgment against Williams in 1842 and purchased property at a sale in April 1845 under this judgment as well as under a second judgment of the federal government against the State Bank in 1846. (Trapnall conveyed his interest in part of the property to Watkins.)

Wassell contracted to repair the buildings by agreement with the Byrds and with the knowledge and agreement of the State Bank with which the Byrds had entered mortgages in 1843. These repairs continued until mid-1845, when Wassell abandoned the project for lack of materials and filed a lien on the property.

The real question was whether the contract with Wassell would take precedence over the prior judgments against the property under which Trapnall and Watkins had made their purchases. Trapnall was apparently aware of the contract at the time of his purchases; Watkins was not. The basic rule is that the interest of the creditor in the real estate is limited to that of the debtor at the time of the judgment. In this case the interest acquired by Trapnall in 1846 was subject to the existing lien of Wassell.

Underlying many of the debtor-creditor disputes was the question of the extent to which a court, acting in equity, could either modify or restrict enforcement of a judgment obtained at law. This issue came to the fore and was discussed extensively in *Hempstead & Conway v. Watkins* in 1845.[20] There the plaintiffs, who had signed as sureties for a loan to one Donald McDonald, sued to block enforcement of a judgment entered at law. They raised defenses to enforcement of the judgment of a procedural nature that had not been raised at the prior suit and claimed that a lack of good faith toward the sureties in the transactions between the creditor and the debtor should relieve them of any obligation.

The question became whether a court of equity could consider the defenses since they were not raised in the action at law. The court concluded that the sureties were not required to raise their defenses earlier, and, if they had been required, the chancery court would have been "ousted of portions of their ancient and intrinsically original jurisdiction."[21] The ultimate result was that in debt collection cases, equity still had a role and parties (debtors or sureties) could raise equitable defenses in some circumstance even if a judgment had been entered in an action at law.

The debate over the role of equity jurisprudence in commercial law had continued during the antebellum period. The resistance was based on a fear of "judicial aggrandizement" due to perceived imprecision in the principles of equity.[22] However, much of the concern was not with equity but with "the nonscientific practice of it in America."[23] As R. Kent Newmyer points out, Justice Joseph Story's influential work on equity jurisprudence, cited by the Arkansas court in *Hempstead & Conway v. Watkins*, had recognized the role equity could play in assisting American business in commercial matters.[24] The need for equity to untangle the complex business arrangements, as illustrated in the above cases, was clearly advantageous.

> The business community and its lawyers had only to be assured that equity would not undercut title to property or obliterate or diminish contractual sanctity.[25]

Equity, in Story's view, should not detract from the will theory of contract but also should not reward "the sloppy, slothful, irresponsible adventures at the expense of "real business men."[26]

Another area in the legal development of commercial law that was the subject of debate was the balance between the federal government's authority under the commerce clause to regulate commercial matters, such as debt and contract, and that retained and jealously guarded by the states. The United States Supreme Court had, in 1824, in *Gibbons v. Ogden,* permitted Congress to claim supremacy in areas of interstate commerce that encouraged the creation of national markets.[27] States continued to assert control over matters within the confines of a particular state.

On two occasions the Arkansas court dealt with the commerce clause of the United States Constitution, both involving contracts with Indians. In the first, *Clark v. Crosland,* the court interpreted a federal act that made all executory contracts entered into by any Indian "null and void" and of "no binding effect whatsoever."[28] This act, largely focused on the sale of "spiritus liquors," was given a broad interpretation and made applicable to all contracts, not just those involving liquor sales. Since the Indians were under the "parental guardianship" of the government, "being an inferior race, many of them ignorant and easily imposed upon," Congress passed this act for their protection.[29]

A different attitude was exhibited a few short years later when this same act was before the court again. This time the contract had been entered into within the state of Arkansas (unlike in *Crosland*).[30] The court, in an opinion of Justice Henry Rector, talked of the Indians as an "educated and intelligent people," "owners of large estates," and "having a need for credit . . . as any other class of persons."[31] The focus of the case was whether Congress was empowered by the US Constitution to enact laws invalidating contracts entered into within the confines of a sovereign state. The court recognized that the United States Supreme Court had interpreted the commerce clause in *Gibbons v. Ogden* as reserving to the states the power to regulate the "completely internal commerce of a State."[32]

> Certainly, nothing could more seriously trench upon the attributes of State sovereignty, than to concede the power in the general government to invalidate contracts entered into by the citizens within the borders of his own State.[33]

Justice Rector, going beyond this, also indicated that "commerce could not as a matter of government policy be applicable to the ordinary business transactions occurring between individuals."[34] The view expressed by Rector was an echo of the political discourse current in the South regarding limits on the power of the national government and of the more general debate concerning what was meant by "commerce."

In *Newton v. Tibbatts,* the court was confronted with a question that reflected not only the interplay of the law of debt and contract but the cautious approach in interpreting any law that might impair the obligation of contract.[35] At issue in this case was the validity of a statute that had repealed all laws authorizing imprisonment for debt except in cases of fraud. This case drew upon the opinion of Justice John Marshall in *Sturgis v. Crowningsheild.*[36] There, the United States Supreme Court had held that imprisonment was not a part of the contract and that state legislatures had the power to abolish imprisonment for debt without impairing the obligation of contracts.[37]

Contract

Lawrence Friedman pegs the nineteenth century as "the century of the contract." It was, he says, "one of the sovereign notions of the nineteenth century."[38] Morton Horwitz ties the rise of the market economy to the development of the "will theory of contract."[39] It was, he says, the period when courts rejected the equitable conception of contract, the belief that contract was "derived from the inherent justice or fairness of an exchange. In its place, they asserted, for the first time, that the source of the obligation of contracts is the convergence of the wills of the contracting parties."[40] It was the market that established what was "fair."[41] While the will theory became the accepted approach for analysis of contract disputes, equity was not ignored. Some have argued that the shift described by Horwitz was more gradual that his narrative suggests.[42]

Supreme Court Justice (and law professor) Joseph Story believed contract law to be "the essence of judicial regulation and the key to republican economic morality."[43] He felt the obligation of contract to be measured not just by "moral law" but also by "universal law" and by the "laws of society."[44] In his mind, the essence of judicial decision-making was to ensure that the "economic process would be orderly, rational, and fair and equitable as well."[45] While Story accepted the need for enforceability of commercial contracts, his work on equity had continued influence during this period.[46] Equity played a role in the administration of contract law.[47] Not only did contract law flourish, it "swallowed up" other areas of law. For example, land sales and dealings were treated contractually.[48]

And contract became a constitutional concept. States were prohibited from impairing the obligation of a contract. The United States Supreme Court gave a broad interpretation to the concept, perhaps as a "metaphor." As Friedman states, "The state was duty-bound to support a broad, free market: To do so, business had to be able to rely on the stability of arrangements legally made, at least in the short and middle run."[49] In the words of Justice Story, laws impairing the obligation of contracts were objectionable because

> they interfere with and disturb, and destroy, private rights solemnly secured by the plighted path of the parties. . . . And they have been truly described as contrary to the first principles of the social compact and to every principle of sound legislation.[50]

Justice Story concluded that no clause of the US Constitution has given rise to a "more acute and vehement controversy." He suggested that any law that changes the "intention of the parties, resulting from the stipulations in the contract" would impair it.[51] Interpretation of this provision became the "root notion" of the law of contracts—legislatures should not "tinker" with bargains freely made; those should be honored by the courts.[52] This involved a body of contract law based on the idea of a true bargain between the parties with relatively few technical rules. By the time the Arkansas Supreme Court began to deal with contract cases, these rules were well accepted and could be applied with conceptual ease in most cases. The Story belief in the contract clause as a restrain on legislatures sounded loudly in his dissent in *Charles River Bridge v. Warren Bridge* in 1837, and never wavered.[53] It was most strongly accepted in other cases, unlike *Charles River Bridge*, where government action affected private contracts.[54]

One of the strongest illustrations of how the restrain on state actions that impaired contracts was viewed by the Arkansas court is seen in *Jacoway v. Denton.*[55] In a postwar three-to-two decision, written by Justice Gregg, the majority found that a provision of the 1868 Arkansas Constitution relating to slave contracts conflicted with provisions of the 1836 Arkansas Constitution and with the contract clause of the US Constitution. The issue arose over a contract entered in October 1860 for the sale of slaves and a debt arising from that agreement. The 1868 Arkansas Constitution specifically declared all such contracts as null and void.

The court went to great pains to express concern over slavery as an institution and to note that the actions of the federal government during the war were governed by the laws of war. Property could be confiscated and seized and title terminated by the conquering power. Thus, the emancipation proclamation, as a war measure, was valid to free slaves and "make any other disposition of them approved by humanity."[56] Therefore, the freedom of the slaves was not traced to either amendments to the US Constitution or enactments in the Arkansas Constitution but to the "sovereign will of the nation, in the assertion of her rights and privileges during active war."[57] Viewed in this light, the provision of the Arkansas Constitution making contracts for the sale or purchase of slaves null and void was intended to have retrospective effect. But, under the United States Constitution, states could not impair the obligation of contracts. This could include actions by a state in adoption of a constitutional provision having this effect, as well as ordinary legislation.

To same effect was *Haskell v. Sevier*, where the court emphasized the difference in an executory contract and an executed one.[58] In this contract the slaves were sold and possession was transferred. The purchase price had not been paid. As an executed contract, only payment remained. Even if the seller warranted them to be slaves for life, as they were at the time, the subsequent exercise of the government's power changed their status, so it was no breach by the seller. A similar result was found in *Anderson v. Mills*.[59] The court, again, held that a mortgage was enforceable even though the security for the mortgage (slaves) was no longer available.

> It is doubtless a misfortune for persons who bought slaves upon credit, and then lost them by emancipation, to have to pay for them. But is now very well settled that the loss falls upon the purchaser and owner and not upon the seller.[60]

This, the court recognized, was "the very ground-work of our system."[61] Any law "releasing a part of an obligation impairs it."[62] The contract here was entered into at a time when it was valid under state law, and it would violate the contract clauses of the federal constitution to permit the state constitution to declare a valid contract null and void.[63]

Even though the concept of will theory of contract had taken firm hold there was still a role for equity in contract law. This could be seen in four areas: specific performance of certain contracts; restrictions on liquidated damages; warranties and misrepresentation; and applications of the custom of the trade.

As a general rule, specific performance of a contract would not be ordered where an adequate remedy at law was available. That is, if damages could be determined and would provide adequate redress, equity would not intervene to order specific performance. For example, in *Cockrell v. Warner*, the parties had agreed that Cockrell would buy livestock (cattle and hogs) from Warner, and he promised to pay with thirty-eight bales of cotton.[64] Warner claimed that Cockrell had baled more than enough cotton to provide the thirty-eight bales but had shipped it to New Orleans rather than transfer it in payment of the debt. He asked that Cockrell be compelled to perform the agreement. The court pointed out that when sales of commodities are involved, if the contract is not performed, the purchaser may, at market price, purchase other commodities of the same kind, description, and quality and sue for damages. Specific performance is not necessary. By contrast, the court recognized in *Jordan v. Deaton* that specific performance was available in a proper case involving land but that the one seeking performance had to be able to show that he had been ready to perform his part of the agreement.[65]

Specific performance may be decreed even if the contract for sale of land is verbal if partial performance has occurred, particularly possession and payment. The Statute of Frauds, which otherwise requires a writing as evidence of a contract for the sale of land, may be satisfied by the partial performance. The court applied these concepts in *Kellums v. Richardson*, an 1860 case in which the "entrance money" for public land had been repaid and possession had been taken of the land.[66] The possession must be connected with the contract and in consequence of it and with either permission or knowledge of the seller. The Statute of Frauds, requiring a writing, may be overcome when it "would be a fraud upon the purchaser to permit the vendor to avail himself of the benefit of the statute." The exception operates to prevent the statute from becoming an "instrument of fraud" itself.[67]

Specific performance was treated as an appropriate remedy in slave sale cases because damages at law would not be adequate compensation. The "intellectual and moral" qualities of slaves and their "social qualities" (skill, fidelity, and gratitude) and their capacity for labor made relief in equity appropriate.

Another area where equity was applicable was where the parties included a provision for stipulated or liquidated damages in the contract in case of breach, as in *Williams v. Green*.[68] Here, the court emphasized that parties were free to make any contracts they wished, "provided they be not illegal, immoral, or against public policy."[69] Thus, the parties might include provisions for stipulated damages but such contracts were "narrowly watched, because of the facility they may afford of being used as a cover for penalties in disguise."[70] The court suggested that if damages would be difficult to ascertain, the parties should be permitted to stipulate them. Furthermore, the court recognized that no uniform or intelligible rule could be readily applied.

The court was able to make the distinction in *Haldeman v. Jennings & Co.*[71] Here, a contract for the manufacture and delivery of staves included a stipulated damages provision calling for payment of $500 for failure to perform by either party. In evaluating the contract, the court concluded that the obligation was not mutual. One party could be required to pay a larger sum (the $500) for non-performance when the total due under the contract would have been less. This turned the stipulated damages clause into a penalty as to that party but not the other, so it was not enforceable.

A third area where equity still played a role in contracts was with regard to implied warranties, as in *Turner v. Huggins.*[72] The court explained that at common law there was no implied warranty of a "sound article" if a chattel was sold for a "sound price."[73] However, the common law also "requires good faith and fair dealings" between the parties to a contract, and the sale could be avoided for "fraudulent concealment of a defect known to the vendor, and not discoverable on ordinary inspection by the vendee."[74]

The court applied this concept in the sale of a horse that, it was alleged, had defective eyes and, in the summer after the sale, went totally blind. However, there was evidence to support the jury's finding that the seller knew of the defect, so the rule was applied to find for the plaintiff-buyer. The court found an express warranty to be present where a seller, even though not using the word "warrant," made a sufficient affirmance of a fact. The seller in *Buckman v. Haney* had told the plaintiff at the time of a horse swap that one of the horse's eyes was blind but the other eye "was as good as any horse's."[75] This was sufficient to make a contract of warranty.

A more significant misrepresentation, such that it is a material inducement, may be grounds for rescission. However, if the buyer has ready access to information and by diligence should be expected to become informed, misrepresentation is not a basis to rescind. For example, in *Yeates v. Pryor* the buyer, Pryor, alleged two separate grounds for fraud in a land sale.[76] Pryor claimed Yeates had indicated that the lands were above overflow of the Mississippi River and that adjacent "back lands" were subject to location of donation claims. These back lands were apparently subject to overflow in 1828, 1832, and 1836 and only a portion could be considered "good dry bottom land free from ordinary overflow." Pryor made no examination of the land until after the purchase, and only two years later did he complete a full examination of the quality of the back lands. However, Yeates apparently also misrepresented the nature of the interest he held in the lands at the time. He could not, at that time, convey any title to Pryor in these lands, although he later perfected his title. Pryor was entitled to rescind the entire contract.

As indicated in the previous chapter, the question of implied warranty did not arise in slave sale cases; the issue of express warranty did. The basic rule applied was that an express warranty of "soundness" did not cover obvious or apparent defects. If an express warranty was present, the court was reluctant to permit actions for fraud or deceit. In such cases, the seller must know that the representation was false.

Another concept adopted by the Arkansas court in contract cases was "custom in trade." Commercial custom became a means of explaining intent of the contracting parties.[77] The idea was that certain terms would be presumed to be a part of the contract because the parties would be familiar with commercial practices and would be presumed to know of customs of the trade (and any exceptions). In the case of *Walsh v. Frank,* the plaintiff was a merchant in St. Louis; the defendant, a merchant in Arkansas.[78] Goods were ordered and shipped upon a steamboat that sunk in the Mississippi River. The question was whether the plaintiff should have insured the goods. The parties had dealt on twelve prior occasions and no shipments had been insured. The custom was not to insure goods unless specifically ordered by the buyer; but, if this occurred even once, the presumption was that all future orders would be insured. The defendant's belief was contrary. The court found that the course of dealing would have indicated to the Arkansas trader the custom (of no insurance) and that "it [was] incredible that such a thing would have escaped an honest man's attention for a dozen consecutive times."[79]

One area where equity is reluctant to intervene is with regard to mistake. In cases where a court of equity is requested to reform a contract due to mistake, it will do so only if the mistake is mutual. When the parties are honestly mistaken as to the meaning of the other, reformation is possible. But where only one party is mistaken in some fact related to the contract, especially where the mistake could have been discovered by "vigilant exercise of due caution," no reformation is possible. This principle is illustrated by *Wilson v. Strayhorn.*[80] Here the parties entered into an agreement for the sale of lots in Dardanelle that were enclosed by a fence. The defendant claimed that he did not realize that a portion of the enclosed land belonged to the city for alleys and roadways. The plaintiff denied representing that he owned all the land that was enclosed by the fence, only that shown on a map.

> All towns have streets and alleys. The citizen of one state is as much presumed to know this as the citizen of another and that the lots are not always uniform in size throughout a state. . . . If a man of ordinary business tact and prudence would have inquired as to the location of streets, courts and alleys in a strange town, before making a purchase, then Wilson would be bound by the rule. In our opinion, a man of ordinary prudence would feel some interest in knowing something about the streets, courts and alleys contiguous to his property.[81]

Most cases dealing with contracts before the Arkansas Supreme Court were resolved by applying the accepted and relatively simple rules of contract law. While contract law remained a matter of state law and there could be state-by-state variation, the overriding concepts were generally consistent. An example of such a general rule is that both parties must have the legal capacity to enter into agreements. This was sometimes an issue with regard to married women and whether they could enter contracts separate from their husbands, as discussed earlier.

An example of this legal incapacity was addressed in *Rogers v. Phillips and Wife.*[82] There the wife had employed the plaintiff to build a two-story frame building on a lot she and her husband owned together. Her husband was apparently absent for long periods and she acted on his behalf. The plaintiff attempted to enforce a mechanics lien to collect the construction debt. The court found that a contract entered by one without capacity was not enforceable. The wife was a *feme covert* and could not act as a *feme sole.*

> Marriage suspends or merges the legal existence of the woman, and, during converture, she must perform everything under the wing and protection of her husband.[83]

Mental competency is also required. This was addressed in *Thompson v. Gossitt.*[84] It was alleged that the seller of land was, at the time of making the contract, in a "low state of health and consequent mental imbecility." Little proof was offered except one witness who said the seller's memory was "treacherous." The court said that partial loss of memory is one of the infirmities of old age, but "such infirmity does not, in contemplation of law, nor in fact, render the aged man incapable of making contracts, whilst the other facilities remain unimpaired."[85]

A good example of how mental incapacity could release one from performance of a contract is *Beller v. Jones.*[86] Jones had apparently been suffering from "great depression of spirits and distress of mind from unhappy domestic relations."[87] Those who knew him best found him to be "impaired in mind" and "unfit for the management of his affairs."[88] He agreed to convey to Beller all his lands, Negroes, and other effects in exchange for Beller taking the five children of Jones to raise until they were age twenty-one or married, at which time Beller agreed to give each child $500. The court said that the evidence of Jones's state of mind, standing alone, might not be sufficient to excuse his performance but, when coupled with the terms of the agreement itself, mental incapacity was clear.

> It is such a contract as no man in his sense, and with right feelings would have proposed; and it ought not to have been accepted. A court of chancery would never enforce the performance of a contract by which children were to be torn from their home and their only parent, and committed to the care of one who might have no feeling for them and whose interest was to have them refuse to live with him, that he might be free from an onerous part of the agreement.[89]

In *Clinton v. Estes,* the court considered the health, appearance, conduct, habits, and such for some time both before and after the making of the contract to determine mental capacity.[90] The plaintiff had owned slaves in Missouri but apparently was presented a bill of sale to his son, to which the plaintiff had added his mark. The son and others took the slaves to Arkansas, where they ended up in the hands of the defendant. At the time of execution of the bill of sale, the plaintiff was described by witnesses as "laboring under the effect of a recent attack of fits, and his mind was not in a condition to consummate a contract of so much importance."[91] According to the witnesses, he was "silent, listless, stupid and childish in his appearance and conduct."[92] While the case was submitted to the jury primarily focused on a claim of fraud, an issue related to that claim was the mental capacity of the plaintiff.

Another type of incapacity to contract is that a minor, ordinarily, cannot enter into a valid contract. Such contracts are normally only enforceable after the minor reaches the age of majority and ratifies or confirms the contract. The court found an exception in *Woodruff v. Logan,* where the minor voluntarily bound himself, in writing, to Woodruff to learn the art of printing.[93] This apprenticeship commenced when the minor was seventeen, and he abandoned his service before he reached the age of majority (then twenty-one). The court found that a minor who bound himself as an apprentice was acting "manifestly for his benefit" and the agreement was binding. Another basic concept in contract law is that the terms of the agreement must be reasonably definite and certain so that it is capable of performance. This is illustrated by *Lyle v. Jackson County,* in which a contractor agreed to build a county jail and a jailor's house.[94] The plans and specifications for the jail itself were detailed and seemingly clear; those for the jailor's house were not. The court said these specifications were so uncertain and indefinite that the contractor would not have been able to construct a building from those specifications.

With regard to the requirement of consideration in contracts, the court emphasized the "will theory" and left it to the parties to "be the sole judges of the benefits to be derived from their own bargains" and would not evaluate the adequacy or appropriateness of the bargained-for consideration. Oral evidence might be admitted to show no consideration or illegal consideration or to show fraud, but not to vary or contradict the terms of the writing.[95]

Mutual promises are sufficient consideration.[96] For example, when the plaintiff promised to have a boat ready at a particular place to haul freight for the defendant, this was sufficient consideration, but if there was no specific time for performances shown, the contract could not be enforceable. An example of how lack of consideration may be the basis for rescinding a contract is shown in the postwar case of *Steele v. Richardson*.[97] In that case the parties had entered into an agreement on April 1, 1865, for the sale of a tract of land and other property valued at $10,000. The defendant transferred six slaves in exchange for the property. Apparently, the plaintiff was unaware that slavery had been abolished by the 1864 Arkansas Constitution and that the slaves were long since free. It was clear that the plaintiff contracted upon a mistake of fact or law. While normally this would not excuse a contract, equity will sometimes make exceptions, especially where one party benefits and the other receives nothing. That was the situation in this case. Because one party received nothing, it was without consideration, and "consideration is an essential requisite to all contracts."[98]

Another well-settled rule in contract cases was recognized by the Arkansas court—the parol evidence rule. This rule essentially provides that where a contract is reduced to writing, oral (parol) evidence is not admitted to vary or contradict the terms of the written agreement. In *Jordan, Ad. v. Femo*, this concept was reaffirmed in a situation where one party wished to introduce evidence that a writing evidencing a debt was not intended to be for the amount stated.[99] The court would not permit use of the "secret or oral agreement or understanding."[100]

Another settled concept is the Statute of Frauds, which requires a writing as evidence of the contract in specified situations. One such situation is that the traditional Statute of Frauds required promises to answer for the debt of another to be evidenced by a signed writing. The Statute of Frauds was the focus of *Kurtz v. Adams*.[101] There was a promise by Adams to answer for debts incurred by one John M. Young at the business of Kurtz. The promise in this case was oral, therefore the statute applied and the obligation was not recognized absent proof in writing.

Summary and Conclusions

From a review of the cases before the Arkansas Supreme Court in the early years, it is clear that the court spent considerable time on debt and contract disputes. Indeed, there were more cases of this type than any other category. While many were routine, requiring more time for the court to unravel the complexities of the underlying transactions than to apply the law, others served to develop the law of debtor-creditor relations or to solidify established contract law doctrine.

In spite of the court's allegiance to the "will theory of contract" concept, the role of equity in contract law continued to be of importance. This is illustrated by the application of rules related to specific performance, liquidated damages, warranties, custom of the trade, and mistake. General rules of contract law, like those related to legal capacity, terms of the agreement, consideration, parol evidence, and the Statute of Frauds, were clearly adopted and applied by the court.

CHAPTER 9

"A Stronghold of Legal Puritanism"

Cases, Controversies, and Conflicts Involving Criminal Law and Procedure

Lawrence M. Friedman indicates that the Revolutionary leaders viewed abuse of criminal laws by government as oppression and included a "minicode" of criminal procedure in the Bill of Rights as a way to curb government power.[1] There was an element of Enlightenment thinking in early statehood constitutions and legislation in "a revolt against bloodthirsty criminal codes."[2] In some states, criminal juries were to be judge of both law and fact.[3] Likewise, a growing sentiment for codification was an effort to curb the power of judges to define new crimes.[4]

While the primary goal of criminal law prior to the Revolution was to define morality, following the Revolution there evolved the rise of economic crime, a concern for "protection of private property and measures to make the economy grow."[5] Friedman writes,

> Consequently the main emphasis on the law shifted to the encouragement of economic activity, rather than enforcement of the ideal moral code.[6]

Further, he suggests criminal law became used as a sort of "crude, undifferentiated administrative agency" to allow for public prosecution, if necessary, of "regulatory crimes" that were not especially regarded as immoral and were not meant to be rigorously enforced but to serve as "a club over the head of persistent and flagrant violators."[7]

Kermit L. Hall continues this theme and points out that colonial Americans "equated criminal behavior with sin" and believed the purpose of the criminal law was to punish and deter.[8] The republican values and economic forces of the Revolution "placed great value on holding and using private property for individual gain" and criminal law adapted to the change. "Americans of post-revolutionary era sought to reconcile these competing demands of liberty and social stability."[9] He points out that criminal law involved the power of the state to deprive a person of liberty and property and social stability requires that the liberty of some be "checked in the interests of the public."[10]

William E. Nelson agrees with this analysis and indicates that after the Revolution, prosecutions for crimes against property increased while those for offenses "against God and religion" decreased. Nelson refers to Blackstone's classification scheme, which would have been known to Revolutionary-era lawyers. As he describes the scheme,

> it included offenses against God and religion, offenses against government, offenses against public justice, offenses against public trade and health, homicide, offenses against the person, and offenses against habitations and other private property.[11]

Among the "offenses against God and religion" were fornication, Sabbath breaking, adultery, drunkenness, gambling, lewdness, and "social vice and illegitimacy."[12] Nelson indicates that the shift in criminal law was, by 1810, toward a concern for punishment of theft.[13] "The end result was that criminal law became secularized; its purpose came to be seen not as the preservation of morality, but rather as the protection of social order and property."[14]

David H. Flaherty agrees with Nelson and says that new philosophical conceptions of law and morals in the second half of the eighteenth century lent support to the separation of criminal law and the enforcement of morals.[15] He cites Bentham and the utilitarians and calls this their basic contribution to jurisprudential thought.[16] Taking a different view are James W. Ely and David J. Bodenhamer. They indicate that, at least in the South, crimes of morality continued to be prosecuted. They question the interpretation that post-1800 criminal process favored protection of property. They acknowledge that theft and other property crimes occupied a share of criminal prosecutions but emphasize that gaming, liquor-related offenses, and sexual immorality continued to be prosecuted in the South even if the patterns in other states differ.

> These findings suggest modifications of traditional interpretations that emphasize southern laxity in crimes against morality and of recent arguments that post-1800 criminal process ignored such crimes in its attempt to protect the economic order. Perhaps crime as theft replaced crime as sin in the criminal codes and prosecution patterns of other states, but southern courts continued the effort to maintain a common morality.[17]

What is missing in any of these interpretations is that the continued emphasis of the prosecution of crimes of morality in the South, and in Arkansas, in particular, may have been an explicit effort to protect the existing economic order. If slavery was the "essence of morality in human relationships," the elite, through political action, could assert their moral authority.[18] One way to assert this authority would be to insist on a common morality.

Beyond the legislative and judicial efforts directed at the institution of slavery in Arkansas, one of the most reflective "mirrors" of social ideology was the continued focus on public morality, as seen in cases reaching the Arkansas Supreme Court. In each of the decades prior to the Civil War, and especially in the 1850s, cases involving gambling, liquor, Sabbath breaking, and other "immoral" conduct were before the court regularly. Most telling is that a greater number of these cases reached the court than did property crimes such as theft. If nothing else, this pattern suggests the importance placed on the prosecution of such crimes and the emphasis on public morality in the greater society.

Criminal Cases in the Ringo Years, 1836–1844

During the tenure of the first chief justice, Daniel Ringo, the court was primarily focused on jurisdictional and procedural matters. Of 168 written opinions, only 5 dealt with criminal law. Even where the underlying case was related to criminal law, the procedural or jurisdiction questions were at the forefront. For example, *Graham v. State* raised the question of whether an act incorporating the City of Little Rock could, without conflicting with the constitution, grant jurisdiction to the city court in certain criminal matters.[19] John E. Graham had been prosecuted and convicted for playing faro in violation of a city ordinance and state statutes prohibiting gaming. The court found that the indictment was proper but that the fine imposed was not in accordance with the power granted the city court. Moreover, the legislature had transferred jurisdiction in such cases to the Pulaski County Circuit Court as of February 21, 1838. The case was remanded to that court.

However, the case was back before the court the next year and the court revisited the jurisdictional questions.[20] The basic question was whether the Arkansas Supreme Court had been granted appellate jurisdiction in criminal cases in light of references to "exclusive" jurisdiction in the circuit courts. By statute, the legislature had specifically authorized appeal to the Supreme Court in criminal matters.

> What, then, was the object of the legislature in enacting the provisions before us? The evil thought to exist, and which it was the principal design to remedy, by these provisions, it is confidently believed counted in the great uncertainty and contrariety of decision, in the different courts in criminal matters, arising from the fact of their being no superior tribunal authorized by law to reverse their adjudications, and thereby establish a uniform rule of decision in that class of cases throughout the State; and therefore with a view to the accomplishment of this most desirable object, the appellate power of the Supreme Court was extended by the act under consideration, to this class of cases.[21]

The court then commented on what it saw as "great lenity and indulgence" toward those accused of crime, which too often allowed many "wicked and notorious offenders" to escape "richly merited punishment."[22] The court suggested that no rational person could believe there had been any "undue rigor or oppression towards the accused, either on the part of the courts or juries."[23]

The state court did address the question of a federal constitutional right in *State v. Buzzard*, involving the Second Amendment's right to bear arms.[24] This may have been (according to the court, it was) the first case addressing such a question in state or federal courts. The challenge was to a statute making the wearing of a concealed weapon a penal offense. According to Chief Justice Ringo, neither the United States Supreme Court nor a federal court nor any other state court had attempted to define the right secured by the Second Amendment. Chief Justice Ringo and Justice Townsend Dickinson, in separate opinions, upheld the validity of the state statute. Justice Thomas Lacy dissented, arguing for its unconstitutionality.

Even in criminal law cases, the court at this juncture was more concerned with jurisdictional questions and procedure than with the development of criminal law itself. As indicated above, the court expressed its view of criminals and the role of law in dealing with offenders in the dicta of *Graham v. State*. Otherwise, criminal law was of no great note as an appellate matter during this period.

Interestingly, even if few criminal cases reached the supreme court, crime at the local level was a concern. The *Arkansas Gazette*, in an editorial in June 1838, suggested that crime would continue until courts and officials enforced the law.[25] During the 1830–1839 period the paper carried stories related to eighty-nine separate murders; in 1840 there were six; twelve in 1841, eighteen in 1842, three in 1843, and four in 1844. This coverage was included with some reluctance. In December 1838 the editor suggested that publishing accounts of murders only caused more crime.[26]

Not only did the paper carry accounts of homicide, there were sporadic reports of robberies or other thefts. In 1837 mention was made of a warehouse larceny in Little Rock and a store robbery.[27] In the same year there was a daring escape on a skiff of robbers who had invaded a plantation in Mississippi County.[28] Horse thefts were noted in Little Rock as being as the rise in 1842.[29] Counterfeiting and forgery were mentioned from time to time, and the whipping of a counterfeiter by Benton County residents was reported with relish in 1842.[30]

As indicated above, it was during this period that the court was primarily dealing with procedural matters. This, too, was the focus of legislation. In 1838 the *Gazette* reprinted the entire text of an act regulating proceedings in criminal cases.[31] However, the greater focus of the court during this period, and the matter receiving extensive press attention, was litigation involving control of the State Bank and the Real Estate Bank. The banks, created during the first legislative session, immediately became the center of a political struggle between the predominant Democrats and the economically powerful Whigs in the state. The struggle for control of the banks continued throughout the period, and, ultimately, the court became embroiled in the controversy, causing two of the initial members to forfeit re-election.[32]

The Era of "Extreme Fussiness": Thomas Johnson's Years, 1845–1852

As the state entered a second decade, economic progress was evident. Agricultural expansion, especially in the lowlands, was well underway. Unfortunately, the banking fiasco impeded economic development, and, without banks in the state, resort to out-of-state financial institutions was necessary.[33] Transportation infrastructure was poorly developed with the river system providing the only real access to markets.[34] Commercial centers developed along the river systems.[35]

The economic expansion was tied to cotton and slavery. This, in turn, tied Arkansas economically and culturally to the other slaveholding states. Southern rights became the rallying cry of the state's political leaders. However, many of the leaders' constituents were less interested in the national debate over slavery. As Thomas A. DeBlack notes, "most Arkansans were too preoccupied with their own survival in the frontier society to worry too much about the threat to slavery."[36] But for the political elite, the "fanaticism" of northern abolitionists had to be confronted and the southern way of life preserved.

Arkansans, like all white southerners, began to defend their way of life. This entailed the need to reflect high moral standards.

This is eloquently stated by Walter Lee Brown (referring to the South):

> Her sectional consciousness was intensified in the 1830's and 1840's by the virulent attacks of northern abolitionists not only upon slavery but upon southern society in general. Thereafter, no matter how much southern Democrats and Whigs might disagree on national political views, they inevitably mustered to the defense of their way of life. . . . [T]hey evolved a wonderful apologia for nearly every phase of southern life.[37]

The state's second decade saw a dramatic increase in criminal cases on appeal to the highest court. Of the total of 802 written opinions issued by the court during this period (1845–1852), 55 dealt with criminal law and procedure. In many of these cases the court was interpreting procedure for the benefit of lower courts and of litigants and in doing so illustrated the "extreme fussiness" characteristic of early courts.[38] For example, in the only criminal case of the July 1848 term, *Yoes v. State,* the defendant had been charged with assault and battery.[39] He had been convicted by a jury that had been charged to the effect that if the defendant had "called Hughs (the victim) out for the purpose of having difficulty with him," the jury should find the defendant guilty. The supreme court found the instruction to be erroneous in that going to a place with the intention of doing an unlawful act is insufficient for a conviction. Unless the defendant carried his intention into effect, he could not be convicted. The conviction was reversed.

In a case involving technical requirements in an indictment, *State v. Hand,* the court upheld a lower court's decision that an indictment in a criminal case (obtaining money by false pretense) was insufficient because only the first name of the defendant was used in the first part of the indictment.[40] Another criminal case involved one William Gabe, *alias* Santa Anna, who had been charged with possessing a counterfeit bank note.[41] It was determined that the indictment was deficient in not alleging intent. Similarly, a second case involved a charge against Gabe for passing counterfeit coin.[42] Gabe argued that the state failed to prove that the Christian name of the victim was "Eli," as alleged in the indictment. The court, in a hyper-technical application of the rules, found that the state had only shown that the crime was committed against a "Clemens" or "Mr. Clemens," but not specifically "Eli Clemens" as charged. This judgment, too, was reversed.

The court overturned another indictment for counterfeiting because it failed to specify the manner of use of an instrument intended for the purpose of counterfeiting coin. It was not clear whether the instrument was used to forge the coin or to alter or adulterate a coin.[43] The court also noted that the jury was not properly sworn (an improper oath was used). As a sidelight, the defendant had also asked for a new trial on the basis that some members of the jury apparently left the panel and went to a grocery in company with the officer in charge and "drank ardent spirits." One juror swore this was for reasons of health and that they did not discuss the case.[44] This matter was not pursued on appeal.

In another case, a conviction for murder was overturned because the jury was improperly sworn.[45] The oath used referred only to their duty to "speak the truth." The court found that the jury, as judges of both the law and the evidence, should be sworn to decide according to both.[46]

A series of criminal cases, most involving gambling, reflects the court's struggle to guide public prosecution of violations of offenses against public morality. The slightest defect could result in the overturning of a conviction. On August 10, 1844, in *Mayers v. State,* an indictment was issued for keeping a billiard table.[47] Trial was held in August 1845. However, the specific offense had been repealed January 8, 1845. The court found that since the legislature had made no provision for punishment of offenses committed before the repeal, the offense itself could no longer be prosecuted. It was an offense "unknown at the time of conviction." In *Hany v. State* the defendants were charged with betting "divers other large sums of money" (25 cents and 50 cents) at card games ("seven-up" and "three-up").[48] The court found the offenses were charged in an "unnecessarily complicated" manner as to be "extremely difficult of proof" and reversed the conviction, a seemingly technical reading of the law. In another gaming case, *Parrott v. State,* the court found that the state's failure to prove that all the persons named in an indictment for betting at cards actually played at the game at the same time was enough to overturn the conviction.[49] Apparently, no proof was submitted that one of the persons named, Thomas B. Hanley, played the game with the other defendants, so the conviction of this defendant could not stand.[50]

The state was more successful in *Drew v. State*.[51] Here the indictment was challenged for failure to state the names of the persons with whom the defendants had bet. The indictment simply stated that the defendants bet a "large sum of money, to wit, the sum of one dollar," at an unlawful game called faro and other amounts at a "game of chance" or on a "gambling device." The court found that reference to betting on a gambling device described as a "faro bank" or "game of faro" was a sufficient description of the prohibited conduct. The court referred to such devices and games of chance as an "Ishmaelietish class."[52] Also, in *Brown v. State*, the court affirmed a conviction of the defendant for keeping a faro "bank" although the indictment referred to a faro "table."[53] The court felt the charge sufficiently complied with the statute and the evidence supported the conviction.

Two cases involved "Sabbath breaking." In the first of these, *Shover v. State*, the defendant was charged with both keeping a grocery open on Sunday and selling spirits on that day as well.[54] The defendant argued that the act under which these charges were brought was unconstitutional. Chief Justice Thomas Johnson, writing for the court in upholding the law, stated:

> The system of religion is recognized as constituting a part and parcel of the common law, and as such all of the institutions growing out of it, or, in any way, connected with it, in case they shall not be found to interfere with the rights of conscience, are entitled to the most profound respect, and can rightfully claim the protection of the law-making powers of the state.[55]

The court, however, reversed the conviction for lack of evidence that the defendant was in control of the grocery and, thus, had actually kept it open on Sunday.

In a second Sabbath-breaking case, *Brittan v. State*, a conviction was upheld over arguments that there should have been a criminal intent element in the statute.[56] In a related situation, a defendant was charged with disturbing a religious congregation by "profanely swearing." (This congregation was using the courthouse as a meeting place.) Since the profane language was not set out, the lower court quashed the indictment. The state appealed. The supreme court reversed, indicating that it was the disturbance that was the gist of the offense; the "contemptuous and profane" swearing was merely the instrument of disturbance, so the indictment should not have been quashed.[57] In what may have been the most important criminal case of this period, *White Ex Parte*, an unusual concurring opinion by Justice Christopher C. Scott was included.[58] He agreed with the outcome but did not entirely concur in all the views expressed by Chief Justice Johnson in the main opinion. The defendant was indicted as an accessory before the fact to murder. He requested bail, which was denied by the lower court. The issue involved a provision of the Declaration of Rights to the state constitution that provided for bail except in cases of capital offenses "where the proof is evident or the presumption great." The defendant argued that he was entitled to bail as a matter of right because the indictment alone raised no presumption of guilt. He further argued that "ancient authorities," including the King's Bench in England, had the power to set bail for any crime whatsoever and that this same power rested in Arkansas courts. The court indicated that a mere allegation of innocence was insufficient; some particular facts would have to be alleged for the court to go beyond the indictment.

Ex Parte Amour Hunt dealt with the power of the governor to pardon convicts and the conditions that could be imposed on the pardon.[59] In this case, the governor had issued a pardon upon condition that the convict leave the state. The defendant apparently did so but later returned and was detained and sought release by *habeas corpus* writ filed in the supreme court. Justice David Walker delivered the opinion of the court, in which Justice Scott concurred. Walker concluded that the pardon issued was under the inherent, discretionary authority of the governor and not under a special statute. (The statute required the convict's agreement to the condition that he not return to the state or face imprisonment.) In this case, the governor's pardon made no mention of any restriction on the convict's returning to the state. Justice Scott agreed that the result was correct under existing law but wrote a lengthy objection to the court even exercising original jurisdiction in such matters. He believed that the constitution set out a scheme under which the supreme court should not exercise original jurisdiction except in specified situations. The lower courts, he believed, were equipped to handle writs of *habeas corpus* or *quo warranto*. The supreme court, he pointed out, has "two great powers: the one appellate purely, and the other a general power of superintending and control over all inferior jurisdictions."[60] He believed that the reference in the constitution to the supreme court's authority to issue writs was remedial in nature, that is, could be exercised as necessary after application had first been made to a subordinate court: in other words, the reference in the constitution to writ power should be read in conjunction with the grant of appellate jurisdiction only.

Among other questions was whether the trial court acted properly in dismissing a juror who had previously served on the grand jury that had issued the indictment (he had); whether a witness's wife, who was living separate and apart, could testify to contradict her husband (she could, because it did not incriminate the husband); and whether the jury should have stayed together during the time of deliberation. (They should have, but unless some influence or improper exposure occurred, no harm resulted.)

Amusing sidelights were added when one witness was asked if he threatened to kill the defendant after learning he had been released on bail. The witness said that he did not, but if he did, he "was in liquor" and did not recollect. A second witness (one of those who watched a defendant kill the cow) had apparently been arrested subsequently for hog stealing.

During the chief justiceship of Thomas Johnson, an increasing number of criminal cases were before the court. With the exception of a small number of violent crimes (rape, murder, and mayhem), the majority involved crimes against "morality," that is, gambling, liquor, and Sabbath breaking. None could be classified as related to protection of property except the single case involving "marking" hogs, one of horse stealing, and one of larceny of a cow, along with the counterfeiting cases.

What is evident from this review of criminal cases before the court during this period is that the court dealt primarily with procedural questions. The procedural questions often arose in the public morality cases, but the guidance from the court was applicable to the prosecution of all criminal matters in the lower courts. Furthermore, as summarized by Friedman, the fussiness gave the appearance of "meticulous justice," an "exaggerated image of justice." In these cases the court was trying to send a message to the profession and to the outside world. "The message was this: our system is dedicated to fairness; it is absolutely obsessed with the rights of defendants."[61]

Whether this message was meaningful to the greater public is an open question. Almost no press attention was directed to the cases heard by the court. One exception was in 1845 when the court was criticized for delay in the appellate process. At the forefront was a case in which the court had reversed a conviction on technical grounds. The problem was that the defendant had already completed his prison term before the decision was rendered.[62]

The *Arkansas Gazette* did cover murder cases in the state for a time. For example, four murders were covered in the newspaper for 1845.[63] Subsequent stories apparently caused the editors to rethink the policy of reporting violent crime, and in October a short statement indicted that the newspaper did not report on such matters because such reports "demoralize readers."[64]

Little mention was made of property crimes prior to 1850. Horse stealing was mentioned in one story.[65] Two burglaries were also reported.[66] The following year four stories related to burglary or theft.[67] In 1851 the first mention was made of attempts to steal slaves.[68] Similar stories appeared in 1852.[69] A reward was offered in 1853 in Arkansas County for information relating to a robbery and the stealing of Negroes.[70]

Interestingly, the coverage related to crimes of public morality was limited, except liquor-related offenses. The temperance movement continued to attract attention. Elbert English, who would soon be elected to the Arkansas Supreme Court, presented a lecture in Little Rock on temperance.[71] As a result, he was asked to lecture throughout the state.[72]

Given the attacks of northern abolitionists on southern society, one aspect of which was the violent ways of southerners, the press attention to crimes of slaves is not surprising. A part of the apologia that evolved was the continued need for guidance and direction by paternalistic slaveholders. As noted by the number of public morality cases reaching the court, the perceived need for high moral standards was beginning to be reflected in the prosecution of public morality offenses. The next decade would see significant expansion in the number of such cases.

The Watkins and English Years, 1853–1860

The prewar years, 1853–1860, were a time of continued economic expansion in Arkansas. Maturation of the plantation economy in the lowlands, accompanied by subsistence farming elsewhere, made the state an agricultural success story.[73] The growth in the economy was related, in large part, to the expansion of slavery and the domination of cotton production, although corn and livestock were important as well.[74] Carl H. Moneyhon has noted:

> New lands, more slaves, and good prices for cotton produced a steady expansion of wealth for all sorts of people and produced an expanding social order.[75]

The upper classes grew in both numbers and strength economically, socially, and politically. As Moneyhon points out, "shared backgrounds, common life-style, and the existence of opportunities for economic success and upward social mobility provided the basis for a social ideology that made sense in the stratified-democratic society."[76] The social ideology called for the protection of slavery and the defense of the southern way of life.

The systematic defense of slavery was seen as necessary to refute "ceaseless attacks" from outside the South.[77] A typical example of southern reaction was an editorial in the *Arkansas Gazette* in 1855 justifying slavery as morally and legally right.[78] A part of this defense of slavery was an emphasis on the need for maintaining public morality. As indicated earlier, the elite could assert their moral authority through political action by insisting on a common morality. In doing so, and by using the legal system to enforce that standard, they could protect their view of themselves and the social ideology they represented. This is illustrated by the significant focus on crimes involving gambling, Sabbath breaking, immoral conduct, and liquor. Crimes of violence dominated press coverage, but criminal offenses relating to public morality were frequently prosecuted and made up a significant portion of the workload of the Arkansas Supreme Court during this period.[79]

By the time that Chief Justice George C. Watkins assumed his duties in 1853, many of the procedural issues and questions involving the jurisdiction and authority of various courts had been resolved. However, the court continued its close attention to detail and technical reading of procedural requirements. Likewise, fewer bank cases occupied the court's time. As fewer procedural and bank questions reached the court, these were replaced with a greater number of cases dealing with property, particularly slaves. In addition, more criminal matters were appealed. Of 1,023 opinions issued during the 1853–1860 period, 137 were criminal cases. Of those, 61 dealt with questions of public morality; only 7 dealt with property crimes.

Commencing in a series of cases in the January 1853 term, the court was called upon to clarify some of the statutory prohibitions regarding the popular activity of gambling. The statutory scheme prohibited the keeping of certain gaming devices or tables and punished anyone who was "interested" or "concerned" in the prohibited gaming or bet on any of the games.

In *Smith v. State* the issue was whether it was necessary to name those persons with whom the defendant was charged with joining in an unlawful game of cards ("pocre").[80] The scheme made it illegal for the owner or occupant of a house, building, or vessel to permit certain gaming activities to be carried on. The question was whether this applied to the keeping of the games, tables, and devices or the actual playing or betting. If the first, the indictment would not have to name other persons involved; if the latter, then it would have to specify those who were involved. A prior decision, *State v. Mathis*, had gone too far, according to the court, and had given the statute too broad a construction.[81] The conviction was reversed. In *Johnson v. State*, a similar technical reading of the statute also caused reversal of a conviction.[82] The indictment had mentioned joint betting and, as a result, the proof had to show that all named were concerned with the betting.

In the following year the court again encountered gaming in a case involving the game of "rondo" (a game played by rolling billiard balls, in which players bet against each other). The owner received a "commission" for the use of his table. The court found that the statute did not embrace this game and the owner did not engage in an indictable offense (it was more like a raffle or lottery).[83] In yet another case challenging the sufficiency of the indictment, the court reversed a conviction for violation of the statute because the named participants in the indictment did not correspond to those shown by proof at trial to have been the participants.[84]

Two years later the court continued to struggle with the difficulty of correctly indicting defendants in gaming cases. In *Stockden v. State*, the accused was indicted for playing cards on the Sabbath.[85] The question was whether the indictment had to aver that the defendant played cards for amusement or for wager. The court felt that playing cards on the Sabbath was the gist of the offense and "whether the playing be for wager or amusement [was] not material."[86] Similarly, the court in another case upheld an indictment for betting on a gambling device "commonly called a Faro Bank."[87]

In another gaming case the defendant was less successful.[88] The indictment was sufficient in that it referred to betting on a game of cards. It was not necessary, said the court, that it specify the nature of the game as one of "hazard or skill."[89]

The technicalities became too much for the court later in 1859. In *Beneux v. State*, the defendant argued that he was indicted under the name "Bennaux" but his name was "Beneux."[90] He argued that, in French, according to the rules of orthography and pronunciation, the two names were wildly different. The court said this might be true to the "ears and understanding of a Frenchman," but the names would be "*idem sonans*" in English. Furthermore, the court stated:

> The decisions have already gone as far as may be allowed in support of such technicalities, which do but tend to produce delay in the administration of the law, and should rather be modified than extended further.[91]

Some gaming cases could be classified as Sabbath-breaking cases.[92] So too could some cases involving the sale of liquor—a good example was *State v. Parnell* in 1855.[93] There the court emphasized that "the gravamen of the charge is desecration of the Sabbath, an offense against public morals."[94]

Two cases in 1853 involved churches or restrictions on activities on the Sabbath. The first was *Stratton v. State*.[95] Here a conviction for disturbing a religious congregation was reversed because it was shown that the defendant had used "indecent gestures and threatening language" toward the preacher (who was of a different denomination) because of some statement the preacher had made. The interruption caused much "confusion and disturbance" in the congregation. The court found that while it was sufficient to charge the offense in the words of the statute without specifying the exact words or particular gestures used, the indictment was not specific enough in that the "church" where the worship was underway was actually a place in the open air some forty yards from the meeting house. There was no proof that what the defendant said and did amounted to indecent gestures or threatening language. The actual offense was something else entirely. The court seemed to indicate that it might be an offense to cause such a disturbance by objecting to the religious tenets of others in this way, but that was not what was specified in the indictment.

On the other hand, a conviction for breaking the Sabbath was upheld where the evidence indicated that a witness came to the defendant's store on a Sunday and had asked to buy goods and was refused. The witness then helped himself to the goods and left without paying. He paid for the goods later, although they were not actually charged to his account. The court found that a jury could have determined that the defendant considered the transaction to be a sale.[96]

Another unusual case was *State v. Goff.*[97] The defendant was convicted of laboring on the Sabbath by cutting and binding wheat. He argued that he did so as a matter of necessity in order to preserve his property. He said he was poor and did not own a cradle for harvesting wheat; he swapped work with a neighbor to procure the use of a cradle; when his neighbor quit harvesting on Saturday he got the cradle to use. His wheat was apparently quite ripe and ready for harvest. The court did not feel this justified his Sunday work and said:

> The husbandman should look forward to the ripening of his grain as an event which must happen, and should make such timely provisions for the harvest as not to violate the Sabbath. This is a duty enjoined alike upon the poor and the rich.[98]

Convictions for liquor offenses were frequently on appeal. Some of these were prosecuted as Sabbath-breaking cases; others, as statutory violations of various liquor laws. While the number of liquor-related cases indicates the public concern with prosecution of offenses, most of these cases were of little legal significance and were often affirmed by the court with little discussion.[99]

In the July 1857 term the court resolved two criminal cases related to indictments of a couple accused of living together as husband and wife without being married.[100] The convictions were reversed because the state had not been required to prove that the parties were not married. The burden had been placed on the defendants to prove that they were husband and wife. The court felt that the state should establish at least *prima facie* evidence that the couple was not married. A similar case was before the court in 1860.[101] A conviction was reversed because the indictment did not specify if it was the first or second offense.

An unusual criminal case was *State v. Mary Hazle.*[102] Here the defendant was accused of two separate counts: appearing in public, partly naked, with the intent of "making a public exhibition of her nudity" and "making an obscene exhibition of her person." The court found the first count insufficient because it did not include the words "against the peace and dignity of the State" and the second sufficient because that part of the statute referred only to "obscene exhibition" (one "offensive to chastity and delicacy, impure, foul, filthy, offensive, disgusting"). Nothing more was necessary since the magic words "against the peace and dignity of the State" appeared in the indictment.[103]

In *Crouse v. State* an indictment for adultery and fornication was found to be defective since there was no statute making this an indictable offense.[104] Language in the indictment alleging that the defendant "unlawfully and wickedly did bed to, and live with . . . a certain man" was insufficient because the charge did not allege that the parties lived together as husband and wife without being married.[105]

During this period, the court dealt with an increasing number of cases involving violent crime ranging from maiming to rape and murder. A number of those cases involved slaves as defendants.

In *Guest v. State,* the court found an indictment for "maiming" to be legally sufficient even though the indictment did not specifically set out the crime as being of the particular grade declared.[106] Three other cases of a technical nature involved indictments for murder or assault with intent to murder.[107] In the first of these the argument was proposed that the indictment was insufficient because the victim was not identified by name but only as a "Wyandott Indian." The suggestion was that the court could not take judicial notice that the words "Wyandott Indian" meant a human being. The court rejected this argument. In the second murder case, the question was raised as to whether a potential juror who was opposed to capital punishment should have been excluded from the jury. While this was seen as error by the judge, it would not have prejudiced the defendant. Other errors by the trial court resulted in a reversal. The assault case was also reversed due to the exclusion of certain testimony by the trial court.

The court was more sympathetic regarding a jury verdict in a prosecution for "maiming" where the jury found the defendant not guilty of the felony offense yet convicted him of a misdemeanor apparently because they believed the fight was by "mutual agreement." The jury's verdict was not clearly expressed but was sufficient to uphold the conviction.[108]

In *Keefe v. State* the court apparently regarded the offense more seriously than had the jury.[109] The defendant had drawn his pistol, cocked it, and pointed it toward the victim, stating, "If you do not pay me my money, I will have your life." This was over a boarding bill. He was found guilty of assault, assessed one hour's imprisonment and a fine of fifty dollars. In affirming the conviction the court said:

> It can hardly be true that the sense of justice of any reasonable man was shocked by the verdict. The only matter of surprise is, that the jury did not inflict a greater punishment than they did, in order to impress it upon the mind of the appellant that in a country governed by a constitution and laws, he should resort, in the future, to the legal mode of enforcing demands and not to the means employed by the barbarian or the robber.[110]

In the January 1860 term the court considered whether when a wife voluntarily committed a crime, the mere presence of the husband could excuse her.[111] The evidence showed that the wife had helped hold the victim while her husband stabbed him eight or ten times. (They had been drinking together.) A statute excused women from criminal responsibility if "acting under the threats, commands and coercion of their husbands."[112] That statute did not apply to excuse the wife in this case.

Criminal cases of interest in the next term included an assault where a "boy" was "whipped unmercifully" for being in the defendant's watermelon patch.[113] And one was a murder case.[114] The murder case involved the critical issue of whether evidence should have been allowed relating to the conduct and motives of the deceased before the killing. His death was the result of a dispute (originally over a debt and "offensive remarks"), in which both parties were armed and had made threats and engaged in "hostile conduct." The deceased had the reputation "of a desperado." He had apparently killed several men and was considered dangerous.

Here the defendant shot first, and there was no direct evidence of any threats having been communicated to the defendant (the usual requirement for the admission of such evidence). The witness could verify what they had seen as part of the *res geste* to prove the conduct of both parties immediately before the killing.[115]

The case receiving the most debate (and a difference of opinion on the court) was a theft case involving a horse, *Golden v. State.*[116] A mistake in the indictment (related to the defendant's first name) did not mean the case could not proceed since the defendant pled not guilty under the original name. He was then estopped from complaining.

In the first case in which a female had been sentenced to the penitentiary, a husband and wife were charged with stealing three pieces of calico and seventeen "hawks" of cotton.[117] The case was reversed because the indictment failed to identify the property with a degree of legal certainty, and, in a rare finding, the court indicated there was an "utter failure of proof" at the trial. Another theft case involved the stealing of bacon.

While many of the procedural questions were resolved in the court's first two decades, constitutional questions remained. And some basic criminal procedural issues continued to arise in the context of the various types of cases. In the area of protection of individual rights during criminal prosecutions, the court addressed specific constitutional rights: the protection against self-incrimination and the necessity that confessions be voluntary.

The court addressed basic evidentiary questions in a murder case involving multiple defendants. At issue was the extent to which the statements of one defendant could be given in evidence against another. The case involved defendants named Doghead Glory, George Potato, Cassalowa, Young Bird, and Moses Glory, charged with the murder of David Scentie. Statements made by Cassalowa to one Adair (who was also a victim of an attack with knives) were admitted into evidence. The deceased was left alone while the attack on Adair occurred by the group of defendants, but that fight was followed immediately by the death of Scentie. All defendants were observed fleeing into the woods, although no one saw the actual attack. The court felt the jury could properly weigh the evidence and there was no error.[118]

In *State v. Quarles* the defendant was indicted for betting on a game of chance ("pocre").[119] At trial another person who had been charged with the same offense was called as a witness after the state entered a motion to *nolle prosequi* (which the court granted). He refused to testify on the basis of the Fifth Amendment. The court refused to compel his testimony. The jury acquitted the defendant and the state appealed. The basis for the appeal was a state statute that allowed a co-defendant to testify but prohibited his testimony from being used against him for this same offense. The court reviewed the basis for the constitutional protection against self-incrimination, saying:

> And it is founded upon the general sense of enlightened men, that compulsory self-accusation of crime is not only at war with the true charities of religion, but has been proven to be impolitic by the truths of history and the experience of common life.[120]

In this situation, since the witness could invoke the privilege if asked about any matters other than the matter before the court and since the statute protected the witness with regard to the testimony at hand, no violation of the constitutional protection was involved. The lower court should have compelled the witness to answer.

Jury misconduct was at issue in a murder case, *State v. Stanton*.[121] A member of the jury apparently left the jury room during deliberations for some time. Another juror signed an affidavit to this effect and claimed the absent juror was gone for about two hours and could not be found by the officer in charge of the jury. The defendant attempted to use this to overturn the jury verdict, suggesting the juror might have been exposed to "injurious influences" while absent. The juror in question responded with an affidavit in which he claimed that he had suffered from a violent headache from noise in the jury room and had gone into the nearby hallway "for relief" and had laid down on a table there for about an hour. He denied seeing anyone during this time. The court refused to overturn the guilty verdict on this basis.

In *Coker v. State* a killing had occurred in the presence of a justice of peace following a trial in which $2.50 was in dispute.[122]

Following the hearing, the parties argued over the testimony of the victim; and following the scuffle, Coker used a Bowie knife to stab the victim. The primary legal question grew out of the trial of the defendant in circuit court. Witnesses submitted affidavits stating they had seen about one-half of the jurors separated from the others during the time they were to deliberate their verdict. The "settled practice" was for all members to remain together once the case was submitted for deliberation unless the court gave leave for the jurors to separate. An appropriate explanation for what the witnesses had observed was found to exist and nothing improper was seen in the action of the jury:

> It is a very common practice for juries, during the day time, to retire to the woods which are adjacent to most of our court-houses, for the purposes of making up their verdicts, whilst the officer in charge stations himself at a respectful distance from them, so as not to intrude upon their deliberations himself, but to guard them from the approach of others. And where the jurors are confined to a room during the night, which is usually the case, they are not unfrequently permitted, by the officer, to retire to the woods in the morning. It is more than probably that the jury, in this case, after having been left in a room during the night, were allowed, by the officer, to retire to the woods on the morning of the 9th of January for a sufficient reason; and, perhaps if the affiants had ascertained and stated all the facts, in their affidavits, the cause of some of the jurors being out of sight would have been accounted for.[123]

Jury conduct was also in question in *Collier v. State,* another murder case.[124] The jury was seen on the porch in front of the hotel rooms engaged in singing. With them at the time were two prominent members of the bar, Pleasant Jordan and Lafayette Gregg. Jordan was, at the time, assisting in the prosecution of the case. He and Gregg had adjoining rooms and upon hearing the jury singing on the porch had joined in. Jordan said he did so because it did not seem that "they carried the bass well," and he told them he could "give it the proper air" and had done so five or six times. Gregg had joined in for three or so songs. No witness heard the case discussed, and while the court found this to be misconduct and that the officer in charge of the jury should be subject to punishment, there was no evidence of any improper influence on the jury.[125]

In *State v. King*, the court took the opportunity to emphasize that, in criminal cases, the accused is entitled to the benefits of all reasonable doubt.[126] And jurors, in no case, should "return a verdict against the accused where they really have a reasonable and well founded doubt of his guilt."[127]

The court adopted the general rule that no confession could be used in evidence unless "freely and voluntarily" made. Confessions made under influence of threats or promises were inadmissible in evidence. Subsequent confessions were rejected on the same basis.[128] In this case, the confession of the defendant was obtained after a "committee of three" from a crowd of 150 to 200 people told the defendant the crowd was satisfied he had committed a murder. He was assured of some protection from those who "might be incensed at him or should desire to injure him on account of this confession."[129] Later, while still in jail, he admitted he had shot the deceased (for fifteen dollars). The question was whether this later confession could be used in evidence. The court had no trouble in determining that the statements to the "committee" could not be used (and the state did not attempt to introduce them) but struggled with the matter of the subsequent confession. In the end the court found that it too should be excluded as being the result of a promise of protection. The earlier influence was presumed to continue to the time of the second confession unless shown to have been removed.[130] The court concluded:

> Confessions are rejected or received in evidence with caution, not from tenderness which the law has for the life and liberty of an alleged criminal . . . but because it distrusts the truth of confessions extorted by fear, or induced by the hope of avoiding an accusation, or escaping an apprehended punishment. . . . [T]here is no safety for the greater portion of society, that is the observers of the law, without preserving with integrity of legal rules that protect against perjury and wickedness, as well as against the weakness of those who are wrongfully suspected or accused of criminal acts.[131]

What is obvious by this summary review of the 137 criminal cases addressed by the court during this period is not only the increased number of cases involving crimes of violence but the continued focus on crimes against morality. Not only were these crimes prosecuted, many were appealed. Economic and property crimes were still a minor part of the court's overall workload. The court, during this period, still spent considerable time on technical procedural questions, on evidentiary issues, and in protecting the rights of the accused.

Much of the public attention in this period was on the public debate surrounding slavery and national events. Camden lawyer John W. Brown expressed concern in 1856 that unless some "providential change" took place, "our Union cannot stand five years longer."[132] His prediction proved correct. By 1860 the secession crisis dominated the news, and the election of 1860 brought a political crisis to the state. Whether Arkansas should follow the lead of South Carolina was the question. The danger posed by secession was unclear; the effect on the economy was a great concern and the chances of southern success if war followed appeared questionable. "Things still more gloomy," reported John W. Brown in late November 1860.[133] In May 1861 Arkansas was out of the Union and at war.[134]

During the Civil War and Reconstruction, 1861–1874

The Civil War caused considerable disruption in the Arkansas Supreme Court's functions. Not only would the court's workload be reduced, but the types of cases would change as well. And, eventually, as the war continued, the court would cease appellate functions altogether. This is a reflection of the fact that local courts were, for the most part, closed during much of the period and disputes were often settled in extra-legal ways.[135] Little appellate review was brought to the supreme court. It did continue its functions relating to "writs" and special questions. For example, in the fall of 1864 the court (at least members English and Pike) was called upon to decide a question related to a quorum requirement of the Confederate state legislature.[136]

A second state supreme court was established by the constitution of 1864 in those areas of the state under federal control.[137] This court, elected in March 1864, began to function only in late 1865 after local courts were reestablished in the state. The appellate caseload grew steadily as government began to function at the local level.[138] The appellate workload increased significantly when a completely new court was elected in 1866 as Democrats asserted control of the civil government in the elections of that year.

The types of cases before court are reflective of the period. Just prior to the Civil War, the court dealt with an array of matters —many involving procedural questions, as would be expected in a court barely twenty years old. A number of "slave" cases occupied the court's attention as well. As war commenced, immediate political questions were before the court arising out of the adoption of a secession constitution in 1861 and the legislation of the Confederate state government under that constitution. In the aftermath of the conflict, when courts were reestablished, a set of new questions arose directly from developments associated with the war itself. These included important questions on the legal effect of secession, limitations on court actions, the effect of emancipation, seizure of property by military authorities, and the legal status of ex-slaves. A limited number of criminal cases reached the court at any point.

Of the 114 cases reported in the January 1861 term only 7 dealt with criminal matters. Two involved the sale of liquor.[139] One involved gaming.[140] One of these cases involved statutory interpretation, where the court found that a criminal statute making it an offense to sell "ardent spirits" to a slave "without permission of the master, mistress, overseer, or person having charge of said negro or mulatto slave" required that the charge plainly state not only that the sale was made but that the permission of all the designated persons was *not* obtained.[141] In another, the defendant was granted a new trial because he was so intoxicated during his initial trial as to be unable to understand the proceeding.[142] The remaining cases involved a robbery, a shooting, and the question of assault and battery versus murder.[143]

No criminal cases were heard in the May 1861 term, but five

were before the court in the December term. One of these was a gambling case.[144] Another was assault and battery.[145] Two were related to road overseers who had been indicted for allowing a road to be obstructed.[146] The last case arose as a criminal matter, but the legal issue before the court was who was to pay jury costs.[147] The only criminal case heard in the duration of the war was the December 1862 case of *State v. Mary*, in which an indictment for arson of a house was found to be defective.[148]

As 1866 drew to a close it was clear that the workload of the Arkansas Supreme Court was returning to prewar levels. The types of cases presented soon reflected the reestablishment of a court system within the state and the return to routine cases. The reestablishment of local courts resulted in increasing resort to the courts to resolve pending disputes. Several courts were faced with backlogs of cases numbering several hundred. Many of these would eventually reach the supreme court.[149] In the June 1867 term twenty-six cases were reported by the court, only one of these involving matters arising directly out of the conflict itself.[150] Otherwise, the court's caseload dealt with the usual procedural questions, property and contract matters, and a limited number of criminal law questions.

Of the eight criminal cases, four involved procedural defects in the indictments or in the selection of juries.[151] A third case was reversed because the trial court would not permit a child witness to testify.[152] Also at issue was whether one who cohabitated with the defendant (but not married) was disqualified as a witness. (The court said no.) This case involved a black soldier who was accused of murder.

In the December 1868 term only one criminal case was before the court.[153] The defendant, a Union soldier charged with murder, claimed to have been acting under orders of his superior officer when the offense for which he was now being prosecuted occurred. General Order No. 3 of the military commander had provided that acts done in a military capacity were not subject to civil prosecution and the case was dismissed by the circuit court. This decision was affirmed on appeal.

The June 1869 term saw eight criminal cases appealed. Two

of those dealt with the military/civil authority relationship and held that during the 1869 period when civil government was provisional, military authorities had authority to arrest and imprison citizens.[154] The court dealt with a series of technical questions arising in these criminal cases. One case was dismissed for lack of jurisdiction.[155] Another was dismissed because the venue was not proved.[156] Another was reversed because a change of venue should have been granted.[157] All three involved serious felonies: an assault with deadly weapon, an assault with intent to commit rape, and a murder. On the other hand, the court upheld two murder convictions. In one, the judge had made a "loose remark" to the jury telling them they were "both the judges of the law and the facts."[158] In the second, the trial court had permitted a child witness (under ten) to testify.[159]

No criminal cases were before the court in December 1869, and the court held no term until December 1870. Two cases in the December 1870 term related to the effect of the 1864 constitution after federal authority was reasserted in the state. In one of these, *State v. Nichols,* the legislature of 1867, assembled under the 1864 constitution, had passed a "pardon and amnesty" act that purported to grant a full pardon for all crimes, except rape, committed after May 6, 1861, and before July 4, 1865, for which there was no conviction prior to the passage of the act.[160] Differences on the court were apparent. Justice John McClure argued for the majority that the legislature had the power to pardon *before* conviction; Justice Lafayette Gregg argued that the legislature could never grant pardons, that this was an executive function. The case in issue was a murder indictment for an event that occurred during hostilities.

In addition to this case, the court heard six other criminal cases in this term, four of which also involved murder. Two were reversed because the jury verdict failed to specify the degree of murder.[161] In another, the case was reversed because after the initial trial had commenced, with a jury empaneled, a witness sworn, and opening statements made to the jury, the state moved to *nolle prosequi* due to an error in the indictment. A second trial resulted in a guilty verdict. The defendant appealed and successfully argued that double jeopardy attached under these circumstances. The court, with McClure and Gregg dissenting, agreed.[162] The remaining murder case involved a sanity issue. The defendant claimed incapacity due to his use of intoxicants. This was an issue for the jury to decide and it was not conclusively shown that excusable sanity would flow from the use of intoxicants so the conviction was affirmed.[163]

One non-murder case involved a prosecution for illegal cohabitation (reversed because the indictment did not charge the parties as being of the opposite sex).[164] Another was an assault case where the question was the jurisdiction of circuit courts to hear cases of assault and battery.[165] The constitution had granted jurisdiction in all criminal cases below felonies to justices of the peace. However, this was not exclusive, according to the supreme court, so such matters could also be heard in circuit court.

In the June 1871 term the court decided five criminal cases, two of which were murder cases, reversed, as in previous terms, due to the failure of the verdict to find a degree.[166] However, the court was more amenable to a jury's failure to enumerate a grade in a fraudulent practice case. There they determined that the highest grade charged attached to the verdict unless the jury departed specifically from a general verdict.[167] The two remaining cases involved prosecutions for sale of liquor without a license and the keeping of a "grocery" without a license. Both were affirmed.[168]

In the June 1872 term only three criminal cases were heard. All involved prosecution for gambling. All were affirmed.[169] And, while the court only addressed three criminal cases in the December 1872 term, these were for more serious crimes and involved more important legal principles. In *State v. Steck* the issue of double jeopardy was addressed.[170] In this case, the initial trial had not progressed beyond jury selection. A sick witness caused delay and the matter was rescheduled. When not all of the jurors showed up, a new jury panel was selected and the trial proceeded. This was not double jeopardy. The prosecution was for malfeasance in office.

The court had spoken more thoroughly on the issue of double jeopardy in 1870 in *Lee v. State*.[171] There, in a trial for murder, the jury had been impaneled, witnesses sworn, and opening statements given by the attorneys. The prosecutor noticed a variance in the dates of the alleged offense between the indictment and the original affidavit. The court dismissed the indictment and referred the matter to a grand jury, which then presented a new indictment of the defendant for the offense. A second trial proceeded and the jury found the defendant guilty of murder.

In reviewing the state of the law under the US Constitution and those of the states, the court found uncertainty as to when jeopardy attaches. Some states had found it necessary for a verdict to be rendered; others found jeopardy once a jury was sworn. The Arkansas Constitution permitted a retrial of a defendant if the first jury was divided in opinion. The court found that while the constitutional provision appeared to specify the situations in which double jeopardy might apply, it was not intended to deprive a defendant of a common law right. The concept of double jeopardy was drawn from the common law and was intended to protect the citizens from the "encroachments of tyranny," so the constitutional provision must be read narrowly, to permit a retrial only in the stated situations—where the jury was divided or where the trial could not proceed due to illness of a juror. In all other cases, jeopardy would attach once the trial commenced.

Justices Gregg and McClure dissented. In their view, the 1868 constitutional provision was specific in referring to "after having been once acquitted by a jury" as the time when jeopardy attaches. They believed that this specified the time when jeopardy attaches—once a verdict was rendered. They acknowledged that their "strong inclination not to allow one, perhaps guilty of a heinous crime, to go free, upon a mere error of the inferior court" might have influenced their construction of the provision, yet they did not see that the rights of an accused were infringed by this interpretation.[172]

A different constitutional question arose in *State v. Carroll.*[173] Here a state statute prohibiting the carrying of concealed weapons was upheld against a constitutional challenge that it violated the US Constitution's Second Amendment right to bear arms. The court found that this right did not prohibit the legislature from enacting a police regulation for the good of society.

In the most serious case, a wife was being prosecuted for murder and argued that her husband's presence during the shooting suggested she was acting under "threats, commands or coercion." The court indicated that this could not be presumed but could arise only if all facts and circumstances so indicated.[174]

The June 1873 term found five criminal cases decided on appeal; the December term, another seven. Four of those were matters related to bonds and their validity.[175] Two cases related to public officials charged with wrongdoing in office.[176] One case related to gambling and another regarded the keeping of a grocery for retail of ardent spirits without a license.[177] In an unusual dispute over ownership of cotton, the defendant prevented two bales from being shipped and a "violent confrontation" resulted. While his conduct was "quite reprehensible and merited punishment," the court determined that it did not constitute robbery.[178]

The final three cases were of a more serious nature. All were for murder. In *State v. Kee* the defendant wounded the deceased with a knife.[179] Contrary to medical advice, the deceased was moved to a residence some distance away from the store where the incident occurred and may not have had the wound properly attended. It became infected with maggots, and he died some time later. The defendant argued that he was not the "mediate" cause of death and could not be convicted of murder (second degree). The court reviewed the existing law in some detail and held that the wound need only be *causa causati* and need not have been the next proximate cause. The case was reversed, however, because the trial court refused to permit the defendant to present evidence of his good character to rebut the presumption of malice on his part. An interesting side note in the appeal was the objection to the jury having during deliberation adjourned to a saloon at which the sheriff paid for drinks for the group. Two black members of the jury were separated to "take refreshments" in a different room of the hotel. The court observed that the jury conduct was "very reprehensible" but did not reverse on this basis.

The last of the three murder cases of importance in 1873 was *State v. Wallace.*[180] Here the court reviewed issues of admissibility of evidence. The court reviewed the grounds under which a judgment of conviction could be reversed on appeal (finding none here) and pointed out that the criminal code had been largely copied from Kentucky and referred to Kentucky court decisions in construing the law.

During the Reconstruction period the increased violence and criminal activity throughout the state was evident in press reports. Murders and attempted murders increased significantly, as evidenced by stories in the *Arkansas Gazette*. There were 142 reports in the 1866–1869 period. There were countless reports of robberies and thefts throughout the state, and destructive fires, many assumed to be arson, were frequently reported.

In the early 1870s criminal activity of all types continued to be reported. Each issue of the *Gazette* carried stories of robberies, burglary, and theft. The *Gazette* mentioned in March of 1870 that these were becoming a serious problem in Little Rock.[181] In 1873 mention was made of horse and cattle theft as being a more common occurrence.[182] In 1872, there were increased references to cotton theft. Not all crimes were violent. Gambling was noted from time to time.[183] A bill in the legislature in 1871 forbid open and notorious adultery and fornication.[184] Apparently, this was not regarded as terribly serious, at least not in Fayetteville. A couple convicted of adultery were lodged in the same jail cell.[185]

A telling feature relating to criminal activity during the period was the annual report of the inspection of the penitentiary. In 1870 this report indicated that 95 inmates were incarcerated.[186] In 1871 the number was 220 (80 whites, 130 blacks, and 6 Indians).[187] The number of inmates in 1872 was 277 (117 whites, 143 blacks, 17 Indians, and 1 woman).[188]

Interestingly, of the thirty-nine criminal cases addressed by the court during this period fully one-third were appeals of convictions for murder. Other serious felonies, such as assault, were also before the court. Continuing also was the prewar attention to gambling, liquor sales, and cohabitation cases, but the number of such cases was far lower than in prewar years. The remainder of the cases involved misconduct in office and a single accusation of robbery growing out of a dispute over ownership of cotton and one case involving fraudulent practice. Perhaps, this is reflective of the violence prevalent in postwar Arkansas and the absence of a fully functioning economy. The courts would, naturally, be more involved in "law and order" issues than in "protecting morals."

Summary and Conclusions

Lawrence M. Friedman suggests that in the first two-thirds of the nineteenth century criminal justice became more and more focused on crimes against property, that is, burglary and theft. He asserts,

> Property crimes were the most frequently punished crimes—or, at least, the most frequently punished *serious* crimes, disregarding the countless minor crimes of liquor violations, drunkenness, disturbing the peace, vagrancy, and minor assault—the ordinary harvest of petty crime.[189]

These crimes, along with those regulating the economy, took on greater importance as "a natural reflex of the increase in the density of economic life, the rise of big business, the explosion of city growth, mass production, the flowering of industry and commerce."[190] Friedman explains that all criminal law is, in a sense, economic: "its rules are attempts to fix prices or ration behavior."[191] Criminal law is also "moral law" in that it describes some behavior as wrong, either inherently so or because of its consequences.[192] Thus, "crimes against morality" or crimes against the "moral sense of the community," laws such as those against adultery and fornication, gambling, and liquor, remained on the books but were not as rigorously enforced.[193]

William E. Nelson reaches a similar conclusion using Blackstone's classification of offenses. He says that the "offenses against God and religion," which included fornication and adultery, were, in Massachusetts at least, the most frequently prosecuted crimes in the pre-Revolutionary period. After the Revolution, prosecution for these offenses decreased and those for property crimes increased.[194]

James W. Ely Jr. and David Bodenhamer suggest that in the South these conclusions are questionable. They point out that crimes against morality continued to be prosecuted. They question the conclusion that post-1800 criminal process favored protection of the economic order except to the extent slavery was given preferred status.[195] They recognize that slaves were elevated to a superior position in the law of property and that criminal law was used to foster the maintenance of the social order in the slaveholding areas.

The explanation in these regional differences may be found in the underlying attitude toward the legal system. According to Edward L. Ayers, formal written law never attained the same weight in the South as in the North.[196] There was a southern preference for personal rather than formal justice, especially when honor was at stake.[197] Ely and Bodenhamer attribute this to the intense individualism found in the South. An ineffective legal system intensified the combativeness of southern society. An effective legal system, then, was "neither expected nor desired."[198]

The criminal law of slavery in the South (the "slave codes") favored the power of the owners and masters and encouraged non-court-imposed punishment and "correction."[199] In Arkansas, for example, masters were encouraged to settle with victims of slave crimes then punish their own slaves without resort to legal proceedings.[200] For major crimes, the ordinary criminal courts did exercise jurisdiction, but it would be the rare case involving a black defendant that would reach the appellate level.

In the early years of its function the Arkansas Supreme Court reflected a certain attention to detail of procedure and pleadings. Friedman has characterized this as "extreme fussiness."[201] But it was not unlike that of many developing courts. He adds,

> The profession believed in strict procedural justice. Hypertrophic appeals gave the *appearance* of meticulous justice. . . . These cases were trying, in their own clumsy way, to send a message to the profession, and to the outside world. The message was this: our system is dedicated to fairness: it is absolutely obsessed with the rights of defendants.[202]

In the early years, the Arkansas Supreme Court had to resolve jurisdictional questions concerning not only its own role but that of the circuit courts. These decisions, in the criminal context, involved both minor crimes (e.g., gambling) and a more serious offense (e.g., accessory to murder). However, in the first eight years (1836–1844) the court was preoccupied with other procedural questions and with cases involving the controversy over the state's banks. Criminal law and procedure was rarely addressed.

In the second period, 1845–1852, the court continued to deal with constitutional questions relating to various courts, some of which arose in a criminal law and procedure context. The total number of appealed cases and the total number of criminal cases increased dramatically during this period. Of 802 written opinions, 55 dealt with criminal law and procedure. Many of these illustrate the "extreme fussiness" of the court in applying of technical rules that were interpreted for the benefit of lower courts and of litigants. With the exception of a few cases involving violent crimes (rape, mayhem, murder, and assault), the vast majority dealt with "moral crimes": gambling, liquor violations, and Sabbath breaking. A limited number dealt with theft or related property crimes.

The prewar years, 1853–1860, saw an increase in total cases to 1,023 with 137 dealing with criminal issues. Crimes of violence (murder, maiming, rape, assault) continued to increase, some of which involved slaves as defendants. In those cases the court dealt with the constitutionality of statutes that punished slaves more severely than whites who committed the same offense; the question of whether a master could testify on behalf of a slave accused of crime; the question of whether a master would have to be informed of an alleged transgression of a slave and be given the option of paying damages and then "chastising his own slave"; and the basic question of whether a slave could even be indicted since they were "mere chattels." Gambling, Sabbath breaking, immoral conduct, and liquor offenses, combined, constituted a greater number of cases than those involving violence. Beyond these cases, the court addressed a few property crimes (e.g., one involving killing animals, one was for stealing bacon, one was for stealing cloth, and a few were counterfeiting cases).

As is obvious, the war years caused a total disruption in legal proceedings. The caseload of the Arkansas Supreme Court declined and only increased again in the aftermath of the conflict, when courts were reestablished. From 1861 to 1867, of a total of 276 cases, only 21 criminal cases were addressed by the court (more correctly, by a series of different courts). More important than the criminal cases were the court's decisions relating to political questions such as the legal effect of secession, the effect of emancipation, the validity of legislation relating to pending court actions at the outbreak of the war, the seizure of property by military authorities, and the rights of ex-slaves.

During the Reconstruction era, 1868–1874, the court saw a significant increase in cases involving serious crimes: assault, assault with intent to commit rape, attempted murder, and murder. A single cohabitation case reached the court, as well as four involving gambling and three liquor sales cases. Although cases related to property rights were often before the court, no property crimes reached the court except for a single case of fraudulent practices and one arising out of a dispute over cotton ownership. The turmoil and unsettled conditions following the war contributed to the increase in violent crime. According to Ayers, during the Reconstruction era, courts, of necessity, spent more time on serious crimes of violence and those against property. This "deflected" attention from the crimes of morality. Although these crimes were still denounced, courts were preoccupied with "more urgent matters."[203]

What does review of the work of the Arkansas Supreme Court during this period reveal? It suggests, at least, that Ely and Bodenhamer's assertion is more accurate in Arkansas than the Friedman-Nelson claim concerning the nature of criminal law and procedure in the early nineteenth century. Prosecution of "moral crime" continued in Arkansas especially in the prewar years. Following the Civil War, violent crime increased dramatically, as evidenced by the number of appeals and by the number of newspaper reports of these crimes.[204] While crimes against property increased as well, these crimes remained a relatively insignificant portion of the total court caseload.

Four explanations may be offered for these patterns. First, evangelical reformers were particularly active in the prewar period in supporting public laws that honored the Sabbath, were against gambling, and were in support of temperance. The greater presence and activity of religious groups as a societal force may have contributed to the continued focus on morality. Southern evangelicalism came to Arkansas, and organized religion expanded rapidly. There were 362 organized churches in the state in 1850; the number grew to 1,008 by 1860.[205] Moral reform was a goal of Arkansas evangelicals, who supported laws to outlaw gambling and to honor the Sabbath. Temperance, too, was a major concern.[206] No doubt, prosecution of violators was encouraged, and this may help account for the continued number of these cases that reached the supreme court.

Second, Arkansas slave laws effectively discouraged prosecution of slaves except for the most serious offenses. By 1860 over one-fourth of the state's population consisted of slaves—and over 80 percent in some counties.[207] If slaves in Arkansas could be assumed to have engaged in the same criminal activity as evidenced in other states—most often, theft—then this crime category would be underrepresented in the number of cases reaching the supreme court.[208] Interestingly, following the war, a significant number of the defendants in serious cases were black.

Third, as a "frontier" with a developing economy, Arkansas would not reflect the same society as the developed Northeast, such as in Massachusetts, where the observations of the Friedman-Nelson pattern were focused. The economy in Arkansas was primarily agricultural with land and slaves as the primary assets. Criminal law would not necessarily be seen as playing a role in protecting the market economy. This was accomplished in the structure of the economic system of slavery itself. In those areas where slavery did not predominate, an even more basic agricultural system operated, one in which resort to legal proceedings was neither necessary nor desired.

Fourth, and perhaps most convincing, the elite in the antebellum period regarded their support of slavery as of the highest moral order. The system they defended was necessary to provide moral discipline and guidance to the slaves. But, to justify this position it was also necessary that morality in the greater society be strictly regulated. Courts served as one vehicle for enforcing this moral code. The antebellum southern aristocracy was concerned with the "orderliness" of society. Legal discipline could be used to provide this order, to an even greater extent than the church.[209] As stated by Bertram Wyatt-Brown,

> So long as the South was functioning on the basis of slavery, so long as its culture remained chiefly rural and ascriptive in orientation, the legal system was obliged to mirror stability.[210]

The criminal justice system could be used to set "ground rules of public behavior" to aid in the community's need for stability.[211]

One reason that the slaveholding elite was concerned about preserving order in their society was in reaction to the criticism of southern society by the northern abolitionists. Those attacks suggested that slavery had so contaminated southern society that law was but a tool for perpetrating the inhumanity of slavery. Southerners feared that these attacks on the law of slavery could destroy a society they had come to believe represented perfection. As defenders of that system, they reacted by emphasizing order. One aspect of that emphasis would be to support the enforcement of law related to morality and to contrast the order and control in southern society to the licentiousness of the North.

Alfred L. Brophy suggests that this perspective affected the manner in which proslavery jurists viewed law. They construed this role narrowly. A "rigidly logical" approach of deciding cases led to a mode of reasoning ("formalism") that applied beyond slavery but to other areas of law as well.[212] This view contributed to the attitude that laws designed to preserve public morality were deserving of application and enforcement but, at the same time, should be scrutinized closely to make sure they were interpreted correctly and applied appropriately. In Arkansas, this attitude contributed to a comforting sense of "legal puritanism" in the minds of the antebellum elite.[213]

CHAPTER 10

"Rights of Belligerents"

Cases, Controversies, and Conflicts during the War Years and in the War's Aftermath, 1861–1867

As the Civil War opened in 1861, the Arkansas Supreme Court, then consisting of three members elected to the court by the legislature under the original 1836 Arkansas Constitution, was confronted with an array of cases typical for the time. The court spent considerable time on procedural matters related to the operation of the legal system, particularly civil matters. Property disputes, contractual matters, inheritance questions, and questions related to land conveyances occupied the majority of the court's caseload. Relatively few criminal matters were brought to the court.[1]

Predictably, the court was also called upon to resolve a number of issues related to slaves, particularly questions involving property rights in slaves and the responsibilities of slave owners.[2] For example, in the case of *Graham v. Roark* the court was called upon to interpret a statute placing responsibility on the slave owner for damage to land caused by the trespass of slaves.[3] The court held the owner responsible even though unaware of the activities causing the damage. In another case involving statutory interpretation, the court found that a criminal statute making it an offense to sell "ardent spirits" to a slave "without permission of the master, mistress, overseer, or person having charge of said negro or mulatto slave" required that the charge plainly state not only that the sale was made but that the permission of all the designated persons was *not* obtained.[4]

Questions involving slave ownership were also before the court during this time. In *Phillips v. Grayson* the question arose as to the effect of a gift of a slave by a deed that restricted the interest to the grantee and the "heirs of her body" and specified that the slave not be subject to the debts or to disposition by the grantee's husband.[5] The question was whether this restriction applied to the second husband of the grantee. The court, in one of its most detailed opinions of the term, found that the wife acquired a separate interest in the slave and her increase and this interest was never subject to the control of the second husband, nor to his debts. Further, in *Curtis v. Daniel* the court applied general principles of property law relating to adverse possession to slaves to resolve an ownership question.[6] "Peaceable, continuous, uninterrupted and adverse possession" of the slaves for more than five years conferred title on the possessor.[7]

Two slave cases in 1861 involved questions of warranties. In *Thompson v. Bertrand*, an agreement for the sale of a slave contained a warranty of soundness of body.[8] The court found that the buyer could rely on the warranty and was not required to examine the slave to try to uncover any defects. Similarly, in *Sessions v. Hartsook* a bill of sale contained a warranty of soundness but included a special provision that the buyers could return any which were unsound and the seller would substitute other slaves.[9] The court held this contractual remedy to be exclusive and would not allow adjustment even if the sellers were not residents, making return of the slave to the seller difficult. The contract was mutually binding on the parties. In the most interesting of the 1861 slave cases, *Daniel v. Guy*, a legal action had been brought by the slaves themselves in a "suit for freedom," alleging that the plaintiffs were white.[10] The court approved the decision of the trial court to permit the jury to examine the feet and to otherwise inspect the plaintiff and her children.

The treatment of the "slave" cases as routine illustrates that the Arkansas Supreme Court harbored no sentiment toward recognition of slaves as anything more than another class of property at this point. This approach was, of course, in line with legal principles affirmed by the United States Supreme Court itself in the Dred Scott decision of five years earlier.[11]

During the December term of 1861, the court reported 61 cases. Since Justice Hulbert Fairchild had served as chancellor in Pulaski County prior to his appointment to the court in July of 1860, a number of the cases heard by the Arkansas Supreme Court in 1861 involved appeals from Justice Fairchild's own decisions. He did not sit in those cases. He was also absent when three cases were heard and was not mentioned as being involved in six others.[12] Justice Fairchild may have been absent during some of those cases because of his torn loyalties during the war. He continued to sit during all of 1862 and early 1863, but after the state government moved from Little Rock to Washington he resigned from the court and left the state.[13]

Fairchild did play an important role during the war years because two of the decisions he authored were critically important to the functioning of the state government prior to federal occupation of the capital. For example, he authored the opinion in the June 1862 term that dealt with the important question of whether the secession constitution had vacated the office of governor. This case, *Danley and Johnson Ex Parte*, was necessary to interpret a provision of the 1861 constitution that indicated that civil and military officials would continue in office until superseded by provisions of the constitution itself or by ordinances passed to carry out the constitution.[14] The constitution specifically called for continuation of some offices for specified periods, for example, supreme court justices. For offices "not otherwise herein provided," an election was to be held in October of 1862 to fill those positions. For some reason, perhaps intentionally, the office of governor was not specifically provided for although many lesser offices were to continue.[15] A question arose as to whether the office of governor was necessary.[16]

In a related case in the December 1862 term, the court was called upon to interpret another provision of the 1861 secession constitution dealing with the continuation in office of state senators. In this case, *State v. Clendenin*, it was indicated that all state senators had been elected in the October 1862 election although it was an error to have done so.[17] While the court gave no guidance as to how the error was to be corrected, it did indicate that the election had been improper. The dispute arose over the election, by the general assembly, of Oliver H. Oates to the office of secretary of state. Oates had been elected as a state senator in 1860. Under the prior constitution, and the language was continued in the 1861 version, no state senator could be elected to any office "within the gift" of the senate during a term to which he was elected. Under this language, it would appear that Oates's selection as secretary of state would have been invalid. However, the court, in a creative effort to accommodate legislative wishes, indicated that since Oates was of that group who should not have been reelected in 1862, his term should have continued for the full four years (until 1864). And, the adoption of the 1861 constitution effectively terminated the term to which he had been originally elected and gave him a "new commission" to hold office for two more years. This was no disqualification to his selection as secretary of state since he had not been *elected* to this new commission.

Another important issue resolved in a case in which Justice Fairchild wrote the opinion, *Burt v. Williams*, was the effect of legislation enacted by the state legislature after secession in which the legislature attempted to continue all court proceedings until after peace was ratified.[18] The act applied to all "suits at law or equity now pending, or hereafter to be commenced in any of the courts of this state." The supreme court found this legislation to be in violation of the constitution of 1861 in that it violated the right to a speedy trial in criminal cases and violated the provision related to the impairment of the obligation of contracts in civil cases. In addition, it was seen by the court as improper exercise of legislative authority since continuances were exclusively judicial acts. The court saw the legislation as effectively closing the courts during the conflict, which would have disregarded the rights of both plaintiffs in civil cases and defendants in criminal matters.

Burt v. Williams was one of eleven cases decided in the June 1863 term prior to the removal of state government from Little Rock.[19] The other cases during that term involved the usual conflicts in business and property matters. One involved the title to slaves under a will. Another was the continuing saga in *Daniel v. Roper* of a claim for freedom of a woman as white and her efforts to recover property taken by her enslaver.[20] No cases were reported during the remainder of 1863 or in all of 1864, but the court apparently sat in Washington during this period.[21]

Justice Fairchild was, in 1864, replaced on the court by Albert Pike.[22] Albert Pike was a natural replacement for Justice Fairchild. He, like Fairchild, was a man of significant ability. He was regarded before the war as a major literary figure, especially for his poetry, and had been a military commander during the Pea Ridge battle. Interesting, Pike was asked after the war to write a short autobiography. He included his opinions concerning various leading members of the bench and bar and praised a number of his contemporaries but never mentioned his own service on the court.[23]

The Confederate court continued to hold sessions until January of 1865, and a number of cases were pending in 1864 when a new constitution was adopted under federal military auspices. These cases were initially held to be "null and void" by the new "federal" court.[24] But a subsequent order indicates that these cases were re-docketed and considered and the opinions were adopted and recorded as the opinions of the Arkansas Supreme Court.[25] This notation was by yet another court, one elected in 1866 after the cessation of hostilities. As a result, some seven cases were reported as in the December 1866 term but were actually cases decided by the Confederate court in late 1864 and early 1865. The seven cases heard by this court, composed of Justices Elbert English, Freeman Compton, and Pike, involved property questions, except for one that was a suit on a debt and another related to an evidentiary question. Four of these opinions were prepared by Albert Pike and reflect his literary skills and depth of analysis.[26]

After Little Rock was occupied by federal troops, an election was conducted in March of 1864 under the supervision of the military authorities for the adoption of a new constitution. This constitutional election, in which only federal soldiers and those who had taken an oath of allegiance to the Union could vote, was adopted, and the secession action of March 4, 1861, declared null and void as never "binding and obligatory upon the people."[27] The constitution was almost identical to the original 1836 constitution but included an article prohibiting slavery and declared as invalid all debts contracted by the Confederate state government.[28] This constitution called for the election of supreme court members by "qualified" voters. At this election, T. D. Yonley, C. A. Harper, and Elisha Baxter were elected to the Arkansas Supreme Court.[29] This court named Judge Yonley as chief justice. Baxter apparently never actually served on the court and resigned to accept election to the US Senate but never served in that capacity either.[30] This court held no sessions in 1864 or in the June term of 1865. In December of 1865, it did decide one case, *Rison v. Farr*.[31] This involved the construction of new constitutional provisions related to voter qualifications. This decision became one of the most critical relating to the conflict. The dispute arose over the question of whether an oath could be required of voters that they had not aided or abetted the Rebel cause after April 1864—the date the new "federal" government took office. The court found this voter qualification requirement to be in conflict with the 1864 constitution, which specified the only requirements for voting to be race (white), sex (male), age (over twenty-one), and residency for a specified period (six months).[32]

The limited service of Justices Yonley and Harper is reflected in the dearth of reports of cases in which they rendered decisions. Judge Yonley had been a Unionist when the war commenced. He apparently left Little Rock for a period and returned only after Little Rock fell to the federals. He was a member of the 1864 constitutional convention and served on the court until the summer of 1866. He was then appointed chancellor of Pulaski County.[33] Judge Harper had lived in Van Buren, perhaps for only two years, and he, too, was a Union man who had been born in New Hampshire. After he resigned office in 1866, he returned to the North.[34]

Justices Yonley and Harper decided only five cases in the June 1866 term, then resigned.[35] Baxter had resigned earlier.[36] In their stead, three new members were elected in August 1866.[37] Those included Chief Justice David Walker, who had served on the court prior to the war, Justice Freeman Compton, who was serving on the court at the time the war commenced and continued to serve under the secession constitution of 1861, and Justice John J. Clendennin, who had previously served as a circuit court judge of the Fifth

Circuit Court until vacation of that office by the adoption of the 1864 constitution. In the war's aftermath, a number of significant issues were before the court, growing out of the conflict itself. These involved questions related to the effect of the 1864 constitution on actions of the Confederate state government and the validity of its actions, the statutes of limitations for court actions, the effect of the Emancipation Proclamation on transactions prior to the end of the conflict, property disputes arising from military seizures during the war, and the status or rights of ex-slaves. These issues, among a number of ordinary questions, were all addressed in the December 1866 term by the newly elected court.

One of the critical questions arising after the end of the war was the question of the validity of actions taken by the Confederate state government under the constitution of 1861. The central issue was whether a state government actually existed from the time of the attempted secession until the adoption of the constitution of 1864. The constitutional convention of 1864 had expressly repudiated and declared "null and void" all legislative and judicial acts under the constitution of 1861.[38] The court addressed this question in one of the more detailed opinions, *Hawkins v. Filkins*, in the December 1866 term.[39] This case was widely discussed and was regarded as highly significant at the time.[40] The court premised the entire decision on the conclusion that the state's attempt to withdraw from the compact made with the United States was void. The real question for the court was whether the state government was destroyed by the act of attempted secession and whether this made any acts of the civil government invalid. On this question the court concluded that even if the Civil War suspended the laws of the United States, the people of the state owed obedience to the laws and government under which they lived, either because Arkansas was "conquered territory" or because the existing government was entirely revolutionized and, as such, the people had a right to establish a *de facto* government for themselves. The court's conclusion was that the conflict was a "civil war" in which "rights of belligerents" apply but not rules of conquest over foreign territory.[41] The court referred to President Abraham Lincoln's inaugural address to support the proposition that the union was unbroken in the view of the constitution and the laws. Lincoln had recognized the existence of state governments even after they passed ordinances of secession, until suspended by the new constitution of 1864. As a result, acts of the government during that period were valid and binding; and the language in the 1864 constitution that attempted to declare void the acts of the secession government—which was both a preamble and an independent declaration—was effective only as to the extent the 1861 constitution was in conflict with the Constitution of the United States. The 1864 convention could not, according to the court, declare the 1861 government void *ab initio*. To do so would have allowed its act of secession to destroy all state government.

One question that was not before the court in *Hawkins v. Filkins* was the power of the convention of 1864 to repeal acts of the legislature. This issue was addressed in *Osborn, Ex Parte*.[42] This was another December 1866 case that focused on an ordinance of the Convention of 1864 that had declared that all laws in force as of March 4, 1861 (before secession), were still in force and, by implication, had repealed any subsequent acts of the Confederate state legislature in conflict with those laws. Such laws were not expressly repealed, although the 1864 constitutional language attempted to declare them "null and void."[43] The court found the declaration to be effective but repeated that all laws of the secession legislature not in conflict with the code of laws of March 4, 1861, were valid under the logic outlined in *Hawkins v. Filkins*.

The Confederate Supreme Court of Arkansas had ruled in *Burt v. Williams,* in the June 1863 term, that a legislative attempt to continue court actions until after the conflict was invalid.[44] Following the war, the court was faced with the question of what effect was to be given a later act of the Confederate state legislature that suspended the statute of limitations as to all debts. This act was effective as of December 1, 1862, and remained in effect until the adoption of the 1864 constitution (March 16, 1864), which repealed all such statutes. For this reason, the court in *Bennett v. Worthington* permitted this space of time to be disregarded in calculating the time period within which court actions would be required to be brought.[45] In fact, the courts in the county where the dispute arose

(Chicot) were closed from October 1861 to October 1865, so there was no court in which the plaintiff could assert a right. The court would not find an exception to the statute of limitations on this basis but did so because of the legislative act of 1862.

The court also addressed the validity of an act of the "federal" legislature that prohibited the collection of any debts by any person who had aided or abetted the rebellion, violated an oath of allegiance, was in the Confederate army, was a Rebel in a federal prison, or had abandoned his or her home for the protection of the Confederacy.[46] In *Vernon v. Henson*, the court found this act to be in clear conflict with the US Constitution's prohibition against laws impairing the obligation of contracts.[47]

Another issue arising from events occurring during the war had to be resolved following the Emancipation Proclamation of September 1, 1862.[48] The issue was first raised in *Dorris v. Grace.*[49] This case, in the December 1866 term, involved a transaction that had occurred in August of 1863 between parties residing in a part of Jefferson County that was not yet under federal control. The transaction involved a written instrument evidencing a debt of $3,000, which was apparently issued as consideration for the sale of a slave. The defense argued that the obligation was not enforceable because the slave sold by Grace was not property subject to sale as a result of the proclamation of President Lincoln. The precise question was the effect of the Emancipation Proclamation on the rights of owners of slaves who resided with their owners beyond the lines of federal occupation. The court, in an opinion by Justice Walker, found that those rights were not affected by the proclamation since it was issued as a war measure under the president's authority as commander-in-chief in time of civil war. If the president had acted in any other capacity, the proclamation would have been unconstitutional. Thus, the obligation was considered valid since, at that time in that location, the slave was still considered property.

The court was faced in *Steele v. Richardson* with a related question.[50] Was a contract for the exchange of land for slaves valid when executed on April 14, 1865, after the constitution of 1864 had abolished slavery in Arkansas?[51] The landowner had been unaware of the action of the 1864 constitution and apparently relied on the representations of the other party concerning the slaves. The court found that the slaves were not property subject to sale and held that the transaction should be set aside, especially in light of the complainant's ignorance and the defendant's misrepresentation.

A series of cases were before the court related to the effect of seizure of property by military authorities (both Federal and Confederate) during the conflict. The first of these, *McCaudle v. Stafford*, did not directly involve seizure by military authorities but was an interesting situation in which the defendant had sold bales of cotton belonging to an estate because they was being destroyed by cattle, had been left unattended, and would have been a total loss had they not been taken care of.[52] There were no courts in operation to authorize the handling of estate property. He admitted selling the cotton bales but proposed as his defense the fact that the proceeds had been soon thereafter stolen from him by federal soldiers and that their officer refused a request for search for the money. At an initial trial this defense had prevailed due to instructions given to the jury, but the supreme court found the decision of the jury exonerating the defendant to be unsupported and remanded the case for a new trial.

In a case directly involving the seizure of property by a soldier in the Confederate army, *Hardage v. Coffman*, the defendant was sued for taking horses belonging to the plaintiff.[53] His defense was that he took the property as a soldier in the Confederate States service upon the direct order and direction of a superior officer. This case, too, was remanded to permit the defendant to introduce evidence concerning the officer in question who had "assumed command as colonel and was recognized as such."

In *Taylor v. Jenkins*, the court stated that soldiers could justify the taking of property under orders of their commanding officer in certain circumstances but could be liable if this was done without sufficient cause.[54] In the particular case in issue, mules were taken from their owner by a federal scout and placed in charge of the US quartermaster. A particular mule from the group was later discovered in possession of Rebel scouts, identified, and returned to the original owner. An intervening purchaser (who lost the mule to the Rebels) claimed the mule. The original owner, Taylor, was located near Pine Bluff and the taking had occurred after federal occupation of that area in 1863. The court found that Taylor was not, based on any evidence presented, an "enemy" of the federal government and that the capture of his property could not be justified as the seizure of "enemy's property." He was entitled to the protection of the law as a citizen of territory reclaimed by the United States forces. As such, his title to the mule was not divested by the capture or affected by the subsequent second capture by a Confederate scout from the intervening purchaser.

In the last of the seizure cases, *Trammell v. Bassett*, it was contended by Confederate soldiers that they seized property of the plaintiff under order of their commanding officer.[55] The court held that they should be allowed to present, as justification, their duty to obey a superior officer.

Before the war the court dealt with a number of issues involving property rights in slaves. After the war questions began to arise as to the status and rights of the former slaves themselves. The constitution of 1864 failed to provide any positive statement regarding civil rights of ex-slaves.[56] It was supposed that abolition of slavery had given some rights, such as the right to sue and be sued and to acquire and dispose of property. Former Justice C. A. Harper, in statements in a report to the US Congress on the formation and operation of the state government under the constitution of 1864, indicated that ex-slaves were not discriminated against except as to suffrage and bearing arms.[57] To have done so would have been a major political mistake.[58] Yet the question remained as to what rights such persons now had.

The Arkansas Supreme Court was faced with a narrow question related to this broad issue in *Milan v. State*.[59] Here, Milan—a man of color—was convicted of assault with intent to kill. In his motion for a new trial, Milan asserted that jurors who had been called had indicated that it would require less evidence to convict the accused than it would a white man on trial for the same offense. The court indicated that constitutional provisions requiring impartial juries would call for rejection of such jurors but that the issue of their actual bias was a matter for the trial judge to decide and would not be reviewed by the appellate court.

The 1865 decision of *Rison v. Farr* had paved the way for ex-confederates to reassert political power in Arkansas.[60] It ruled unconstitutional the law requiring an oath that a prospective voter had not taken up arms or supported the Confederacy since April 1864 as a prerequisite to voting.[61] In the election of August 1866 the ex-Confederates had gained control of the legislature as "Conservatives." The supreme court operating in December of 1866 was one selected by this new legislature.[62]

As 1866 drew to a close it was clear that the workload of the Arkansas Supreme Court was returning to prewar levels. The types of cases presented soon reflected the reestablishment of a court system within the state and the return to routine cases. The reestablishment of local courts resulted in increasing resort to the courts to resolve pending disputes. Several courts soon were faced with backlogs of cases numbering several hundred. Many of these would eventually reach the supreme court.[63] In the June 1867 term, twenty-six cases were reported by the court and only one of these involved matters arising directly out of the conflict itself.[64] That was the case of *Denton v. Brownlee, Homer & Co.*, relating to the suspension of the statutes of limitation against debts of those in military service while still in service.[65] Otherwise, the court's caseload dealt with the usual procedural questions, property and contract matters, and a limited number of criminal law questions.

However, this return to normalcy was not to last, nor would this court remain in office much longer. On March 2, 1867, Thaddeus Stevens of Pennsylvania introduced the first Reconstruction Act, which declared that no legal state government existed anywhere in the South. Arkansas, along with Mississippi, was placed in a military district, and the military commander was empowered to substitute trials before a military commission for civil courts. New constitutions were demanded of the southern states. The members of the Arkansas Supreme Court were removed from office.[66] Congressional Reconstruction had arrived.

CHAPTER 11

"Usurpation and Treachery"

Cases, Controversies, and Conflicts in the Arkansas Supreme Court during Reconstruction, 1868–1874

On Tuesday, February 14, 1871, the Arkansas House of Representatives adopted a resolution to establish a committee of inquiry to ascertain "in what instances and under what circumstances" judges of the Arkansas Supreme Court had or were "corruptly" using their offices "either for personal advantage, or from political bias and partisanship, or to gratify the wishes, or to serve the purposes of the present Executive."[1] This resolution was directed at Chief Justice John McClure and his relationship with the Republican administration of Governor Powell Clayton. Two days later articles of impeachment were submitted against Clayton. Four days later impeachment charges were submitted against McClure.[2] These charges came amidst the turbulent struggle for control of state government and would occupy much of the time of the legislature during the remainder of the 1871 session. McClure's involvement in this struggle is but one aspect of the history of the Arkansas Supreme Court during the Reconstruction period, particularly those years, 1868–1874, when he was a member of the court.

Congressional control of Reconstruction and the acts that followed included Arkansas in the states that were declared to have no legal state government and required a new constitution be adopted. This constitution, submitted to the voters on March 14, 1868, along with a slate of Republican officers, was approved. The constitution provided that the governor would appoint the chief justice and four members would be elected to serve on the court.

As might be expected, this Reconstruction court was often embroiled in the political controversies surrounding the administration of the Republican state government. At the same time, it was obligated to resolve a number of politically sensitive questions that arose in the aftermath of the Civil War, and these, along with more mundane legal issues, occupied much of the court's time during this period.

The political questions faced by the court provide the best illustration of how the court, and its individual members, became increasingly embroiled in state political controversies. By the end of the Reconstruction period the court was, due to the actions of McClure and his close associates on the court, little more than a political tool of one faction of the Republican Party. At the same time the court had to resolve a number of routine matters ranging from questions of procedure to debt collection, property conveyancing, and a few criminal matters. While these cases were of importance to the parties involved and, in some cases, established precedent for future cases, it was the cases involving political issues that were given the most attention by the court; that is, the opinions reflected greater thought and analysis and sometimes generated vigorous dissenting opinions, especially as the major split in the Republican Party developed in the early 1870s.

The cases that involved important political issues can be classified into five major categories. First, the court dealt with a series of cases involving questions related to currency. Contracts entered into during the war often referred to "dollars" or "Confederate money." The legislature had attempted to deal with such questions in the Confederate Money Act of March 5, 1867, but questions continued to arise as to the effect of obligations incurred during the conflict where specific currency was contemplated. A second group of important cases dealt with questions arising out of contracts entered during wartime. Some contracts involved the use of property for war purposes and others were for the sale of slaves. The court wrestled with the issue of enforceability of such contracts for some time before eventually resolving all the questions.

A third group of cases arose out of local political disputes and conflicts between various groups who were vying for control of county government. Questions involving the payment of county obligations, taxes, and the issuance of bonds occupied considerable court time. Those conflicts were of particular consequence because of Republican actions undertaken to finance various government programs and the growing opposition to these programs at the local level. A fourth category focused on the legal effects of secession and the effects of federal action on Arkansas citizens, such as the Civil Rights Act and the Emancipation Proclamation, and the validity of actions of the Confederate state government. The most important category dealt with political controversies and centered on the supreme court's power to issue original writs to state officials, such as *mandamus*, *quo warranto,* and other remedial writs demanding that the officials take specified action. This issue became of critical importance as the court became involved in election disputes, the rights of individuals to hold office, and contests for offices, including the contest between Joseph Brooks and Elisha Baxter for the governorship.

Currency

The first case decided by the new court was a currency case, *Moody v. Hawkins.*[3] It was framed as a usury issue in that at the time the obligations were incurred, repayment was anticipated in "Confederate money" or "Treasury notes of the Confederate States of America." Due to depreciation, the value of the notes was only 20 percent of the nominal value. This, it was alleged, created a contract that was usurious and void. The court, however, found that the fact that Confederate money was greatly depreciated was not sufficient, alone, to establish that a contract for more than the legal rate of interest was intended. A similar result was reached in *Jordan v. Mitchell.*[4]

The most important of the currency cases was *Leach v. Smith and wife.*[5] Here the court considered the validity of the Confederate Money Act of 1867. In that act the legislature had provided that in any suit to recover payment of a bill, promissory note, or contract for the payment of money, if the parties had agreed that repayment was to be in Confederate money, the recovery could be had in gold or silver or United States legal tender and the amount of the recovery would be based on the *value* of the Confederate money "as estimated in the community at the time and place of making of the agreement." Further, if the agreement did not mention the kind of money, the defendant could introduce evidence as to the intent.

In *Leach v. Smith and wife* notes were executed on August 1, 1862, but no mention was made of the specific kind of money anticipated. The court found that it was necessary to determine whether the legislation was proper under the state and federal constitutions "as a pure question of constitutional law."[6] The court found the act to be repugnant to both state and federal constitutions because it impaired the obligation of contracts. The court's interpretation was that since the parties originally agreed to payment in a fluctuating currency, the maker of the note was entitled to repay in that currency even if it had depreciated during the period. The effect was to leave those who held such notes with no real remedy—a result that would have the greatest effect on those former Confederates who might have had money to lend during the rebellion. The court mentioned, but did not decide, the issue of whether contracts payable in Confederate money would be considered legal at all—a matter to be dealt with in future cases. The same issue was addressed in a June 1869 Confederate money case in which the court affirmed its opinion in *Leach v. Smith and wife* holding the 1867 legislation unconstitutional.[7]

The December 1869 term of court saw the court still dealing with difficulties related to Confederate money. In that term the court finally focused on the question of legality of contracts payable in Confederate currency. In *Latham v. Clark,* at issue was a note dated March 1, 1863, payable in "Confederate money."[8] In a long opinion by Chief Justice William Wallace Wilshire, the court addressed the single question of the legality of a contract for payment of Confederate money. The court reviewed the history of the conflict between the states and simply declared that Confederate money would now be treated as having been issued without authority of law since it was issued solely for the purpose of aiding and carrying on the rebellion. As such, the rebellion would have quickly failed if the people had refused to receive and use the currency to carry on business transactions. Its illegality tainted all such contracts between individuals and rendered them void as opposed to the public policy of the nation.

Justice William Harrison dissented and argued that to hold the contracts invalid would require a finding that the illegality would have to be so "immediately connected with the transaction as to be in aid and furtherance of it; or, in other words, the illegality must be inherent and constitute a part of it."[9] The majority view was then used to resolve questions in *Ford v. Ragland* and in two cases involving the same parties, *Glenn v. Case* and *Glenn v. Case,* where the parties were left "in the condition in which they have put themselves and in which the courts find them."[10]

The decision in *Latham v. Clark* made it easy for the court to dispose of cases on this issue in the December 1870 term.[11] One Confederate money case was disposed of under the ruling of *Leach v. Smith and wife*.[12] The court, in June 1871, had occasion to reaffirm its earlier decisions that contracts in which Confederate money were the consideration were null and void.[13] The court in the December 1871 term had the opportunity to once again affirm its view related to Confederate money. In *Cooksey v. McCrery* a note was alleged to have been paid with Confederate money to officers of the Confederate state government. The court refused to recognize the payment as satisfaction of the debt.[14]

Wartime Contracts

The second group of important cases focused on the effect of various contracts incurred during the war years and their enforceability. In the court's first term two cases involved contracts for the sale of slaves, a matter that had been before the prior court on at least two occasions.[15] In the first of these, *Johnson v. Walker*, a suit was brought to rescind a contract for the sale of a farm along with implements, crops, and slaves.[16] The attempt to rescind was apparently in large part due to the fact that the slaves were freed prior to the date of the transaction. However, the court refused to intervene because the parties had equal familiarity with "certain transactions and acts" which affected the situation. The court did not touch the issue of when slaves in Arkansas became free, a matter addressed by the previous court and to be addressed in future cases. In the second case involving the sale of slaves, *Goolidge v. Burnes*, a defense to an obligation was raised alleging that the original sales contract failed for lack of consideration since the slaves had been freed on January 1, 1863, by the decision of President Abraham Lincoln.[17] Again, the court avoided the issue because, in this case, the legal instruments involved did not directly involve the transfer of the slaves to the parties in the dispute.

In the one case during the June 1869 term involving a promissory note for the sale of slaves, a provision of the 1868 constitution making such contracts null and void and unenforceable was held inapplicable to an original judgment on the note entered before the adoption of the new provision.[18] These cases indicate no shift in views of the court and are consistent with the decisions of the first term.

Contracts for the sale of slaves still continued to haunt the court in the December 1869 term, so it finally squarely faced the question of legality of these contracts. The developing split on the court is illustrated by the most important decision related to these contracts, *Jacoway v. Denton*.[19] Justice Lafayette Gregg delivered the opinion of the majority of the court regarding the 1868 constitutional provision prohibiting the enforcement of such contracts—a matter previously addressed but not firmly resolved by the court. Gregg examined the prospective effect of this provision and determined that a contract entered into in 1860 created vested property rights, valid at the time. The national constitutional prohibition against state law that would impair the obligation of a contract was seen as directly contradictory to the state constitutional provision and, as a result, the state provision would fail. Justice John McClure, joined by Justice Thomas Bowen, vigorously dissented and argued that the court had no jurisdiction to declare the state constitution void. Bowen simply argued that it was against public policy to enforce contracts for the sale of slaves.

In the December 1870 term two cases related to contracts for the sale of slaves were disposed of by the authority of *Jacoway v. Denton*.[20] The court had more difficulty with a case involving a sale of a slave on July 10, 1863, and the effect of the Emancipation Proclamation on such sales. According to the earlier decision of *Dorris v. Grace*, the proclamation did not liberate or free slaves outside the lines of federal occupation.[21] In this case it was not clear if the transaction occurred within the territorial lines, although Justice McClure felt the facts were obvious—that federal forces were in place in the county in question on the date of the transaction.[22] Similarly, in *Pillow v. Brown & Childress*, the court relied on *Jacoway v. Denton* to resolve questions related to contracts for slave sales that occurred in 1860 and in 1862.[23] However, a more difficult question related to whether the debtor was entitled to abatement of interest during the war when he was prevented from paying the debt due to the separation of the parties. (One lived within federal lines; the other was a Confederate officer outside the federal lines). The majority found that no abatement was due since there was no evidence that an attempt to pay the debt was ever made. Justice Gregg agreed with the conclusions but not the logic of the majority decision. Justice McClure dissented on a basis similar to his dissent in *Jacoway v. Denton* and argued that since the contract was made in Tennessee, the courts of Arkansas should not be available to enforce it even if the contract could be considered valid under the *Jacoway v. Denton* approach. He would have applied the Arkansas constitutional prohibition.

In still another case involving contracts for the sale of slaves, the court, in June 1873, found that where a seller took a mortgage to secure the payment of the purchase money, the debt still remained even though the slaves were freed by emancipation. The loss fell on the buyer, not the seller.[24] Justice McClure and Justice J. E. Bennett dissented.

A second type of contract that occupied the court's attention involved sales of property to be used to support the Confederate cause. In two such contract cases during the December 1868 term, the court had the occasion to rule on the validity of contracts for sale of guns and horses used in Confederate service. In *Tatum v. Kelly*, a contract dated July 11, 1861, was for the sale of guns to be used to arm men engaged in the rebellion.[25] It was alleged that the plaintiff knew of the intent and purpose of the transaction and, as a result, the contract should be considered illegal. The court found the contract to be "so connected with an illegal transaction as to be inseparable from it."[26] Since the payee "actively promoted the unlawful and treasonable purpose of the defendants," the court would not come to his aid to enforce the collection of the note.[27]

A similar result was attained in *Ruddell v. Landers.*[28] Here it was shown that the contract at issue was for the sale of horses for the "express and well understood purpose" of providing mounts to men engaged in the rebellion. The payee of the note was a captain of a company of cavalry who agreed to endeavor to collect money from his soldiers to pay for the horses. To induce the owner to provide them to the maker, and others, who were not actually engaged to the rebellion, the captain agreed to become responsible for a share of the obligation. The court found the whole transaction to be "contrary to public policy" and "palpably illegal and treasonable from its inception" and held the transaction to be void.

In three cases involving contracts for sale of horses to be used in Confederate service, the court in the June 1869 term affirmed its decision in *Tatum v. Kelly* and held such contracts invalid or unenforceable.[29] In an interesting, related case, *Smith v. Graves,* the court dealt with the question of whether a Confederate soldier could keep a horse taken from behind Federal lines under authority of his commanding officer.[30] The case had been twice tried before local juries and in both cases the defendant/ex-soldier had prevailed. The court remanded the case for another trial but indicated that the jury should be instructed that the taking of the horse under these circumstances did not confer title to defendant.

In the June 1871 term the contract issue was before the court again, but the court simply reaffirmed its earlier decisions involving contracts for the sale of property for use in Confederate service and indicated that it had settled these issues, along with those relating to the sale of slaves.[31]

In the December 1871 term the court had to decide the validity of a contract between a citizen of the State of Minnesota and a citizen of Arkansas that was entered into during the conflict, on

February 7, 1865. Justice Harrison argued that any such contracts were void and invalid as against public policy on the principle that they were contracts made with a "public enemy."[32] Justice McClure dissented and argued that the date on which restrictions on trade were removed should have been recognized as effective once the "loyal citizens" of Little Rock had formed the 1864 government under federal auspices. Since the power and authority of the United States had been reestablished at the date of the making of the note, he would have upheld its validity. The note was apparently granted in the employment of counsel for one imprisoned as a Rebel and McClure was not inclined to be sympathetic to his cause. He chastised the majority "in their desire to aid a man who flaunts his treason in their face as a reason why he should not pay his debts" and considered the plea as one "the contents of which are known to be false, and contradicted by the public history of the times."[33]

Conflicts Involving Local Officials

The third set of cases of political significance grew out of the efforts of Governor Clayton to improve the economic situation in the state, to provide schools, railroads, and internal improvements.[34] Conflicts grew with local officials over taxation to pay for the social, educational, and economic programs advocated by the Republicans.[35] Of particular concern were the state's financial picture and the use of scrip issued to meet the government's expenses when revenues fell short.[36]

In late 1868 the state had developed a revenue deficiency and had issued scrip to meet expenses of government. The scrip (treasury certificates) was made receivable for tax payments. Speculators had purchased the scrip at discounts and sold it to others for use in tax payments. Public reluctance to accept scrip created a financial crisis. In addition, the legislature had approved a bond program to fund state debt and to finance the building of railroads and levees.[37] Charges of corruption and dishonesty were rampant. Justice McClure was apparently intimately involved in these activities, and he and others closely associated with the Clayton administration were accused of mismanagement at best. The controversy led to a schism in the Republican Party that was soon exploited by the Democrats and culminated in conflicts between Clayton and his former associates.[38] Realignment within the ranks of the Republicans was soon to come. The beginning of the schism was reflected in the division on the court between McClure and Gregg and Harrison. Wilshire and Bowen would soon end their service on the court and played lesser roles.

An example of the reluctance of local officials to wholeheartedly endorse the goals of the Republicans is provided in the December 1868 term in *Fletcher v. Oliver.*[39] Here a taxpayer filed for an injunction to prevent the tax collector from collecting a road tax assessed in Pulaski County on property within the city of Little Rock. The 1868 constitutional provisions mandated that all real property be taxed by uniform rule and allowed an exemption, by legislative act, of up to $500 of personal property. In the case at hand, a city charter attempted to limit taxation of property of city inhabitants. In an opinion by Justice McClure the court upheld the dismissal of the complaint and upheld the road tax.

A continuing problem also concerned the issuance of local scrip intended to circulate as currency. In the city of Little Rock, an effort was apparently made to issue city bonds, which might have circulated as currency. The court, in *Jones v. City of Little Rock,* recognized that no authority existed for such issuance but refused to approve injunctive relief against the city council.[40] The court had previously refused to issue an injunction, indicating that the supreme court had no constitutional power to issue injunctive relief and, in the present case, would not issue a writ of mandamus to compel a lower court to grant the requested relief.[41]

In a related matter the court had refused to interfere in a decision by the treasurer of Pulaski County to refuse to pay certain county scrip because the county court had required that all such scrip be presented on or before February 13, 1867, for classification and reissuing.[42] The majority of the court upheld the right of the county to refuse to recognize scrip that was not timely presented, but Justice McClure, in the first dissenting opinion of the 1868 court, argued that the treasurer had no authority to refuse to redeem the scrip and expressed his opinion of the local officials:

> To say that a county may have dishonest, incompetent and unfaithful officers, as it appears was the case in this instance, and that the county authorities, who are charged with the protection of its interest, can set idly by and see an application made for a mandamus against the treasurer, to compel the payment of the scrip that they have ordered refunded, without taking steps to restrain the payment, certainly shows a dereliction of duty that deserves a severe reprimand, rather than the sympathy expressed by the majority of the court.[43]

It is not clear whether McClure had some reason, not reflected in the opinion, for encouraging the payment of the scrip. He was often involved in unsavory activities and became notorious for his involvement in a number of financial schemes involving local internal improvements.[44]

In the June 1871 term, conflicts involving local officials are illustrated by six cases from Chicot County. Three of the Chicot County cases arose out of the issuance of bonds by the county to the Mississippi, Ouachita, and Red River Railroad Company in 1860. Payment of the principal and interest on the bonds was now being sought. The court determined that the county court had no authority to issue bonds for any purpose and certainly not to pay for stock in a railroad company.[45] Also, from Chicot County appeals were taken from decisions in the local courts related to efforts to restrain the collection of a school tax. The Court refused to hear the matters since they were not yet finally decided at the local level.[46] And the court, in *Hays, Ex parte,* refused to issue a writ of mandamus against the circuit judge of Chicot County compelling him to grant an injunction restraining the Chicot County local officials from receiving scrip.[47] These cases are illustrative of the turmoil that existed in many counties, particularly with regard to financing of local governmental operations and schools.[48]

As indicated earlier, one of the programs of the Republican administration of Clayton was the establishment of schools. Some local opposition was apparent, particularly when it was made clear that the intent was to establish schools for both white and black children. Some counties attempted to avoid the required taxation to support the schools. One such attempt is illustrated by *County*

Court of Union County v. Robinson.[49] Here the trustee had determined that there were 397 youths in the district and only four schools had been provided and that there should have been ten schools and sufficient taxes to support that number. The electors of the county had refused to establish the number of schools necessary or sufficient tax levy to support them. The trustee had then brought the matter to the county court and it, too, had failed to establish adequate support for the schools. The trustee sought a writ of mandamus to compel the county court to act, but the supreme court indicated that the writ was not the proper remedy and that the matter should have proceeded by appeal. One interesting aspect of the case was the court's discussion of the necessity of establishing separate schools for whites and blacks. This matter would be back before the court again in future years.

The December term 1872 found the court with a new member. The term of Justice Harrison expired on January 1, 1873. Marshal L. Stephenson was elected to fill the vacancy. Stephenson had served as a circuit judge in eastern Arkansas. Justice Stephenson's first opinions were in routine matters, but by the end of the term he was called upon to write the opinion in one of the term's most controversial cases, *Floyd v. Gilbreath*, a case involving a question of the legality of taxes levied in Scott County.[50] The crucial issue dealt with the power of the chancery courts to grant relief in cases where the taxes were unauthorized by law. Justice Stephenson used the occasion to attempt to define the boundaries between the law and chancery courts. He found that it was not proper for the chancery court to grant the relief requested and that the law provided adequate remedies. Justice Gregg disagreed and would have allowed the exercise of equity jurisdiction to provide relief to the taxpayers.

In a second case involving a controversy over taxes, *Wells v. Cole*, the court had to deal with the question of whether state scrip could be used to pay county taxes or school taxes.[51] The issue was of some consequence because of the Republican attempts to finance public programs and to cover state budget deficits by the issuance of scrip, which had generally been acceptable as a means of paying state taxes. The legislature had authorized the issuance of the

"Treasurer's certificates" in 1868 and in 1871 had authorized their use in paying state and county taxes. Justice McClure felt that it was not within the authority of the legislature to require the counties to accept the scrip. Justice Gregg, dissenting, argued that the legislature could lawfully determine how such instruments could be used. Logically, he said, if the legislature could create counties and other subdivisions of government, the legislature could prescribe the powers and duties of these entities.

In the December 1873 term of the supreme court, a total of sixty-four opinions were issued. In none of these was a written dissent reported. Most of the decisions were on routine matters, sparking little controversy. Three dealt with the continued problem of scrip. In *Seymour v. Jefferson County,* a question was addressed involving county scrip and the authority of the county judge to issue bonds in exchange for the scrip.[52] It was apparently the duty of the county clerk, not the county judge, to issue the bonds, and the court so found. In *Coit v. Claw* the question was presented as to the authority of the county board to declare what taxes could be paid in what funds.[53] The court determined that the county board had no discretion in the matter. Finally, in *English v. Oliver*, the court affirmed its previous decision that the county must accept state scrip in payment of county taxes under prior law but that under a new act passed April 29, 1873, this could no longer be compelled for certain taxes.[54] The legislature, not the court, had finally resolved the difficulties surrounding the use of scrip.

Legal Effect of Secession

In one of the more important cases of the June 1869 term the court had to determine the effect of the federal Civil Rights Act with regard to statutes in place in Arkansas directly in conflict with the federal act.[55] Prior state statutes had prohibited testimony by members of the African or Negro race in any cause where a white person was interested in the outcome. The federal legislation of April 9, 1866, the Civil Rights Act, determined that citizenship extended to people of every race and color and that all citizens could give evidence. The majority in *Kelly v. State* took the occasion to review the power of the federal government to act and to emphasize that former laws of the states that had seceded were forever abolished.[56] In addition, the court emphasized the view that actions of the Confederate state government were null and void. Justice McClure dissented, not because he disagreed with the outcome but because he thought it unnecessary to set out an elaborate discussion of a question that he saw as plainly settled by the outcome of the war.

Two cases in the December 1870 term related to the effect of the 1864 Arkansas Constitution after federal authority was reasserted in the state and a "provisional" government established. In one case, the actions of a local probate official under the Confederate government were successfully challenged as being invalid because a new constitution (that of 1864) had been adopted prior to the action.[57] In the second case, *State v. Nichols,* the legislature of 1867, assembled under the 1864 constitution, had passed a "pardon and amnesty" act that purported to grant a full pardon for all crimes, except rape, committed after May 6, 1861, and before July 4, 1865, for which there was no conviction prior to the passage of the act.[58] Again, the differences on the court were apparent. Justice McClure argued for the majority that the legislature had the power *before* conviction; Justice Gregg argued that the legislature could never grant pardons, that this was an executive function.

The most interesting cases of the June 1871 term focused on the legal effect of secession. This matter had been addressed by the prior court in *Hawkins v. Filkins* in 1866.[59] Justice David Walker, writing for that court, had concluded that even if the Civil War had suspended the laws of the Untied States, the people of the state owed obedience to the laws and government under which they lived. The court concluded that the government of the state continued *de facto* from the time of attempted secession until suspended by the new constitution of 1864 and, as a result, the acts of the Confederate state government during the period were valid and binding. The 1864 convention could not declare the 1861 government void *ab initio*.

The issue was back before the court in *Penn v. Tolllison* with regard to the validity of actions taken by state courts during the Confederate period.[60] Justice McClure took the opportunity to review the earlier decision of *Hawkins v. Filkins* in light of the language of the 1868 constitution. He declared that there was no such thing as a *de facto* state and that the government formed in 1861 could in no way be considered a state *de jure* in any sense of the word. As a result, he could find no basis for validity of any actions of courts during the war. The Confederate Constitution of 1861 was characterized as one that "simply sprang into being through usurpation and treachery of men who betrayed the trust reposed in them by their constituents. The courts that existed under the constitutions of 1836 and 1868 were created by the people; the courts, existing under the Constitution of 1861, were creatures of the individuals who comprised the Convention; the former from the sovereignty, and the latter from usurpation and violence."[61] Justice Harrison dissented without comment.

The precedent laid down by Justice McClure was used by Justice Gregg in another case during the term in which the same issue was raised.[62] Gregg upheld the 1868 constitutional provision declaring the actions of the Confederate government to be void. Justice Bennett then used both cases to reach a similar result in *Timms v. Grace*.[63]

The court in the December 1871 term was again faced with the question of the validity of actions of courts taken during the rebellion under the Confederate state government. In *Carroll v. Boyd* the court restated its opinion that proceedings of the courts of the state under Confederate authority were void.[64] In *Vinsant v. Knox*, the court had the opportunity to clarify the effect of its previous cases, *Penn v. Tollison* and *Thompson v. Mankin*, on decisions taken during the time when the ruling of *Hawkins v. Filkins* was presumed to be the law.[65] The court indicated that the two later cases absolutely overruled *Hawkins v. Filkins* and that no one could acquire any rights by virtue of the rulings and assumptions of the court in that case. As a result, the granting of letters of probate by a court under the Confederate state government were null and void and creditors against the estate were not prevented from asserting claims as late as 1871.

The last case reported in the December 1872 term was *Metropolitan National Bank of New York City v. Gordon*.[66] Here the court revisited an important issue arising out of the war. In this case the bank sued on an obligation dated April 16, 1860, and the question was whether the statute of limitations ran during the war. The predecessor court had delivered an opinion in *Bennett v. Worthington* holding that the statute of limitations ran even if courts were closed during the war.[67] Justice Gregg indicated his "high respect" for the prior court but overruled the prior decision and held that the statute of limitations was suspended during the hostilities.

Civil Rights

Congress enacted the Civil Rights Bill on April 9, 1866, which declared all persons born in the United States, regardless of race or color, to be citizens and extended the rights enjoyed by white citizens to all citizens. This included the right to make contracts, to bring lawsuits, and to enjoy equal protection of the law. Later that year in a trial in Pulaski County black witnesses (including the robbery victim) testified against the defendant, who was white. This was challenged on appeal; the defendant argued that the prior statutes of the state prohibited such testimony and challenged the congressional act as unconstitutional.[68]

The court pointed out that under the supremacy clause of the federal constitution, laws of Congress are the supreme law of the land and state courts are bound by them regardless of state law to the contrary. Furthermore, the court went on to emphasize that states were not permitted to secede from the union, although by rebellion the states could destroy their own government, invoking the power of the federal government to suppress insurrections to guarantee each state a republican form of government.[69] Justice McClure, in dissent, agreed with the outcome .but argued the case was moot given that the defendant had long since been pardoned and that rights of blacks to testify had been well established and that the "progress of events" made the decision unnecessary and of no consequence.[70]

Political Controversies

While the other categories involved questions of political importance, one category involved the court, directly, in the increasingly bitter political controversies during the period. In what would prove to be an important case in the future, the court, in the 1868 term, had to interpret its own constitutional authority to grant original writs. In *Price & Barton v. Page*, Justice McClure examined the language of the 1868 constitution that appeared to permit the granting of "writs of error and supersedeas, certiorari and habeas corpus, mandamus and quo warranto, and other remedial writs."[71] Similar language in the original 1836 constitution had been interpreted by the 1851 court to apply only to means of "superintending control" of inferior courts and in the aid of appellate jurisdiction of the court. The court, in *Price & Barton v. Page*, held that the decision of 1851 was incorrect and that, especially with changes made in the 1868 constitution, the court clearly had jurisdiction to issue remedial writs. But, in the case at hand, the court refused to issue a writ of mandamus directed to the state treasurer. Judges Gregg and Harrison dissented and argued that the older case interpreting substantially similar language in the 1836 and 1868 constitutions was correct and that the supreme court should not assume original jurisdiction with regard to writs. In any event, they agreed that the statute in question did not prohibit the challenged action of the state treasurer—the issuance of interest-bearing certificates when the state treasury was bare. The importance of this case would become obvious in the turmoil surrounding the struggle for control of state government following 1870 and the 1872 elections.

The Republican Party by late 1869 was split into three factions, and the Democrats were poised to reassert influence. One group under the leadership of Lieutenant Governor James Johnson formed a new party designated the "Liberal Republicans." The remainder were split between the Clayton forces, called "Minstrels," who remained in control of state government, and the "Brindletails," headed by Joseph Brooks, insurgent Radicals concerned with the leadership of Clayton and his overtures to the Democrats.[72]

The Brooks faction created an anti-Clayton slate of candidates for the 1870 election.[73] In the end, some compromise was reached between the Clayton and the Brooks factions—at least to the extent that only one Republican candidate was finally offered for each position.[74] However, after the election Clayton made concessions to the Democrats to gain their support for his election to the US Senate.[75] Eventually, this effort also failed because of Clayton's determination that Lieutenant Governor Johnson not succeed him as governor.[76] This controversy was the basis for the impeachment charges against both Clayton and McClure in the 1871 legislature.

Following this turmoil the supreme court issued opinions in sixty-eight cases during the December 1870 term. A significant number dealt with political questions growing out of the 1870 election. These included a series of cases related to the duties of registrars, election returns, and the attempted impeachment of Lieutenant Governor Johnson. Probably the most significant decisions of the court during this term focused on voting rights and elections. In a series of three cases involving the actions of registrars in refusing to list individuals as qualified voters, the court determined that the registrars were acting in an executive capacity in carrying out the duties of registering voters. As such, according to the court, no appeal could be taken to a court from the rulings of an executive officer under the "separation of powers" concept embodied in the constitution in spite of legislation specifying judicial review of the actions of the registrars. In this neat side step the court was able to avoid ruling on the constitutionality of the required oath for electors.[77]

A particularly bitter election squabble developed during the 1870 election in Pulaski County. The governor was empowered to appoint election officials, including registrars and elections judges. In Pulaski County, Clayton obtained the agreement of the Democrats not to run candidates in return for a fair registration process. In Pulaski County the opposition Republicans (Brindletails) attempted to establish control of the polling places with a goal of preventing the appointed officials from performing their duties, which would have allowed the local precinct voters to select election judges. In five of the Pulaski County townships they were successful in controlling the polling places, but the Clayton-appointed officials set up competing voting boxes, so two sets of returns were developed.[78]

The certification of returns gathered at the Brindletail polling places would have meant the election of the opposition slate. The Clayton forces filed an action in the supreme court for a writ of mandamus to force the county clerk to certify the regular returns. In *Howard v. McDiarmid*, Justice McClure asserted the jurisdiction of the court with regard to the issuance of writs, as earlier determined in *Price & Barton v. Page*, to find that mandamus was proper to compel the clerk to certify the returns as reported by the regular officials.[79] He went to great pains to find it the duty of the clerk to determine which of the returns were legitimate and to assert that only the "regular" returns constituted a legal poll. Justices Gregg and Harrison dissented on the same basis as in *Price & Barton v. Page*, arguing that the court had no original jurisdiction to hear the issue. Justice Gregg went further and argued that election matters were to be free from control of the judiciary and executive departments and left solely under the control of the legislative branch.

The significance of the court's exercise of original jurisdiction in such cases became obvious with the efforts of the Clayton forces to prevent Lieutenant Governor Johnson from becoming governor upon Clayton's election to the US Senate. The Conservatives were willing to support Clayton's election with the hope that Johnson would become governor.[80] Impeachment charges were filed against Johnson in the legislature; this failed by one vote.[81] *Quo warranto* proceedings were filed in the supreme court, and Clayton's political ally, McClure, rendered the opinion of the court in *State v. Johnson*.[82] McClure reasserted the court's jurisdiction to hear the matter as an original proceeding under *Price & Barton v. Page* and then proceeded to evaluate the validity of the cause against Johnson. The charge was that Johnson had failed to qualify for his office within fifteen days of the election as required by the constitution. McClure and the majority issued the writ, which required Johnson to show that he had complied with all requirements of the law. The proceedings ran over a six-day period in February of 1871, following which the court found that Johnson was, in fact, entitled to the office. As before, Justice Gregg dissented from the exercise of the power but agreed with the outcome on the facts. This was but the final salvo in the battle between Clayton and Johnson. Johnson agreed to accept appointment as secretary of state after having been offered other appointments and a bribe of several thousand dollars as compensation.[83]

State v. Johnson was Justice McClure's first case as chief justice. For reasons never fully explained but no doubt a part of the political intrigue surrounding the episode, just prior to the filing of the proceeding against Johnson, Chief Justice Wilshire and Associate Justice Bowen resigned. McClure was appointed chief justice and J. E. Bennett and E. J. Searle were appointed to the court.[84] Both were firmly in the Clayton camp and were apparently close to McClure. Bennett was a New Yorker and had served as a colonel of Illinois infantry. He came to Little Rock in 1868 and was appointed federal judge. Searle was from Ohio and had also served in the Union army. He came to Arkansas in 1865 and had served as both a prosecuting attorney and a circuit judge.[85]

Their appointments coincided with efforts in the House of Representatives to impeach Justice McClure for conspiring to remove Johnson from office. The House also accused McClure of bargaining "for pay and bribes" to influence actions and decisions.[86] The impeachment trial before the Senate came after the compromise with Johnson, but because it was publicly viewed as important, the Senate went through the motions of a trial in March 1871. McClure made a lengthy opening statement in his own defense and admitted the essential facts of the charge, that he had issued a temporary restraining order against Johnson but, he argued, for such an act to be unlawful it had to be accompanied by an "unlawful or corrupt" intent. He was unanimously acquitted by the Senate, which then voted to pay him $2,000 for costs. Five thousand copies of the report of the trial, including his full statement in his own defense, were ordered printed by the state contract printers (McClure held such a contract himself).[87]

During the remainder of 1871, the anti-Clayton forces attacked Clayton relentlessly. He was indicted and acquitted on charges of election fraud; he was investigated by the US Senate, and his fitness to sit was challenged because of his certification of results in the

1870 election. He was eventually exonerated from these charges.[88] The Republican Party in the state remained bitterly divided, and the 1872 campaign would feature Joseph Brooks as the candidate favored by the anti-Clayton Republicans and the Conservatives. Clayton chose Judge Elisha Baxter to head the "Minstrel" ticket.

It was in this atmosphere that the Arkansas Supreme Court entered the June 1871 term. The Clayton trio of McClure, Bennett, and Searle, along with the old line Republican Gregg and the moderate Republican Harrison, who would eventually desert the Republican Party altogether for the Democrats, faced continuing political conflicts but none of the nature of the proceeding against Johnson of the prior term. Two cases involved the court's power to issue writs. These were, in actuality, a continuation of the battle in Pulaski County related to election returns. George W. McDiarmid, as county clerk, had been before the court earlier in the proceeding to force him to certify the "regular" election returns in the 1870 election. In March of 1871 the state legislature had appointed a circuit clerk of Pulaski County and had designated him as the official county recorder. McDiarmid had apparently refused to turn over the official county records to the new circuit clerk. A petition for a writ of mandamus was filed against him in *Fitch v. McDiarmid,* and the court was faced with the question of whether this proceeding was proper.[89] Justice Bennett, following the example of McClure in earlier cases, again reiterated the basis for the court's jurisdiction, and Gregg, again, dissented. The majority, however, indicated that the proper writ was in *quo warranto*, not mandamus. The attorney general then filed a motion for *quo warranto* against McDiarmid, which was granted in *State v. McDiarmid.*[90] Justice Gregg objected on familiar grounds.

In the December 1871 term, the most controversial were cases related to the continuing saga of the battle over the 1870 election in Pulaski County and the power of the supreme court to exercise original jurisdiction in such matters. In two of the first cases of the term the court dealt with the question of whether the writ of *quo warranto* could be issued at the request of private persons. The court indicated that only the attorney general could bring an action for the writ. Individuals were provided the option of bringing other actions to determine their rights to a contested office.[91] Because the dispute in Pulaski County had not been resolved in the prior term, the matter was before the court once again in *McDiarmid v. Fitch*.[92] Here the court evaluated the response of the registrar in Pulaski County related to his failure to deliver the original voter registration books to the county clerk for more than a year after the election. Since no reason was given for the delay, the court issued a writ of mandamus, and even Justice Gregg agreed that it was proper, although he restated his opinion that the court's jurisdiction did not extend to cases of this nature.

Following the decision that only the attorney general could file a *quo warranto* request, action was taken against McDiarmid, commanding him to show by what authority he held the office of recorder in Pulaski County. Justice McClure indicated that the legislature had approved an act on March 16, 1871, transferring the duties of recorder from the county clerk to the circuit clerk in counties of a population of fifteen thousand or more (Pulaski County was probably the only county affected). Fitch had been appointed circuit clerk by the governor and had demanded that McDiarmid deliver all books and documents related to the office of recorder. McDiarmid refused to do so. Since under the constitution of 1868 the legislature could establish the duties of offices such as county clerk or circuit clerk, it was proper for the legislature to transfer the duties of the office of recorder from one clerk to the other. The court ordered that a judgment of ouster be entered against McDiarmid. The same issues were presented in cases from Jefferson County and were decided on the same basis.[93]

In the June 1873 term the court became embroiled in the contest over the governorship between Joseph Brooks and Elisha Baxter. This was, no doubt, the major issue of the entire Reconstruction period. In the election of 1872 Brooks had garnered the support of Liberal Republicans, former Whigs, Conservative Democrats, and the anti-Minstrel Republicans. Baxter was the candidate of the Minstrels. The official returns reflected that Baxter had won, 41,681 to 38,415. The Brooks supporters insisted that the official returns were incorrect and that massive fraud had denied Brooks the election. Since the constitution called for disputed elections to be decided in the legislature, it was unlikely that Brooks would be afforded a fair hearing in that forum since the legislature was controlled by the Minstrels.[94]

Baxter took office in January and immediately thereafter political realignment began to occur. He made overtures to the Democrats, and a struggle for control of the legislature ensued. McClure, as editor of the *Republican* and leader of the Minstrels, began to try to stop the growing influence of the Democrats over Baxter. By April the split between Baxter and McClure was public. McClure then began to push the claim of Brooks to the governorship. By then the Democrats in the legislature had reservations about Brooks and preferred to take their chances with Baxter. It appeared that Baxter's position was secure.[95]

In June the attorney general asked the supreme court for leave to file a *quo warranto* proceeding against Baxter, requiring him to prove the validity of his claim to the governorship. This matter was heard by the court and the writ was denied on June 4.[96] The opinion of the court was written by Justice Gregg in *State v. Baxter.*[97] The majority indicated that the determination of the question was vested solely in the legislature and no court had jurisdiction to decide the matter. Justice McClure argued that the court should decide the issue, although no written dissent was filed.[98] The matter would rest for some months with that action. Brooks then filed an action in Pulaski Circuit Court alleging that Baxter had usurped the office. No action was taken for some ten months by the court.[99]

By the close of 1873 it appeared that Brooks had been deserted by all except McClure and a few others of those determined to stop Baxter and the Democrats. The Democrats were beginning to talk of a constitutional convention to revise the basic form of government. Baxter appeared to favor this move as well, and the anti-Baxter Republicans became apprehensive that he would call the legislature into session for the purpose of voting on whether to call for a convention.[100]

As the state moved into the new year, Brooks was still maneuvering to assume the governorship. In April the judge of the Pulaski County Circuit Court, John Whytock, a close associate of McClure, called the case of *Brooks v. Baxter,* which had lain dormant for ten months. He declared that Brooks was entitled to the office of governor. McClure administered the oath of office to Brooks to install him as governor. The Arkansas Supreme Court was brought into the fray by arrangements made by Brooks's supporters (obviously, McClure and his associates). The arrangement was that the court would reverse its prior decision and pass directly on the jurisdiction of the Pulaski County Circuit Court. On May 7, 1974, four members of the court acted to find that the decision of the lower court was proper and that Brooks was entitled to the office of governor.[101] Brooks then drove Baxter from the capitol by a show of force, and this action precipitated an event that would result in the complete reassertion of control by the Democrats—the Brooks-Baxter war.

Baxter attempted to obtain assistance from President Ulysses S. Grant, but Grant's initial reply was that the matter should be left to the courts of the state. Brooks also tried to obtain assistance from Grant but was rebuffed as well.[102] The Arkansas delegation in Washington, with the exception of former chief justice Wilshire, now a US representative, attempted to influence the Grant administration on Brooks's behalf. Delegates pushed for resolution in the state courts.[103] The effort of four members of the court to resolve the controversy failed since the full court was not involved. The conflicting claims continued until a compromise was finally reached whereby the legislature would be called into special session. On May 14 the legislature assembled and Baxter was recognized as governor by both houses.[104] At that point President Grant issued a proclamation ordering Brooks and his party to disband. Both sides agreed to disband and to send home the troops each had assembled.[105]

Once Baxter was reinstalled in the capitol as governor, the state officials who had supported Brooks resigned or vacated their offices upon the threat of impeachment.[106] Chief Justice McClure and Justices Stephenson and Bennett were among those who were impeached by vote of the House. They vacated their offices and the governor appointed Democratic replacements: E. H. English, J. T. Bearden, and F. W. Compton.[107] They would serve on the court until the election of new members in the fall

While the legislature was in session, a call for a constitutional convention was issued and a bill was passed providing for an election in June on the question and to elect delegates to such a convention.[108] The June 30 vote on the constitutional convention resulted in an overwhelming victory for the measure: 80,259 for, 8,607 against. The Democrats elected over seventy of the ninety-one delegates.[109]

In October a vote on the proposed constitution and on all state constitutional officers was held. The new constitution reduced the supreme court to three members, all elected. The Republicans denied the validity of the constitutional convention and refused to offer candidates in the election.[110] The constitution was ratified and all Democratic candidates easily won election.[111] E. H. English was elected chief justice; David Walker, who had twice served on the court, was elected associate justice, along with William Harrison, the Republican turned Democrat whose term had expired only the previous year.[112] Later in the fall this new court, with a change in members, ruled that the Circuit Court of Pulaski County had no authority to resolve the disputed election.[113]

Interestingly, two of these new justices had been supporters of Brooks during the contest for the governorship. David Walker had continued to believe that Brooks had been legitimately elected and had refused to join the Democratic support of Baxter.[114] William Harrison had not only supported Brooks but continued to do so after the election. He was among a group that included McClure who went to Washington to appear before a congressional committee investigating political affairs in Arkansas. There they presented the argument that Baxter had never been legitimately elected. The congressional investigation resulted in a recommendation to Congress in early 1875 that advised against any interference in Arkansas affairs by the national government. This report was adopted by Congress as a whole, and, as a result, the Republicans finally capitulated.[115] The Democrats had returned to power, the new constitution was recognized, and Reconstruction in the state was at an end.

Summary and Conclusions

From this review of the activities of the Arkansas Supreme Court during congressional Reconstruction, it is clear that the court was unable to remain above the political struggle that was underway in the state. The ties of individual court members to competing factions influenced many of the decisions of the court, particularly on controversial political issues. While the court's workload consisted primarily of routine matters and these appear to have been decided by impartial application of the law, those cases involving political questions often served as the forum for individual justices to express their prevailing political philosophies. And most justices made overt efforts to use the power of office to support (or obstruct) the goals of varying political factions in the state. At perhaps no other period in the state's history has the court been the focus of equivalent efforts to manipulate the outcomes of individual cases for such blatant political purposes.

In *Democracy in America* Alexis de Tocqueville was intrigued by the "immense political influence" of American judges. He referred to the difficulty a stranger might have in understanding the judicial organization of the United States:

> He hears the authority of a judge involved in the political occurrences of every day, and he naturally concludes that in the United States the judges are important political functionaries; nevertheless, when he examines the nature of the tribunals, they offer at the first glance nothing that is contrary to the usual habits and privileges of those bodies; and the magistrates seem to him to interfere in public affairs only by chance, by a chance that recurs every day.[116]

No better example could be provided to reinforce this view of de Tocqueville's than the actions of the Arkansas Supreme Court during the Reconstruction period.

CHAPTER 12

"Distinguishing the Righteous from the Roguish"

Summary and Conclusions

Slavery, including the social and economic system it supported, was defended by white southerners not only as a constitutionally protected right but as a "socially beneficial institution," a "positive good."[1] The defense of slavery took on a moral tone. Southerners believed in what Bertram Wyatt-Brown summarizes as a "rule of honor," the moral code to which they adhered. Reputation was evidence of character.[2] This personal attribute of honorable character was one of the "psychological and social underpinnings of Southern culture."[3]

The planters constituted a small portion of the population but dominated southern politics and society.[4] The slaveholding elites would, naturally, wish to preserve their ordered society and would comfortably exercise social control through the legal system. As Wyatt-Brown notes, "the law served to distinguish the righteous from the roguish," and the worthy members of the community were invested with " collective power in the name of tradition and order."[5] Eugene D. Genovese refers to this as a "hegemonic function of the law," where the legal system becomes an "instrument" by which the socioeconomic class of slaveholders "imposes its viewpoint upon the class as a whole and the wider society."[6] It was the opinions of a relatively few that mattered, but these few, acting to preserve their own image of self-worth (honor), could assert their moral authority by rendering powerless those who questioned "the premises of the social order."[7] One such premise was the morality of the slave economy. They came to see slavery as the "very foundation of a proper social order and therefore as the essence of morality in human relationships."[8]

The prewar years were a time of continued economic expansion in Arkansas. Maturation of the plantation economy in the lowlands, accompanied by subsistence farming elsewhere, made the state an agricultural success story.[9] The growth in the economy was related, in large part, to the expansion of slavery and the domination of cotton production, although corn and livestock were important as well.[10] Carl H. Moneyhon has noted,

> New lands, more slaves, and good prices for cotton produced a steady expansion of wealth for all sorts of people and produced an expanding social order.[11]

The upper classes grew in both numbers and strength economically, socially, and politically. As Moneyhon points out, "shared backgrounds, common life-style, and the existence of opportunities for economic success and upward social mobility provided the basis for a social ideology that made sense in the stratified democratic society."[12] The social ideology called for the protection of slavery and the defense of the southern way of life.

As a "frontier" with a developing economy, Arkansas would not reflect the same society as the developed Northeast. The economy in Arkansas was primarily agricultural, with land and slaves as the primary assets. The market economy was protected in the structure of the economic system of slavery itself. In those areas where slavery did not predominate, an even more basic agricultural system operated.

Morton J. Horwitz argues that the early years of the nineteenth century in the United States evidenced the emergence of an "instrumental conception of law." This, he says, "encouraged innovation," and judges acted on a "self-conscious consideration of social and economic policies."[13] In a real sense, the legal system was used to promote economic growth and encourage social change. Judges saw themselves as agents of change with a new policy orientation.[14] Lawrence M. Friedman adds that the thrust of law during this period was "promotion of enterprise." The aim was to provide a basis for economic growth. For example, government was to provide transport, currency, and credit to aid in the growth and expansion of the economy. This transformation, he suggests, is seen the areas of debt and contract, banks and banking, business entities, public land and settlement policies, and real property.

James W. Ely and David J. Bodenhamer agree with much of the analysis of Horwitz and Friedman. They suggest that the South, however, was different. The southern system was more inclined to protect landed and slaveholding interests.[15] It may have operated to actually retard non-plantation economic development. The unusual degree of attention in the South to matters of race and caste curtailed legal experimentation. "Indeed, any change in the status quo was viewed with suspicion."[16] Southern law became a collection of "archaic provisions and conservative rulings." Ely and Bodenhamer attribute this not only to the undue attention to race and caste but also to other southern characteristics: "a rural culture, a hierarchical society, and pervasive localism."[17] Tony A. Freyer agrees but suggests that southern law, particularly in the areas of transportation, credit, and property, accommodated diverse class interests. In doing so, social and political stability was preserved at the expense of non-plantation economic development.[18]

This can be no better illustrated than in the attention southern law focused on the protection of landed interests and slaveholders, the "hegemonic function" described by Genovese.[19] There is some academic debate with regard to the sufficiency of this interpretation, whether it is explicitly Marxist or merely "instrumental reductionism," that is, "adopting a view of American legal history that reduces American law to a mere instrument of dominant classes."[20]

> Legal enactments are partly ideological and partly political forms. In their ideological being, they exist as discourses. In their most developed form these discourses are written down and carefully circumscribed. They take on a magical form as sacred texts: the canons of social order.[21]

During the critical period of the Arkansas's development, 1836–1874, the work of the Arkansas Supreme Court reflects not only social change but the development of the legal system in the new state and the role the judiciary was to play. Genovese suggests that in the South the dominant social and economic class of slaveholders could impose its viewpoint on the wider society. If this is true, Genovese's concept of "hegemony" should be evident in the opinions of the court.[22] The cases reaching the Arkansas Supreme Court dealing with issues surrounding the settlement of public lands, banks and banking, internal improvements (such as transportation), and slaves and slavery provide a basis for analysis of whether promotion of enterprise or hegemony was the goal. In addition, cases involving family law and family property, debt and contract, and, finally, criminal law and criminal procedure reflect the view of the court as to the proper social order—whether any change from the status quo was appropriate.

The Court's Legacy

A. LAND TITLES

One of the least challenged assertions of James Willard Hurst is that in the nineteenth century law was used by Americans to "facilitate their economic ambitions."[23] Hurst drew two "working principles" concerning the uses of law:

> (1) The legal order should protect and promote the release of individual creative energy to the greatest extent compatible with the broad sharing of opportunity for such expression. . . . (2) The legal order should mobilize the resources of the community to help shape an environment which would give men more liberty by increasing the practical range of choices open to them and minimizing the limiting force of circumstances.[24]

For Hurst, public land policy provided a perfect example of how the law could aid in the "immediate exploitation of resources and the freeing of men's energies."[25] The withholding of large blocks of land by private speculators was discouraged, just as disposal of public land was encouraged. This, Hurst argues, was to favor legal doctrines and policies to delegate resources and power to private entrepreneurs.[26]

Prior to Arkansas statehood, the uncertain nature of land titles in the territory contributed to the failure of plantation agriculture to expand significantly.[27] The question of land titles continued into the statehood period. The Arkansas Supreme Court handled sixty-three public land cases from 1836 through 1861. These included disputes arising from holders of preemption certificates, New Madrid certificates, military bounty claims, claims on Indian land, and, later, claims on swampland. Some of the state's most prominent political figures were involved in these contests, often as speculators who had acquired the rights of holders of various types of claims. For example, Chester Ashley was reported to be the largest landowner in the state by shrewd dealing and wise investment. He was a frequent litigant in land cases. In this litigation, as with much of that before the court, the dispute was often between Ashley and other speculators.

The attitude of the court in public land cases seems to parallel that of the South generally. Over time a certain lack of sympathy toward preemption claimants can be detected. At the same time the ultimate resolution of some of the disputes over title by application of the concept of adverse possession reflects a view that protection of the existing order was more important, that disruption might occur if those in occupancy were displaced.

B. BANKS AND BANKING

Those who maintain that the antebellum South was a "dual economy" with "yeomen" farmers, largely self-sufficient and removed from the credit economy and dominated by the plantation sector both economically and politically, could be describing antebellum Arkansas.[28] This "conflict and collaboration" could be no better illustrated than in the political and economic collusion resulting from the creation of two state banking institutions in Arkansas immediately after statehood. These institutions were promoted successfully by the slaveholding power elites and the ruling political dynasty. The political battles that ensured were often between those in control of the banks and the factions, primarily from the upcountry, who opposed the state's involvement in the credit market.

Through questionable lending practices, favoritism and abuse, outright corruption, and mismanagement, the banks failed. This financial irresponsibility, combined with the federal banking policies of the Jackson administration that left state banks unregulated, meant the institutions were to be short lived.

The fiasco not only left the state in debt but resulted in hundreds of lawsuits, many of which reached the Arkansas Supreme Court.[29] The court handled 159 banks and banking cases in the antebellum years. This does not include a number of debt cases or procedural cases in which the banks were only mentioned in passing. Nor is it possible to accurately characterize all "banks and banking" cases as involving issues that were in any way unique to the state institutions. These were cases in which the institutions were prominently involved, either in conflicts over control or when conflicts arose involving one of the banks as a prominent party in the litigation. While the banks were created by and for the politically connected—the powerful, ruling elites—as the scandal evolved, the political "dynasty" became disenchanted and, ultimately, became "anti-bank" and supported the efforts to wind down the state's involvement in the banking business.

C. TRANSPORTATION

However, without state-sponsored banking institutions the state became almost totally dependent on out-of-state sources of credit, and economic development was retarded. This affected the availability of basic services, as well as internal improvements such as roads, levees, and railroads, and deterred the development of a system of education—all necessary for economic success.[30]

Efforts to use revenues from the sale of public lands were unsuccessful. Speculators stepped in to grab large tracts of swampland and overflowed lands when those sources of funds were made available to support internal improvements and railroads. Title disputes, fraud, and incompetence, coupled with localism, meant the "energy" was dissipated. Localism also determined that road and railroad construction efforts would also be unfruitful.

The Arkansas Supreme Court had an important role in this saga. However, because the disputes coming to the court were often centered on fights among the acquisitive speculators or between large tract holders and the state, the court could in no way be seen as an "instrument of change." In any event, attention soon turned to much more compelling interests—the threat of the antislavery movement and the emergence of the Republican Party.

D. SLAVERY

From statehood until the first year of the Civil War, the Arkansas Supreme Court heard 109 cases involving slaves in some way. The number is actually higher if cases are counted where slaves were mentioned but were not the focus of the case. For example, in many of the debt cases, slaves were mentioned as being collateral for the property on which execution was sought.[31]

Slaves were the focus in a few criminal cases, although the actual number is relatively small. This is probably because criminal activity by slaves was often handled by the master, outside formal legal process.[32] And the Arkansas court also dealt with suits for freedom by slaves and a limited number of slave cases that focused on other issues, such as liability for acts of slaves and liability for injuries to slaves.[33]

What is most telling about the slave cases is the rise in the number as slavery expanded in the state and as the debate over slavery as an institution intensified. In Justice Daniel Ringo's years, 1836–1844, the court heard only seven slave cases; in Thomas Johnson's years, 1845–1852, there were thirty-five cases that might be properly classified as slave cases. In the prewar years, 1853–1861, the number increased to seventy-seven. And in a number of these cases questions arose as to the correct rules applicable to slaves as property. This reflected the struggle the court was having in determining exactly how to treat slaves. Which property rules applied? Real property? Personal property? In some cases the court could turn to statutes for answers since the early legislatures attempted to deal with the same questions. In others, the court struggled to apply common law concepts of property law to this peculiar form of property.

It is in this arena that the Arkansas Supreme Court could be said to have used the law to further the economic interests of the slaveholder class and to have acted to preserve the institution itself. This is in accord with what Paul Finkelman calls "fidelity to slavery," which he asserts became more important than "fidelity to abstract concepts of law" in the South.[34] Finkelman's conclusion has been criticized by A. E. Keir Nash as an "oversimplification" and based on a premise that southern judges were placed in an "awkward position" of having to make such choices "by the force of greater historical events."[35] In fact, Nash argues that Arkansas judges strove for neutrality in judicial decision making although "sympathetic to the peculiar institution and much aware of the external premises upon it."[36] However, Nash bases this conclusion on language in a few cases dealing with slaves suing for freedom and not on an examination of all types of cases involving slaves as property. In the cases involving slaves as property, the hegemonic function of law, as suggested by Genovese, is clear.

E. FAMILY LAW AND FAMILY PROPERTY

Landowners were, of course, interested in preserving family property. In the patriarchal and hierarchical tradition, the husband was head of the household and he and his spouse were considered one flesh, which meant he acquired the right to use her real estate during her life and controlled all rents and profits from it. Her personal property came under his exclusive control. Various arrangements evolved to create a separate estate in the form of trusts or by a marriage settlement entered into prior to marriage. In the absence of such arrangements, creditors of the husband could look to the property of the wife to pay the debts of the husband.

In this context Arkansas was one of the early states to adopt a form of a married women's property law that permitted married women to own property in their own names free of the liability of the debts of their husbands. The operative section of this law made specific reference to slaves. This was, in part, a form of debt relief that provided some security to female children.[37] The impetus for such legislation was, in part, the desire of planters who wished to protect property from the mismanagement of their daughter's husbands. Later enactments were also a type of debtor protection and dealt with dower rights for widows and homestead exemptions. These provisions, as well, were supported by landowners who were creditors but often debtors as well.

The Arkansas Supreme Court dealt with these provisions and,

generally, took an expansive view of family property and interpreted the laws to afford the broadest protection. In line with southern paternalism, the court was sympathetic to efforts to protect family property. And, clearly, the court recognized the realm of the wife in planting "seeds of domesticity" in other areas of family law.

F. DEBT AND CONTRACT

Arkansas, like much of the South, was credit dependent in the early nineteenth century. An intricate web of contractual rights and obligations grew from this dependency. The courts were central to enforcement of those often-complex contractual arrangements. Civil dockets were dominated by debt collection cases. At the appellate level, the first issue for the court was often to unravel the complicated arrangements and to determine the priorities among competing claimants.

Much of the law of debtor-creditor contracts grew out of existing business practices. Negotiability was the underlying key to making credit transactions viable. The Arkansas Supreme Court, like the United States Supreme Court, approved this concept, along with others, which aided a functioning credit economy.

Merchants and wealthier planters supplied credit to the non-propertied classes. These creditors were themselves debtors who obtained credit through factors, often out of state. This created a degree of social independence and gave "non-slaveholders a stake in the slaveholder's world."[38]

During this same period the concept of the "will theory" of contract emerged. The rise of a market economy was tied to the development of this concept.[39] The source of obligations was the convergence of the wills of the contracting parties. The role of the courts was to enforce that will as expressed in the contract itself. Equity played a lesser role. The contract cases before the Arkansas Supreme Court reflect this view of contract. The essence of judicial decision-making, according to Arkansas supreme court justice Joseph Story, was to ensure an orderly and rational economic process, but one that was fair and equitable as well.[40] This became the hallmark of interpretation and enforcement of contract cases in the Arkansas court, along with a strict interpretation of the prohibition on impairing the obligation of a contract.

G. CRIMINAL LAW AND CRIMINAL PROCEDURE

As the focus of the early nineteenth century shifted to the encouragement of economic activity and protection of private property, the focus of the criminal law shifted as well—away from preservation of morality. Or so the argument goes.[41] However, in the South crimes of morality continued to be prosecuted even if patterns in other states differed.[42]

The record of the Arkansas Supreme Court indicates this to be true. Cases involving gambling, liquor, Sabbath breaking, and other "immoral" conduct were before the court regularly. A greater number of these cases reached the appellate court than did property crime such as theft, which suggests the importance placed on the prosecution of such crimes and the emphasis on public morality in the greater society.

While a number of explanations may be forwarded for this pattern, most convincing is that the elite, slaveholding class believed that morality in the greater society should be strictly regulated, in part, to justify their view of their duty to provide moral discipline and guidance to slaves. Antibellum southern aristocracy was concerned with "orderliness" of society, and the criminal justice system could be used set rules—to aid in the communities' goal of stability. By an emphasis on order, the "perfection" of southern society could be contrasted to the licentiousness of the North.

"Lords of the Soil"

By the 1850s the "lords of the soil" had their land. Many title disputes had been resolved. They had the slaves, an essential means to wealth. Legal controversies involving slaves and slavery were increasing, and protection of slavery was seen as necessary for survival of the economic and social system in the state. Agriculture was expanding. That is to say, cotton production and plantations were expanding. Poor transportation and geographic limitations did pose some restrictions on continued growth of the cotton culture. However, the real problem was lack of readily available credit. The collapse of the banking institutions meant the state lost much of its economic independence. For individual planters, farmers, and businessmen, the hardships that resulted when prices dropped or when weather conditions were unfavorable could mean disaster. Moneyhon targets the problem:

> Each January 1, the money made by Arkansans from their crops and produce went to pay off their debts, then moved out of state as merchants settled their obligations. As a result, the state was left with no cash and little accumulated capital.[43]

A contemporary observer of the state's plight was John W. Brown of Camden. Brown had moved to Arkansas from Memphis and located first near Princeton in Dallas County, where he maintained a plantation. Later he rented out the land, hired out his slaves, and moved to Camden to practice law and enter business. He owned properties throughout the state as a land speculator. In 1860 he owned over ten slaves, placing him in a group of only about two thousand such slaveholders.[44] He was each year concerned about balancing his income to meet his obligations in advances and interest. A drop in cotton price, transportation difficulties on the Ouachita River, death of a slave, or unpaid taxes were all subjects of travail and comment. These troubles, combined with Brown's increasing pessimism regarding the preservation of the republic and impending conflict, would elicit cogent comments in Brown's diary. These entries reflect that not all "lords of the soil" were in a position to take advantage of the expansion of the economy and that conditions in the late 1850s were worse than often acknowledged.[45]

Following the election of Franklin Pierce as president in 1852, Brown lamented that Henry Clay and Daniel Webster were no longer living:

> I fear it will be some time before we shall have three or even one other patriot who will be able to save the Union, and the principles of our happy government from destruction.[46]

In January 1853 he was commenting on the leaders of Arkansas as "selfish and unscrupulous" and on the state's lack of "commercial facilities, without capital, without enterprise."[47] He commented on his personal financial situation later in the year.

> I am getting out of my indebtedness rapidly but still the claimants are so urgent, mainly from need, that it almost distracts me. The country is so poor in the way of money that to be in debt even with large means is disturbing to my sensibilities and leads to unpleasant feelings.[48]

In early 1854 Brown moved to Camden and, while still concerned about the "losing year," expressed hope that things would be better in another year.[49] By the end of the year he had invested in an insurance company but was distressed by crop failure and the lack of skill of the overseer at the plantation. "So in a pecuniary view I am left in difficulty and am short of the expected means of payment nearly $1000 while my expenses have increased."[50]

The insurance business seemed to do well over the next few months, although his law practice was a disappointment. By midyear 1856 Brown was expressing optimism with regard to his finances. However, he was distressed by the election prospects.

> I have declined buying any more property until I see some further developments. I am satisfied that if some providential change does not take place, our Union cannot stand five years longer, and when ever the Union is dissolved, there is an end to all safety on the rights of property or security for its peaceful possession.[51]

By the end of 1857 he was expressing concern over the economic situation in the county: "The whole Union is in a panic and perhaps the World as far as commerce extends."[52] Difficulties in the insurance business meant the loss of salary and some continued conflicts with other investors. But he said he was "turning over debts to meet debts" and felt he could "avoid distress in the present crisis."[53] By the end of the year he was expressing relief. "My pecuniary affairs are somewhat improved and my circumstances easier than ever before, but without any great increase."[54] The next year was "reasonably prosperous."[55] In early 1860 he entered a partnership in an "Exchange and Brokerage" business, which was "encouraging." However, by April he was concerned about commission merchants "below" (New Orleans) who would not accept or pay on the faith of cotton, of which there was overproduction.[56]

Following the election of 1860, he expressed distress over the "fire eaters" in the South who were pushing for secession. On election day he said, "Today will in all probability be made the pretext for destroying the only Republican form of government on earth."[57] On January 1, 1861, with secession looming, he addressed the question of slavery.

> I look upon the question of Slavery, the all absorbing question now, powerful as it is, as only a pretext for the overthrow of this government.[58]

As the war commenced, one of Brown's continuing concerns was the lack of ready money. He could not collect on debts owed him and the shift to Confederate Treasury notes proved unreliable. He complained of the "demoralization" displayed regarding "contracts, debts and promises."[59] State scrip was practically worthless and Confederate Treasury notes depreciated rapidly. Gold was at a premium.[60]

A federal blockade meant that supplies could not be obtained. Farms were converted from cotton to grain, corn, and oats. Cotton could not be sold past the blockade, but it was traded for sugar and molasses in New Orleans.[61] However, the federal seizure of New Orleans meant loss of Confederate control of Mississippi and this brought dependency regarding the prospects for the South.[62] Camden became a military post, and Confederate soldiers passing through, Brown observed, were "equal to the locusts in Egypt in eating out almost every thing as they go."[63] Brown was able to engage a steamboat to bring unshucked corn from Monroe, Louisiana, to Camden. He managed to secure several thousand bushels with the "corn boat" and to see to its distribution at "reasonable rates."[64] He used the Confederate money to purchase property for investment, no one "wishing to lay away" confederate currency.[65] While the family struggled, they had the necessities of life and fared much better than most others west of the Mississippi.

Brown complained that "speculation and fraud" of government officials acted to the detriment of the South.[66] As Confederate currency declined in value, prices for goods increased. Brown, in July 1863, paid $9 to $10 for a bushel of salt; corn was $3.50 a bushel, and flour was 25¢ a pound.[67] When the federals gained control of Little Rock and Pine Bluff, concern mounted that they would advance to Camden. Brown closed his office and divided all specie coin and Louisiana bank paper with his partner.[68]

In December 1863 Brown complained about the lack of discipline among the Confederates stationed in Camden and how the citizens had been "pillaged, taxed and plundered by soldiers and army stragglers who never fought a battle nor advanced on an invading foe."[69] He saw the war as hopeless and the citizens "without protection, almost without resources, and living as slaves to the military power."[70]

In April 1864 the Confederate army left Camden in anticipation of the federal occupation. On the fifteenth they arrived "infuriated by combat and hunger." Following the initial demand for and theft of foodstuffs, order was soon restored. The slaves were "instantly told they were as free as we."[71] Otherwise, federal officers provided security to the Brown home while boarding there. The federals left Camden "quietly and in perfect order" on April 26.[72]

In June 1864 Brown accepted an appointment as financial agent for the Confederate Trans-Mississippi Department's Treasury Agency. His job entailed the exchange of old Confederate currency for a new issue and the exchange of gold for Confederate paper currency.[73] By September the new issue of Confederate currency had depreciated greatly and scarcely anything could be bought with the notes.[74] By December supplies were exhausted and the Browns were down to "Hog and Hominy" and flour once a day.[75] Brown's son, Henry Clay (named for Brown's idol), returned from fighting in Missouri, wounded but alive, in December 1864. Spirits lightened somewhat, but the "surest symptom" of the Confederacy's failure was seen in the continued decline in confidence in Confederate currency.[76]

In April 1865 word reached Camden that the Confederate Congress had passed legislation putting a quota on slaves from each state who were to enter the army in exchange for freedom. Brown remarked that this was "virtually giving up the principles upon which we went into the war."[77] News of Robert E. Lee's surrender reached Camden in late April and the war was over. As

Brown saw it, "Our so-called Confederacy is gone," and the United States was again united.[78] Brown called in witnesses to observe his burning of the now worthless Confederate paper currency in his hands.[79] He used much of his last salary to buy federal greenbacks, which placed him in a better position financially. But, he said, he had lost fully one-half of his estate during the war.[80]

As civil government was restored under federal control, small business reopened, supplies began to arrive, and the distress for food was relieved. "I have occasionally too some returning hopes of better times to come," he said.[81] He indicated that he was "looking into" some law questions that would arise out of "the new State of things." He had hoped not to practice law again but saw that it was likely to be necessary. He concluded:

> There will be a good deal of litigation here of which I have a fair chance for good share.[82]

Because Brown had served in an official capacity for the Confederate government, he did not qualify for amnesty but had to prepare a special application to President Andrew Johnson. That application was completed and sent to Washington.[83] Brown's diary abruptly ended July 13, 1865, so he did not relate the outcome of his application, nor did he record events during Reconstruction.

John W. Brown was not a true plantation aristocrat; he was not one of the powerful elite, in part because he was a Whig, not a Democrat; he was not a "fire eater" screaming for secession. He was, like many Arkansans, caught in the middle of a controversy that he found distressing. This "lord of the soil" had survived the ups and downs of difficult and uncertain land ventures and credit and debt crises but recognized that the third element of the southern economy—slavery—would result in disunion and disaster for the country he loved. Like many of his class, he lost much during the war but survived financially and was in a position to move forward afterward.

As Carl Moneyhon has shown, the state's landed interests prevailed in the political drama that played out in the state between 1867 and 1874. They ultimately managed to regain control of the state government and to "use it to protect themselves."[84] As he succinctly states, "the return of the Democrats in 1874 for all practical purposes restored Arkansas to those who had dominated it before the war."[85] Of this, John W. Brown would have been, no doubt, dismayed. Earlier he had summarized his news of what these "Fire Eaters" had sought in their "pretext for dissolution." They had "vainly hoped," he said, "to set up for themselves a Government under their own control—In which they could have matters all their own way, build up whatever they desired, and pull down whomsoever and whatsoever their own selfish ambitions and wreckless passions dictated."[86] Their hegemony had failed to preserve the premises of the old social order, but, in the end, returned them to power.

NOTES

Preface

1. Bertram Wyatt-Brown, *Southern Honor: Ethics and Behavior in the Old South* (New York: Oxford University Press, 2007), 369.

2. Stephen A. Smith, "Arkansas Advocacy: The Territorial Period," *Arkansas Law Review* 31 (1977): 449.

3. Ibid., 450.

4. Lynn Foster, "Courts and Lawyers on the Arkansas Frontier," *UALR Law Review* 26 (2004): 543.

5. Morris S. Arnold, *Unequal Laws unto a Savage Race: European Legal Traditions in Arkansas, 1686–1836* (Fayetteville: University of Arkansas Press, 1985), 207.

6. Ibid., 198.

7. L. Scott Stafford, "Slavery and the Arkansas Supreme Court," *UALR Law Journal* 19 (1997): 413.

8. Ibid., 423.

9. Ibid., 433. Stafford also contributed two important works dealing with the court's work in the aftermath of the Civil War. See his "Judicial Coup D' Etat: Mandamus, Quo Warranto and the Original Jurisdiction of the Arkansas Supreme Court," *UALR Law Journal* 20 (1998): 891–984; and "The Arkansas Supreme Court and the Aftermath of the Civil War," *UALR Law Review* 23 (2001): 355–407.

10. Morton Gitelman, "The Separation of Law and Equity and the Arkansas Chancery Courts: Historical Anomalies and Political Realities," *UALR Law Journal* 17 (1995): 215; and Morton Gitelman, "The First Chancery Court in Arkansas," *Arkansas Historical Quarterly* 55 (1996): 357.

11. C. R. Stevenson, *Arkansas Territory—State and Its Highest Courts* (Little Rock: Clerk of the Supreme Court, 1946).

12. Walter Lee Brown, *A Life of Albert Pike* (Fayetteville: University of Arkansas Press, 1997) 213–17, 426–28.

13. Jeannie M. Whayne, Thomas A. DeBlack, George Sabo III, and Morris S. Arnold, eds. *Arkansas: A Narrative History* (Fayetteville: University of Arkansas Press, 2002); S. Charles Bolton, *Arkansas, 1800–1860: Remote and Restless* (Fayetteville: University of Arkansas Press, 1998); and John Gould Fletcher, *Arkansas* (Fayetteville: University of Arkansas Press, 1989).

14. A better mirror would be trial court records showing all cases, not just those that were appealed. Unfortunately, these records do not exist in most counties for this time period.

15. Some cases are, no doubt, mentioned only because of the reviewer's own quirky interests.

16. Robert A. Kagan, Bliss Cartwright, Lawrence M. Friedman, and Stanton Wheeler, "The Business of State Supreme Courts, 1870–1970," *Stanford Law Review* 30 (1977): 44.

CHAPTER 1

"A Hegemonic Function of the Law": An Introduction

1. Wythe Holt, "Now and Then: The Uncertain State of Nineteenth-Century American Legal History," *Indiana Law Review* 7 (1974): 113.

2. Wyatt-Brown, *Southern Honor*, 3.

3. Ibid., 15.

4. Ariela J. Gross, *Double Character: Slavery and Mastery in the Antebellum Southern Courtroom* (Athens: University of Georgia Press, 2000), 47–48.

5. Wyatt-Brown, *Southern Honor*, 14–15, 22.

6. Eugene D. Genovese, *The Political Economy of Slavery: Studies in the Economy and Society of the Slave South*, 2nd ed. (Hanover, CT: Wesleyan University Press, 1989), 28.

7. Wyatt-Brown, *Southern Honor*, 369.

8. Eugene D. Genovese, *Roll, Jordan, Roll: The World the Slaves Made* (New York: Random House, 1976), 27.

9. Ibid.

10. Genovese, *The Political Economy of Slavery*, 8. Southerners drew support from some northern supporters of slavery. For example, Bishop John Henry Hopkins, presiding bishop of the Episcopal Church, defended slavery as based on biblical teachings: "Where is the 'law' which is higher than the code laid down by the Deity? Where is the rule of morals which shall claim supremacy over the Word of God?" John Henry Hopkins, *The American Citizen: His Rights and Duties According to the Spirit of the Constitution of the United States* (New York: Pudney and Russell, 1857), 125.

11. Gross, *Double Character*, 49–50.

12. Edward L. Ayers, *Vengeance and Justice: Crime and Punishment in the 19th-Century American South* (New York: Oxford University Press, 1984), 31, quoting Wilber J. Cash, *The Mind of the South* (New York: Vintage Book Reprint, 1969), 31–32.

13. James W. Ely Jr. and David J. Bodenhamer, "Regionalism and the Legal History of the South," in *Ambivalent Legacy: A Legal History of the South*, ed. James W. Ely Jr. and David J. Bodenhamer (Jackson: University Press of Mississippi, 1984), 19.

14. United States v. Dickinson, *Hempstead's Reports* 1. The territorial legislature had provided for this punishment in the criminal law. See Act of Nov. 4, 1808. The report indicates that the governor pardoned the defendant and the sentence was not carried out.

15. University of Arkansas at Little Rock, William H. Bowen School of Law, "Arkansas Territorial Briefs and Records," http://www.law.ualr.libguide.com/records and briefs (accessed December 20, 2015).

16. Elizabeth Gaspar Brown, "Law and Government in the Louisiana Purchase: 1803–1804," *Wayne State Law Review* 2 (1956): 178.

17. Dueling among planters and politicians was, according to Edward L. Ayers, "the most rationalized manifestation of a set of values accepted in every part and by every class of the antebellum South." It was the "heart of honor." See Ayers, *Vengeance and Justice*, 15–16.

18. Fletcher, *Arkansas*, 64–65. Also see Brown, *The Life of Albert Pike*, 162–64. Albert Pike was one of the attorneys engaged by the local prosecutor, John Clendenin, to assist in the prosecution of John Wilson.

19. Arnold, *Unequal Laws*, 183.

20. Henry R. Schoolcraft, quoted in Arnold, *Unequal Laws*, 184.

21. Ibid.

22. Ibid., 186

23. Thomas Nuttall, *A Journal of Travels into the Arkansas Territory during the Year 1819* (Fayetteville: University of Arkansas Press, 1999), 179.

24. Ibid., 248–49.

25. United States v. Dickinson, *Hempstead's Reports* 1.

26. Nuttall added praise for the "penitentiary law of confinement" successfully adopted in New York and Pennsylvania, as an "improvement in jurisprudence, which deserves to be adopted in every part of the United States." See Nuttall, *A Journal of Travels*, 248.

27. Fletcher, *Arkansas*, 55.

28. Ibid. For more detail on legal developments in the pre-1819 period, see Arnold, *Unequal Laws*. Also see Foster, "Courts and Lawyers on the Arkansas Frontier," 543.

29. Waddy W. Moore, "Some Aspects of Crime and Punishment on the Arkansas Frontier," *Arkansas Historical Quarterly* 23 (1964): 50–64. Not the least of these difficulties was that the locations of county seats changed frequently (ibid., 61–62).

30. Smith, "Arkansas Advocacy," 452–54.

31. Diane D. Blair, *Arkansas Politics and Government: Do the People Rule?* (Lincoln: University of Nebraska Press, 1988), 24–30.

32. Fletcher, *Arkansas*, 91. The term "fine Arkansas gentlemen" is derived from a song composed by Albert Pike to honor Elias Rector, a prominent "plantation magnate" of the antebellum years. See Fletcher, *Arkansas*, 103–8.

33. Blair, *Arkansas Politics and Government*, 24.

34. Ibid., 29. The Ozark highlanders may not have fit the "traditionalistic" political culture description because their "aggressively independent" and deliberate "quest for remoteness" may have resulted in anarchistic attitudes toward government and, in particular, legal institutions. Blair, *Arkansas Politics and Government*, 31.

35. Thomas A. DeBlack "The Rights and Rank to Which We Are Entitled: Arkansas in the Early Statehood Period," in *Arkansas: A Narrative History*, ed. Whayne et al., 117–18.

36. Bolton, *Arkansas, 1800–1860*, 53–54.

37. Carl Moneyhon, *The Impact of the Civil War and Reconstruction on Arkansas: Persistence in the Midst of Ruin* (Fayetteville: University of Arkansas Press, 2002), 36–37.

38. Ibid., 53.

39. Ibid., 80.

40. Genovese, *Roll, Jordan, Roll*, 4. According to Genovese, this paternalism grew out of need to "discipline and morally justify a system of exploitation," not out of "benevolence, kindness and good cheer (ibid., 4)."

41. Brown, *A Life of Albert Pike*, 107.

42. Ibid.

43. Ibid., 282.

44. Ibid.

45. Ibid., 284–85.

46. Ibid., 291.

47. Martin J. Horwitz, *The Transformation of American Law, 1780–1860* (Cambridge: Harvard University Press, 1977), 2.

48. Ibid., 3.

49. Ibid., 23–25.

50. Lawrence M. Friedman, *A History of American Law,* 3rd ed. (New York: Simon and Schuster, 2007), 121–22.

51. Ibid., 70.

52. James Willard Hurst, *Law and the Conditions of Freedom in the Nineteenth-Century United States* (Madison: University of Wisconsin Press, 1967), 7, 10.

53. Ibid., 33.

54. Genovese, *The Political Economy of Slavery*, 27.

55. Ibid.

56. Ibid., 24.

57. Ely and Bodenhamer, "Regionalism and the Legal History of the South," 7–9.

58. Ibid., 4.

59. Ibid., 7.

60. Ibid.

61. Ibid., 9–10.

62. Tony A. Freyer, "Law and the Antebellum Southern Economy: An Interpretation," in *Ambivalent Legacy: A Legal History of the South*, ed. James W. Ely Jr. and David J. Bodenhamer (Jackson: University Press of Mississippi, 1984), 49–68.

63. Ibid., 63.

64. David Y. Thomas, *Arkansas and Its People: A History, 1541–1930,* vol. 1 (New York: American Historical Society, 1930), 86–89.

65. Bolton, *Arkansas, 1800–1860*, 14.

66. Ely and Bodenhamer, "Regionalism," 5.

67. Ibid., 6.

68. Genovese, *The Political Economy of Slavery*, 27.

69. Hugh Collins, *Marxism and Law* (New York: Oxford University Press, 1984), 43.

70. Ibid., 29, 43, 73.

71. Olufemi Taiwo, *Legal Naturalism: A Marxist Theory of Law* (Ithaca, NY: Cornell University Press, 1996), 88–89.

72. S. Charles Bolton, *Territorial Ambition: Land and Society in Arkansas, 1800–1840* (Fayetteville: University of Arkansas Press, 1993), 57, quoting the *Arkansas Advocate* of January 1831.

73. Bolton, *Arkansas, 1800–1860*, 53–54.

74. Jeannie M. Whayne, "The Turbulent Path to Statehood: Arkansas Territory, 1803–1836," in *Arkansas: A Narrative History*, ed. Whayne et al., 93.

75. Bolton, *Arkansas, 1800–1860*, 61.

76. Thomas A. DeBlack "Prosperity and Peril: Arkansas in the Late Antebellum Period," in *Arkansas: A Narrative History*, ed. Whayne et al., 141.

77. Ibid.

78. Orville W. Taylor, *Negro Slavery in Arkansas* (Fayetteville: University of Arkansas Press, 2000), 47–58.

79. Ibid., 58.

80. Bolton, *Arkansas, 1800–1860*, 57.

81. Thomas A. DeBlack, "'The Rights and Rank to Which We Are Entitled': Arkansas in the Early Statehood Period," in *Arkansas: A Narrative History*, ed. Whayne et al., 111.

82. Bolton, *Arkansas, 1800–1860*, 56.

83. Ibid.

84. DeBlack, "'The Rights and Rank,'" 111.

85. Bolton, *Arkansas, 1800–1860*, 59–61.

86. Friedman, *A History*, 169.

87. Ibid., 170.

88. Bolton, *Arkansas, 1800–1860*, 16–17.

89. Friedman, *A History*, 170.

90. Hurst, *Law and the Conditions of Freedom*, 5.

91. Friedman, *A History*, 171.

92. Horwitz, *Transformation*, 31.

93. Friedman, *A History*, 177.

94. Horwitz, *Transformation*, 31.

95. Friedman, *A History*, 196–97.

96. Ibid., 197.

97. Ibid., 238.

98. Moneyhon, *The Impact of the Civil War*, 28–33.

99. Ibid.

100. Ibid., 34.

101. Ibid., 90.

102. Ibid., 240.

103. Taylor, *Negro Slavery in Arkansas*, 47.

104. Ibid., 48.

105. Ibid., 50.

106. Ibid., 93–94.

107. Ibid., 118–30.

108. Genovese, *The Political Economy of Slavery*, 28.

109. Bolton, *Arkansas, 1800–1860*, 64–65.

110. Taylor, *Negro Slavery in Arkansas*, 130.

111. Bolton, *Arkansas, 1800–1860*, 138.

112. Ely and Bodenhamer, "Regionalism," 5.

113. Michael Grossberg, *Governing the Hearth: Law and the Family in Nineteenth-Century America* (Chapel Hill: University of North Carolina Press, 1985), 17.

114. Ibid., 30.

115. Horwitz, *Transformation*, 173.

116. Freyer, "Law and the Antebellum Southern Economy," 59.

117. Horwitz, *Transformation*, 160, 173.

118. Ayers, *Vengeance and Justice*, 141.

119. Kenneth M. Stampp, *America in 1857: A Nation on the Brink* (New York: Oxford University Press, 1990), 42.

120. Ibid., 39, 42.

121. Ely and Bodenhamer, *Ambivalent Legacy*, 20–21.

122. See, e.g., William E. Nelson, "Emerging Notions of Modern Criminal Law in the Revolutionary Era: A Historical Perspective," *New York University Law Review* 42 (1967): 452.

123. 23 Ark. 161 (1865).

124. Moneyhon, *The Impact of the Civil War*, 263.

125. Ibid., 268–69.

126. Ibid., 4.

127. Kagan et al., "The Business of State Supreme Courts," 123.

128. Ibid., 153. In her study of trial court records in five Black Belt states, and, in particular, those in Adams County, Mississippi, Ariela J. Gross concludes: "Cases appealed to high courts were more representative of the typical trial than one might imagine today. All five state supreme courts were required to hear every appeal that came before them, unlike today, when only a small fraction of appeals are accepted for a hearing. . . . A comparison of the five-state sample with Adams County sample of unappealed cases revealed no important differences; appealed suits did not even involve larger amounts of money, nor were the appellants who took cases to a higher court themselves wealthier than other plaintiffs." Gross, *Double Character*, 7.

CHAPTER 2

"Peculiar Province and Duty": Organization, Procedures, and Trends in the Early Arkansas Courts

1. Kagan et al., "The Business of State Supreme Courts," 204.

2. Josiah H. Shinn, *Pioneers and Makers of Arkansas* (Baltimore: Genealogical Publishing Company, 1967), 202–6.

3. Ibid., 93–94.

4. Ibid., 201.

5. John Hallum, *Biographical and Pictorial History of Arkansas* (Albany, NY: Weed Parsons and Company, Printers, 1887), 137.

6. Ibid., 120.

7. For an intriguing look at this practice, see Diana Sherwood, "Code Duello in Arkansas," *Arkansas Law Review* 31 (1977), 449.

8. Smith, "Arkansas Advocacy," 449.

9. Arnold, *Unequal Laws*, 198–99.

10. Ibid., 58.

11. Ibid., 175.

12. Ibid., 58.

13. Ibid., 138.

14. Ibid., 143–46.

15. Ibid., 140–42.

16. Ibid., 142–48.

17. Elizabeth Gaspar Brown, "Law and Government in the 'Louisiana Purchase': 1803–1804," *Wayne State Law Review* 2 (1956): 173.

18. Arnold, *Unequal Laws*, 149–50.

19. Ibid., 174-175. Arkansas was permitted to continue slavery as a part of the Missouri Compromise. Bolton, *Territorial Ambition*, 24.

20. Ibid., 6.

21. *Hempstead's Reports* 27.

22. *Hempstead's Reports* 105.

23. Arnold, *Unequal Laws*, 193.

24. The issue was raised again in an early case after statehood, Small v. Strong, 2 Ark 198 (1838).

25. Hallum, *Biographical and Pictorial History*, 42–63.

26. Thomas, *Arkansas and Its People*, 9.

27. Ibid., 92.

28. Blair, *Arkansas Politics and Government*, 24–30.

29. Fletcher, *Arkansas*, 91. The term "fine Arkansas gentlemen" is derived from a song composed by Albert Pike to honor Elias Rector, a prominent "plantation magnate" of the antebellum years. (ibid., 103–8).

30. Blair; *Arkansas Politics and Government,* 24.

31. Ibid., 29. The Ozark highlanders may not have fit the "traditionalistic" political culture description because their "aggressively independent" and deliberate "quest for remoteness" may have resulted in anarchistic attitudes toward government and, in particular, legal institutions. Blair, *Arkansas Politics and Government,* 31.

32. DeBlack, "'The Rights and Rank,'" 117–18.

33. Bolton, *Arkansas, 1800–1860*, 53–54.

34. Moneyhon, *The Impact of the Civil War*, 36–37.

35. Donald P. McNeilly, *The Old South Frontier: Cotton Plantations and the Formation of Arkansas Society* (Fayetteville: University of Arkansas Press, 2000), 180.

36. Ibid., 53.

37. Ibid., 80.

38. Thomas, *Arkansas and Its People*, 96.

39. Ibid., 105.

40. Ibid., 111.

41. Ibid., 119.

42. Thomas A. DeBlack, *With Fire and Sword: Arkansas, 1861–1874* (Fayetteville: University of Arkansas Press, 2003), 105.

43. Ibid., 106.

44. 24 Ark. 161 (1865). The third member elected was Elisha Baxter, who did not serve. He was selected by the legislature as US senator but was never allowed to serve in that capacity.

45. The legislature elected in 1866 may have contributed to the later inclusion of Arkansas in the congressional declaration of Reconstruction. That legislature declined to ratify the Fourteenth Amendment to the US Constitution because it called for "equal protection of the law" and expressed confidence

in President Andrew Johnson; both actions were repugnant to the hardliners in congress. Paige E. Mullholian, "Arkansas General Assembly of 1866 and Its Effect on Reconstruction," *Arkansas Historical Quarterly* 20, (1961): 331–43.

46. Eugene G. Feistman, "Radical Disfranchisement in Arkansas, 1867–1868," *Arkansas Historical Quarterly* 12 (1953): 127–28.

47. Ibid.,129; 14 Stat. 428–429 (March 2, 1867).

48. 15 Stat. 2–5 (March 23, 1867).

49. 15 Stat. 14–16 (July 19, 1867).

50. Feistman, "Radical Disfranchisement," 134–36.

51. Ibid., 138.

52. For a complete list of delegates, see Feistman, "Radical Disfranchisement," 161–63.

53. Feistman, "Radical Disfranchisement," 152.

54. Ibid., 153.

55. Ibid., 155.

56. Ibid.

57. Ibid., 154.

58. Stevenson, *Arkansas Territory*, 39.

59. Jesse Turner, "The Constitution of 1836," *Arkansas Historical Association* 3 (1911): 106.

60. Constitution of 1836, Article VI, § 7.

61. Constitution of 1836, Article VI, § 2

62. Stevenson, *Arkansas Territory,* 25.

63. Constitution of 1836, Article VI, § 3.

64. Ibid.

65. Ibid.

66. Constitution of 1836, Article VI, § 10.

67. Constitution of 1836, Article VI, § 6.

68. Stevenson, *Arkansas Territory*, 24.

69. State v. Ashley, 1 Ark. 279 (1939); and State v. Ashley, 1 Ark. 513 (1839).

70. 5 Ark. 709 (1844).

71. 3 Ark. 532 (1841).

72. Robert Frail, Ex Parte, 3 Ark. 561 (1841): 564.

73. 1 Ark. 21 (1837). "Mandamus" is an order to a public official to perform a legally required act or to refrain from an illegal action. See current law at Ark. Code Ann. § 16-115-101.

74. Hawkins v. The Governor, 1 Ark J70 (1839).

75. 5 U.S. 137, 1 Cranch 137, 2 L. Ed. 60 (1803).

76. 1 Ark. at 591.

77. Friedman, *A History*, 299.

78. Ibid.

79. Semon v. Hill, 7 Ark. 76 (1846).

80. Ibid., 74.

81. 6 Ark. 317 (1845).

82. Ibid., 327.

83. Ibid., 366.

84. 11 Ark. 627 (1851).

85. Sparks v. Beaver, 11 Ark. 630 (1851).

86. Moneyhon, *The Impact of the Civil War*, 103–4.

87. Ibid., 107.

88. Ibid., 110.

89. Ibid., 111.

90. These cases are Trapnall v. Burton, 24 Ark. 371 (1866); Rice v. Harrell, 24 Ark. 402 (1866); Marshall v. Green, 24 Ark. 410 (1866); Branch v. Mitchell, 25 Ark. 431 (1866); Busby v. Treadwell, 24 Ark. 456 (1866); Twomby v. Kimbrough, 24 Ark. 459 (1866); and Gaines v. Craig, 24 Ark. 477 (1866).

91. 24 Ark. 161.

92. Fletcher, *Arkansas*, 203.

CHAPTER 3

Finding "Repose" from the "Nagging Concern" of Title Insecurity: Cases, Controversies, and Conflicts Relating to Land Titles

1. Charles S. Sydnor, "The Southerner and the Laws," *Journal of Southern History* 6 (1940): 8.

2. Ibid.

3. Ibid.

4. Ely and Bodenhamer, "Regionalism," 4.

5. Friedman, *A History*, 172.

6. Ibid., 176.

7. Ibid., 177.

8. Ibid., 171.

9. Ibid., 172.

10. Ibid., 176.

11. Ibid., 310.

12. Ibid. Some states later added a requirement of payment of taxes. "An adverse claimant was not suppose to be a mere squatter (ibid., 310)."

13. John G. Sprankling, "An Environmental Critique of Adverse Possession," *Cornell Law Review* 79 (1994): 843.

14. Bolton, *Arkansas, 1800–1860*, 15.

15. Paul W. Gates, "Federal Land Policies in the Southern Public Land States," *Agricultural History* 53 (1979): 225.

16. Whayne, "The Turbulent Path to Statehood," 92.

17. For example, all but 5 percent of the military bounty lands was held by speculators. Gates, "Federal Land Policies," 225.

18. Craig Thompson Friend, "Liberty Is Pioneering: An American Birthright," *OAH Magazine of History*, 19 May 2005, 16.

19. Ibid.

20. John R. Van Atta, "'A Lawless Rabble': Henry Clay and the Cultural Politics of Squatters Rights, 1832–1841," *Journal of the Early Republic* 27 (Fall 2008): 339.

21. Mark T. Kanazawa, "Possession Is Nine Points of the Law: The Political Economy of Early Public Land Disposal," *Explorations in Economic History* 3 (1996): 234.

22. Ibid., 231. Previously, special exemptions on a selective basis had been granted, especially in Ohio and Mississippi.

23. Friedman, *A History*, 169; Friend, "Liberty Is Pioneering," 19.

24. Friedman, *A History*, 170.

25. Friend, "Liberty Is Pioneering," 16.

26. Van Atta, "'A Lawless Rabble,'" 363.

27. S. Charles Bolton, "Jeffersonian Indian Removal and the Emergence of Arkansas Territory," in *A Whole Country in Commotion: The Louisiana Purchase and the American Southwest*, ed. Patrick G. Williams, S. Charles Bolton, and Jeannie M. Whayne (Fayetteville: University of Arkansas Press, 2005), 87.

28. Jeannie M. Whayne, "A Shifting Middle Ground," in *A Whole Country in Commotion*, ed. Williams, Bolton, and Whayne, 75.

29. Whayne, "The Turbulent Path to Statehood," 93.

30. The story by Thomas James in *Three Years among the Indians and New Mexicans* is related in some detail in Fletcher, *Arkansas*, 56–64. The name "Arkopolis" was apparently suggested but never used for the new capital, which became known as "Little Rock," referring to the first rock outcropping on cliffs near the Arkansas River, moving east to west.

31. See Robert L. Jones and Pauline H. Jones, "Stephen F. Austin in Arkansas," *Arkansas Historical Quarterly* 25 (1966): 345–46.

32. *Hempstead's Reports* 3.

33. Lonnie J. White, *Politics on the Southwestern Frontier: Arkansas Territory, 1819–1836* (Memphis: Memphis State University Press, 1964), 30-31.

34. Francis Ross, "Some Arkansas Cases," *Arkansas Lawyer*,19 (April 1985), 75-77, quoting Dallas T. Herndon, *Why Little Rock Was Born* (Little Rock, 1933), 139–40.

35. White, *Politics on the Southwestern Frontier*, 32.

36. United State v. Samperyac and Stewart, *Hempstead's Reports* 118.

37. *Hempstead's Reports* 118.

38. *Hempstead's Reports* 118 at 144.

39. United States v. Sampeyreac and Stewart, 7 *Peters* 222 (1833). For some reason, the report on the case in the Supreme Court uses a different spelling of "Samperyac."

40. Wynn v. Morris, 16 Ark. 414 (1855); Wynn v. Garland, 16 Ark. 440 (1855).

41. 16 Ark. at 438. Apparently, Justice English was mistaken in his prediction.

42. The court detailed a colorful account of Mrs. Taylor's "clandestine" flight from the state to get to the "Spanish country" in order to elude service. The reasons for her flight were not given. 16 Ark. at 426.

43. 16 Ark. at 438.

44. Ibid., 474.

45. 12 Ark. 296 (1851). The transcript of this case was 856 pages! It was set out in anticipation of an appeal to the United States Supreme Court, which did occur.

46. 12 Ark. at 308–9.

47. Cunningham v. Ashley and Beebe, 13 Ark 653 (1853).

48. Cunningham v. Ashley, 16 Ark. 168 (1855).

49. Cunningham v. Ashley, 16 Ark. 181 (1855). Cunningham died before the litigation was concluded.

50. Cunningham v. Brumback, 23 Ark. 336 (1861) at 340.

51. Ibid., 338.

52. Beebe's role in the saga was not quite over. In 1883 the attorney general filed suit in United States Circuit Court for the Eastern District in Arkansas, alleging that the original "pre-emption float claims" recognized in Beebe had been procured by fraud. The allegation was that certain New Madrid certificates vested in W. M. O'Hara (who subsequently conveyed these to, among others, Chester Ashley) had predated the Beebe patent and the lands (about 480 acres upon which Little Rock was partly built) were legally appropriated to the New Madrid certificate holders. The government argued that the United States was not bound by any statute of limitations nor barred from asserting a public right. The case was heard by the United States Supreme Court in 1888. (Beebe was deceased.) The court inspected the record in the case and determined that the government was not the real party in interest but had filed the suit at the behest of private individuals who had acquired presumptive interests in the land by a series of transfers and devisees. (These individuals were residents of Galesburg, Illinois, and Troy, New York.) The attorneys for the claimants had, in fact, managed the case. Since the government was merely a "conduit" for the private litigants, the court applied principles of equity to give effect to the statute of limitations, "laches," and lapse of time to dismiss the suit. The court stated: "More than forty-five years ago, the complainants in this bill could have instituted their action. The death of the parties charged with the fraud, and also of most, if not all, of the witnesses having personal knowledge of the transaction, the fact that a city has been built upon the land in question, the occupation of large portions of it by hundreds of innocent purchasers, the homesteads of many families covering other portions of it, the uninterrupted possession maintained for more than a generation, are resting upon faith in the patent issued by the United States Government, constitute reasons more than sufficient for the refusal of the court to set aside such patent at the suit of a party who has so long slept upon his alleged rights." United States v. Beebe, 127 U.S. 338 (1888): 348.

53. At one point Justice McLean referred to Cunningham as carrying on the controversy with "a commendable energy." 13 Ark. at 665.

54. 12 Ark. 9 (1851).

55. 4 Stat. 473 (March 3, 1831). This act was followed by subsequent land grants for other public purposes.

56. 13 Ark. at 34–35.

57. 17 Ark. 608 (1857).

58. Ibid., 610.

59. Ibid., 622. "Champerty" is involved where an attorney agrees to receive as compensation part of the litigation recovery; the "purchase" of a lawsuit by the attorney. This was a common law concept.

60. Ibid., 635.

61. Ibid., 639.

62. Ibid., 702–3.

63. Ibid., 703–4.

64. 20 Ark. 359 (1859).

65. 20 Ark. at 379.

66. Bolton, *Arkansas, 1800–1860*, 5. Hot Springs (near the Ouachita River) became a noted health resort and was eventually preserved as Hot Springs National Park. See Ruth Irene Jones, "Hot Springs: Ante-Bellum Watering Place," *Arkansas Historical Quarterly* 14 (1955): 3–4. "Thermopolis" was the name first used for the village.

67. 16 Ark. 9 (1855). These were the heirs of Ludoricus Belding, who established the first hotel at the springs in 1828. Jones, "Hot Springs," 8.

68. Burke v. Gaines, 16 Ark. 27 (1855), was decided on the same basis.

69. Jeannie M. Whayne, "Henry Massie Rector," in *Arkansas Biography*, ed. Nancy A. Williams (Fayetteville: University of Arkansas Press, 2000), 234.

70. Rector v. Gaines, 19 Ark. 70 (1857) at 81.

71. Other cases following this principle were Hunter v. Gaines, 19 Ark. 92 (1857), Hale v. Gaines, 19 Ark. 94 (1857), Butler v. Gaines, 19 Ark. 95 (1857), and Sweeptzer v. Gaines, 19 Ark. 96 (1857).

72. 19 Ark. at 84.

73. 19 Ark. 94 (1857).

74. 19 Ark. 96 (1857).

75. Gaines v. Hale, 16 Ark. 9 (1855).

76. N. Williams, *Arkansas Biography*, 234.

77. Brown, *A Life of Albert Pike*, 449.

78. Ibid.

79. Ibid.

80. After the Civil War, Rector attempted to pursue his claims again. He, along with other claimants, brought suit in the US Court of Claims, and it was heard in 1874. The government took the position that the original interpretation was correct; the lands in that region were unsurveyed in 1820 and, therefore, not authorized to be sold. No New Madrid location could be made at that time, and since it had not been perfected by 1832, the reservation took precedence. Rector, represented by Albert Pike, argued to no avail that his father, Elias, had done everything he could to perfect the claim. The US Court of Claims seemed reluctant to reverse the interpretation given the act by the attorney general in 1820 and, also, recognized that to rule otherwise would contradict a number of decisions of the United States Supreme Court. (Brown, *A Life of Albert Pike*, 450–451.) Hot Springs Cases, 10 Ct. 345 (1874). The Supreme Court addressed the issue in 1876 and confirmed the decree of the US Court of Claims. (Hot Springs Cases, 92 U.S. 698 [1876].) Rector's claim had never been perfected, so the reservation of 1832 applied. During the pendency of this litigation, a compromise had been reached so that Gaines controlled the lower part of the valley; Hale, the center; and Rector, the upper. They, in turn, leased the land to others, many of whom ultimately received title when a commission was set up in 1877 to finally resolve title questions. (Jones, "Hot Springs," 25.) These tenants argued, successfully, that Rector had been a trespasser on public land, so the leases were not binding, and that they, as actual occupiers, had the

better claim. Walter L. Brown, "The Henry M. Rector Claim to the Hot Springs of Arkansas," *Arkansas Historical Quarterly* 15 (1956): 281–92.

81. Whayne, "The Turbulent Path to Statehood," 97.

82. Ibid., 99–100. Also see Joseph Patrick Key, "Outcasts upon the World," in *A Whole Country in Commotion*, ed. Williams, Bolton, and Whayne, 100.

83. Whayne, "The Turbulent Path to Statehood," 98–99. Also see Lonnie J. White, "Arkansas Territorial Indian Affairs," *Arkansas Historical Quarterly* 21 (1962): 203, 208.

84. Whayne, "The Turbulent Path to Statehood," 99.

85. Key, "Outcasts," 95–96, quoting, in part, a letter written by one of the early arrivals.

86. Dale E. Edward, "Arkansas and the Cherokees," *Arkansas Historical Quarterly* 8 (1940): 96.

87. Daniel F. Littlefield Jr. and Lonnie E. Underhill, "The Cherokee Agency Reserve, 1828–1886," *Arkansas Historical Quarterly* 31 (1972): 178–79.

88. 1 Ark. 313 (1839).

89. 9 Stat. 520 (September 28, 1850).

90. Sidney F. Ansbacher and Joe Knetsch, "Negotiating the Maze: Tracing Historical Title Claims in Spanish Land Grants and Swamp and Overflowed Lands Act," *Journal of Land Use and Environmental Law* 17 (2002): 353.

91. Robert W. Harrison and Walter M. Kollmorgan, "Land Reclamation in Arkansas under the Swamp Land Grant of 1850," *Arkansas Historical Quarterly* 6 (1947): 371–72.

92. William E Colby, "III Mining Law in Recent Years: Land Grants to States (Cont'd), Swamp and Overflowed Lands," *California Law Review* 37 (1959): 595.

93. Harrison and Kollmorgan, "Land Reclamation," 374.

94. Ibid., 377.

95. Quoted in Ibid., 378.

96. Ibid., 379.

97. Ibid., 381–82.

98. Bolton, *Arkansas, 1800–1860*, 16–17.

99. Following the Civil War, this action was challenged on constitutional grounds. The effort at untangling the land titles continued into the new century. Harrison and Kollmorgan, "*Land Reclamation*," 387–88, 405, 412–15.

100. Harrison and Kollmorgan, "*Land Reclamation*," 416.

101. Hempstead Land Agent v. Underhill's Heirs, 20 Ark. 337 (1859).

102. 13 Ark. 198 (1853).

103. Ibid., 206.

104. State v. Arkansas v. County Court of Crittenden County, 19 Ark. 360 (1858).

105. Ibid., 364. Also see Barnard v. Lafayette County, 19 Ark. 509 (1858).

106. McGehee v. Mathis, Sheriff, 21 Ark. 40 (1860).

107. Ibid., 58–59.

108. Ibid., 58.

109. Ibid., 59.

110. McDermott v. Mathis, Sheriff, 21 Ark. 60 (1860). Four additional cases were resolved on the same basis.

111. 20 Ark 100 (1859).

112. 20 Ark 337 (1859).

113. Underhill Heirs v. Howard 20 Ark 663 (1859).

114. 22 Ark 344 (1860).

115. A similar result was found in Cheatham v. Phillips, 23 Ark 80 (1861), where the purchaser, Cheatham, was caught in the 1853 change-over in authority.

116. 23 Ark 313 (1861).

117. 23 Ark 653 (1861).

118. United States v. Pillerin et al., 13 How. 261, 54 U.S. 9 (1851). The court confirmed previous rulings that French grants of land in Louisiana made after the territory was ceded to Spain are void unless confirmed by the Spanish government before the cession to the United States. Continuous possession from the time of the grants would be the foundation for an assertion of title.

119. The other swampland cases included *Gaster's Heirs v. Gaines* (23 Ark. 712 [1861]), in which the court re-emphasized that the presentation of accounts for levee work with an application to purchase lands was not a sale. It might be subsequently accepted or rejected by the swampland commissioners. A similar outcome was determined in *Beckham v. Worthen* (23 Ark. 270 [1861]). The only difference was that the certificate of application made reference to the deposit of scrip in payment. This was not sufficient to evidence a sale.

120. 24 Ark. 33 (1862).

121. 24 Ark. 38 (1862).

122. 24 Ark. 40 (1862).

123. 24 Ark. 109 (1863).

124. Schaer v. Gliston, 24 Ark. 137 (1863).

125. Pike v. Underhill, 24 Ark. 124 (1863).

126. 24 Ark. 431 (1866). This is one of the seven opinions of the Confederate court, rendered before 1864, that was published by order of the court in 1866.

127. 24 Ark. 402 (1866), rendered before 1864.

128. 26 Ark. 54 (1870).

129. 27 Ark. 152 (1871).

130. 27 Ark. 385 (1872).

131. Ibid., 391.

132. 28 Ark. 235 (1873).

133. Ibid., 236.

134. Van Atta, "A Lawless Rabble," 356.

135. Kanazawa, "Possession," 247–48.

136. Friend, "Liberty Is Pioneering," 16.

137. 12 Ark. 33 (U.S. Sup. Ct. Opinion by Justice McLean).

138. Paul Finkelman, "John McLean: Moderate Abolitionist and Supreme Court Politician," *Vanderbilt Law Review* 62 (2009): 521.

139. Ibid., 536.

140. John G. Sprankling, "The Anti-Wilderness Bias in American Property Law," *University of Chicago Law Review* 63 (1996): 538–39.

141. Ibid.

142. Ibid., 819.

143. 17 Ark. 608 (1857).

144. 23 Ark. 336 (1861).

145. Brown, *A Life of Albert Pike*, 37, 120–21, 192.

146. Ibid., 42–43.

147. Thomas A. DeBlack, "Prosperity and Peril: Arkansas in the Late Antebellum Period," in *Arkansas: A Narrative History*, ed. Jeannie M. Whayne, Thomas A. Deblack, George Sabo III, and Morris S. Arnold (Fayetteville: University of Arkansas Press, 2002), 157–58.

CHAPTER 4
"Coon Skins and Peltry": Cases, Controversies, and Conflicts Related to Banks and Banking

1. Cited in Timothy S. Huebner, *The Southern Judicial Tradition: State Judges and Sectional Distinctiveness, 1790–1890* (Athens: University of Georgia Press, 1999), chapter 2: "John Catron, Jacksonian Jurisprudence, and the Expansion of the South," 51.

2. Ibid., 61–63.

3. Ibid., 69.

4. Charles Sellers, *The Market Revolution: Jacksonian America, 1815–1846* (New York: Oxford University Press, 1991), 70.

5. Freyer, "Law and the Antebellum Southern Economy," 54–55.

6. Tony A. Freyer, *Producers versus Capitalists: Constitutional Conflict in Antebellum America* (Charlottesville: University Press of Virginia, 1994), 38.

7. Ibid.

8. Constitution of the State of Arkansas, 1836, Article VII, "Establishment of Banks," Section 1.

9. Fletcher, *Arkansas*, 64–65; Philip Durham, "The Desperado as Hero," *Arkansas Historical Quarterly* 14 (Autumn 1964): 347. As an interesting sidelight, Absolom Fowler, one of the attorneys for Wilson, brought suit against Wilson to recover a $1,000 fee for defending him. Albert Pike and Frederick W. Trapnall testified for Fowler that the fee was reasonable. Chester Ashley testified for Wilson and indicated that he, too, had represented Wilson but for a fee of $500. He apparently believed $500 to be adequate since Wilson had employed four attorneys in the case. The matter was before the Arkansas Supreme Court on a question of proper venue. Wilson v. Fowler, 3 Ark. 463 (1841).

10. See the *Journal of the Proceedings of the Senate* (Tuesday, October 4, 1836), 51; and the Constitution of the State of Arkansas, Article VII, "Establishment of Banks," Section 1.

11. See Ed Stebbins, "Early Banking in Arkansas," *Arkansas Historical Quarterly* 13, no. 4 (1954): 409–13. Also see Bolton, *Arkansas, 1800–1860*, 56.

12. Larry Schweikart, "Southern Banks and Economic Growth in the Antebellum Period: A Reassessment," *Journal of Southern History* 53, no. 1 (1987): 19–36; also see Freyer, "Law and the Antebellum Southern Economy," 56.

13. James M. Woods, *Rebellion and Realignment: Arkansas's Road to Secession* (Fayetteville: University of Arkansas Press, 1987), 22.

14. *Journal of the Proceedings of the Senate* (Tuesday, October 4, 1836), 51.

15. Thomas, *Arkansas and Its People*, 91–92; Ted R. Worley, "The Arkansas State Bank: The Ante-Bellum Period," *Arkansas Historical Quarterly* 23 (Spring 1964): 65–73; Ted R. Worley, "The Control of the Real Estate Bank of the State of Arkansas, 1836–1855," *Mississippi Valley Historical Review* 37 (1950): 413–14.

16. *Journal of the Proceedings of the Senate* (Tuesday, November 7, 1837), 9–10.

17. Ibid., 68.

18. Ibid., 71.

19. *Journal of the Proceedings of the Senate* (Tuesday, November 14, 1837), 25.

20. *Journal of the Proceedings of the Senate* (Monday, November 13, 1837), 23–24.

21. Woods, *Rebellion and Realignment*, 22–23.

22. Worley, "The Arkansas State Bank," 66–67.

23. Ibid., 73.

24. Fletcher, *Arkansas*, 132–33.

25. State v. Ashley, 1 Ark. 279 (1839).

26. State v. Ashley, 1 Ark. 513 (1839).

27. 3 Ark. 570 (1841).

28. Thomas, *Arkansas and Its People*, 98.

29. "Governor's Message," *Appendix to the Journals of the House of Representatives* (November 8, 1842), 1–15.

30. "Report of the Committee on the Real Estate Bank," *Appendix to the Journals of the House of Representatives* (1842), 60–68.

31. Thomas, *Arkansas and Its People*, 99. These trustees included former governor James S. Conway and Carey Harris, the principal in the prior case. Ten of the trustees were members of the Central Board of the Real Estate Bank, which had made the assignment, and a number were themselves indebted to the Real Estate Bank. Conway, Ex Parte, 4 Ark. 302 (1842).

32. 4 Ark. 302 at 406–7.

33. Hallum, *Biographical and Pictorial History*, 79.

34. Ibid., 79–80.

35. 4 Ark. 44 (1842).

36. 4 Ark. 44 at 54–55.

37. See, e.g., Webster v. State Bank, 4 Ark. 423 (1842).

38. Mahony v. State Bank, 4 Ark. 620 (1842).

39. 5 Ark. 93 (1843).

40. 5 Ark. 558 (1844).

41. Brian G. Walton, "Ambrose Hundley Sevier in the United States Senate, 1836–1848," *Arkansas Historical Quarterly* 32 (1973): 38.

42. Ibid., 141.

43. Thomas, *Arkansas and Its People*, 99.

44. Ibid., 100.

45. 5 Ark. 595 (1844).

46. Hallum, *Biographical and Pictorial History*, 56–57.

47. 5 Ark. 595 (1844).

48. 6 Ark. 135 (1845).

49. Duncan v. Biscoe et al. Trustees R. E. Bank, 7 Ark. 175 (1846).

50. Roane et al. Trustees R. E. Bank v. Brodie, 7 Ark. 264 (1847).

51. 8 Ark. 236 (1847).

52. Woodruff v. Trapnall, 51 U.S. 190 (1850).

53. 9 Ark. 205 (1848).

54. 51 U.S. 218 (1850).

55. Stevenson, *Arkansas Territory*, 31.

56. Harry G. Heiss, "The Public Career of David Walker: The Antebellum Years" (MA thesis, University of Arkansas, 1983), 82–83.

57. Ibid., 85, 91–94.

58. Ibid., 94–96.

59. 11 Ark. 44 (1850).

60. 7 Ark. 175 (1846).

61. 11 Ark. 44 at 51.

62. 12 Ark. 321 (1851).

63. Hallum, *Biographical and Pictorial History*, 276–78.

64. 13 Ark. 563 (1853).

65. 51 U. S. 190 (1850).

66. Cotheal v. Biscoe et al., Trustees R. E. Bank, 13 Ark. 591 (1853); Cocks v. State Bank, 13 Ark. 592 (1853).

67. 15 Ark. 20 (1854).

68. Woodruff v. Trapnall, 51 U.S. 190 (1850); Danley v. Pike, 15 Ark. 141 (1854).

69. State v. Trustees of the Real Estate Bank of the State of Arkansas, "Bill in Chancery," reprinted in Senate Appendix, *Journal of the Proceedings of the Senate*, 1854, 315–47.

70. Hallum, *Biographical and Pictorial History*, 57, 367.

71. Heiss, "The Public Career," 117.

72. "Report of Gordon W. Peay," *Appendix to the Journal of the House of Representatives*, 1856, 142–71.

73. "Report of the Accountants of the Real Estate Bank of Arkansas," *Appendix to the Journal of the House of Representatives*, 1856, 173–369.

74. Ibid., 226.

75. "Report of the Joint Committee on the Affairs of the Bank of the State of Arkansas," *Appendix to the Journal of the House of Representatives*, 1856, 389–98.

76. *Journal of the House of Representatives* (Wednesday, November 8, 1859), 17–33. But not all bank matters had been resolved by the end of Governor Conway's term. The issue of the Holford bonds re-emerged after the Civil War. The Republicans attempted to fund all state debt in 1869 at face value, including the unpaid bonds. After Reconstruction, a constitutional amendment, which passed by a margin of eight to one, repudiated the state's obligation on these bonds along with levee and railroad bonds issued during the Republican era. This repudiation did not include the undisputed debt represented by bonds issued by the State Bank and the Real Estate Bank. These obligations were eventually paid, in part, by a special tax levied by the legislature and, in part, by a compromise reached with the federal government, which held state bonds issued by the long since defunct State Bank. Garland E. Bayliss, "Post Reconstruction Repudiation: Evil Blot or Financial Necessity?," *Arkansas Historical Quarterly* 23 (1964): 243–59. Also see Thomas, *Arkansas and Its People*, 271–373.

77. 24 Ark. 22 (1862).

78. 27 Ark. 425 (1872).

79. 27 Ark. at 435.

80. The court carefully distinguished the five hundred bonds "hypotheticated" for $121,356.59 (the "Holford" bonds), indicating that the 1861 legislation assumed these bonds were illegally disposed of and that the state was not liable for their payment. 27 Ark. at 439.

81. 27 Ark. 667 (1872).

82. Elsie M. Lewis, "Economic Conditions in Ante-Bellum Arkansas, 1850–1861," *Arkansas Historical Quarterly* 6 (1947): 268.

83. Ibid.

84. Ibid., 269.

85. Worley, "The Control of the Real Estate Bank," 426.

CHAPTER 5

"Pervasive Localism": Cases, Controversies, and Conflicts Relating to Transportation

1. Friedman, *A History*, 120; Hurst, *Law and the Conditions of Freedom*; Horwitz, *Transformation.*

2. Friedman, *A History*, 121.

3. Ibid., 125.

4. Ely and Bodenhamer, "Regionalism," 4.

5. Genovese, *The Political Economy of Slavery*, 31.

6. Moneyhon, *The Impact of the Civil War*, 25.

7. Ibid., 26.

8. Ibid., 83.

9. Mattie Brown, "River Transportation in Arkansas, 1819–1890," *Arkansas Historical Quarterly* 1 (1942): 342–43.

10. Walter Moffatt, "Transportation in Arkansas, 1819–1840," *Arkansas Historical Quarterly* 15 (1959): 19.

11. Ibid., 191.

12. State v. Stroope, 20 Ark. 202 (1859).

13. See, e.g., State v. Hester, 21 Ark. 193 (1860).

14. Lewis, "Economic Conditions," 270, quoting the *Washington Telegraph*, July 21, 1852.

15. Brown, *A Life of Albert Pike*, 285.

16. Moneyhon, *The Impact of the Civil War*, 87.

17. Ibid., 88–89.

18. Ibid., 87–90.

19. 20 Ark. 204 (1859).

20. Stephen E. Wood, "The Development of Arkansas Railroads, Part I," *Arkansas Historical Quarterly* 7 (1948): 104. This company was in conflict with the Cairo and Fulton Railway Company (and with Governor Conway) over the congressional land grants that were to fund the roads and, eventually, was unable to compete. The Cairo and Fulton appeared to be supported by the governor (ibid., 111).

21. Wood, "The Development of Arkansas Railroads," 107.

22. Ibid., 108, 112.

23. Ibid., 114.

24. Ibid., 115.

25. See Mississippi, Ouachita & Red River R.R. Co. v. Gaster, 20 Ark. 455 (1859); and five other cases at 20 Ark. 461 (1859), and one at 20 Ark. 462 (1859). Also see M.O. & R.R.R. Co. v. Gaster, 22 Ark. 361 (1860).

26. 20 Ark. 463 (1859).

27. This result was applied in sixteen other cases: in 20 Ark. 494 (1859) and in M.O. & R.R.R.R. Co. v. Turrentine, 21 Ark. 445 (1860).

28. 20 Ark. 443 (1859).

29. Following the war, state aid was granted to help in construction. The line was eventually consolidated with another line with former governor Powell Clayton as president. However, foreclosure and sale followed. Wood, "The Development of Arkansas Railroads," 137.

30. Wood, "The Development of Arkansas Railroads," 123.

31. 24 Ark. 96 (1863).

32. In Dartmouth College v. Woodward, 4 Wheaton 518 (1819), the United States Supreme Court determined that a private corporation, though created by state law, was entitled to protection of the contract clause of the United States Constitution. States could not later "impair" the obligation of the contract.

33. English & Wilshire v. Chicot County, 26 Ark. 454 (1871).

34. 28 Ark. 460 (1873).

35. Ibid., 463.

36. 27 Ark. 564 (1872).

37. Ibid., 566.

38. 20 Ark. 561 (1859).

39. 20 Ark. 573 (1859).

40. This was the issue in the famous United States Supreme Court case of *Charles River Bridge v. Warren Bridge* (11 Pet. 420 [1837]), in which the court determined that the granting of a second franchise did not interfere with vested rights of the first since nothing in the charter indicated that it was exclusive. Arkansas law was to the opposite effect.

41. 23 Ark. 514 (1861).

42. For a discussion of the postwar history of ferry franchises and toll bridges in Arkansas, see Michael B. Dougan, "The Doctrine of Creative Destruction: Ferry and Bridge Law in Arkansas," *Arkansas Historical Quarterly* 39 (1980): 136–58.

43. 25 Ark. 26 (1867).

44. 26 Ark. 464 (1871).

45. Ibid., 467.

46. 25 Ark. 474 (1869).

47. Ibid., 476.

48. 26 Ark. 3 (1870).

49. Reed v. Hanger, 20 Ark. 625 (1859).

50. Ibid., 628. The later conflicts between toll bridge operations and

holders of ferry franchises is reviewed in Dougan, "The Doctrine of Creative Destruction."

51. Memphis & St. Francis Plank Road Co. v. Rives, 21 Ark. 322 (1860).

52. Harry L. Watson, "Conflict and Collaboration: Yeomen, Slaveholders, and Politics in the Antebellum South," *Social History* 10 (1985): 273–98.

53. Ibid., 283.

54. Ibid.

55. Ibid., 294.

56. Ibid.

57. Moneyhon, *The Impact of the Civil War*, 85.

58. 19 Ark. 308 (1858).

59. DeBlack, "The Rights and Rank," 121.

60. Lewis, "Economic Conditions," 273.

61. Moneyhon, *The Impact of the Civil War*, 90.

62. McNeilly, *The Old South Frontier*, 180.

63. Ibid., 186.

CHAPTER 6

"Inspecting the Negro Foot": Cases, Controversies, and Conflicts Relating to Slaves and Slavery

1. Gross, *Double Character*, 3.

2. Ibid., citing, in particular, Genovese, *Roll, Jordan, Roll*. See also Mark V. Tushnet, *Slave Law in the American South:* State v. Mann *in History and Literature* (Lawrence: University Press of Kansas, 2003).

3. Tushnet, *Slave Law*, 82–83.

4. Ibid., 13.

5. Mark Tushnet, "Slave Law as Contract and Hierarchy," review of *Southern Slavery and the Law, 1619–1860*, by Thomas D. Morris, *Reviews in American History* 24 (1996): 590–95.

6. Ibid., 592.

7. Walter Johnson, "Inconsistency, Contradiction, and Complete Confusion: The Everyday Life of the Law of Slavery," Review of *Slavery and the Law, 1870–1860,* by Thomas D. Morris, *Law & Social Inquiry* 22, no. 2 (1997): 412; also see Horwitz, *Transformation*.

8. Thomas D. Morris, "Society Is Not Marked by Punctuality in the Payment of Debts: The Chattel Mortgages of Slaves," in *Ambivalent Legacy*, ed. Ely and Bodenhamer, 164–65.

9. Ibid., 155, 164–66.

10. Ibid., 149–50.

11. Ibid., 152.

12. Ibid., 153.

13. Claire Priest, "Creating an American Property Law: Alienability and Its Limits in American History," *Harvard Law Review* 120 (2006): 417–25.

14. Ibid., 440–41.

15. Ibid., 455–56.

16. Morris, "Society Is Not Marked by Punctuality," 150–53. While the

title theory suggests title was transferred to the lender, in reality, the borrower retained possession until default or foreclosure. See Ann M. Burkhart, "Lenders and Land," *Missouri Law Review* 64 (1999): 266–68.

17. Trapnall's Adx. v. The State Bank, 18 Ark. 53 (1856) at 61.

18. Porter v. Clements, 3 Ark. 364 (1841).

19. Ibid.

20. 5 Ark 321 (1844).

21. 5 Ark. 321 at 339–40, quoting Chapman v. Turner, 1 Call Va. Rep. 281 (Va. Court of Appeals).

22. 19 Ark. 278 (1857).

23. Ibid., 281.

24. Blakemore v. Byrnside, 7 Ark. 505 (1847).

25. Scott, White & Co. v. Henry & Cunningham, 13 Ark. 112 (1852), 117.

26. Trammell v. Thurmond, 17 Ark. 203 (1856). Other ownership disputes were resolved in Blagg v. Hunter, 15 Ark. 246 (1854), McNeill v. Arnold, 17 Ark. 154 (1856), Arnold v. McNeill, 17 Ark. 179 (1856), and McDaniel v. Crabtree, 21 Ark. 431 (1860).

27. 9 Ark. 112 (1848).

28. Cunningham v. Brumback, 23 Ark 336 (1861), 338.

29. Gullett and Wife v. Lamberton, 6 Ark. 109 (1845); and Gullett and Wife v. Saffold, 6 Ark. 123 (1845).

30. Dixon v. Thatcher's Heirs, 8 Ark. 134 (1847).

31. Humphries v. McCraw, 9 Ark. 91 (1848).

32. Wallace v. Brown, 17 Ark. 449 (1856). Another replevin case was Cornish v. Keesee, 17 Ark. 391 (1856).

33. State Bank v. Williams, 6 Ark. 156 (1845).

34. Ryburn v. Pryor, 14 Ark. 505 (1854).

35. 16 Ark. 154 (1855).

36. Carr v. Crain, 7 Ark. 241 (1847).

37. Ibid.

38. 16 Ark. 628 (1856).

39. See Spencer v. McDonald, Adm., 22 Ark 466 (1861). Some slave cases were mere routine disputes over ownership. Rheubottom v. Sadler, 19 Ark. 491 (1858) and 19 Ark. 496 (1858); Anderson v. Dunn, 19 Ark. 650 (1858); Morine v. Wilson, 19 Ark. 520 (1858).

40. 16 Ark 671 (1856).

41. Ibid., 694. Also see Crabtree v. McDaniel, 17 Ark 222 (1856), and Machin v. Thompson, 17 Ark 199 (1856).

42. 20 Ark 136 (1859).

43. Ibid., 143.

44. Ibid., 144.

45. Ibid.

46. Gross, *Double Character*, 122. She cites statistics from the Supreme Court of Louisiana and from Adams County, Mississippi, to bolster this claim.

47. Ibid., 144.

48. Horwitz, *Transformation,* 59–62.

49. Ibid., 167.

50. Andrew Fede, "Legal Protection for Slave Buyers in the U.S. South: A Caveat Concerning *Caveat Emptor*," *American Journal of Legal History* 31 (1987): 324. See also Robert E. Mensel, "A Diddle at Brobdingnag: Confidence and Caveat Emptor during the Market Revolution," *University of Memphis Law Review* 38 (2007): 104–10.

51. Horwitz, *Transformation*, 180.

52. Fede, "Legal Protection for Slave Buyers," 324.

53. Ibid., 330.

54. Ibid., 335.

55. Ibid., 331–34.

56. Ibid., 340. Fede suggests this path was akin to modern sales law under the Uniform Commercial Code.

57. Fede, "Legal Protection for Slave Buyers," 346.

58. Ibid., 350.

59. 19 Ark 447 (1858).

60. Ibid., 460.

61. Ibid.

62. Ibid., 460–61.

63. 22 Ark 517 (1861).

64. "Trover" is a common law tort action "to recover damages for wrongful conversion of personal property or to recover actual possession of such property." Steven H. Gifis, *Law Dictionary*, 3rd ed. (New York: Barons' Educational Services, 1991), 501.

65. 11 Ark 139 (1850).

66. Tatum v. Mohr, 21 Ark 349 (1860).

67. Previously, the court had approved jury instructions that stated that the measure of damages was the difference between the price paid and the actual value. Johnson v. Ashley, 7 Ark 470 (1847). The emphasis here was the difference in "worth" as warranted and actual value. Price would be an indication of the worth.

68. 23 Ark 730 (1861).

69. Ibid., 734.

70. Ibid., 732.

71. 4 Ark 563 (1842).

72. Ibid., 564–65.

73. Ibid., 570.

74. Johnson & Grimes v. McDaniel, 15 Ark 109 (1854); and Plant v. Condit, 22 Ark 454 (1861).

75. Fede, "Legal Protection for Slave Buyers," 349.

76. Ibid., 354.

77. Ibid., quoting Summers v. Bean, 54 Va. 162 (1856).

78. 20 Ark 618 (1859).

79. Ibid., 613, quoting Henderson v. Vaulx and Wife, 18 Tenn. 30 (1836).

80. Ibid., 614.

81. Fede, "Legal Protection for Slave Buyers," 356.

82. Stafford, "Slavery and the Arkansas Supreme Court," 449.

83. Ibid., 449.

84. Constitution of 1836, Act VII § 1.
85. Ark. Rev. Stat. Ch 56 § 1 (1838).
86. Ark. Rev. Stat. Ch 66 § 1 (1838).
87. Act 68 of 1859 Ark. Acts.
88. Aramynta v. Woodruff, 7 Ark. 422 (1849).
89. Wilson v. Dean, 10 Ark. 308 (1850).
90. Campbell v. Campbell, 13 Ark. 513 (1853).
91. 18 Ark. 399 (1857).
92. Ibid., 403.
93. Ibid., 413.
94. Harriet and Others v. Swan & Dixon, 18 Ark. 495 (1857).
95. 19 Ark. 121 (1857).
96. Ibid., 130.
97. 19 Ark. 580 (1858).
98. 19 Ark. 121.
99. 19 Ark. 583.
100. 19 Ark. 424 (1858).
101. Phebe v. Quillin, 21 Ark. 490 (1860).
102. Ibid., 500.
103. 23 Ark. 50 (1861).
104. Ibid., 52.
105. 24 Ark. 131 (1863).
106. Ibid., 135.
107. 15 Ark. 151 (1854).
108. Ibid., 157.
109. Ibid., 158.
110. 15 Ark. 159 (1854).
111. Ibid., 161.
112. 23 Ark. 19 (1861).
113. Ibid., 22.
114. 18 Ark. 114 (1856).
115. Ibid., 117.
116. Ibid., 118.
117. 15 Ark. 162 (1854).
118. Ibid., 165.
119. Ibid., 166.
120. Ibid., 168.
121. Watkins v. Bailey, 21 Ark. 274 (1860).
122. 21 Ark. 509 (1860).
123. 21 Ark. 512 (1860).
124. State v. Cadle, 19 Ark. 613 (1858).
125. Ibid., 621. See Medlock v. State, 18 Ark. 363 (1857); and State v. Parnell, 16 Ark. 506 (1855).
126. State v. Alford, 22 Ark. 186 (1860).
127. Ibid., 388.
128. 8 Ark. 400 (1848).
129. 11 Ark. 389 (1850).

130. 11 Ark. at 405.
131. 11 Ark. at 410.
132. Pleasant v. State, 13 Ark. 360 (1853).
133. State v. Charles, 11 Ark. 389 (1850).
134. 13 Ark. at 376.
135. 14 Ark. 552 (1854).
136. Ibid., 561.
137. Ibid., 565, quoting from a Tennessee case.
138. 15 Ark 624 (1855).
139. See 13 Ark 360 (1853).
140. See 14 Ark. 552 (1854).
141. Ibid., 644.
142. Bone v. State, 18 Ark. 109 (1856).
143. Ibid., 111.
144. Fede, "Legal Protection for Slave Buyers," 356.
145. Stafford, "Slavery and the Arkansas Supreme Court," 413, 417.

CHAPTER 7

"Affording Peace and Quiet": Case, Controversies, and Conflicts Relating to Family Law and Family Property

1. Grossberg, *Governing the Hearth*, 17.
2. Ibid., 4–6.
3. Ibid., 12–14.
4. Ibid., 30.
5. Ibid., x–xi.
6. G. Edward White, *Land in American History*, vol. 1: *From the Colonial Years through the Civil War* (Oxford: Oxford University Press, 2012), 9.
7. Ibid., 79.
8. Ibid., 57.
9. Grossberg, *Governing the Hearth*, 101.
10. Ibid., 104.
11. Ibid., 21–23.
12. Ibid., 24.
13. Ibid., 105–20.
14. Ibid., 120–26.
15. Ibid., 129–40.
16. Friedman, *A History*, 142–45.
17. Hendrik Hartog, *Man and Wife in America: A History* (Cambridge: Harvard University Press, 2000), 71–74.
18. Ibid., 73.
19. Ibid., 74.
20. Peter W. Bardaglio, *Reconstructing the Household: Families, Sex, and the Law in the Nineteenth-Century South* (Chapel Hill: University of North Carolina Press, 1995), 33–34
21. Ibid., 34. It can be argued that this actually reinforced the southern

view of family hierarchy by "bolstering contemporary notions of wifely and husbandly behavior.

22. Bardaglio, *Reconstructing the Household,* 33.

23. Allen v. Allen (1827), Arkansas Territorial Briefs and Records, William H. Bowen School of Law, University of Arkansas at Little Rock.

24. Friedman, *A History*, 143.

25. Article IV § 24.

26. Article IV § 23.

27. Revised Statutes of the State of Arkansas, Ch. 51, Sec. 1 (1838).

28. 9 Ark. 507 (1848).

29. Ibid., 512.

30. Ibid., 516.

31. Ibid., 517.

32. Welch v. Welch 16 Ark. 527 (1855).

33. 18 Ark. 320 (1856).

34. Ibid., 330.

35. 14 Ark. 267 (1853).

36. Simpson v. Simpson, 25 Ark. 487 (1869).

37. Ibid., 490.

38. 25 Ark. 615 (1861).

39. Ibid., 616.

40. Ibid., 617.

41. Ibid.

42. Ibid., 619.

43. Ibid., 621. The plaintiff's cause was not strengthened by evidence that he had told others that he was "under engagement to another lady residing in Louisiana." The defense of condonation has since been eliminated. See Arkansas Code Annotated § 9-12-325.

44. Bardaglio, *Reconstructing the Household*, 81.

45. Grossberg, *Governing the Hearth*, 237.

46. Bardaglio, *Reconstructing the Household*, 81.

47. Ibid., 82–84.

48. Ibid., 86, 89–90. Illegitimate children were normally left with the mother (ibid.).

49. Bardaglio, *Reconstructing the Household*, 95.

50. 24 Ark. 55 (1862).

51. Ibid., 65.

52. Ibid., 66.

53. Kelly v. Neely, 12 Ark. 657 (1852).

54. Ibid., 663.

55. 26 Ark. 470 (1871).

56. 26 Ark. at 475. This is consistent with the modern privilege.

57. 26 Ark. at 472.

58. Dunnahoe v. Williams, 24 Ark. 264 (1866).

59. Friedman, *A History*, 146.

60. Marylynn Salmon, *Women and the Law of Property in Early America* (Chapel Hill: University of North Carolina Press, 1986), 15.

61. Friedman, *A History*, 88–90.
62. Salmon, *Women and the Law*, 12.
63. Ibid., 93.
64. 27 Ark. 288 (1871).
65. Michael B. Dougan, "The Arkansas Married Woman's Property Law," *Arkansas Historical Quarterly* 46 (1987): 3–26.
66. Ibid., 14–15.
67. Ibid., 11, 14.
68. Ibid., 15.
69. 14 Ark. 339 (1854).
70. Sanders v. Sanders, 20 Ark 610 (1859).
71. Ibid., 611.
72. Ibid., 612.
73. Ibid., 614.
74. 19 Ark. 66 (1857).
75. Phillips v. Grayson, 23 Ark. 769 (1861).
76. 19 Ark. 66 (1857).
77. Howell v. Howell, 19 Ark. 339 (1858), 344.
78. Ferguson & Neill v. Moore and Wife, 19 Ark. 379 (1858), 394–95.
79. Allen v. Hightower, 21 Ark. 316 (1860); and Kirkpatrick v. Buford, 21 Ark. 268 (1860).
80. 1868 Constitution, Article 7, §6.
81. 1874 Constitution, Article 9, §7.
82. 25 Ark. 223 (1868).
83. 28 Ark. 351 (1873).
84. Chaplin v. Holmes, 27 Ark. 414 (1872).
85. Lawrence M. Friedman, *Dead Hands: A Social History of Wills, Trusts, and Inheritance Law* (Stanford: Stanford Law Books, 2009), 19–23.
86. Ibid., 27, 42, 47–48.
87. Ibid., 24.
88. Kelly's Heirs v. McGuire, 15 Ark. 555 (1855).
89. Ibid., 582.
90. Ibid., 587, quoting from Chancellor Kent (4 Kent 404).
91. Ibid.
92. Ibid., 588.
93. Ibid.
94. Ibid.
95. Ibid., 589.
96. Ibid., 592.
97. Ibid., 596.
98. Ibid., 600.
99. Ibid., 599–600.
100. Lofting v. Glass, 15 Ark. 680 (1855); West v. Williams, 15 Ark. 682 (1855); and Scull v. Vaugine, 15 Ark. 695 (1855).
101. 27 Ark. 65 (1871).
102. 27 Ark. 445 (1872).

103. Friedman, *A History*, 36.
104. Ibid., 35.
105. Ibid., 31.
106. Salmon, *Women and the Law*, 16.
107. Ibid., 142.
108. Ibid., 141.
109. Friedman, *A History*, 162.
110. Ibid., 23–24.
111. Ibid., 24–25.
112. Salmon, *Women and the Law*, 142.
113. Hartog, *Man and Wife in America*, 145–46.
114. Ariela R. Dubler, "In the Shadow of Marriage: Single Women and the Legal Construction of the Family and the State," *Yale Law Journal* 112 (2003): 1647, 1667.
115. 5 Ark. 608 (1844); Dougan, "The Arkansas Married Woman's Property Law," 10.
116. 5 Ark. 608 at 611.
117. Ibid., 613.
118. Ibid., 616.
119. Ibid., 628.
120. 12 Ark. 381 (1851).
121. Ibid., 388.
122. 8 Ark. 9 (1847).
123. See, e.g., 5 Ark. 629 (1844). This was but one chapter in the long saga relating to the estate of Dr. Nimrod Menifee, a wealthy landowner in Conway County.
124. 9 Ark. 46 (1848).
125. Welch v. Cole, 14 Ark. 400 (1854).
126. Ibid., 402.
127. Thorn and Wife v. Ingram, 25 Ark. 52 (1867).
128. Street, Trustee v. Saunders, 27 Ark. 554 (1872).
129. 27 Ark. 554 (1872). The court referred to the suit as "amicable," obviously filed to settle the issue.
130. 28 Ark. 256 (1873).
131. Jones v. Jones, 28 Ark. 19 (1872).
132. Ibid., 21.
133. Ibid., 25.
134. Joseph W. McKnight, "Protection of the Family Home from Seizure by Creditors: The Sources and Evolution of a Legal Principle," *Southwestern Historical Quarterly* 86 (1983): 369–99.
135. Ibid., 375.
136. Ibid., 377.
137. Ibid., 378. Austin was himself being pressed for payment of personal debts (ibid., 377).
138. McKnight, "Protection of the Family Home," 382.
139. Ibid., 390.

140. Ibid.

141. Ibid., 393. This followed the 1836 Constitution of Texas as well as the Constitution of the United States.

142. McKnight, "Protection of the Family Home," 397.

143. Paul Goodman, "The Emergence of Homestead Exemption in the United States: Accommodation and Resistance to the Market Revolution, 1840–1880," *Journal of American History* 80 (1993): 470–98.

144. Ibid., 471.

145. Ibid., 476. Southern paternalism did not extend to slaves, who were never included in classes of protected property (ibid., 480).

146. Goodman, "The Emergence of Homestead Exemption," 487.

147. 24 Ark. 255.

148. Ibid., 279 *et seq.*

149. Alison D. Movantz, "There's No Place Like Home: Homestead Exemption and Judicial Constrictions of Family in Nineteenth-Century America," *Law and History Review* 24 (2006): 245–95.

150. 24 Ark. at 158.

151. Wassell v. Tunnah, 25 Ark. 101 (1867).

152. Ibid., 103.

153. 27 Ark. 648 (1872).

154. 28 Ark. 485 (1873).

155 A prior case, *Tumlinson v. Swinney* (22 Ark. 400 [1860]), had permitted a claim on the day of sale. This was, however, under the original 1852 act, which contained no provision setting out a method for asserting the right.

CHAPTER 8

"The Key to Republican Economic Morality": Cases, Controversies, and Conflicts Relating to Debt and Contracts

1. Brown v. Wright, 17 Ark. 9 (1856). The case report includes the following recipe for the tonic:

5 Gallons Precipitated Bark
4 pounds Willow inner bark, fresh
4 pounds Cherry inner bark, fresh
4 pounds Dogwood inner bark, fresh
4 pounds Sarsaparilla in root

5 pounds Boneset—fresh-boiled in as much clear water as will cover the articles. Boil down to one gallon, then strain through a fine cloth, and add 4 gallons American Brandy; then take 6 or 8 ounces of extract of barks dissolved in the brandy, 1 ounce of the oil cinnamon, 1 pint of alcohol, make an essence, then mix all together, and is ready for use.

2. Friedman, *A History*, 196–97.

3. Freyer, *Producers versus Capitalists*, 38.

4. Thomas D. Russell, "The Antebellum Courthouse as Creditors' Domain: Trial-Court Activity in South Carolina and the Concomitance of Lending and Litigation," *American Journal of Legal History* 40 (1996): 332.

5. Ibid., 334.

6. Ibid., 336.
7. Freyer, "Law and the Antebellum Southern Economy," 59.
8. Ibid., 55–57.
9. Ibid., 55–56.
10. Ibid., 57.
11. Ibid., 57–58.
12. Russell, "The Antebellum Courthouse as Creditors' Domain," 352–55.
13. 13 Ark. 150 (1852).
14. 16 Peters 1 (1842).
15. Freyer, *Producers versus Capitalists*, 55.
16. Ibid., 166.
17. 12 Ark. 421 (1851).
18. Ibid., 589.
19. 15 Ark. 73 (1854).
20. 6 Ark. 317 (1845).
21. Ibid., 367.
22. R. Kent Newmyer, *Supreme Court Justice Joseph Story: Statesman of the Old Republic* (Chapel Hill: University of North Carolina Press, 1985), 293.
23. Ibid.
24. Ibid.
25. Ibid., 292.
26. Ibid., 294.
27. 9 Wheaton 1 (1824).
28. 17 Ark. 43 (1856).
29. Ibid., 44.
30. Hicks v. Ewhartonah, 21 Ark. 106 (1860).
31. Ibid., 108.
32. Ibid., 109.
33. Ibid., 108.
34. Ibid., 107.
35. 7 Ark. 150 (1846).
36. Sturgis v. Crowningsheild, 4 Wheat. 200.
37. A similar statute applying to debts of those in "Indian country" was applied in 1856 in *Sutton v. Hays* (17 Ark. 412 [1856]).
38. Friedman, *A History*, 404.
39. Horwitz, *Transformation*, 173.
40. Ibid., 160.
41. Ibid., 181.
42. See James W. Fox, "The Law of Many Faces: Antebellum Contract Law Background of Reconstruction-Era Freedom of Contract," *American Journal of Legal History* 49 (2007): 61–112.
43. Newmyer, *Supreme Court Justice Joseph Story*, 150.
44. Ibid., 151.
45. Ibid., 150.
46. Fox, "The Law of Many Faces," 71–78.
47. Ibid., 73.
48. Friedman, *A History*, 203.

49. Ibid.

50. Joseph Story, *A Familiar Exposition of the Constitution of the United States* (Washington, DC: Regnery Publishing, 1986), 193.

51. Ibid., 197.

52. Friedman *A History*, 203.

53. Charles River Bridge v. Warren Bridge, 11 Peters 420 (1837).

54. *Charles River Bridge* was Story's attempt to "apply the law of private contract to governmental economic activities" as previously done in *Dartmouth College*. Newmyer, *Supreme Court Justice Joseph Story*, 231.

55. 25 Ark. 625 (1869).

56. Ibid., 629.

57. Ibid., 631.

58. 25 Ark. 152 (1867).

59. 28 Ark. 175 (1873).

60. Ibid., 187.

61. Ibid., 640.

62. Ibid., 642.

63. This was reaffirmed the next year in *Pillow v. Brown & Childress* (26 Ark. 240 [1870]).

64. 14 Ark. 345 (1854).

65. 23 Ark. 704 (1861).

66. 21 Ark. 137 (1860).

67. McNeill v. Jones, 21 Ark. 277 (1860), 278.

68. 14 Ark. 315 (1854).

69. Ibid., 319.

70. Ibid.

71. 14 Ark. 329 (1854).

72. 14 Ark. 21 (1853).

73. Ibid., 25.

74. Ibid., 26.

75. 11 Ark. 339 (1850).

76. 11 Ark. 58 (1850).

77. Horwitz, *Transformation*, 192.

78. 19 Ark. 270 (1857).

79. Ibid., 277.

80. 26 Ark. 28 (1870).

81. Ibid., 32.

82. 8 Ark. 366 (1848).

83. Ibid., 367–68.

84. 23 Ark. 175 (1861).

85. Ibid., 177–78.

86. 22 Ark. 92 (1860).

87. Ibid., 94.

88. Ibid.

89. Ibid., 99.

90. 20 Ark. 216 (1859).

91. Ibid., 248.

92. Ibid.
93. 6 Ark. 276 (1845).
94. Ibid., 177–78.
95. Cheney v. Higginbotham, 10 Ark. 273 (1850).
96. Speer v. McLaughlin, 11 Ark. 732 (1851).
97. 24 Ark. 365 (1866).
98. Ibid., 372.
99. 13 Ark. 593 (1853).
100. Ibid., 598.
101. 12 Ark. 175 (1851).

CHAPTER 9

"A Stronghold of Legal Puritanism": Cases, Controversies, and Conflicts Involving Criminal Law and Procedure

1. Friedman, *A History*, 207.
2. Ibid.
3. Ibid., 211.
4. Gordon S. Wood, *Empire of Liberty: A History of the Early Republic, 1789–1815* (New York: Oxford University Press, 2009), 403. Jefferson apparently felt that the judge should be in "a mere machine" (ibid.).
5. Friedman, *A History*, 218.
6. Lawrence M. Friedman, "Notes toward a History of American Justice," *Buffalo Law Review* 24 (1974–1975): 117.
7. Friedman, *A History*, 218. In today's lexicon, these would be "consumer protection" laws, and these are largely enforced by administrative agencies rather than the courts. Friedman gives as an example an Indiana statute that prohibited the sale of merchandise not made in the United States without a license (ibid., 217).
8. Kermit L. Hall, *The Magic Mirror: Law in American History* (New York: Oxford University Press, 1989), 169.
9. Ibid., 168.
10. Ibid.
11. Nelson, "Emerging Notions of Modern Criminal Law," 452.
12. Ibid., 455–58.
13. Ibid., 466.
14. Ibid., 450, 466.
15. David H. Flaherty, "Law and the Enforcement of Morals in Early America," *Perspectives in American History* 5 (1971): 203.
16. Ibid., 337–38.
17. Ely and Bodenhamer, *Ambivalent Legacy*, 20–21.
18. Genovese, *The Political Economy of Slavery*, 8.
19. 1 Ark. 171 (1838).
20. State v. Graham, 1 Ark. 428 (1839).
21. Ibid., 433.
22. Ibid., 434.
23. Ibid., 433–34.

24. 4 Ark. 18 (1842). This question arose again in 1872, when a state statute prohibiting the carrying of concealed weapons was upheld against a constitutional challenge that it violated the Second Amendment. The court found that this right did not prohibit the legislature from enacting a police regulation for the good of society. See State v. Caroll, 28 Ark. 99 (1872).

25. *Arkansas Gazette*, June 20, 1838.

26. Ibid., December 19, 1838.

27. Ibid., December 5, 1837, and August 29, 1839.

28. Ibid., April 4, 1837.

29. Ibid., February 2, 1842.

30. Ibid., May 25, 1842.

31. Ibid., March 28, 1838.

32. The story of the banks and the legal struggle is related in detail in Brown, *A Life of Albert Pike*.

33. Bolton, *Arkansas, 1800–1860*, 61. The legislature in 1846 adopted a constitutional amendment to prohibit the establishment of banks in the state.

34. Bolton, *Arkansas, 1800–1860*, 55, 66.

35. DeBlack, "Prosperity and Peril," 138.

36. Ibid., 153.

37. Brown, *A Life of Albert Pike*, 241

38. Lawrence M. Friedman, *Crime and Punishment in American History* (New York: Harper Collins, 1993), 256.

39. 9 Ark. 42 (1848).

40. 6 Ark. 165 (1845). Hand was found not guilty in a second case involving an indictment for passing a forged certificate of deposit. State v. Hand, 6 Ark 169 (1845).

41. Gabe, alias Santa Anna v. State, 6 Ark. 519 (1846).

42. Gabe, alias Santa Anna v. State, 6 Ark. 540 (1846).

43. Smith Bell v. State, 10 Ark. 536 (1850).

44. Ibid., 10 Ark. at 537.

45. Patterson v. State, 7 Ark. 59 (1846).

46. This is a correct application of the understanding of the role of the jury in the sense that the jury is to apply the law as explained by the judge to the evidence (the facts). It does not suggest that juries were to decide what law to apply. This division of function had become clear by the early nineteenth century—at least in theory. See Friedman, *Crime and Punishment*, 104.

47. 7 Ark. 68 (1846).

48. 9 Ark. 193 (1848).

49. 10 Ark. 574 (1850).

50. It is not clear if this defendant is the same as the later Arkansas Supreme Court justice Thomas B. Hanly.

51. 10 Ark. 83 (1849).

52. Ibid., 84.

53. 10 Ark. 607 (1850).

54. 10 Ark. 259 (1850).

55. Ibid.

56. 10 Ark. 299 (1850).

57. State v. Ratliff, 10 Ark. 530 (1850).

58. 9 Ark. 222 (1848).

59. 10 Ark. 284 (1850).

60. 10 Ark. at 291.

61. Friedman, *Crime and Punishment*, 257–58.

62. *Arkansas Gazette*, July 14, 1845.

63. Ibid.; *Arkansas Gazette,* May 26, 1845, July 14, 1845, and December 15, 1845. As indicated in the discussion above, few of these were appealed.

64. *Arkansas Gazette*, October 27, 1854.

65. Ibid., May 3, 1850.

66. Ibid., June 14, 1850; September 13, 1850.

67. Ibid., August 15, 1851; September 12, 1851; October 31, 1851.

68. Ibid., June 20, 1851; January 16, 1852.

69. Ibid., January 16, 1852.

70. Ibid., October 28, 1853.

71. Ibid., February 23, 1846.

72. Ibid., March 2, 1846.

73. See Bolton, *Arkansas, 1800–1860*, 61–65.

74. Ibid., 64–66.

75. Moneyhon, *The Impact of Civil War*, 53.

76. Ibid., 56.

77. Stampp, *American in 1857*, 113–15.

78. *Arkansas Gazette*, April 6, 1855.

79. The October 1854 *Arkansas Gazette* policy that it would no longer report on murder and other outrageous acts because such reports "demoralize readers" changed by 1858 when six murders were reported along with an accidental killing in a fight "between friends" in Ashley County. *Arkansas Gazette*, October 9, 1858.

80. 13 Ark. 680 (1853).

81. 3 Ark. 84 (1840).

82. 13 Ark. 684 (1853).

83. State v. Hawkins, 15 Ark. 299 (1854).

84. Jester v. State, 14 Ark. 552 (1854).

85. 18 Ark. 186 (1856).

86. Ibid at 187.

87. Warren v. State, 14 Ark. 195 (1856).

88. Orr v. State, 18 Ark. 540 (1857).

89. Ibid., 545. Similarly, in *Medlock v. State* (18 Ark. 363 [1857]) it was not necessary to prove the exact amount of money alleged in the indictment, only that betting of money occurred.

90. 20 Ark. 97 (1859).

91. Ibid. Four gaming cases were before the court in the second 1860 term, but none were reversed on technical grounds. Dixon v. State, 22 Ark. 213 (1860) ("chuck-a-luck"); State v. Hollard, 22 Ark. 242 (1860) (faro betting); Dudney v. State, 22 Ark. 251 (1860) (keeping a gaming house); and State v. Martin, 22 Ark. 420 (1860) (betting on dice).

92. See, e.g., Stockden v. State, 18 Ark. 186 (1856), or State v. Grace, 21 Ark. 138 (1860) (playing cards on Sunday).

93. 16 Ark. 506 (1855).

94. 16 Ark at 507.

95. 13 Ark. 688 (1853).

96. Bennett v. State, 13 Ark. 694 (1853).

97. 20 Ark. 289 (1859).

98. Ibid., 291.

99. See, e.g., State v. Adams, 16 Ark. 497 (1855); and Edwards v. State, 22 Ark. 253 (1860).

100. Hopper v. State, 19 Ark. 143 (1857); and Parker v. State, 19 Ark. 147 (1857).

101. State v. Burgett, 22 Ark. 323 (1860).

102. 20 Ark. 156 (1859).

103. Ibid., 159.

104. Crouse v. State, 16 Ark. 566 (1855).

105. Ibid.

106. 19 Ark. 405 (1858).

107. Reed v. State, 16 Ark. 499 (1855); Hofler v. State, 16 Ark. 334 (1855); and Atkins v. State, 16 Ark. 568 (1855).

108. Strawn v. State, 14 Ark. 549 (1854).

109. 19 Ark. 190 (1857).

110. Ibid., 192.

111. Freel v. State, 21 Ark. 212 (1860).

112. Ibid., 218.

113. Swinney v. State, 22 Ark. 215 (1860).

114. Pitman v. State, 22 Ark. 354 (1860).

115. Ibid., 357.

116. 19 Ark. 590 (1858).

117. Holeman v. State, 13 Ark 105 (1853). The governor apparently pardoned Mrs. Holeman before the court heard the case.

118. Doghead Glory v. State, 13 Ark. 236 (1853).

119. 13 Ark 307 (1853).

120. 13 Ark. at 311.

121. 13 Ark. at 317 (1853).

122. 20 Ark 53 (1859).

123. Ibid., 61.

124. 20 Ark. 36 (1859).

125. Ibid., 50.

126. 20 Ark. 166 (1859).

127. Ibid., 167.

128. Love v. State, 22 Ark. 336 (1860).

129. Ibid., 339.

130. Ibid., 340.

131. Ibid., 343.

132. John W. Brown Diary, August 9, 1856, Microfilm Collection, Arkansas History Commission, Little Rock.

133. Ibid., November 29, 1860.

134. See Carl Moneyhon, "1861: 'The Die Is Cast,'" in *Rugged and Sublime: The Civil War in Arkansas*, ed. Mark K. Christ (Fayetteville: University of Arkansas Press, 1994), 1–19.

135. John W. Brown recorded in March 28, 1862, that courts were not held in their circuit due to "absence of parties and witnesses" and the general "engrossment of the public mind by the war." John W. Brown Diary, March 28, 1862. A year later he did attend court in Columbia County and was pleased to see a grand jury functioning there, particularly in light of the "tendency toward military usurpation." John W. Brown Diary, April 21, 1863.

136. Dallas T. Herndon, *Centennial History of Arkansas* (Chicago: S. J. Clarke Publishing Co., 1922), 1:289.

137. Ruth Caroline Cowen, "Reorganization of Federal Arkansas, 1862–1865," *Arkansas Historical Quarterly* 18 (1959): 132–57.

138. See *Arkansas Reports*, vol. 24.

139. State v. White, 23 Ark. 275 (1861); and State v. Omey, 23 Ark. 281 (1861).

140. State v. Rhoda, 23 Ark. 156 (1861).

141. State v. Omey, 23 Ark. 281 (1861).

142. State v. Taffe, 23 Ark. 34 (1861).

143. State v. Ross, 23 Ark. 198 (1861); State v. Cooper, 23 Ark. 278 (1861); and State v. Pack, 23 Ark. 235 (1861).

144. State v. Rorie, 23 Ark. 726 (1861).

145. State v. Branum, 23 Ark. 540 (1861).

146. State v. Moore, 23 Ark. 550 (1861); and State v. Hagood, 23 Ark. 553 (1861).

147. Bates v. Independence County, 23 Ark. 722 (1861).

148. 24 Ark. 44 (1862).

149. *Arkansas Gazette*, February 12, 1867.

150. That was the case of *Denton v. Brownlee, Homer & Co.*, relating to the suspension of the statutes of limitation against debts of those in military service while still in service. 24 Ark. 556 (1867).

151. State v. Green, 24 Ark. 591 (1867) (defective indictment); State v. Scott, 25 Ark. 107 (1867) (prosecutor did not endorse indictment); State v. Harper, 25 Ark. 83 (1867) (jury not properly sworn); and State v. Lawson, 25 Ark. 106 (1867) (jury not sworn).

152. State v. Flanagin, 25 Ark. 92 (1867).

153. State v. Cheek, 25 Ark. 206 (1868).

154. State v. Belding, 25 Ark. 315 (1869); State v. Belding, 25 Ark. 318 (1869).

155. State v. Jones, 25 Ark. 375 (1869).

156. State v. McQuistian, 25 Ark. 435 (1869).

157. State v. Edwards, 25 Ark. 444 (1869).

158. State v. McAdams, 25 Ark. 405 (1869).

159. State v. Warner, 25 Ark. 447 (1869).

160. 26 Ark. 74 (1870).

161. State v. Thompson, 26 Ark. 323 (1870); and State v. Allen, 26 Ark. 333 (1870).

162. State v. Lee, 26 Ark. 260 (1870).

163. State v. McKenzie, 26 Ark. 334 (1870).

164. State v. Dunn, 26 Ark. 34 (1870).

165. State v. Smith, 26 Ark. 149 (1870).

166. State v. Trammell, 26 Ark. 534 (1871); and State v. Neville, 26 Ark. 614 (1871).

167. State v. Curtis, 26 Ark 439 (1871).

168. State v. Scott, 26 Ark. 521 (1871); and State v. Henry, 26 Ark. 523 (1871).

169. State v. Tremble, 27 Ark. 355 (1872); State v. Portes, 27 Ark. 360 (1872); and State v. Tremble, 27 Ark. 397 (1872).

170. 28 Ark. 113 (1872).

171. 26 Ark. 260 (1870).

172. Ibid., 275–76.

173. 28 Ark. 99 (1872).

174. State v. Edwards, 27 Ark. 493 (1872).

175. State v. Jones, 28 Ark. 119 (1873); State v. Sugarman, 28 Ark. 142 (1873); State v. Pinson, 28 Ark. 397 (1873); and State v. Moore, 28 Ark. 480 (1873).

176. State v. Mahar, 28 Ark. 207 (1873) (constable withheld fines, penalty, and forfeiture); State v. Coit 28, Ark. 417 (1873) (circuit clerk indicted for forgery).

177. State v. Seabrosh, 28 Ark. 396 (1873); and State v. Brandon, 28 Ark. 410 (1873).

178. State v. Brown, 28 Ark. 126 (1873).

179. 28 Ark. 155 (1873). Also see Runnells v. State, 28 Ark. 121 (1873).

180. 28 Ark. 531 (1873).

181. *Arkansas Gazette*, March 6, 1870.

182. Ibid., May 13, 1873; May 18, 1873.

183. Ibid., January 5, 1872, and frequently in 1873.

184. Ibid., March 19, 1871.

185. Ibid., May 24, 1871.

186. Ibid., February 24, 1870.

187. Ibid., September 21, 1871.

188. Ibid., July 16, 1872.

189. Friedman, *Crime and Punishment*, 109.

190. Ibid., 114–15.

191. Ibid., 107.

192. Ibid., 125.

193. Ibid., 139.

194. Nelson, "Emerging Notions of Modern Criminal Law," 450–51.

195. Ely and Bodenhamer, *Ambivalent Legacy*, 20.

196. Ayers, *Vengeance and Justice*, 23.

197. Ibid.

198. Ely and Bodenhamer, *Ambivalent Legacy*, 18–19.

199. Friedman, *Crime and Punishment*, 85. Also see Moore, "Some Aspects of Crime and Punishment," 56.

200. Friedman, *Crime and Punishment*, 86.

201. Ibid., 256.

202. Ibid., 257–58. Friedman adds that the message never got through and that the public never knew or cared about such technical matters.

203. Ayers, *Vengeance and Justice*, 181.

204. Bolton, *Arkansas, 1800–1860*, 116–17. John Brown related his personal story of temperance frequently, starting with his initiation into a division of the Sons of Temperance in Camden. John W. Brown Diary, January 14, 1854.

205. Bolton, *Arkansas, 1800–1860,* 115.

206. Ibid., 116–17.

207. Ibid., 127.

208. Friedman cites a localized study from South Carolina showing that from 1818 to 1860, 43.3 percent of blacks accused of crime were accused of crimes against property. Friedman, *Crime and Punishment*, 87.

209. Wyatt-Brown, *Southern Honor*, 392.

210. Ibid., 395.

211. Ibid., 399.

212. Alfred L. Brophy, "Over and above . . . there broods a portentous shadow, —the shadow of law: Harriet Becher Stowe's Critique of Slave Law in *Uncle Tom's Cabin*," *Journal of Law and Religion* 12 (1995–96): 457. The influence of such proslavery thought on the rise of legal formalism has been largely ignored. See, e.g., Horwitz, *Transformation*. Horwitz devotes an entire chapter to the rise of formalism, but his focus is on the shift to a market-oriented society, and he does not discuss any influence of proslavery thought.

213. Lawrence M. Friedman, "The Law between the States: Some Thoughts on Southern Legal History," in *Ambivalent Legacy*, ed. Ely and Bodenhamer, 42.

CHAPTER 10

"Rights of Belligerents": Cases, Controversies, and Conflicts during the War Years and in the War's Aftermath, 1861–1867

1. In the January term of 1861, only 6 cases involved criminal matters out of 114 total cases decided by the court during this term. *Arkansas Reports*, vol. 22, vol. 23.

2. Of the 114 cases in the January term, 12 involved questions related to slaves. *Arkansas Reports*, vol. 22, vol. 23.

3. 23 Ark. 19 (1861).

4. Omey v. State, 23 Ark. 28 (1861).

5. 23 Ark. 769 (1861).

6. 23 Ark. 362 (1861).

7. 23 Ark. at 368.

8. 23 Ark. 731 (1861).

9. 23 Ark. 519 (1861).

10. 23 Ark. 50 (1861). This case had previously been before the court on another issue. Daniel v. Guy, 19 Ark. 121 (1857). It would appear later on still yet another question. Daniel v. Roper, 24 Ark. 131 (1863). For a full discussion of the factual background, see Robert S. Shafer, "White Persons Held to Racial Slavery in Antebellum Arkansas," *Arkansas Historical Quarterly* 49 (1985): 134–55.

11. Dred Scott v. Sandford, 19 Howard 393 (1856). See Florence R. Beatty-Brown, "Legal Status of Arkansas Negroes before Emancipation," *Arkansas Historical Quarterly* 28 (1969): 6–13.

12. *Arkansas Reports*, vol. 23.

13. Stevenson, *Arkansas Territory*, 31.

14. 24 Ark. 1 (1862).

15. *Arkansas State Gazette*, August 16, 1862. Danley was the editor of the *Gazette* and fully supported the court's decision.

16. 24 Ark. 78 (1862).

17. 24 Ark. 91 (1862).

18. 24 Ark. 91 (1862).

19. The Arkansas Supreme Court apparently moved with the government to Washington and continued the June term in October. Stevenson, *Arkansas Territory*, 33. This move was by authority of legislation enacted the prior year, which empowered the governor to move the seat of government in case of imminent danger. Leo Elmer Huff, "Confederate Arkansas: A History of Arkansas during the Civil War" (MA thesis, University of Arkansas, 1964), 21–22. A May 1862 move of state archives and of some state officials to near Hot Springs following the Pea Ridge conflict had created political difficulties for Governor Rector. This move was apparently made without official notice to the Arkansas Supreme Court. *Arkansas State Gazette*, June 28, 1862.

20. 24 Ark. 131 (1863).

21. Fay Hempstead, *Historical Review of Arkansas* (Chicago: Lewis Publishing Co., 1911), 1:252.

22. Fay Hempstead, *A Pictorial History of Arkansas* (St. Louis: N. D. Thompson Publishing Company, 1890), 585. Justice Fairchild resigned on June 8, 1864. Stevenson, *Arkansas Territory*, 33. Pike was confirmed by the Confederate state legislation when called in September 1864 by Governor Flanigan. Huff, "Confederate Arkansas," 30–31.

23. Albert Pike, "Autobiography," included in Hallum's *Biographical and Pictorial History*, "Confederate Arkansas," 215–21. This autobiography is in the nature of a letter from Pike to Hallum, dated August 15, 1886, while Pike was in Washington, D.C. Hallum included a number of his own observations concerning Pike and called him "without doubt or rival, the greatest of American poets." Hallum, *Biographical and Pictorial History*, 22. Pike also contributed a number of other sketches to Hallum's work.

24. A notation in court records of June 8, 1864, states: "The proceedings subsequently recorded in this Record Book, having taken place since the adoption of the Constitution of the 16th of March, 1864, are considered to be null and void, and so treated by the Supreme Court." Stevenson, *Arkansas Territory*, 33.

25. *Arkansas Reports*, vol. 24.

26. These opinions are also longer than the typical opinion of the time. See Trapnall v. Burton, 24 Ark. 371 (1866); Marshall v. Green, 24 Ark. 410 (1866); Branch v. Mitchell, 24 Ark. 433 (1866); and Twombly v. Kimbrough, 24 Ark. 459 (1866).

27. Constitution of the State of Arkansas of 1864, Preamble: "We the

people of the state of Arkansas, having the right to establish for ourselves a constitution in conformity with the constitution of the United State of America, recognizing the legitimate consequences of the existing rebellion, do hereby declare the entire action of the late convention of the state of Arkansas, which assembled in the city of Little Rock on the 4th day of March, 1861, was, and is, null and void, and is not now, and never has been, binding and obligatory upon the people." Reprinted in Edward W. Gantt, *Gantt's Digest of the Statutes of Arkansas* (Little Rock: Little Rock Printing and Publishing Company, 1874), 115–25.

28. Cowen, "Reorganization of Federal Arkansas," 132–57.

29. Stevenson, *Arkansas Territory*, 36.

30. Ibid., 37.

31. 23 Ark. 161 (1865).

32. Constitution of the State of Arkansas of 1864, Article IV, Section 2.

33. Stevenson, *Arkansas Territory*, 78.

34. Ibid., 68. Thomas Staples, *Reconstruction in Arkansas, 1862–1874* (Gloucester: Peter Smith, 1964; repr., New York: Columbia University Press, 1924), 28.

35. Staples, *Reconstruction in Arkansas*, 81.

36. Stevenson, *Arkansas Territory*, 37.

37. Staples, *Reconstruction in Arkansas*, 109.

38. Constitution of the State of Arkansas of 1864, Preamble.

39. 24 Ark. 286 (1866).

40. *Daily Arkansas Gazette*, February 10, 1867. A large number of the members of the Arkansas General Assembly attended the court's announcement of the opinion and the House ordered five thousand copies of the opinion printed, to be distributed throughout the state.

41. "No government can, properly speaking, conquer its own territory." 24 Ark. at 310.

42. 24 Ark. 479 (1866).

43. Constitution of the State of Arkansas of 1864, Preamble.

44. 24 Ark. 91 (1863).

45. 24 Ark. 487 (1866).

46. This act was passed by a vote of 51–0 in the House of Representatives and was signed by the governor, May 31, 1864. *Journal of the House of Representatives*, Session of 1864 (Little Rock: Price & Burton State Printers, 1870), 165.

47. 24 Ark. 242 (1866).

48. The entire Emancipation Proclamation was set out in *Arkansas State Gazette*, October 11, 1862, along with an editorial criticizing the action.

49. 24 Ark. 326 (1866).

50. 24 Ark. 365 (1866).

51. Constitution of the State of Arkansas of 1864, Article V, Section 1.

52. 24 Ark. 224 (1866).

53. 24 Ark. 256 (1866).

54. 24 Ark. 337 (1866).

55. 24 Ark. 499 (1866).

56. Constitution of the State of Arkansas of 1864, Article II.

57. Staples, *Reconstruction in Arkansas*, 81–82.

58. Sidney Crawford, "Arkansas Suffrage Qualifications" *Arkansas Historical Quarterly* 2 (1943), 331–339.

59. 24 Ark. 346 (1866).

60. 24 Ark. 161 (1865).

61. Staples, *Reconstruction in Arkansas*, 79.

62. Fletcher, *Arkansas*, 202–3.

63. *Daily Arkansas Gazette*, February 12, 1867.

64. *Arkansas Reports*, vol. 24.

65. 24 Ark. 556 (1867).

66. Fletcher, *Arkansas*, 203.

CHAPTER 11

"Usurpation and Treachery": Cases, Controversies, and Conflicts in the Arkansas Supreme Court during Reconstruction, 1868–1874

1. *Journal of the House of Representatives*, State of Arkansas, 18th session, 337.

2. Ibid., 395.

3. 25 Ark. 191 (1868).

4. 25 Ark. 258 (1868).

5. 25 Ark. 246 (1868).

6. Ibid., 252.

7. Woodruff v. Tilley, 25 Ark. 309 (1869).

8. 25 Ark. 574 (1869).

9. Ibid., 598.

10. Ford v. Ragland, 25 Ark. 612 (1869); Glenn v. Case, 25 Ark. 616 (1869); Glenn v. Case, 25 Ark. 620 (1869); ibid., 620.

11. Jordan v. Walker, 26 Ark. 1 (1870); King v. Carnall, 26 Ark. 36(1870); George v. Terry, 26 Ark. 160 (1870).

12. Green & Wilson v. Roane & Bell, 26 Ark. 15 (1870).

13. Waymack v. Heilman, 26 Ark. 449 (1871).

14. 27 Ark. 303 (1871). This issue resurfaced one last time in the June 1872 term in *Carllee v. Carlton* (27 Ark. 379 [1872]). And as late as December 1873 similar questions still plagued the court. In *Tucker v. Horner* (28 Ark. 335 [1873]), the court ruled that Confederate war bonds could not serve as valid consideration for a promissory note.

15. Dorris v. Grace, 24 Ark. 326 (1866); Steele v. Richardson, 24 Ark. 365 (1866).

16. 25 Ark. 196 (1868).

17. 25 Ark. 241 (1868).

18. Russell v. Shute, 25 Ark. 469 (1869).

19. 25 Ark. 625 (1869).

20. Sevier v. Haskell, 26 Ark. 133 (1870); Buchanan v. Nixon, 26 Ark. 47 (1870).

21. 24 Ark. 326 (1866).

22. Kaufman & Co. v. Barb, 26 Ark. 24 (1870).

23. 26 Ark. 240 (1870).

24. Anderson v. Mills, 28 Ark. 175 (1873).

25. 25 Ark. 209 (1868).

26. Ibid., 211

27. Ibid., 212.

28. 25 Ark. 238 (1868).

29. McMurtry v. Ramsey, 25 Ark. 349 (1869); Hanover v. Gray, 25 Ark. 350 (1869); Portis v. Green, 25 Ark. 376 (1869).

30. 25 Ark. 458 (1869).

31. Contracts involving sale of property for use in Confederate service were unenforceable. Booker v. Robbins & Page, 26 Ark. 660 (1871). Issues regarding contracts for the sale of slaves were settled. Sheppard v. Thomas, 26 Ark. 617 (1871).

32. Rice v. Shook, 27 Ark. 137 (1871).

33. Ibid., 146–47.

34. Orval Truman Driggs Jr., "The Issues of the Powell Clayton Regime, 1868–1871," *Arkansas Historical Quarterly* 8 (1949): 37.

35. Ibid., 52–53.

36. Ibid., 54.

37. Ibid., 55–57.

38. Ibid., 62–63.

39. 25 Ark. 289 (1868).

40. 25 Ark. 301 (1868).

41. Jones v. City of Little Rock, 25 Ark. 284 (1868).

42. Parsel v. Barnes, 25 Ark. 261 (1868).

43. Ibid., 270.

44. Everette Swinney, "*United States v. Powell Clayton*: Use of the Federal Enforcement Acts in Arkansas," *Arkansas Historical Quarterly* 26 (1867): 143–54.

45. English & Wilshire v. Chicot County, 26 Ark. 454 (1871); Chicot County v. Tilghman, 26 Ark. 461 (1871); Chicot County v. Tilghman, 26 Ark. 463 (1871).

46. Citizens' Bank of Louisiana v. Walker, 26 Ark. 469 (1871); Reynolds v. Craycraft, 26 Ark. 469 (1871).

47. 26 Ark. 510 (1871).

48. See Driggs, "The Issues," 42–44.

49. 27 Ark. 116 (1871).

50. 27 Ark. 675 (1872).

51. 27 Ark. 603 (1872).

52. 28 Ark. 254 (1873).

53. 28 Ark. 516 (1873).

54. 28 Ark. 317 (1873).

55. 14 Stat. 27–30 (April 9, 1866).

56. 25 Ark. 392 (1869).

57. Page v. Cook, 26 Ark. 122 (1870).

58. 26 Ark. 74 (1870).

59. 24 Ark. 286 (1866).

60. 26 Ark. 545 (1871).

61. Ibid., 585.

62. Thompson v. Mankin, 26 Ark. 587 (1871).

63. 26 Ark. 598 (1871).

64. 27 Ark. 183 (1872).

65. 27 Ark. 266 (1872).

66. 28 Ark. 115 (1872).

67. 24 Ark. 487 (1866).

68. Kelley v. State, 25 Ark. 392 (1869).

69. Ibid., 397.

70. Ibid., 403.

71. 25 Ark. 527 (1869).

72. The Clayton faction took its name from the fact that a prominent member had once been associated with a minstrel troupe. The Brooks faction took its name from a nickname applied to Brooks, "old Brindletail," which he had received from a reference to his speechmaking capabilities by a local Negro orator who had declared that Brook's voice reminded him of an "old brindletail bull." James H. Atkinson, "The Arkansas Gubernatorial Campaign and Election of 1872," *Arkansas Historical Quarterly* 1 (1942): 307–8. One illustration of the court's involvement in the conflict is found in the fact that Justice Bowen had apparently acted as an intermediary between the Clayton people and the Democrats. Driggs, "The Issues," 63.

73. Driggs, "The Issues," 65.

74. Ibid., 67

75. Ibid., 69.

76. Ibid., 69–70.

77. Allen, Ex Parte, 26 Ark. 9 (1870); O'Bar, Ex Parte, 26 Ark. 14 (1870); Byers, Ex Parte, 26 Ark. 15 (1870).

78. Swinney, "*United States v. Powell Clayton*: Use," 147–48.

79. 26 Ark. 100 (1870).

80. Swinney, "*United States v. Powell Clayton:* Use," 149.

81. Driggs, "The Issues," 70.

82. 26 Ark. 281 (1870).

83. Driggs, "The Issues," 70–71.

84. Staples, *Reconstruction in Arkansas*, 385.

85. Stevenson, *Arkansas Territory*, 63. 75.

86. John M. Harrell, *The Brooks-Baxter War: A History of the Reconstruction Period in Arkansas* (St. Louis: Slawson Printing, 1893), 98.

87. Ibid., 102–3.

88. Driggs, "The Issues," 72–73.

89. 26 Ark. 482 (1871).

90. 26 Ark. 480 (1871).

91. Ramsey v. Carhart, 27 Ark. 12 (1871); Campbell v. Goodrich, 27 Ark. 14 (1871).

92. 27 Ark. 106 (1872).

93. White v. Prigmore, 27 Ark. 188 (1872); and White v. Prigmore, 27 Ark. 189 (1872).

94. George H. Thompson, *Arkansas and Reconstruction: The Influences of Geography, Economics, and Personality* (Port Washington, NY: Kennikat Press, 1976), 97–105.

95. Ibid., 108–23.

96. Staples, *Reconstruction in Arkansas*, 403–4.

97. 28 Ark. 129 (1873).

98. Staples, *Reconstruction in Arkansas*, 404.

99. Ibid.

100. Ibid., 409.

101. Staples, *Reconstruction in Arkansas*, 409–16. Also see L. Scott Stafford, "Significant Decisions of the Supreme Court of Arkansas: *Brooks v. Page* (May 7, 1874)," *Arkasnsas Lawyer 46* (Fall 2001): 40.

102. Harrell, *The Brooks-Baxter War*, 211.

103. James H. Atkinson, "The Brooks-Baxter Contest," *Arkansas Historical Quarterly* 4 (1945): 128–29.

104. Ibid., 143.

105. Ibid., 145.

106. Staples, *Reconstruction in Arkansas*, 421

107. Thompson, *Arkansas and Reconstruction*, 158.

108. James J. Atkinson, "The Adoption of the Constitution of 1874 and the Passing of the Reconstruction Regime," *Arkansas Historical Quarterly* 5 (1946): 288–96.

109. Thompson, *Arkansas and Reconstruction*, 164.

110. Staples, *Reconstruction in Arkansas*, 424–31.

111. Thompson, *Arkansas and Reconstruction*, 163.

112. Ibid., 155.

113. Brooks v. Baxter, 29 Ark. 173 (1874). The prior decision in Brooks v. Page was expunged from the case reports.

114. Atkinson, "The Brooks-Baxter Contest," 295–96

115. Thompson, *Arkansas and Reconstruction*, 169.

116. Alexis de Tocqueville, *Democracy in America* (New York: Vintage Books, 1956), 1:102.

CHAPTER 12
"Distinguishing the Righteous from the Roguish": Summary and Conclusions

1. Stampp, *America in 1857*, 113.

2. Gross, *Double Character*, 47–48.

3. Wyatt-Brown, *Southern Honor*, 14–15, 22.

4. Genovese, *The Political Economy of Slavery*, 28.

5. Wyatt-Brown, *Southern Honor*, 369.

6. Genovese, *Roll, Jordan, Roll*, 27.

7. Ibid.

8. Genovese, *The Political Economy of Slavery*, 8. Southerners drew support from some northern supporters of slavery. For example, Bishop John Henry Hopkins, presiding bishop of the Episcopal Church, defended slavery as based on biblical teachings: "Where is the 'law' which is higher than the code laid down by the Deity? Where is the rule of morals which shall claim supremacy over the Word of God?" Hopkins, *The American Citizen*, 125.

9. See Bolton, *Arkansas, 1800–1860*, 61–65.

10. Ibid., 64–66.

11. Moneyhon, *The Impact of Civil War*, 53.

12. Ibid., 56.

13. Horwitz, *Transformation*, 2.

14. Ibid., 23–25.

15. Ely and Bodenhamer, "Regionalism," 7–9.

16. Ibid., 7.

17. Ibid., 4.

18. Freyer, "Law and the Antebellum Southern Economy," 49–68.

19. Genovese, *The Political Economy of Slavery*, 27.

20. A. E. Keir Nash, "*In re* Radical Interpretations of American Law: The Relation of Law and History," *Michigan Law Review* 82 (1983): 275–76.

21. Colin Sumner, "The Ideological Nature of Law," in *Marxism and Law*, ed. Piers Beirne and Richard Quinney (New York: John Wiley & Sons, 1982), 257.

22. See Genovese, *Roll, Jordan, Roll*, 27, 147–48.

23. This characterization of Hurst's thesis is from Thomas D. Russell, "The Antebellum Courthouse as Creditor's Domain: Trial Court Activity in South Carolina and the Concomitance of Lending and Litigation," *American Journal of Legal History* 40 (1996): 334.

24. Hurst, *Law and the Conditions of Freedom*, 6.

25. Ibid., 68.

26. See Harry N. Scheiber, "Back to 'The Legal Mind'? Doctrinal Analysis and the History of Law," *Reviews in American History* 5, no. 4 (1977): 463. Also see Harry W. Scheiber," Property Law, Expropriation, and Resource Allocation by Government: The U.S., 1789–1910," *Journal of Economic History* 33 (1973): 232–51.

27. Whayne, "The Turbulent Path to Statehood," 93.

28. Watson, "Conflict and Collaboration," 274–98.

29. DeBlack, "The Rights and Rank," 111–13.

30. Moneyhon, *The Impact of the Civil War*, 83.

31. In Arkansas, as in other states, civil litigation was the primary focus of the litigation, and most civil litigation was over debts. As summarized by Russell in "The Antebellum Courthouse," these might be characterized as "account, assumpsit, attachment, bill of exchange, case, covenant, debt, due bill, guaranty, note, obligation, order and single bill," but the core circumstance was that "the defendant owed money to the plaintiff." Russell, "The Antebellum Courthouse," 345.

32. Stafford, "Slavery and the Arkansas Supreme Court," 432.

33. Ibid., 446–47.

34. Paul Finkelman, *An Imperfect Union: Slavery, Federalism, and Comity* (Chapel Hill: University of North Carolina Press, 1981), 182.

35. Nash, "*In re* Radical Interpretations," 309–10.

36. Ibid., 307–8.

37. See Dougan, "The Arkansas Married Women's Property Law."

38. Freyer, "Law and the Antebellum Southern Economy," 59.

39. Horwitz, *Transformation*, 173.

40. Newmyer, *Supreme Court Justice Joseph Story*, 150.

41. See, e.g., Friedman, *A History*, 218; Nelson, "Emerging Notions of Modern Criminal Law," 452.

42. Ely and Bodenhamer, *Ambivalent Legacy*, 20–21.

43. Ibid., 31.

44. Horace Adams, "An Arkansas Alderman, 1857," *Arkansas Historical Quarterly* 11 (1952): 80, 100.

45. Ibid., 98.

46. John W. Brown Diary, Sunday, November 14, 1852.

47. Ibid., Saturday, January 1, 1853.

48. Ibid., Wednesday, March 16, 1853.

49. Ibid., Wednesday, May 17, 1854.

50. Ibid., Monday, January 1, 1855.

51. Ibid., Saturday, August 9, 1856.

52. Ibid., Tuesday, October 20, 1857.

53. Ibid., Thursday, January 14, 1858.

54. Ibid., Saturday, January 1, 1859.

55. Ibid., Sunday, January 1, 1860.

56. Ibid., Friday, April 27, 1860.

57. Ibid., Tuesday, November 6, 1860.

58. Ibid., Tuesday, January 1, 1861.

59. Ibid., Tuesday, February 4, 1862.

60. Ibid., Monday, December 9, 1861, and Tuesday, January 7, 1862.

61. Ibid., Wednesday, March 5, and Monday, March 17, 1862.

62. Ibid., Friday, May 10, and Friday, June 21, 1862.

63. Ibid., Tuesday, September 16, 1862.

64. Ibid., Monday, December 15, 1862.

65. Ibid., Monday, March 16, and Thursday, March 26, 1863.

66. Ibid., Thursday, March 19, 1863.

67. Ibid., Tuesday, July 14, 1863.

68. Ibid., Monday, October 5, 1863.

69. Ibid., Saturday, December 12, 1863.

70. Ibid., Friday, January 8, 1864.

71. Ibid., Friday, April 15, 1864.

72. Ibid., Tuesday, April 26, 1864.

73. Ibid., Monday, June 27, 1864.

74. Ibid., Wednesday, September 7, 1864.

75. Ibid., Thursday, December 14, 1864.

76. Ibid., Monday, February 13, 1865.

77. Ibid., Thursday, April 6, 1865.

78. Ibid., Thursday, May 19, 1865.

79. Ibid., Tuesday, May 24, 1865.

80. Ibid., Friday, June 3, 1865.

81. Ibid., Tuesday, July 11, 1865

82. Ibid., Saturday, July 8, 1865.

83. Ibid., Thursday, June 16, 1865.

84. Moneyhon, *The Impact of the Civil War*, 240.

85. Ibid., 263.

86. John W. Brown Diary, Tuesday, April 26, 1865.

BIBLIOGRAPHY

Official Records, Legal Codes, and Statutes

4 Stat. 473 (March 3, 1831).

9 Stat. 520 (September 28, 1850).

14 Stat. 27–30 (April 9, 1866).

14 Stat. 4–19, 28–429 (March 2, 1867).

15 Stat. 2–5 (March 23, 1867).

15 Stat. 14–16 (July 19, 1867).

Arkansas Constitutions of 1836, 1864, 1868, and 1874.

Arkansas Reports, vols. 1–29.

"Arkansas Territorial Briefs and Records." University of Arkansas at Little Rock, William H. Bowen School of Law. http://www.ualr.libguide.com/records and briefs. Accessed December 20, 2015.

Hempstead's Reports, vols. 1–279.

Historical Report of the Secretary of State, University of Arkansas Press, 2008.

Journal of the Proceedings of the Arkansas Senate, October 4, 1836, October 5, 1836, November 4, 1837, November 7, 1837, and November 13, 1837.

Journals of the Arkansas House of Representatives, 1842, 1856, 1859, 1864, and 1871.

Revised Statutes of the State of Arkansas, ch. 51, sec. 1 (1838).

United States Reports, vols. 5, 7, 51, 54, 92, and 127.

Books

Arnold, Morris S. *Unequal Laws unto a Savage Race: European Legal Tradition in Arkansas, 1686–1836*. Fayetteville: University of Arkansas Press, 1985.

Ayers, Edward L. *Vengeance and Justice: Crime and Punishment in the 19th-Century American South*. New York: Oxford University Press, 1984.

Bardaglio, Peter W. *Reconstructing the Household: Families, Sex, and the Law in the Nineteenth-Century South*. Chapel Hill: University of North Carolina Press, 1995.

Blair, Diane D. *Arkansas Politics and Government: Do the People Rule?* Lincoln: University of Nebraska Press, 1988.

Bolton, S. Charles. *Arkansas, 1800–1860: Remote and Restless*. Fayetteville: University of Arkansas Press, 1998.

———. *Territorial Ambition: Land and Society in Arkansas, 1800–1840*. Fayetteville: University of Arkansas Press, 1993.

Brown, Walter Lee. *A Life of Albert Pike*. Fayetteville: University of Arkansas Press, 1997.

Cash, Wilber J. *The Mind of the South*. New York: Vintage Book Reprint, 1969.

Chambliss, William J. *Making Law*. Bloomington: Indiana University Press, 1993.

Collins, Hugh. *Marxism and Law*. New York: Oxford University Press, 1984.

DeBlack, Thomas A. *With Fire and Sword: Arkansas, 1861–1874*. Fayetteville: University of Arkansas Press, 2003.

De Tocqueville, Alexis. *Democracy in America*. New York: Vintage Books, 1956.

Finkelman, Paul. *An Imperfect Union: Slavery, Federalism, and Comity*. Clark, NJ: Lawbook Exchange, Ltd., 2000. First published 1981 by University of North Carolina Press.

Fletcher, John Gould. *Arkansas*. Chapel Hill: University of North Carolina Press, 1947.

Freyer, Tony A. *Producers Versus Capitalists: Constitutional Conflict in Antebellum America*. Charlottesville: University Press of Virginia, 1994.

Friedman, Lawrence M. *Crime and Punishment in American History*. New York: Harper Collins, 1993.

——. *Dead Hands: A Social History of Wills, Trusts, and Inheritance Law*. Stanford: Stanford Law Books, 2009.

——. *A History of American Law*. 3rd ed. New York: Touchstone, 2007.

Genovese, Eugene D. *The Political Economy of Slavery: Studies in the Economy and Society of the Slave South*, 2nd ed. Hanover: Wesleyan University Press, 1989.

——. *Roll, Jordan, Roll: The World the Slaves Made*. New York: Random House, Inc., 1976.

Gifis, Steven H. *Law Dictionary*, 3rd ed. New York: Barons' Educational Services, 1991.

Gross, Ariela J. *Double Character: Slavery and Mastery in the Antebellum Southern Courtroom*. Athens: University of Georgia Press, 2000.

Grossberg, Michael. *Governing the Hearth: Law and the Family in Nineteenth-Century America*. Chapel Hill: University of North Carolina Press, 1985.

Hall, Kermit L. *The Magic Mirror: Law in American History*. New York: Oxford University Press, 1989.

Hallum, John. *Biographical and Pictorial History of Arkansas*. Albany: Weed Parsons and Company, Printers, 1887.

Harrell, John M. *The Brooks and Baxter War: A History of the Reconstruction Period in Arkansas*, (St. Louis: Slawson Printing, 1893).

Hartog, Hendrik. *Man and Wife in America: A History*. Cambridge: Harvard University Press, 2000.

Hempstead, Fay. *Historical Review of Arkansas*. Chicago: Lewis Publishing Co., 1911 Vol 1.

———. *A Pictorial History of Arkansas*. St. Louis: N. D. Thompson Publishing Company, 1890.

Herndon, Dallas T. *Centennial History of Arkansas*, vol. 1. Chicago: S. J. Clarke Publishing Co., 1922.

Hopkins, John Henry. *The American Citizen: His Rights and Duties According to the Spirit of the Constitution of the United States*. New York: Pudney and Russell, 1857.

Horwitz, Morton J. *The Transformation of American Law, 1780–1860*. Cambridge: Harvard University Press, 1977.

Howe, Daniel Walker. *What Hath God Wrought: The Transformation of America, 1815–1848*. New York: Oxford University Press, 2007.

Huebner, Timothy S. *The Southern Judicial Tradition: State Judges and Sectional Distinctiveness, 1790–1890*. Athens: University of Georgia Press, 1999.

Hurst, James Willard. *Law and the Conditions of Freedom in the Nineteenth-Century United States*. Madison: University of Wisconsin Press, 1967.

McDougall, Walter A. *Throes of Democracy: The American Civil War Era, 1829–1877*. New York: Harper Collins Publishers, 2008.

McNeilly, Donald P. *The Old South Frontier: Cotton Plantations and the Formation of Arkansas Society, 1819–1861*. Fayetteville: University of Arkansas Press, 2002.

Moneyhon, Carl. *The Impact of the Civil War and Reconstruction on Arkansas*. Fayetteville: University of Arkansas Press, 2002.

Newmyer, R. Kent. *Supreme Court Justice Joseph Story: Statesman of the Old Republic*. Chapel Hill: University of North Carolina Press, 1985.

Novak, William J. *The Peoples' Welfare: Law and Regulations in Nineteenth-Century America*. Chapel Hill: University of North Carolina Press, 1996.

Nuttall, Thomas. *A Journal of Travels into the Arkansas Territory during the Year 1819*. Fayetteville: University of Arkansas Press, 1999.

Reynolds, David S. *Waking Giant: America in the Age of Jackson*. New York: Harper Collins Publishers, 2008.

Salmon, Marylynn. *Women and the Law of Property in Early America*. Chapel Hill: University of North Carolina Press, 1986.

Sellers, Charles. *The Market Revolution: Jacksonian America, 1815–1846*. New York: Oxford University Press, 1991.

Shinn, Josiah H. *Pioneers and Makers of Arkansas*. Baltimore: Genealogical Publishing Company, 1967.

Stampp, Kenneth M. *America in 1857: A Nation on the Brink*. New York: Oxford University Press, 1990.

Staples, Thomas. *Reconstruction in Arkansas, 1862–1874*. Gloucester, MA: Peter Smith, 1964. First published 1924 by Columbia University Press.

Stevenson, C. R. *Arkansas Territory—State and Its Highest Courts*. Little Rock: Clerk of the Supreme Court, 1946.

Story, Joseph. *A Familiar Exposition of the Constitution of the United States.* Washington, DC: Regnery Publishing, 1986.

Taiwo, Olufemi. *Legal Naturalism: A Marxist Theory of Law.* Ithaca, NY: Cornell University Press, 1996.

Taylor, Orville W. *Negro Slavery in Arkansas.* Fayetteville: University of Arkansas Press, 2000.

Thomas, David Y. *Arkansas and Its People: A History, 1541–1930*, vol. 1. New York: American Historical Society, 1930.

Thompson, George H. *Arkansas and Reconstruction: The Influences of Geography, Economics, and Personality.* Port Washington, NY: Kennikat Press, 1976.

Tushnet, Mark V. *Slave Law in the American South:* State v. Mann *in History and Literature.* Lawrence: University Press of Kansas, 2003.

Whayne, Jeannie M., Thomas A. DeBlack, George Sabo III, and Morris S. Arnold. *Arkansas: A Narrative History.* Fayetteville: University of Arkansas Press, 2002.

White, G. Edward. *Law in American History,* vol. 1. New York: Oxford University Press, 2012.

White, Lonnie J. *Politics on the Southwestern Frontier: Arkansas Territory, 1819–1836.* Memphis: Memphis State University Press, 1964.

Williams, Nancy A., ed. *Arkansas Biography: A Collection of Notable Lives.* Fayetteville: University of Arkansas Press, 2000.

Williams, Patrick G., S. Charles Bolton, and Jeannie M. Whayne. *A Whole County in Commotion: The Louisiana Purchase and the American Southwest.* Fayetteville: University of Arkansas Press, 2005.

Wood, Gordon S. *Empire of Liberty: A History of the Early Republic, 1789–1815.* New York: Oxford University Press, 2009.

Woods, James M. *Rebellion and Realignment: Arkansas's Road to Secession.* Fayetteville: University of Arkansas Press, 1987.

Wyatt-Brown, Bertram. *The Shaping of Southern Culture: Honor, Grace, and War, 1760s–1880s.* Chapel Hill: University of North Carolina Press, 2001.

———. *Southern Honor: Ethics and Behavior in the Old South.* New York: Oxford University Press, 2007.

Zainaldin, Jamil. *Law in Antebellum Society: Legal Change and Economic Expansion.* New York: Alfred A. Knopf, 1983.

Chapters in Books

Ely, James W., Jr., and David J. Bodenhamer, "Regionalism and the Legal History of the South." In *Ambivalent Legacy: A Legal History of the South,* edited by James W. Ely Jr. and David J. Bodenhamer, 3–29. Jackson: University Press of Mississippi, 1984.

DeBlack, Thomas A. "Prosperity and Peril: Arkansas in the Late Antebellum Period." In *Arkansas: A Narrative History*, edited by Jeannie M. Whayne,

Thomas A. DeBlack, George Sabo III, and Morris S. Arnold, 135–65. Fayetteville: University of Arkansas Press, 2002.

——. "'The Rights and Rank to Which We Are Entitled': Arkansas in the Early Statehood Period." In *Arkansas: A Narrative History*, edited by Jeannie M. Whayne, Thomas A. Deblack, George Sabo III, and Morris S. Arnold, 109–34. Fayetteville: University of Arkansas Press, 2002.

Freyer, Tony A. "Law and the Antebellum Southern Economy: An Interpretation." In *Ambivalent Legacy: A Legal History of the South,* edited by James W. Ely Jr. and David J. Bodenhamer, 49–68. Jackson: University Press of Mississippi, 1984.

Friedman, Lawrence M. "The Law between the States: Some Thoughts on Southern Legal History." In *Ambivalent Legacy: A Legal History of the South*, edited by James W. Ely Jr. and David J. Bodenhamer, 30–46. Jackson: University Press of Mississippi, 1984.

Key, Joseph Patrick. "Outcasts upon the World." In *A Whole Country in Commotion: The Louisiana Purchase and the American Southwest*, edited by Patrick G. Williams, S. Charles Bolton, and Jeannie M. Whayne, 91–105. Fayetteville: University of Arkansas Press, 2005.

Moneyhon, Carl. "1861: The Die Is Cast." In *Rugged and Sublime: The Civil War in Arkansas*, edited by Mark K. Christ, 1–19. Fayetteville: University of Arkansas Press, 1994.

Morris, Thomas D. "Society Is Not Marked by Punctuality in the Payment of Debts: The Chattel Mortgages of Slaves." In *Ambivalent Legacy: A Legal History of the South*, edited by James W. Ely Jr. and David J. Bodenhamer, 147–70. Jackson: University Press of Mississippi, 1984.

Sumner, Colin. "The Ideological Nature of Law." In *Marxism and Law,* edited by Piers Beire and Richard Quinney, 255–61. New York: John Wiley & Sons, 1982.

Whayne, Jeannie M. "Henry Massie Rector." In *Arkansas Biography*, edited by Nancy A. Williams, 234. Fayetteville: University of Arkansas Press, 2000.

——. "A Shifting Middle Ground." In *A Whole Country in Commotion: The Louisiana Purchase and the American Southwest*, edited by Patrick G. Williams, S. Charles Bolton, and Jeannie M. Whayne, 59–75. Fayetteville: University of Arkansas Press, 2005.

——. "The Turbulent Path to Statehood: Arkansas Territory, 1803–1836." In *Arkansas: A Narrative History,* edited by Jeannie M. Whayne, Thomas A. DeBlack, George Sabo III, and Morris S. Arnold, 73–108. Fayetteville: University of Arkansas Press, 2002.

Articles

Adams, Horace. "An Arkansas Alderman, 1857." *Arkansas Historical Quarterly* 11 (1952): 79–101.

Ansbacher, Sidney F., and Joe Knetsch. "Negotiating the Maze: Tracing

Historical Title Claims in Spanish Land Grants and Swamp and Overflowed Lands Act." *Journal of Land Use and Environmental Law* 17 (2002): 351–73.

Atkinson, James H. "The Adoption of the Constitution of 1874 and the Passing of the Reconstruction Regime." *Arkansas Historical Quarterly* 5 (1946): 288–96.

——. "Arkansas Gubernatorial Campaign and Election of 1872." *Arkansas Historical Quarterly* 1 (1942): 307–21

——. "The Brooks-Baxter Contest." *Arkansas Historical Quarterly* 4 (1945): 124–49.

Bayliss, Garland E. "Post Reconstruction Repudiation: Evil Blot or Financial Necessity?" *Arkansas Historical Quarterly* 23 (1964): 243–59.

Beatty-Brown, Florence R. "Legal Status of Arkansas Negroes before Emancipation." *Arkansas Historical Quarterly* 28 (Spring 1969): 6–13.

Broply, Alfred L. "'Over and above . . . there broods a portentous shadow,—the shadow of law': Harriet Beecher Stowe's Critique of Slave Law in *Uncle Tom's Cabin*." *Journal of Law and Religion* 12 (1995–96): 457–506.

Brown, Elizabeth Gaspar. "Law and Government in the Louisiana Purchase: 1803–1804." *Wayne State Law Review* 2 (1956): 169–89.

Brown, Mattie. "River Transportation in Arkansas, 1819–1890." *Arkansas Historical Quarterly* 1 (1942): 342–54.

Brown, Walter L. "The Henry M. Rector Claim to the Hot Springs of Arkansas." *Arkansas Historical Quarterly* 15 (1956): 281–92.

Burkhart, Ann M. "Lenders and Land." *Missouri Law Review* 64 (1999): 249–315.

Cash, Marie. "Arkansas in Territorial Days." *Arkansas Historical Quarterly* 1 (1942): 223–34.

Colby, William E. "III. Mining Law in Recent Years and Grants to States (Con't), Swamp and Overflowed Lands." *California Law Review* 37 (1949): 592–627.

Cowen, Ruth Caroline. "Reorganization of Federal Arkansas, 1862–1865." *Arkansas Historical Quarterly* 18 (1959): 132–57.

Crawford, Sidney. "Arkansas Suffrage Qualifications." *Arkansas Historical Quarterly* 2 (1943): 331–39.

Currie, David P. "The Constitution in Congress: The Public Lands, 1829–1861." *University of Chicago Law Review* 70 (2003): 783–820.

Dale, Edward E. "Arkansas and the Cherokees." *Arkansas Historical Quarterly* 8 (1949): 95–114.

Dougan, Michael B. "The Arkansas Married Woman's Property Law." *Arkansas Historical Quarterly* 46 (1987): 3–26.

——. "The Doctrine of Creative Destruction: Ferry and Bridge Law in Arkansas." *Arkansas Historical Quarterly* 39 (1980): 136–58.

Driggs, Orval Truman, Jr. "The Issues of the Powell Clayton Regime, 1868–1871." *Arkansas Historical Quarterly* 8 (1949): 1–75.

Dubler, Ariela R. "In the Shadow of Marriage: Single Women and the Legal

Construction of the Family and the State." *Yale Law Journal* 112 (2003): 1641–1715.

Durham, Philip. "The Desperado as Hero." *Arkansas Historical Quarterly* 14 (1964): 340–58.

Ewing, Cortez A. M. "Arkansas Reconstruction Impeachments." *Arkansas Historical Quarterly* 13 (1953): 131–53.

Fede, Andrew. "Legal Protection for Slave Buyers in the U.S. South: A Caveat Concerning Caveat Emptor." *American Journal of Legal History* 31(1987): 322–58.

Feistman, Eugene G. "Radical Disfranchisement in Arkansas, 1867–1868," *Arkansas Historical Quarterly* 12 (1953): 126–68.

Finkelman, Paul. "John McLean: Moderate Abolitionist and Supreme Court Politician." *Vanderbilt Law Review* 62 (2009): 519–65.

Flaherty, David H. "Law and the Enforcement of Morals in Early America." *Perspectives in American History* 5 (1971): 203.

Foster, Lynn. "Courts and Lawyers on the Arkansas Frontier." *UALR Law Review* 26 (2004): 543–72.

Fox, James W. "The Law of Many Faces: Antebellum Contract Law Background of Reconstruction Era Freedom of Contract." *American Journal of Legal History* 49 (2007): 61–112.

Friedman, Lawrence M. "Notes toward a History of American Justice." *Buffalo Law Review* 24 (1974–1975): 111–34.

Friend, Craig Thompson. "Liberty Is Pioneering: An American Birthright." *OAH Magazine of History* 19 (2005): 16–20.

Gates, Paul W. "Federal Land Policies in the Southern Public Land States." *Agricultural History* 53 (1979): 206–27.

Gitelman, Morton. "The First Chancery Court in Arkansas." *Arkansas Historical Quarterly* 55 (1996): 359–82.

———. "The Separation of Law and Equity and the Arkansas Chancery Courts: Historical Anomalies and Political Realities." *UALR Law Journal* 17 (1995): 215–58.

Goodman, Paul. "The Emergence of Homestead Exemption in the United States: Accommodation and Resistance to the Market Revolution, 1840–1880." *Journal of American History* 80 (1993): 470–98.

Harrison, Robert W., and Walter M. Kollmorgan. "Land Reclamation in Arkansas under the Swamp Land Grant Act of 1850." *Arkansas Historical Quarterly* 6 (1947): 369–418.

Holt, Wythe. "Now and Then: The Uncertain State of Nineteenth-Century American Legal History." *Indiana Law Review* 7 (1974): 615–43.

Johnson, Walter. "Inconsistency, Contradiction, and Complete Confusion: The Everyday Life of the Law of Slavery." *Law & Social Inquiry* 22, no. 2 (1997): 405–33.

Jones, Robert L., and Paulene H. Jones. "Stephen F. Austin in Arkansas." *Arkansas Historical Quarterly* 25 (1966): 336–53.

Jones, Ruth Irene. "Hot Springs: Ante-Bellum Watering Place." *Arkansas Historical Quarterly* 14 (1955): 3–31.

Kagan, Robert A., Bliss Cartwright, Lawrence M. Friedman, and Stanton Wheeler. "The Business of State Supreme Courts, 1870–1970." *Stanford Law Review* 30 (1977): 121–23.

Kanazawa, Mark T. "Possession Is Nine Points of the Law: The Political Economy of Early Public Land Disposal." *Explorations in Economic History* 33 (1996): 227–49.

Ledbetter, Cal, Jr. "The Constitution of 1836: A New Perspective." *Arkansas Historical Quarterly* 41 (1982): 213–52.

Lewis, Elsie M. "Economic Conditions in Ante-Bellum Arkansas, 1850–1861." *Arkansas Historical Quarterly* 6 (1947): 256–74.

Littlefield, Daniel F., and Lonnie E. Vanderhill. "The Cherokee Agency Reserve, 1828–1886." *Arkansas Historical Quarterly* 31 (1992): 166–80.

McKnight, Joseph W. "Protection of the Family Home from Seizure by Creditors: The Sources and Evolution of a Legal Principle." *Southwestern Historical Quarterly* 86 (1983): 369–99.

Mensel, Robert E. "'A Diddle at Brobdingnag': Confidence and Caveat Emptor during the Market Revolution." *University of Memphis Law Review* 38 (2007): 97–152.

Moffatt, Walter. "Transportation in Arkansas, 1819–1840." *Arkansas Historical Quarterly* 15 (1956): 187–201.

Moore, Waddy W. "Some Aspects of Crime and Punishment on the Arkansas Frontier." *Arkansas Historical Quarterly* 23 (1964): 50–64.

Movantz, Alison D. "There's No Place like Home: Homestead Exemption and Judicial Construction of Family in Nineteenth-Century America." *Law and History Review* 24 (2006): 245–95.

Mulhollan, Paige E. "Arkansas General Assembly of 1866 and Its Effect on Reconstruction." *Arkansas Historical Quarterly* 20 (1961): 331–43.

Nash, A. E. Keir. "*In re* Radical Interpretations of American Law: The Relation of Law and History." *Michigan Law Review* 82 (1983): 274–345.

——. "Reason of Slavery: Understanding the Judicial Role in the Peculiar Institution." *Vanderbilt Law Review* 32 (1979): 104–23.

Nelson, William E. "Emerging Notions of Modern Criminal Law in the Revolutionary Era: A Historical Perspective." *New York University Law Review* 42 (1967): 452–82.

Priest, Claire. "Creating an American Property Law: Alienability and Its Limits in American History." *Harvard Law Review* 120 (2006): 385–458.

Ross, Francis. "Some Arkansas Cases." *Arkansas Lawyer* 19 (April 1985): 75–77.

Ross, Margaret Smith. "Cadron: An Early Town That Failed." *Arkansas Historical Quarterly* 16 (1957): 3–27.

Russell, Thomas D. "The Antebellum Courthouse as Creditor's Domain: Trial Court Activity in South Carolina and the Circumstance of Lending and Litigation." *American Journal of Legal History* 40 (1996): 331–64.

Scheiber, Harry N. "Back to 'The Legal Mind?' Doctrinal Analysis and the History of Law." *Reviews in American History* 5 (1977): 458–66.

——. "Property Law, Expropriation, and Resource Allocation by Government: The U.S., 1789–1910," *Journal of Economic History* 33 (1973): 232–51.

Schweikart, Larry. "Southern Banks and Economic Growth in the Antebellum Period: A Reassessment." *Journal of Southern History* 53(1) (1987): 19–36.

Shafer, Robert S. "White Persons Held to Racial Slavery in Antebellum Arkansas." *Arkansas Historical Quarterly* 49 (1985): 134–35.

Sherwood, Diane. "Code Duello in Arkansas." *Arkansas Law Review* 31 (1977): 449–76.

Smith, Stephen. "Arkansas Advocacy: The Territorial Period." *Arkansas Law Review* 31 (1977): 449–76.

Spitler, William Hayden. "Over a Century of Doubt and Confusion: Adverse Possession in Arkansas, Intent to Hold Adversely and Recognition of Superior Title in *Fulkerson v. Van Buren*." *Arkansas Law Review* 53 (2000): 459–87.

Sprankling, John G. "The Anti-wilderness Bias in American Property Law." *University of Chicago Law Review* 63 (1996): 519–90.

——. "An Environmental Critique of Adverse Possession." *Cornell Law Review* 79 (1994): 816–84.

Stafford, Logan Scott. "Judicial Coup D'Etat: Mandamus, *Quo Warranto,* and the Original Jurisdiction of the Supreme Court of Arkansas." *UALR Law Journal* 20 (1998): 891–984.

——. "Significant Decisions of the Supreme Court of Arkansas: *Brooks v. Page* (May 7, 1874)." *Arkansas Lawyer* 36 (Fall 2001): 40.

——. "Slavery and the Arkansas Supreme Court." *UALR Law Journal* 19 (1997): 413–64.

——. "Supreme Court Justice and Governor Henry M. Rector." *Arkansas Lawyer* 46 (Winter 2011): 30.

Stebbins, Ed. "Early Banking in Arkansas." *Arkansas Historical Quarterly* 13, no. 4 (1954): 409–13.

Stokes, D. A., Jr. "The First State Elections in 1836." *Arkansas Historical Quarterly* 20 (1961): 126–50.

Swinney, Everette. "*United States v. Powell Clayton*: Use of the Federal Enforcement Acts in Arkansas." *Arkansas Historical Quarterly* 26 (1967): 143–54.

Sydnor, Charles S. "The Southerner and the Laws." *Journal of Southern History* 6 (1940): 3–23.

Turner, Jesse. "The Constitution of 1836." *Arkansas Historical Association* 3 (1911): 74–166.

Tushnet, Mark. "Slave Law as Contract and Hierarchy." *Reviews in American History* 24 (1996): 590–95.

Van Atta, John R. "'A Lawless Rabble': Henry Clay and the Cultural Politics of Squatters' Rights, 1832–1841." *Journal of the Early Republic* 27 (2008): 337–78.

Walton, Brian G. "Ambrose Hundley Sevier in the United States Senate." *Arkansas Historical Quarterly* 32 (1973): 25–60.

Watkins, John J. "Division of Labor between Arkansas's Appellate Courts." *UALR Law Journal* 17 (1995): 177–214.

Watson, Harry L. "Conflict and Collaboration: Yeomen, Slaveholders, and Politics in the Antebellum South." *Social History* 10 (1985): 273–98.

White, G. Edward. "The Appellate Opinion as Historical Source Material." *Journal of Interdisciplinary History* 1 (1971): 491–509.

White, Lonnie J. "Arkansas Territorial Indian Affairs." *Arkansas Historical Quarterly* 21 (1962): 193–212.

Wight, Willard E. "Letters of Thomas B. Hanly, 1863–1864." *Arkansas Historical Quarterly* 15 (1946): 161–71.

Wood, Stephen E. "The Development of Arkansas Railroads, Part I." *Arkansas Historical Quarterly* 7 (1948): 103–40.

Worley, Ted R. "The Arkansas State Bank: The Antebellum Period." *Arkansas Historical Quarterly* 23 (1964): 65–73.

——. "The Control of the Real Estate Bank of the State of Arkansas, 1836–1855." *Mississippi Valley Historical Review* 37 (1950): 403–26.

Master's Theses

Heiss, Harry G. "The Public Career of David Walker: The Antebellum Years." MA thesis, University of Arkansas, 1983.

Huff, Leo Elmer. "Confederate Arkansas: A History of Arkansas during the Civil War." MA thesis, University of Arkansas, 1964.

Manuscript

John W. Brown Diary. Microfilm Collection, Arkansas History Commission, Little Rock.

INDEX

J. W. LOONEY is a retired judge for the Arkansas Eighteenth West Judicial Circuit and emeritus distinguished professor at the University of Arkansas School of Law, where he also served as dean and was founding director of the graduate program in agricultural law.